The Civil War from Its Origins to Reconstruction

D1536836

The Polish American Encyclopedia (2011)

THE CIVIL WAR FROM ITS ORIGINS TO RECONSTRUCTION

James S. Pula

McFarland & Company, Inc., Publishers

Jefferson, North Carolina

LIBRARY OF CONGRESS CATALOGUING-IN-PUBLICATION DATA

Names: Pula, James S., 1946– author.
Title: The Civil War from its origins to Reconstruction / James S. Pula.
Description: Jefferson, North Carolina : McFarland & Company, Inc.,
Publishers, 2019 | Includes bibliographical references and index.
Identifiers: LCCN 2019009756 × ISBN 9781476674117
(paperback. : acid free paper) ∞
Subjects: LCSH: United States—History—Civil War, 1861–1865. |
United States—History—Civil War, 1861–1865—Causes.
Classification: LCC E468 .P34 2019 | DDC 973.7/11—dc23
LC record available at https://lccn.loc.gov/2019009756

BRITISH LIBRARY CATALOGUING DATA ARE AVAILABLE

ISBN (print) 978-1-4766-7411-7
ISBN (ebook) 978-1-4766-3501-9

The front cover image is of the First Connecticut battery, near Fredericksburg,
May 2, 1863, Andrew J. Russell, photographer (Library of Congress)

Printed in the United States of America

McFarland & Company, Inc., Publishers
Box 611, Jefferson, North Carolina 28640
www.mcfarlandpub.com

For Michael Bruce Lynch

Table of Contents

Introduction

The era of Sectionalism, Civil War and Reconstruction was the most traumatic period in American history. Not only were the issues of the day so divisive they could not be peaceably settled, the contending sides could not even agree on what to call the conflict.

"What's in a name?" asks Juliet in Shakespeare's immortal *Romeo and Juliet*. "That which we call a rose by any other name would smell as sweet." Perhaps so, but names are often less than interchangeable. Although it is common today to refer to the bloodbath of the 1860s as the Civil War, it has been referred to by dozens of different appellations. No doubt a major cause for the lack of an agreed upon name for this formative event has been that each variation carries political connotations. A "civil war" implies a war between two groups who are members of the same country, so it was favored by the North which argued secession was illegal. The United States government formally adopted "War of the Rebellion" for its official collection of documents from the Union and Confederate armed forces, the implication again being a rebellion within a single nation. Other Northerners sometimes referred to it as the "War for the Union"; that is, the war to preserve the nation. In each example the name clearly indicated an internal rebellion against a government.

The United Confederate Veterans adopted the term "War Between the States" since it gives primacy to the individual states and the States' Rights philosophy espoused in the South and it reflects the perception of legitimacy for that war that the United States government identified as treasonous rebellion. The terms "War for Southern Independence" and "Second American Revolution" were also common in the South, the latter because it linked secession with the 1776 Declaration of Independence. Among diehard unreconstructed rebels, the "War of Northern Aggression" continued to be a favorite into the middle of the twentieth century.

During the 1880s and 1890s when joint reunions of veterans began to take place, accompanied by efforts to promote national reconciliation, a phrase often heard was "The Late Unpleasantness," an expression of supreme understatement that at the same time remained neutral in the partisan name game. If one wished to avoid provoking an argument or hurt feelings on one side or the other, the fratricidal conflict was simply "The Late Unpleasantness."

—∽∞∽—

The outcome of the Civil War changed the fundamental social, economic and political foundations of the nation, with effects still felt today. The war literally tore families apart, some of which never reconciled. A higher percentage of the population was in uniform during the Civil War than any other war in American history. Estimates of those who died because of the Civil War vary, but most cite a figure around 628,000, nearly as many as all of the American deaths in the Revolution, the War of 1812, the Mexican War, the Spanish-American War, World War I, World War II, the Korean Conflict, Vietnam, and the Middle East added together. More recent estimates place the number even higher.

Economically, the war led to massive government debt, the repayment of which resulted in increases in existing taxes and the implementation of new assessments including the personal income tax. A national paper currency appeared, the United States government acted to create a federal banking system, and the Northern victory brought pro-business control of the national government in place of Southern pro-agrarian interests. Socially, the war paved the way for direct federal aid to higher education, increased career opportunities for women, the creation of West Virginia, institution of the absentee ballot, and the stimulation of the westward movement, facilitated by federal support of the expansion of national railroad systems. Politically, three Constitutional amendments emerged from the wreckage of the war—the Thirteenth, Fourteenth, and Fifteenth—that ended slavery, redefined United States citizenship and reinforced earlier amendments guaranteeing the rights of citizens. The interpretation of the Constitution broadened to favor the implied powers of the central government at the expense of the states and the fundamental control of the federal government changed from Southern Democrats to Northern Republicans for most of the decades through 1932. Further, several Supreme Court cases reshaped the way the nation interpreted some of the powers of the chief executive and Congress, while also stating explicitly that secession had in fact been unconstitutional.

Given the pivotal formative influence of the mid-nineteenth century, it should not be a surprise that more books are published in the United States each year about the American Civil War era than any other topic. This raises the obvious question: Why do we need yet another book on this period? There are two ways to approach this question. First, a large part of the annual publishing output is comprised of biographies, both military and political, and of military history including the macro examination of campaigns and micro history of individual units. Among the more comprehensive histories of these decades, most are designed as textbooks, usually for college-level courses, and focus primarily on the politics of the age. There is a dearth of comprehensive works designed for the general public or for those new to their study of this influential historical period. This book is designed to fill that void by providing explanations and interpretations of the issues and events of the era against a general historical background of the incidents as they unfolded.

The second thing that this book does differently from most is to interweave the military history of the conflict with social, economic, and political events. Several decades ago, when I first began teaching courses on the Civil War, I used this same approach in class and students often commented that they never realized how much military events shaped the actions of Congress and other social, economic, and political affairs. This approach provides an integrated narrative as well as interpretations of cause-and-effect relationships that are not evident when the military dimension is missing or only superficially referenced as is often the case with other publications. To accomplish this, in the chapters covering the wartime years, I first discuss the military campaigns and then the social, economic, and political changes that occurred because of the cause-and-effect relationship.

Finally, books on the Civil War often provide the author's interpretation not only of events, but also of what the primary sources—the building blocks of any serious historical research—have to say on a given issue. In this book I have included direct quotations from pertinent primary sources so that the reader can determine exactly what they say without the mediation of a third party. Further, this approach also provides the casual reader not only with the opportunity to see the differing viewpoints of the actual participants, but also to see how these primary sources can be pieced together into a unified, meaningful historical narrative.

Through the approach outlined above, this book provides an overview of the issues and events that gradually divided the national to the point where compromise, which had successfully averted each previous national crisis, was no longer possible by 1860. It offers interpretations of these questions and incidents, while also providing general interpretations about how and why the process of national disintegration moved seemingly inexorably toward a tremendously destructive national trauma.

—⟋⟍—

I wish to thank the staff of the interlibrary loan office at Purdue University Northwest as well as the Regenstein Library at the University of Chicago, the Library of Congress, the National Archives and Records Administration, and the Hathi Trust, all of which greatly aided in the research for this work. Special appreciation goes to Prof. Saul Lerner for his willingness to read my manuscript and offer insightful suggestions that greatly improved the work. My thanks also to Dr. Richard Sommers, Mr. Frederick Tressler and Mr. Michael Robinson whose assistance was most helpful to the accuracy of the final manuscript.

Where a note number appears next to a name, biographical information may be found in the note. Unless otherwise indicated, information on numbers and casualties are taken from *The War of the Rebellion: A Compilation of the Official Records of the Union and Confederate Armies* (Washington, D.C.: U.S. Government Printing Office, 1882) and Thomas L. Livermore, *Numbers and Losses in the Civil War in America 1861–65* (New York: Kraus Reprint Co., 1969).

1

"To Form a More Perfect Union"

In the early morning hours of April 12, 1861, General Pierre Gustave Toutant Beauregard issued perhaps the most momentous order in American history. Artillery fire exploded from around Charleston harbor, raining shells on Fort Sumter for the next 34 hours and igniting the most destructive war in American history, a conflict that would permanently change the course of the nation's future. Why had it come to this? Why was the country being torn apart by passions too profound to be quenched by compromise? The answer lay in two centuries of history that slowly, imperceptibly at first, led to the development of two separate economic, social and political traditions in the northern and southern regions of English North America.

The Colonial Inheritance

The seeds of discontent were sown with the planting of the first English and Dutch colonies in the "New World." The impetus for this originated in the concept of "mercantilism," the idea that the strength of a nation is determined by its wealth and that wealth is achieved through commerce. To political leaders of the sixteenth century, the truth of this theory had been demonstrated in the rise of the Italian states whose trade with the Middle East and Orient brought them riches which led to political power far beyond their size. When the Portuguese opened a new route around the southern tip of Africa to the rich trade with Asia, Portugal likewise rose to a position of economic and political prominence. The scenario played out yet again when Spain became the richest and most powerful nation in Europe through trade and colonization in the Western Hemisphere and as the gold, silver, and other products of the discovery, exploration, and settlement augmented the wealth of Spain. It was economics that motivated all of this exploration. It was economics that led to European colonization in the Americas. As Richard Hakluyt, advisor to Elizabeth I, asserted in his argument for colonization, such settlements would be the source of valuable raw materials as well as markets for English goods.

It was this drive for economic gain that also propelled English colonization. Yet it was the same imperative that led to somewhat different patterns of economic development. The initial Jamestown colony was established by a joint stock company, the Virginia Company of London, for the express purpose of generating a profit to its investors. To this end, in addition to colonists some of the earliest arrivals were Polish and either Dutch or German artisans who were to establish commercial enterprises. Among the major assets of what came to be Virginia were valuable timber, tar, pitch and other commodities in great demand by the Royal Navy and the growing British merchant fleet. In 1609 John Rolfe began the first commercial cultivation of tobacco. By 1616 the nascent colony produced 2,500 pound of the leafy crop, with the early success encouraging the expansion of the new venture. Within four more years the colony was producing 119,000 pounds of tobacco and was shipping it to a growing English market.[1]

To be profitable, tobacco had to be grown in large quantity for export. But to grow it in bulk required large amounts of land and a sizable labor force. There was land aplenty, and initially indentured servants filled the need for workers, but there were significant drawbacks to this system. An indenture was a legal contract under which people sold their labor for a set period of time after which they were free from any obligation. The indentured person retained all of the rights and legal protections of an English citizen; thus, the worker could not be mistreated or forced to serve beyond the period of the indenture. If tobacco was to be grown in large quantities on huge estates or plantations, another less expensive source of labor was necessary. In 1619 it arrived in the form of the first slaves imported into Virginia. By the latter part of the seventeenth century, slavery provided a large labor force which, once purchased, could be made to serve for life and could produce offspring who continued the source of labor indefinitely. Slaves were not English citizens so they enjoyed none of the legal protections afforded indentured servants. Gradually, slaves were given legal status so that by the latter part of the seventeenth century the slave was identified as property under the designation "chattel." As the English population spread south with the formation of the Carolinas and later Georgia, this same plantation system was well adapted to the production of indigo, rice, and later cotton, all of which proved to be profitable commercial enterprises.

Although the average colonist from the Chesapeake Bay area south was a small independent farmer growing crops to feed his family, with perhaps a little left over to barter for needed supplies, the economic and political power in these colonies rested with the owners of the large commercial plantations along with a few wealthy merchants in seaports like Charleston. The increasing demand for their products led to the spread of commercial plantation agriculture and with it the need for expansion of the labor force. Over time, these "planters" came to control some 75 percent of the wealth of the southern colonies. Political and social life centered in Charleston in the Carolinas and Jamestown, or later Williamsburg, in Virginia. The wealthy hired people to run their plantations so they could reside at the center of social, economic and political life, while those of moderate income resided on their plantations. Often the latter lived at least part time in the seaports during the heat of the summer months. It was this wealthy class that controlled virtually every aspect of life in the southern colonies. Voting and elective office were the preserve of those who held enough property or wealth to qualify for the franchise, while education was reserved for those who could likewise afford it. The well-to-do hired tutors so their younger children could learn the basics of reading, writing and arithmetic. The ideal was to send one's son to England for an "education," which consisted largely of learning how a gentleman was expected to behave in society and making connections that could be useful in future business endeavors. Those who lacked funds for this sent their sons north to be educated at one of the few colleges in existence in the English colonies. The great numerical majority who were independent subsistence farmers had no such opportunity save what they could impart to their children themselves.

To the north, the English colony in Plymouth, and its later expansion into Massachusetts Bay and surrounding colonies in New England, also contained a majority of small farmers, but included a middle class of shop owners, artisans, and entrepreneurs as well as fishermen plying the rich waters off New England and the Grand Banks. Over time a shipbuilding industry developed which employed not only skilled craftsmen but sailors as commercial shipping became an important part of the New England economy. Free public education meant that by 1750 virtually all males and nearly 90 percent of females were literate, higher percentages at that time than in England itself. Unlike the southern regions, there was a much broader franchise in New England where the tradition of town meetings led to widespread participation in the political life of the colonies. Though not completely democratic, it was much more so than the regions farther south.[2]

Between the two areas of English settlement lay the Dutch colony of New Netherland. The Dutch Republic was one of the most important commercial centers of the seventeenth century with trading routes that stretched all over Europe as well as into the Western Hemisphere, Africa and Asia. They knew a good harbor when they saw one and the waters immediately off Manhattan Island provided the best anchorage in all of North America. A lucrative fur trade with the indigenous people quickly led to the establishment of a small colony that grew slowly to include settlements in the immediate area and up the Hudson River to Fort Orange (modern Albany). In an effort to develop the colony the Dutch admitted Waloons, French Huguenots, German Lutherans, Scandinavians, English and Polish Protestants, Portuguese, Jews, and many others. Within a few years some eighteen different languages could be heard in the colony. With an abundance of land, great tracts or patroonships were reserved for "patroons" who would then allow

The Dutch colony of New Amsterdam, now New York, was a bustling commercial center as early as the seventeenth century, joining Boston in New England as the foundations for the growth of the commercial economy of the northern colonies. The importance of commerce in 1656 can be seen in this engraving (Benson John Lossing, ed., *Harper's Encyclopedia of United States History* [vol. 6] [New York: Harper and Brothers, 1912]).

settlers to work their land for rent and often a share of the resulting crop. These were not slaves, but free people who paid rent to live on and work the land much as share croppers did in nineteenth and twentieth century America. The patroons, together with the merchant class, formed the controlling group in Dutch New Netherland, as they continued to do, along with equivalent English landowners and entrepreneurs, once the English took over the Dutch colony in 1664.

Very early in the development of the colonies that would become the United States, one can clearly see the foundation for differences between the northern and southern regions of English/Dutch settlement. To the south, large commercial plantations and their owners dominated, exerting both economic and political control of colonies whose primary residents were poor subsistence farmers and slaves, neither of which enjoyed any meaningful control over their lives. Education was reserved mostly for the upper economic classes, as was political participation. To the north the economy became much more diverse. Small farmers still predominated numerically, but a middle class of entrepreneurs, skilled artisans, and commercial interests also participated in governing a better educated populace than in the southern colonies. Under the British mercantilist system, these differences were not that significant, but once American independence arrived and a new government attempted to legislate for an entirely new nation, the economic differences often meant that proposals beneficial for one section were opposed by the other.

Creating a New Government

Most of the fundamental differences that were to split the nation asunder were in evidence during the American Revolution when representatives of the self-declared independent states attempted to form a unified government. Throughout the pre–Revolutionary era there had been very little cooperation among the thirteen different colonial governments, even when faced with the imminent threats posed by the lengthy series of conflicts generally known collectively as the French and Indian Wars. In fact, when Benjamin Franklin proposed a plan to unify the colonies under a central government to enable them to meet this danger not a single colony agreed to the idea. Each colonial government was quite jealous of its own prerogatives and unwilling to relinquish any of its authority to a central government. This same spirit of individuality hampered efforts to form an effective government once independence was declared in 1776. The resulting Articles of Confederation proved to be exceptionally weak with most authority withheld by the individual states. The new government lacked such essential powers as levying taxes, regulating trade, or even conscripting troops to prosecute the ongoing revolution. It could only ask the states to raise taxes or troops, and they were free to alter the amount requested or to refuse entirely. As a reflection of the jealously guarded prerogatives of each state, nine of the thirteen had to vote in favor of any proposal for it to become law and all thirteen had to agree to any amendment of the Articles, a nearly impossible prospect when judged by previous experience.

When it eventually became evident that this new government was not working, a convention was called to amend the Articles, but it quickly transformed into a movement to draft an entirely new government—the Constitutional Convention. Some of the major obstacles faced by this gathering mirrored the issues that steadily drove a wedge between the newly independent states. At its most fundamental level, formation of the new government was a contest between those who favored a "federation" and those who favored a "national" authority. Gouverneur Morris, who had signed the Articles of Confederation as a representative of Pennsylvania but came to recognize their shortcomings, defined the "federation" as "a mere compact resting on the good faith of the parties" whereas a "national" model implied "a complete and compulsive" submission to the central authority.[3] This was an essential question to answer because most of the delegates had been political or military leaders during the Revolution and recalled all too well the perception of Parliament as an overbearing absentee government that appeared to them to be usurping the prerogatives of the local elected colonial assemblies. Even many of those who wanted a single united government to emerge from the deliberations were nevertheless apprehensive of creating another all-powerful government that would simply recreate Parliament with all the same objections.

While most of the delegates regarded the Articles as insufficient, there was considerable dissent when it came to creating a stronger, more compulsory central government because it required the individual states to relinquish authority. If for no other reason, this conjured up in the minds of many the absentee rule of Parliament they had just fought an eight year war to overthrow, while others simply objected to diminishing the powers of their own state legislatures and elected officials. It was to appease those who feared the development of an overreaching central authority that proponents of the new Constitution agreed to add an amendment to the original proposal limiting the power of this new general government. This eventually became the Tenth Amendment: "The powers not delegated to the United States by the Constitution, nor prohibited by it to the states, are reserved to the states respectively, or to the people."

Another key disagreement occurred over how representation was to be apportioned. The Articles gave each state one vote reflecting the belief that they were each independent and equally important members of the original confederation. Those in the less populated states were adamant that this be preserved, fearing that if it were not their own interests would be submerged under the greater voting strength of their larger neighbors. The representatives of the more populous states, led by Virginia, believed that there ought to be proportional representation based upon population. They feared that without this the smaller states might combine to outvote proposals favored by a majority of the people. This was yet another iteration of the old struggle over political control played out on a more national stage. The result was a series of compromises in which the new congress would be comprised of two branches, a House of Representatives based on the population of each state and a Senate in which each state received two votes regardless of size. Although the division here was between the larger and smaller states, as the nation developed and the population of the northern states increased considerably faster than that of the southern states, this issue of state representation became increasingly important as "the South" used its parity in the Senate to protect against any unfavorable legislation proposed by the more populous "North."

One more aspect of the representation issue emerged with the question of whether or how slaves were to be counted. Here the division in perspective was unmistakably between the northern and southern sections. If slaves were counted those states with large slave populations would be entitled to more representatives, and hence more votes, in the House. Southern states obviously favored this, while those in the north did not. The latter argued that since slaves were not free to participate in the political process they ought not be counted. When the issue of taxation came before the delegates the positions were reversed. Southern states argued that slaves should not be counted because with taxes levied proportionally among the states they would be liable to pay more. Northern states argued that since slaves were an integral part of the commercial plantation economy they ought to be counted for purposes of taxation. After considerable debate attended by rising emotional appeals, compromise prevailed. The delegates agreed to a proposal by James Wilson from Pennsylvania that "representatives and direct Taxes shall be apportioned among the several States which may be included within this Union, according to their respective Numbers, which shall be determined by adding to the whole Number of free Persons, including those bound to Service for a Term of Years, and excluding Indians not taxed, three fifths of all other Persons."[4] Everyone understood that "all other Persons" referred to slaves. Thus the so-called "Three-Fifths Compromise" became the law of the land in the new government.

Yet another divisive issue was the regulation of commerce. The major exports of the new nation came from the southern states—tobacco, rice, indigo and soon to outpace them all, cotton. Naturally delegates from these states feared that the new government might place a tax on exports, thereby cutting into their trade and profits. If Congress could regulate trade, South Carolina's Charles C. Pinckney prophesied, the southern states would become "nothing more than overseers for the Northern States."[5] This was a strong emotional appeal since everyone knew what his warning meant. Plantation owners hired "overseers" to manage their operations, and their labor force, for them. The implication was that if Congress were given the authority to regulate commerce, Southern plantation owners would be reduced to managing the production process for absentee rulers in the North. At the same time, a heated discussion took place about the root cause of much of the dissention, the issue of slavery itself. When Luther Martin of Maryland proposed a tax on the importation of slaves, the result was an emotional exchange on the morality and economics of slavery itself. John Rutledge of South Carolina rose to contest the assertion that slavery was an issue of morality. "Interest alone," he proclaimed, "is the governing principle with nations."[6] Slavery was an economic issue, not a question of morality.

For a time it appeared that this divisive issue would doom the entire proceedings, but eventually compromise again prevailed. Delegates from South Carolina and Georgia approached their New England counterparts with an offer. In exchange for an agreement that the new government would not interfere with the continued importation of slaves for at least twenty years, southern delegates would agree to a provision that a simple majority vote would be necessary for Congress to regulate trade. As a result, among the powers granted to Congress under Article I, Section 8, is the authority "to regulate Commerce with foreign Nations, and among the several States, and with the Indian Tribes." In return, Article I, Section 9, contained the proviso that "the Migration or Importation of such Persons as any of the States now existing shall think proper to admit, shall not be prohibited by the Congress prior to the Year one thousand eight hundred and eight, but a Tax or duty may be imposed on such Importation, not exceeding ten dollars for each Person." Everyone understood that the "such Persons" were slaves even though it would have been much to divisive to actually include the word "slave" in the document.

The significance of all of this is the lingering unanswered questions it bequeathed to future generations. Without compromise there would have been no Constitution and possibly no United States since it took nine of the thirteen states to ratify the new Constitution before it took effect. Even then it would hardly have been effective if the more populous states decided not to join. No matter how one divided the opposing sides—

large state vs. small state or slave state vs. free state—there would not have been enough votes to adopt the new government without compromise. Yet in compromise the immediate issues were addressed without a cure for the underlying causes of potential conflict. The fundamental issues of the scope and authority of the central government, representation, economic policy, and slavery remained. They would recur with increasing divisiveness over the next three-quarters of a century.

The Beginning of Political Factions

Alexander Hamilton found himself faced with an almost insurmountable task when he assumed office as the first Secretary of the Treasury in 1789. The nation was deeply in debt. By the end of the Revolution, Congress had amassed debts of $54 million while the individual states owed another $25 million. Paper currency issued by Congress was nearly worthless and European nations were reluctant to lend money to the untried and sorely pressed government. By 1787 some $3 million in overdue interest could not be paid. The treasury was empty. Creditors were clamoring for payment, not the least of whom were ex-soldiers who had not yet received payment for their Revolutionary War services, some of whom were threatening to march on Congress.

To solve the crisis, Hamilton advocated two moves. The first was funding the national debt. Hamilton feared that if the new government did not pay its debts it would be unable to borrow in the future and the new nation would face bankruptcy. He also believed the nation needed the support of the upper economic class to be successful for it was this group who controlled the funds that could make the new government solvent, if only they could be convinced that their investments would be safe. Therefore the government should guarantee its debts both to assure the availability of future credit and to gain support of the upper economic class without which the government would have difficulty obtaining funds. Under Hamilton's plan, the original certificates of indebtedness issued by the Continental Congress would be recalled and replaced with interest-bearing bonds with a specific maturity date.

His second proposal called for federal assumption of state debts. The purpose was both to make sure that states paid their debts and, perhaps more importantly, to encourage people to look to the federal government to guarantee their debts. By having the federal government guarantee the debts, Hamilton was very subtly changing the focus of people's interest and attention away from state governments and toward the federal government. This fit nicely with his belief in a strong central government. Although Virginia opposed this, since it had already paid off most of its previous debts, as had some other states, Hamilton gained the necessary backing by agreeing to support a permanent move of the nation's capital to the South where Virginia and Maryland donated a ten-square-mile tract of land for that purpose along the banks of the Potomac River. Thus was born the District of Columbia.

More problematic was Hamilton's proposal to coordinate the government's finances through a national bank. The bank could issue loans, regulate currency, and provide the government with a place to deposit money collected from bonds, taxes, the sale of western lands, or other sources. Hamilton proposed that this "bank of the United States" enjoy a monopoly on the deposit of federal money. Critics feared that the proposal would lead to corruption, promote speculation and infringe on the operations of state and local banks, possibly even driving them out of business. Among the leaders opposing Hamilton's plan were James Madison and Thomas Jefferson who argued that such a creation would be unconstitutional since the Constitution did not specifically give Congress the power to create a bank. Hamilton responded by arguing that since the Constitution gave Congress the authority to enact laws to carry out the powers it had, and since Congress had the power to sell lands, tax, and regulate commerce, it had the "implied" power to create a bank to handle these transactions. This was one of the first examples of how the compromises negotiated to gain adoption of the Constitution had failed to solve the basic issues separating the opposing views, a key question being the intended breadth of Congressional powers.

At the heart of the disagreement was the very nature of the federal government. Did the Constitutional Convention intend to create a strong central government with the flexibility to adapt its basic authority to cover new situations or did it intend to create a government whose powers were limited only to those specifically mentioned in the document itself. Surely a close reading of the Constitution would clear up this disagreement, but instead it pointed only to a perplexing ambiguity. The central issue was a seeming contradiction in two portions of the document. Article I, Section 8, stated that "the Congress shall have power.... To make all Laws which shall be necessary and proper for carrying into Execution the foregoing Powers, and all other Powers vested by this Constitution in the Government of the United States, or in any Department or Officer thereof." It was this provision upon which Hamilton rested his argument. Congress could create a bank because it was necessary for the collection of taxes, sale of lands and bonds, and the payment of bills. On the other hand, Madison and Jefferson pointed to the Tenth Amendment which said that "the powers not delegated to the United States by the Constitution, nor prohibited by it to the states, are reserved to the states respectively, or to the people." This had been specifically added to the Bill of Rights to assuage the fears of those who did not want to create an all-powerful central government to replace the one they had just shed in the Revolution. To the two Virginians this amendment clearly interpreted the earlier clause in a most restrictive sense. And therein lay the problem. One could look at either of these to portions of the Constitution and come to entirely different conclusions on the nature of the central government. This dichotomy quickly led to a "loose interpretation" based on Article I, Section 8, which came to be called the "elastic clause" because it could be stretched to cover almost any eventuality, and a "strict" or "States' Rights" interpretation based on the Tenth Amendment. These differing interpretations precluded any easy solution to what was meant. Rather, they had a tendency to prolong the disagreements on not only the national bank but other issues that arose over the following decades.

Hamilton's plan largely solved the nation's economic crisis, but the political differences continued. Following George Washington's decision not to seek a third term as president, the Federalist administration of John Adams adopted the Alien and Sedition Acts which, among other things, made it a crime punishable by fine and imprisonment to "write, print, utter or publish, or shall cause or procure to be written, printed, uttered or published, or shall knowingly and willingly assist or aid in writing, printing, uttering or publishing any false, scandalous and malicious writing or writings against the government of the United States, or either house of the Congress of the United States, or the President of the United States."[7] Jefferson and Madison were appalled by this overt disregard of the freedoms of speech and the press clearly articulated in the Bill of Rights.

Alexander Hamilton solved the financial problems that beset the United States after independence, but his actions exposed some of the fundamental differences of opinion on exactly what the new Constitution meant (Library of Congress).

They responded with the Virginia and Kentucky Resolutions which argued that the Constitution was a compact between the states and that as such the individual states possessed the right to "nullify" any federal law not specifically authorized by the Constitution. That is, states had the right to prevent the enforcement of a federal law within their boundaries if Congress lacked the Constitutional authority to enact the legislation or if the law unfairly aided one section of the country at the expense of another. This was a very clear articulation of the States' Rights position of limited federal authority along with the logical extension of state nullification of laws adopted beyond the scope of Constitutional authority. These theories of States' Rights and Nullification became the basis for Southern opposition to a whole host of federal actions leading up to the final outbreak of civil war.

America's "Peculiar Institution"

There had always been those opposed to slavery, even in the earliest of colonial times. Along with the issue of representation, slavery was one of the most divisive issues faced by the Constitutional Convention. The delegates solved the immediate issue by compromising where necessary and ignoring it when not essential to an agreement. Despite this temporary arrangement, the two issues remained both divisive and intertwined.

The end of the American Revolution removed the British restrictions on movement beyond the Alleghany Mountains and also affirmed American ownership of the land east of the Mississippi River from the Spanish holdings in New Orleans and Florida as far north as the Canadian border. Once the various states agreed to relinquish their western land claims to the federal government the next question to be decided was how this vast land would be opened to settlement. This meant an immediate resurfacing of the slavery issue since southerners migrating west fully expected to take their "property" with them. The issue was solved with relatively little difficulty by passage of the Northwest Ordinance in 1787. This legislation created the "Northwest Territory" from the land north of the Ohio and east of the Mississippi Rivers with the provision that it could later be subdivided into from three and five states. To apply for statehood, any area must have a minimum population of 60,000 and submit a state constitution that guaranteed freedom of religion, the

James Madison, shown here in this Gilbert Stuart portrait, and Thomas Jefferson authored the responses to Alexander Hamilton's broad interpretation of the Constitution. Their arguments became the basis for the States' Rights position taken by the South (Library of Congress).

right to trial by jury, and the prohibition of slavery. Given the sensitivity of the South to the slavery issue, it was understood that since states created north of the Ohio River would prohibit slavery, the "peculiar institution" would be legal in any states created south of that river. The Northwest Ordinance led to an orderly settlement of the Northwest Territory and affectively defused a potential crisis over slavery by creating the Ohio River as the border between future free and slave territory. Nevertheless, the next clash over slavery developed from exactly this issue.

The original thirteen states—seven "Northern" and six "Southern"—were joined by Vermont in 1791, Kentucky in 1792, and Tennessee in 1796 creating an equal balance of eight Northern and eight Southern states. The admission of Ohio in 1803 gave the North a temporary advantage until the entry of Louisiana in 1812. Thereafter, Indiana (1816) and Mississippi (1817) balanced each other while Illinois (1818) and Alabama (1819) did likewise to yield an even eleven "free" and eleven "slave" states. With a very sparse population west of the Mississippi, when Missouri applied for admission in 1819 there appeared to be no other area that could readily be used to balance the state either North or South. Whichever way it entered the Union, free or slave, that side would have a majority for the foreseeable future.

The balance of states was particularly important for political purposes. During the three decades following adoption of the Constitution the population of the "free" states grew much faster than that of the "slave" states, due primarily to the rapidly increasing immigration which mostly settled in northern manufacturing areas or sought land for farming where they would not be faced with competition from slave labor. This increase in population gave the northern states an expanding numerical advantage in the House of Representatives, raising fears in the South that anti-slavery forces might introduce legislation to restrict or eliminate slavery or that Northern manufacturers would be successful in lobbying for higher tariffs or other economic legislation harmful to Southern interests. To prevent this, it became increasingly clear to Southern leaders that they must maintain the balance of power in the Senate. Since each state had equal representation in the upper house of Congress, it was their only legislative hope to prevent any disadvantageous bills adopted by the House from becoming law.

Southern fears appeared justified when in February 1819 the House adopted a bill to allow Missouri to draft a constitution that included an amendment by James Tallmadge of New York to eliminate slavery despite the fact that it already existed there. The bill failed in the Senate but the issue of Missouri's admittance to the Union sparked heated national debate. Southerners were particularly anxious that the North not achieve numerical dominance in the Senate since it would then control both houses of Congress, further jeopardizing Southern wellbeing. The leadership skills of Speaker of the House Henry Clay of Kentucky eventually led to an agreement that satisfied both factions. In its final form, what came to be known as the "Missouri Compromise" contained two parts. First, to settle the short-term issue of political balance in the Senate it was agreed that Missouri could enter the Union as a slave state and Maine, which was until that time land claimed by Massachusetts, would be admitted as a new free state. This would preserve the critical balance of power in the Senate.

Given the sensitivity of the slavery issue, the second part of the agreement was designed as a long-term solution that would prevent an emotional national debate from erupting every time a territory applied for admission in the future. Under this provision, any territory originating from the Louisiana Purchase applying for admission to the

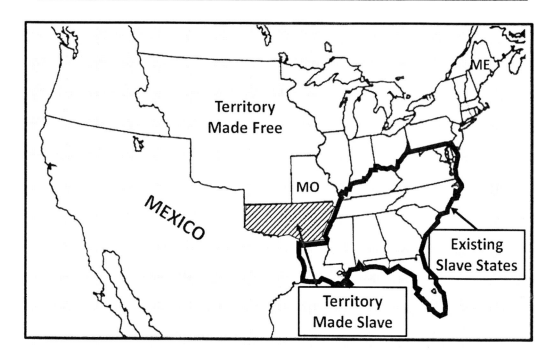

The Missouri Compromise resolved a major crisis by preserving the balance of power between free and slave states in the U.S. Senate and providing a means by which future states could be admitted without a recurring national debate on slavery (James S. Pula).

Union would automatically enter as a free state if it were located north the southern boundary of Missouri (36°30′ north latitude) and any qualified territory located south of that boundary would correspondingly enter as a slave state. This provision was particularly important to the South which was anxious to prevent the slavery issue from becoming the subject of serious national debate given the North's growing political power.

The Missouri Compromise defused a potential major crisis while at the same time effectively preventing the slavery issue from taking center stage on the national level for nearly two decades. "The outbreak" of the crisis, James G. Blaine wrote, "was so sudden, its course so turbulent, and its subsidence so complete, that for many years it was regarded as phenomenal in our politics, and its repetition in the highest degree improbable if not impossible."[8] Others disagreed. Thomas Jefferson feared that the agreement only postponed an inevitable breakup of the Union. "[T]his momentous question," he wrote, "like a fire bell in the night, awakened and filled me with terror. I considered it at once as the knell of the Union. [I]t is hushed indeed for the moment, but this is a reprieve only, not a final sentence. A geographical line, coinciding with a marked principle, moral and political, once conceived and held up to the angry passions of men, will never be obliterated; and every new irritation will mark it deeper and deeper."[9]

The Tariff Controversy

Like the debates over state rights and federal authority and slavery, the competing interests of manufacturing and agriculture also provoked very heated exchanges in the growing North-South rift. One of the major national issues emerging during the mid–1820s involved the tariff. A tariff is a tax on imported or exported goods. In this case, the tariff involved imports. By the 1820s, freed from the mercantilist restrictions of the British Empire by the success of the American Revolution, some of the people in the North began to invest in the development of manufacturing operations. But these businesses were small and often had difficulty competing against imports from England where large, well developed factories with better technology turned out less expensive goods than the smaller American businesses were able to produce. If they could not sell their goods, American business owners could not make a profit. Consequently, Northern manufacturers wanted their representatives to enact protective tariffs that would increase the price of imported goods to a level where they were more expensive for consumers than domestically manufactured products. Southern plantation owners and merchants objected.

At the time, the South was the major exporting area of the country. Southern commercial crops such as cotton, tobacco and rice comprised over half of all American exports. If the U.S. placed a tariff on British goods, it would hurt British manufacturers. Southerners feared that British owners would then pressure Parliament to retaliate by enacting a tariff on American goods; this is called a "reciprocal tariff," a tariff enacted in retaliation for another nation's tariff. Since the South was the major exporting region, these reciprocal tariffs would fall on Southern planters and merchants, reducing their profits. From their standpoint, the American tariff was a discriminatory law that benefited Northern manufacturers at the expense of Southern planters and merchants. Moreover, while Northern manufacturers benefited from the tariff, the tariff resulted in consumers paying higher prices for manufactured goods. Since the South was largely a consumer of manufactured goods, they would be paying higher prices to benefit Northern manufacturers.

To support their anti-tariff argument, Southerners looked to the Constitution. What they found was the Tenth Amendment that Madison and Jefferson had earlier used as justification for their theory of nullification. Southerners reasoned that since the right to enact tariffs had not been given to the federal government in the Constitution, and since it was a discriminatory tax that benefited the North at the expense of the South, the federal tariff was unconstitutional. This left states free to nullify it within their borders. Northerners of course disagreed. The Constitution explicitly gave the federal government the authority to regulate commerce. Northerners argued that the purpose of the tariff was to regulate trade. A high tariff decreased imports, while a low tariff, or no tariff, increased imports. Since the federal government had the authority to regulate commerce, and since it did have the right under Article I, Section 8, to enact laws to carry out that authority, then it had the right to enact a tariff. Who was right? In the end it depended on which interpretation of the Constitution one held. Each side referred to the Constitution as the legal basis for its position.

This difference in interpretation highlighted the growing divide between people who favored a strong central government and those who favored a limited central government with the individual states retaining authority for everything except what was specifically ceded to the federal government. Although these differences existed in all regions of the country, over time there developed a growing chasm between the North and the South over this issue. Southerners argued that the central government was a "confederacy," a group of sovereign states that united for specific purposes (defense, trade, foreign policy), yet otherwise acted as independent states, the so-called States' Rights interpretation. Northerners, who came increasingly to support a strong central government to promote trade and commerce, espoused a "loose interpretation" of the Constitution based on the "implied powers" of the Elastic Clause. They argued, as had Alexander Hamilton, that not every specific power of government necessary in the future could possibly be foreseen and enumerated in the Constitution, but these were granted through the implied powers authorized in Article I, Section 8.

By 1820 the South was becoming increasingly conscious of its unwelcome status as a political minority. Because of the growing divide between the economies of the North and South, the two sections increasingly pursued different political objectives. With the expansion of commerce and manufacturing in the North offering jobs, new immigrants tended to settle mostly in that region greatly increasing its already numerical majority in the House of Representatives. Consequently, the South had no chance whatever to successfully oppose legislation in that chamber. As both a numerical and cultural minority, how could it defend its interests against what it perceived as an increasingly aggressive North? How could it prevent the central government from adopting legislation against the South's best interests?

The growing population of the North made it difficult if not impossible for the South to prevent Northern states from passing any legislation they chose, while the mounting aggressiveness of the North convinced Southerners all the more of their political vulnerability. The person who emerged as the leader of the Southern position was John C. Calhoun. Born in South Carolina, Calhoun graduated from Yale University in Connecticut before becoming an attorney in Charleston. Elected to the South Carolina state legislature, he later served as Secretary of War under James Monroe, Vice President under John Quincy Adams, and U. S. Senator. He is generally considered one of the most able Senators in American history and was the leading architect of the Southern strategy from the 1820s through his death in 1850.

Calhoun realized that the South would never be able to control the House of Representatives, but there were other steps that could be taken to protect Southern interests. For a bill to become law it had to be approved by *both* houses of Congress. Since each state had equal representation in the Senate, as long as there remained at least an equal number of Northern and Southern states the South would be able to protect its interests in the upper house. Thus, the admission of new states would be a major political issue in succeeding decades. Beyond that, control of either the presidency or vice presidency was an important check the South could wield on Northern power. As sectionalism increased there was a general attempt by the Democratic and Whig parties to "balance" a presidential ticket with one person from the North and one from the South. Control of the presidency was the preferred Southern alternative since the president could veto legislation and could also appoint Supreme Court justices, thus insuring that any appeal to the judiciary would be reviewed by a majority favorable to the Southern position. Yet, the vice presidency also wielded some protective power since the vice president served as the presiding officer of the Senate and in cases where there was a tie vote in that house could cast the deciding vote. Throughout the remaining years leading up to the final outbreak of the Civil War, maintaining the balance of power in the Senate and insuring a sympathetic ear in the executive branch became the foremost Southern political strategies to protect their political, economic, and social interests.

The tariff issue began to become a major national issue during the time Calhoun served as Vice President. In 1826, a bill to enact a high protective tariff was introduced into Congress. After being approved in the House of Representatives where the larger population of the North gave it more votes than the South, the measure went to the Senate where the vote resulted in a tie since North and South had an equal number of states. Calhoun, exercising the prerogative of the vice president, voted "nay" causing the bill to fail.

The bill died, but the disagreement did not. It became a major issue in the election campaign of 1828 when John Quincy Adams, the son of former president John Adams, ran for re-election as a Whig against Andrew Jackson of Tennessee. Like his father, Adams believed in a loose interpretation of the Constitution which supported a tariff to protect emerging American industries, nearly all of which were in New England and the Middle Atlantic States. Jackson, the popular hero of the Battle of New Orleans against the British in 1815, although by this time a wealthy planter, styled himself as a "man of the people" and used his residence in Tennessee to portray himself as a champion of the Southern and Western agricultural interests that formerly sup-

John C. Calhoun emerged as one of the most prominent senators in U.S. history through his leadership of South Carolina, and then the entire South, in its political struggle against the North (Library of Congress).

ported Jefferson. Much like the Federalists before them, the Whigs were strongest in the commercial Northeast where they were led by Daniel Webster, but also enjoyed support among middle-class commercial interests promoting internal improvements and ambitious farmers and immigrants in the West led by Henry Clay. Although he gained a reputation for his support of the "common man," Jackson accumulated a fortune from his law practice, speculation in western lands, and as the owner of a productive cotton plantation employing more than 100 slaves. Labeled a "frontier aristocrat" by critics, his followers began calling themselves "Democrats," and the Jacksonian movement is generally considered to be the beginning of the modern Democratic Party.

During the campaign, Jackson's followers introduced a high tariff bill into Congress. They assumed that the South would vote against it and New England in favor of it. If the same scenario developed as it had earlier and the measure failed in the Senate, Jackson's followers would be able to appeal for votes in the North by claiming that they had tried to help manufacturers. It they could attract enough votes there, Jackson, a Southerner, would be elected. Surprisingly, the bill passed despite the high duties and the inclusion of raw materials needed by Northern industries. So onerous was it considered by some people that detractors took to calling it the "Tariff of Abominations."

Appalled by the new law, the South Carolina legislature declared the tariff to be unconstitutional and issued the "South Carolina Exposition and Protest," secretly authored by Calhoun who, as Vice President, did not want to make his authorship public. The document provided a vigorous defense of States' Rights, declared the tariff to be unconstitutional, and recommended state nullification. The Protest argued that the Constitution did not provide the federal government with any authority to levy a tariff, the federal government was not in need of money since it was operating at a surplus, and Northern manufacturers were in no great distress. Thus, there was no valid reason for the tariff. At the same time, cotton prices were down on the world market so that Southern planters found it difficult to operate at a profit. The tariff was both unconstitutional and unfair.

After Jackson won the 1828 presidential election there was a short respite while South Carolina waited to see what would happen under the new administration. Nevertheless, tensions continued. A debate over the sale of western lands in the U.S. Senate quickly turned into an acrimonious exchange over States' Rights. Senator Robert Y. Hayne of South Carolina proposed an alliance between Southerners and Westerners to support a low tariff, a low price for the sale of western lands, and the nullification of attempts by the Northeast to expand the powers of the federal government. Daniel Webster of Massachusetts made an impassioned speech responding to Hayne in which he argued that the federal government had been created by the people, not the states, and that the people had granted legislative authority to Congress and the national government which was supreme over the states in every respect. The Constitution, he further argued, provided an opportunity for states that were unhappy to amend it or to seek redress through the federal court system. There was no provision for a state to nullify a federal law. As the heated debate continued, Hayne accused New England of being disloyal during the War of 1812 and asserted that the right to liberty was foremost over union. Webster replied that the two concepts were inseparable: "Liberty and Union, now and forever, one and inseparable." The debate spilled over into the annual Jefferson Day Dinner in April 1830 when President Jackson rose to offer the toast "our Union: it must be preserved." Not to be outdone, Calhoun rose to offer "the Union, next to our liberty, most dear. May we always remember that it can only be preserved by distributing equally the benefits and burdens of the Union."[10]

In the election year of 1832, with the original tariff bill scheduled to expire the following year, a new bill emerged in Congress to make the tariff permanent. In addition, it would increase some tariffs on imported manufactured goods, while at the same time lowering tariffs on raw materials such as wool and flax needed in the Northern textile industry. Southerners quite naturally were once again aroused by the permanency of the new tariff bill and the changes which they believed only increased its discriminatory nature. The South Carolina legislature responded on November 24 with its "Ordinance of Nullification":

> Whereas the Congress of the United States, by various acts, purporting to be acts laying duties and imposts on foreign imports, but in reality intended for the protection of domestic manufactures, and the giving of bounties to classes and individuals engaged in particular employments, at the expense and to the injury and oppression of other classes and individuals, and by wholly exempting from taxation certain foreign commodities, such as are not produced or manufactured in the United States, to afford a pretext for imposing higher and excessive duties on articles similar to those intended to be protected, hath exceeded its just powers under the Constitution, which confers on it no authority to afford such protection, and hath violated the true meaning and intent of the Constitution, which provides for equality in imposing the burthens of taxation upon the several States and portions of the confederacy; And whereas the said Congress, exceeding its just power to impose taxes and collect revenue for the purpose of effecting and accomplishing the specific objects and purposes which the Constitution of the United States authorizes it to effect and accomplish, hath raised and collected unnecessary revenue for objects unauthorized by the Constitution.
>
> We, therefore, the people of the State of South Carolina in Convention assembled, do declare and

ordain, and it is hereby declared and ordained, that the several acts and parts of acts of the Congress of the United States, purporting to be laws for the imposing of duties and imposts on the importation of foreign commodities, and now having actual operation and effect within the United States, and, more especially, ... [the tariff acts of 1828 and 1832] ... are unauthorized by the Constitution of the United States, and violate the true meaning and intent thereof, and are null, void, and no law, nor binding upon this State, its officers or citizens; and all promises, contracts, and obligations, made or entered into, or to be made or entered into, with purpose to secure the duties imposed by the said acts, and all judicial proceedings which shall be hereafter had in affirmance thereof, are and shall be held utterly null and void.

And it is further ordained, that it shall not be lawful for any of the constituted authorities, whether of this State or of the United States, to enforce the payment of duties imposed by the said acts within the limits of this State; but it shall be the duty of the Legislature to adopt such measures and pass such acts as may be necessary to give full effect to this ordinance, and to prevent the enforcement and arrest the operation of the said acts and parts of acts of the Congress of the United States within the limits of this State, from and after the 1st day of February next, and the duty of all other constituted authorities, and of all persons residing or being within the limits of this State, and they are hereby required and enjoined, to obey and give effect to this ordinance, and such acts and measures of the Legislature as may be passed or adopted in obedience thereto.[11]

The act went on to prohibit any court within the state from recognizing the federal tariff laws or challenging the Ordinance of Nullification and require all civil and military officials to take an oath to "obey, execute, and enforce" the Ordinance. Then, in a final show of defiance it declared that "we, the people of South Carolina,"

do further declare that we will not submit to the application of force, on the part of the Federal Government, to reduce this State to obedience; but that we will consider the passage, by Congress, of any act authorizing the employment of a military or naval force against the State of South Carolina, her constituted authorities or citizens; or any act abolishing or closing the ports of this State, or any of them, or otherwise obstructing the free ingress and egress of vessels to and from the said ports, or any other act on the part of the Federal Government, to coerce the State, shut up her ports, destroy or harass her commerce, or to enforce the acts hereby declared to be null and void, otherwise than through the civil tribunals of the country, as inconsistent with the longer continuance of South Carolina in the Union: and that the people of this State will thenceforth hold themselves absolved from all further obligation to maintain or preserve their political connection with the people of the other states and will forthwith proceed to organize a separate government, and do all other acts and things which sovereign and independent states may of right do.[12]

Clearly, the Ordinance of Nullification was a challenge to federal authority that the president could not ignore. Since he was a Southerner, many people expected Jackson to be conciliatory and act to eliminate or reduce the tariff to appease South Carolina. If they did, they were greatly mistaken. Jackson responded on December 10 with his "Proclamation to South Carolina" in which he observed that

the Ordinance [of Nullification] is founded ... on the strange position that any one state may not only declare an act of Congress void, but prohibit its execution; that they may do this consistently with the Constitution; that the true construction of [the Constitution] permits a state to retain its place in the Union and yet be bound by no other of its laws than those it may choose to consider as constitutional.... Look for a moment to the consequence. If South Carolina considers the revenue laws unconstitutional and has a right to prevent their execution in the port of Charleston, there would be a clear constitutional objection to their collection in every other port; and no revenue shall be collected anywhere.... If this doctrine had been established at an earlier day, the Union would have been dissolved in its infancy....

I consider, then, the power to annul a law of the United States, assumed by one state, incompatible with the existence of the Union, contradicted explicitly by the letter of the Constitution, unauthorized by its spirit, inconsistent with every principle on which it was founded, and destructive of the great object for which it was formed.

In vain these sages [the framers of the Constitution] declared that Congress should have the power to lay and collect taxes, duties, etc.; in vain they have provided that they shall have the power to pass laws which shall be necessary and proper to carry those powers into execution, that those laws and the Constitution should be the "supreme law of the land, and that judges in every state shall be bound thereby...." Vain provisions! ineffectual restrictions! vile profanation of oaths! miserable mockery of legislation! if a bare majority of voters in any one state may, on real or supposed knowledge of the intent with which a law has been passed, declare themselves free from its operation....

The right to secede is deduced from the nature of the Constitution, which they say, is a compact between sovereign states who have preserved their whole sovereignty and are subject to no superior: that because they make the compact they can break it when their opinion has been departed from by other states....

The Constitution forms a government, not a league.... Each state having expressly parted with so many powers as to constitute jointly with other nations, a single nation, cannot from that period, posses any right to secede, because such succession does not break a league, but destroys the unity of a nation.... To say that any state may at pleasure secede from the union is to say that the United States is not a nation.... Because the union was formed by a compact, it is said that the parties to that compact may, when they feel themselves aggrieved, depart from it; but it is precisely because it is a compact that they may not.[13]

Concluding that "the power to annul a law of the United States is incompatible with the existence of the Union and contradicted explicitly by the letter of the Constitution," the president asserted that once a state accepted the Constitution and joined the Union it entered into a "binding obligation" which it was not then free to dissolve.[14] Finally, specifically addressing the threat of military action, Jackson stated in no uncertain terms that any attempt at disunion by armed force was in fact treason. Everyone knew the penalty for treason was death.

In this game of political poker, the president had upped the ante; it was now time for South Carolinians to either fold or raise. They chose to raise the stakes. On December 17 the South Carolina legislature issued a call for a meeting of states to "consider the Federal-State relationship." South Carolina was looking for support from the other Southern states in particular, but few were aroused enough to risk open warfare with the federal government over taxation. Most states, both North and South, condemned the move and the meeting was never held. South Carolina was now out on a limb, having openly defied the president and the federal government, but receiving no substantial support from other states.

At this juncture, Jackson had his supporters in Congress introduce on January 8, 1833, the Verplanck Bill, proposed by Representative Gulian C. Verplanck of New York, to reduce tariffs by 50 percent. About two weeks later, on January 21, they also introduced the Force Bill which would give the president the authority to use force if necessary to enforce his Proclamation to South Carolina. What was happening in this seeming contradiction was that Jackson was offering South Carolina an olive branch, an honorable way out of the predicament, but with the realization that if it is not taken the president reserves the right to use force. Cooler heads in South Carolina prevailed and accepted the Verplanck Bill as a face-saving way out of the crisis. On January 21 the South Carolina legislature suspended the "Ordinance of Nullification." Notice that it did not "repeal" the Ordinance, it merely "suspended" it; no doubt this was a last attempt at defiance by implying that it had the right to nullify but chose to suspend action. Jackson ignored this and further crisis, and the possible early beginning of civil war, was averted. Eventually, a compromise Tariff of 1833 co-authored by Henry Clay and John C. Calhoun provided a gradual reduction on all tariffs above 20 percent until there was no tariff above that level by 1842.

This whole episode was an eerie portent of events to come in the winter of 1860–61. But for the time being an immediate showdown had been averted. Northern politicians could now go back home and run for re-election by telling their constituents that they had stood up to those hot heads down in Charleston and forced them to back down. The tariff was still on the books and being collected in South Carolina. Politicians in South Carolina could run for re-election by telling the folks back home that they had stood up to the might of the entire federal government, all by themselves, and forced the government to lower the tariff by half, a major victory. Everyone was happy—at least until the next crisis.

Andrew Jackson, despite being a slave-owning Southerner, as president acted to assert the authority of the federal government over the individual states (Library of Congress).

2

An Expanding Nation Leads to Expanding Divisions

The Louisiana Purchase of 1803 doubled the size of the United States, but it remained for this land to be settled, made productive, and brought into the fabric of the nation. Land was plentiful, but making it prosperous required better transportation to open the regions west of the Appalachian Mountains, further development of commerce and industry to boost and diversify the economy, and the population to occupy the vast unsettled tracts that were the future of the nation.

Innovations in Transportation

In the wake of the American Revolution, new inventions in transportation spurred both the growth of American manufacturing and the Northern commercial class. In 1775 there were almost no roads connecting American cities. Transportation was usually by sea along the coast from the major Atlantic ports—Savannah, Charleston, Wilmington (NC), Norfolk, Baltimore, Philadelphia, New York, Newport (RI), Providence (RI), and Boston. What roads that did exist were little more than horse trails incapable of serious commercial transportation. In the wake of the War of 1812, the construction of turnpikes began among several cities. These were constructed by private companies under state charter. Turnpikes consisted of logs laid side-by-side, the intervening cracks filled with dirt. Every so often there would be a toll gate where travelers were expected to pay a toll for the use of the road. By 1825, turnpikes linked most major cities in the East. They were relatively effective for moving people, but were not as helpful moving heavy freight which quickly wore out the logs. This, along with natural deterioration and occasional floods necessitated constant repair.

The next major development in transportation was the canal. In 1820, the quickest way for produce from western farmers to get to market was by floating it down the Mississippi River to the port of New Orleans. Travel east across the Great Lakes was possible, but once produce arrived in Lake Erie there was no fast, convenient way to get it to market in the coastal cities. Similarly, eastern manufactured products were difficult to ship west where new markets might be opened. Commercial interests in New York developed the idea of building a canal to connect Lake Erie at Buffalo with New York City via Albany. This would open western trade through New York, with the state reaping the financial rewards. New York applied to the federal government for funding to construct a canal, but was rejected because the project would be within a single state and the decision was that projects within a single state ought to be financed by state resources. New York proceeded anyway, obtaining the necessary loans from other sources. Between 1817 and 1825 construction of the Erie Canal to link various lakes and rivers across the state to Albany, from where products could be shipped down to New York City via the Hudson River, resulted in a water link from Buffalo to New York. Almost overnight, New York City became the preeminent seaport on the Atlantic coast, the gateway to the west. Population and industrial growth followed the route of the canal. Other states were quick to begin their own canals which provided faster, less expensive transportation than did turnpikes and which could also accommodate heavier loads. In the fifteen years between the opening of the Erie Canal in 1825 and 1840, some 3,000 miles of canal were constructed.

Canals, however, also had some disadvantages. It was difficult, if not impossible, and costly to build them over hills and mountains, and they also froze in the winter making transport by canal only a limited seasonal advantage. The next advance to emerge was the railroad. Railroads offered the advantages of being able to go uphill, they were easier to build through rough terrain, they could operate in winter, and they were much faster than canal boats, moving people and freight at breathtaking speeds of 15 to 40 miles per hour. In fact, some physicians warned people against using railroads for fear their inner organs would be squashed from the excessive speed. But railroads could go where canals could not, and they were faster, cheaper and could haul larger amounts of freight than canal boats. Moving a ton of freight by wagon in 1800 cost an average of 15 to 30 cents per ton per mile. By rail in 1860 moving a ton cost only two to four cents per ton per mile.

The remarkable increase in the speed and capacity of shipping, coupled with the dramatic decrease in cost, enabled westerners to move agricultural products east and manufacturers to move their products west. As transportation developed, normal trade routes from the west generally shifted from north-south along the Mississippi River, to east-west along the Great Lakes-Erie Canal route or the numerous railroad connections that soon emerged. This led to a fundamental political shift. The Democratic Republicans of Thomas Jefferson counted their strength among constituencies in the South and the West—including the western region above the Ohio River—thereby linking the South and the Northwest in a political alliance against the Federalist and later Whig factions that were strongest in the Northeast. With the expansion of the canals and railroads the Northwest gradually became economically linked with the Northeast, shattering the previous economic and political linkage between the South and the Northwest. As a result, the Northwest and Northeast gradually merged to form the "North" where two distinct regional sections had previously existed.

Diverging Economies

Once the United States gained its independence, it was no longer subject to the mercantilist restrictions of the British Empire. One of those regulations prohibited colonists from developing any industry that would compete with those in England. With this restriction removed, manufacturing began to expand, especially in the North. Initially small operations that sold their products locally or regionally, very few were large enough to produce merchandise for export. In the antebellum years, the major exporting area of the country remained the South.

Yet manufacturing grew steadily, spurred by a number of inventions. One of the more important was the "cotton gin" developed by Eli Whitney in 1793. The gin was a machine that used comb-like instruments to separate the seeds from the cotton much quicker and with less expense than removing the seeds by hand. Before this innovation one worker could clean one pound of cotton per day; after it the same worker could clean fifty pounds per day. This exerted a major influence on America—both North and South. It extended cotton production over much of the South, resulted in the significant expansion Southern slavery, and shaped Southern culture into one based on a slave society. In the North, the availability of inexpensive, plentiful cotton led to the rapid rise of the textile industry which became the largest manufacturing venture in the nation. The number of spindles in operation in textile mills increased dramatically from 220,000 in 1820, to 800,000 in 1825, 1,750,000 in 1835, and 2,280,000 in 1840. In turn, the demand for cotton to feed these mills and to supply the enormous textile industry in Great Britain made commercial cotton agriculture so profitable in the South that production increased by 800 percent in a single decade.[1]

Throughout the antebellum years, the major segments of the economy continued to grow—both agriculture and manufacturing—but agricultural produce remained the major exports as seen in the following table which compared all manufactured goods to cotton alone.

Year	Manufactured Goods	Cotton
1805	2	9
1810	2	15
1815	2	18
1820	3	22
1825	6	36

In millions of dollars.

By 1860 cotton exports accounted for 60.6 percent of all U.S. exports, and agricultural produce in general accounted for 82 percent of total exports.

With the regions of the country clearly reflecting different economic interests, Henry Clay, an influential U.S. senator from Kentucky, attempted to promote the idea that economic differences between the sections could be developed to overall advantage if each section specialized in something, while linking itself into a general system of cooperation with the other sections. He called this the "American System." In principle this appeared to be a reasonable solution to sectional differences, yet the self-interest of North and South, coupled with the increasing emotionalism of the growing national debates, acted to prevent any such accommodation from taking hold. The North and South would continue to develop along diverging economic paths that only exacerbated the differences between them.

The Growth of Northern Political Power

Internal migration accomplished much of the early settlement of territory between the Appalachian Mountains and the Mississippi River, with people from the southern states generally moving into areas below the Ohio River, as well as the lands north of that waterway in southern Ohio, Indiana and Illinois, but by 1820 a significant influx of immigrants had begun to arrive. Data suggests that between 1816 and 1860 about 70 percent of all Europeans who entered the United States came in through the port of New York. Most of them chose to settle in the northern regions where the beginnings of commercial and industrial development provided jobs and the vast amount of inexpensive, sparsely settled farmlands offered agricultural opportunities where one would not be in competition with slave labor.

Boosted by a massive influx of Irish and Germans, the number of new arrivals continued to increase every decade from 1790 through 1860. By the mid–1850s, with a total population that stood slightly less than thirty million, nearly 10 percent of the population had arrived within the previous decade.

Decade	Immigrants
1790–1800	50,000
1801–10	70,000
1811–20	114,000
1821–30	151,000
1831–40	599,000
1841–50	1,713,000
1851–60	2,314,000

The population density of Ireland was one of the largest in Europe during the 1830s. Absentee landlords controlled most Irish land, making it virtually impossible for ordinary Irish to purchase farms, while at the same time increasing rents, tithes, and taxes made the small farmer unable to compete with large estates and often forced those who did own land to sell it and become landless tenant farmers. These economic factors, coupled with a lack of real political opportunities and the religious annoyance of Catholics having to pay taxes to support the Anglican Church, led many to think of migration elsewhere. The great "Potato Famine" of 1845–49 spurred a movement that had already begun. Between 1845 and 1855, an estimated 750,000 Irish died of famine and disease, while another two million left their homeland. Historians have estimated that nearly half of the entire population of Ireland migrated elsewhere during the nineteenth century, almost four million to the United States forming the largest single immigrant group prior to 1850. From about 6,000 in 1816, Irish immigration rose steadily to 65,000 by 1831; then erupted to 92,000 in 1842, 196,500 by 1847, and 206,000 in 1850.[2]

Most of the Irish settled initially in the large northeastern port cities, especially New York and Boston. Too poor to travel elsewhere, with only limited formal education—if any at all—and no industrial skills, they took unskilled positions in factories or worked as common laborers, settling into the cheapest tenements they could find. In the cities they frequently came into conflict with black workers on the docks and in other undesirable locations where they competed for both jobs and housing. Rivalries among the poor often led to violence between competing groups. Tenements grew to be grossly overcrowded, often with entire extended families living in one room or a basement, causing diseases to spread rapidly. Sanitation and fire protection were rudimentary at best. Life for most of these early Irish immigrants was at or below subsistence level, making each day a dreary life-and-death existence.

But the Irish did have one advantage. They were used to dealing with British control in Ireland, and they fell back on some of the same survival tactics they had used in the

"Old Country" to assist them in their adjustment to life in the underworld of urban America. The first, and probably most important support mechanism was the Roman Catholic Church. As a disenfranchised people in their own native land, the Catholic Church had offered them not only religious solace, but to some extent acted as their liaison with the outside world. People sought advice from the local priest, the illiterate came to have letters or contracts read to them, they sought legal advice, and many other secular services. In America, the Irish quickly gravitated to the Catholic Church for the same functions, to act as an arbiter with the unfamiliar outside world of urban America. Almost immediately, Irish priests began to replace the French who had dominated the Catholic hierarchy in America. By 1836, 35 of the 38 priests in the Diocese of New York-New Jersey were Irish—the other three were Germans. By the end of that decade, the Irish had firm control of the American Catholic hierarchy, a control they still exert to this day. In return, the Church acted as both religious and secular advisor, at once ministering to the spiritual and daily worldly needs of the Irish immigrant communities.

The other advantage the Irish had was that they spoke English. Very soon American politicians began appealing for the votes of Irish immigrants, and a close relationship developed between the Irish and American urban politics. This led to the creation of the famous "political machines" such as "Tammany Hall" that ruled New York City politics for the balance of the century and beyond. While political reformers and Nativists alike bemoaned the "selling of Irish votes" that kept these political machines in power, the relationship was not one-dimensional. The Irish received significant benefit for their political support. Political bosses helped them to obtain what they needed most—jobs. By 1855, 300 members of the 1,100-man New York City police force had been born in Ireland. Jobs in the fire department, on public works projects, and other public payrolls went to Irish immigrants in return for their political support. Politicians obtained pushcart licenses for their supporters, fixed minor problems with the police, sent Christmas turkeys to constituents, provided coal in the winter, paid rents and provided food in emergencies, appeared at their constituents' funerals, saw to it that presents arrived when babies were born, arranged for housing, and in dozens of other ways courted the Irish vote with services and support the immigrants could obtain nowhere else. By 1855, fully 34 percent of the registered voters in New York City were Irish. In time, the Irish themselves grew in political power to control most of the big-city political machines throughout the northeast from Boston through Chicago.

German migration was much more of a cross-section of German society.[3] It contained laborers and farmers, unskilled workers and skilled craftsmen, college professors and newspaper editors. Arriving with much more money per capita than the Irish, many of the Germans traveled inland to purchase farm lands in the Midwest or populate emerging cities such as Cincinnati, Milwaukee or St. Louis. They were the largest single immigrant group every year but three between 1854 and 1894, and are estimated to have been the largest group to arrive in America during the 19th century with over five million people. In 1851, 221,253 Germans arrived, with the 1910 census revealing 8,282,618 people listing "Germany" as their "country of origin." German historian Friedrich Kapp estimated that between 1819 and 1871, 2,358,709 Germans migrated to America bringing with them $500 million in cash and assets and a potential productive capacity of over $1.75 billion.

Because of their stronger financial position, and the cross section of society that migrated, the Germans attempted very early to establish ethnic enclaves in America. In the 1830s there were attempts to settle German colonies in Arkansas and Missouri, and movement to Texas began in the 1840s. By 1843 there were so many Germans in Texas that public laws were published in German. By 1847 approximately 20 percent of all white residents of Texas were Germans or of German origin, and by 1900 some 33 percent of Texans could trace their ancestry to Germany. By 1900, Germans constituted the largest single ethnic group in 27 different states. Unlike the Irish, German immigration contained in addition to Catholics, large numbers of Lutherans and other Protestants, significant numbers of Jews, and a large minority of "freethinkers," the latter being either anti-clerical, anti-religious, or both. Those arriving prior to the "Springtime of Nations" in 1848 were referred to as the "Thirtys" (from the 1830s) or the "Grays." They contained a large number of farmers and so-called "Latin Farmers," educated people who sought an idyllic bucolic life in the open farmlands of the American west (today's Midwest). Their acknowledged leader was Gustav Koerner, a political radical who settled in Illinois and became active in organizing German political strength in the elections of 1840 and 1844. He favored active German participation in American society and politics. In 1852 he switched from the Democratic Party to the new Republican Party because of its anti-slavery position. He was elected lieutenant governor of Illinois in 1856 and became U.S. Minister to Spain in 1862.

Democratic and nationalistic European revolts, including the famous "Springtime of Nations," sent floods of political refugees abroad when the monarchical forces regained control throughout Europe. A large number of the refugees were drawn to the United States by the prospects of inexpensive land, the democratic form of government, public education, and freedom of or from religion. Germans arriving after 1848 were generally referred to as the "Forty-Eighters" (or "Greens"). They included a large number of political radicals who wanted to remake society. Failing in Germany, they brought their penchant for reform to America. Among their leaders were the radical abolitionist editors Karl Heinzen and Bernhard Domschcke, and revolutionaries-turned-political-activists Franz Sigel, Carl Schurz and Friedrich Hecker. Because of their numbers, their relative economic position, and the fact that they were spread over such a wide area of the United States, the Germans became a significant political force in mid-nineteenth century America.

The two largest immigrant groups in antebellum years reacted very differently to the sectional debates that grew in intensity in the years leading up to the outbreak of the Civil War. The Irish, perhaps because they lacked a tradition of political participation in government in Ireland and the difficult, day-to-day existence so many of them faced in America, tended to be more interested in local issues rather than the great national debates. Although the Irish manifested some interest in the "Young Ireland" movement, or later political efforts to free their homeland, they were not strong supporters of the great reform movements of the day in America—temperance, women's rights, or abolitionism. Fervent supporters of the Democratic Party, they tended to either ignore or display hostility toward the growing anti-slavery movement. Situated as most Irish were in a struggle for the lowest paying jobs in society, and the least desirable housing, they frequently found themselves in competition with black residents in the large cities. To the average Irish laborer, the end of slavery would bring with it a massive migration of blacks to the Northern cities that would only stiffen the already competitive environment for life's necessities. Why should they support the anti-slavery movement, they asked, when achievement of its goals could well hurt their own already fragile existence? This did not mean that they favored slavery, only that they were afraid of the consequences for themselves were it eliminated. In 1856 they voted overwhelmingly for the Democratic candidate

James Buchanan. In 1860 their votes went largely to Northern Democrat Stephen A. Douglas, with few votes cast for Republican Abraham Lincoln, who they equated with the abolitionists.

The Germans' perspective was somewhat different. A large number of educated Germans migrated to America as exiles from failed democratic revolutions in Europe; consequently, they tended to support reform movements including the anti-slavery crusade. Quite early, most German-language newspapers in America came out in favor of the anti-slavery movement. At the height of the debate over the Kansas-Nebraska Act, German political leaders met in 1854 to debate a program they could support on the national level. What they developed was the "Louisville Platform," an extremely liberal— one might even say "radical" for that day—document that embraced the abolition of slavery, sought the repeal of the Fugitive Slave Acts, argued for the enfranchisement of women and blacks, and advocated a long list of social legislation including such things as free homesteads, public support for education, and institution of a maximum ten-hour work day. The formation of the Republican Party in the early 1850s split the German communities between the Republicans, known foremost for their anti-slavery and pro-immigrant policies, and the Democrats who were themselves split on both of these issues. Some Germans remained within the Democratic Party while others joined the Republicans, but even those who remained within the Democratic fold often voted with their Repub-

With the arrival of tens of thousands of new immigrants, anti-immigrant feeling increased. In this cartoon an Irish and a German immigrant, depicted in the stereotypes of the era, are seen carrying off a ballot box while disorder erupts in the background (Library of Congress).

lican fellow-immigrants on the key issues of the day. Indeed, many became prominent members of the more radical abolitionist movement.

Among the more prominent German anti-slavery leaders were Karl Heinzen, editor of the radical *Deutsche Schnellpost*, Gustav Koerner who helped to craft the anti-slavery platform of the new Republican Party in the 1850s, early Republican activists Friedrich Hecker and Friedrich Hassaurek, and Carl Schurz who gained a reputation for his anti-slavery rhetoric and became an intimate of Abraham Lincoln. The Polish immigrants Jan Tyssowski, Michael Heilprin, Adam Gurowski, and Marie Zakrzewska were among the more outspoken abolitionists, as was the Norwegian Hans Christian Heg. As veterans of the democratic and nationalistic revolutions that swept Europe in the late 1840s; many of these European immigrants were particularly interested in the cause of freedom that they equated with the anti-slavery movement. Since the large majority of each of these groups settled in the free North, they were able to speak out against slavery and in favor of the Union with little fear of overt retaliation. The German-language press in particular contained a large number of editors and journalists interested in promoting the cause of abolition. In 1860, there were 265 German-language newspapers being published in the United States. All of them favored preserving the Union except three, and the latter were all published in the South.

Immigration thus figured into the North-South dialogue in several important respects. The rapid increase in the population of the regions north of the Ohio River strengthened the hold of the North on the House of Representatives and promoted the early entry of new "free" states into the Union to at first insure parity with the South in the Senate and later to see the North gain a majority in that body as well. These immigrants also stimulated the demand for finished goods that at once promoted the further development of Northern industry and provided the labor force for this expansion. Finally, at least among the Germans, immigration provided vocal leaders who contributed to the rise of the anti-slavery movement and its spread through both the English- and German-speaking North.

The Second Great Awakening

Beginning slowly in the 1790s, expanding rapidly after the mid–1820s, a major religious revival swept Protestant America. While the older dominant religious groups from colonial days—Congregationalists, Episcopalians and Presbyterians—grew slowly, Methodists increased rapidly from 50 congregations in 1780 to some 20,000 by 1860 and Baptists went from 400 to over 12,000. One reason for this was a liberalization movement intent on attracting new members. This was accompanied by increasing use of traveling ministers who spoke at emotionally charged public revivals designed to convert people to their version of Christianity. As some of the more conservative elements in the Protestant churches began to liberalize, one of the most important changes was the transformation of Calvinist theology. Traditional strict Calvinism adhered to the doctrines of predestination and innate depravity. In other words, mankind was innately imperfect and it was only through the will of divine grace that one could enter heaven—only the will of God could lead to salvation and it was predestined when a person was born whether that person would be saved or not. Influenced by the same Enlightenment thought that was a contributing factor to the beginning of the American Revolution,

Protestant theology began to become affected by the growing belief that mankind had a free will and that the power of religious destiny rested with the people, much as the power of political government derived from the people. Salvation was slowly being "democratized."[4]

Although well under way by the 1830s, one of the leaders of the Second Great Awakening was the Presbyterian minister Charles Grandison Finney. Beginning his evangelical career in 1834 in Upstate New York, described for its intense evangelism as "the Burned-Over District" by the historian Whitney Cross, Finney rejected the Calvinist belief in predestination, preaching instead a doctrine of individual responsibility for redemption. The strict Calvinist view maintained that a person could do nothing to gain salvation since only God could ordain salvation. Finney argued just the opposite. Since humans possessed free will, it must have been intended that they use free will to make decisions, and if they could make decisions that must mean that they were capable of influencing events. Far from their ultimate fate being predetermined, Finney reasoned, people, through use of their own free will, could determine their own fate. Further, it was not sufficient for people simply to lead good lives themselves, to earn eternal salvation a person must do good deeds in society. This new view brought with it a closer relationship between the individual and God because Finney's preaching taught that by doing virtuous deeds, by actively participating in the improvement of society, an individual could earn his or her own deliverance. "Unless the will is free, man has no freedom," wrote Finney, "and if he has no freedom, he is not a moral agent."[5] Laced with liberal democratic ideals and anti-aristocratic overtones that fit well with the popular ideas of the day, Finney's ardent preaching struck a responsive chord in an era of religious and social revival. Converts embraced this emphasis on individualism and self-determination, often gaining renewed confidence in themselves and their abilities to shape the world around them.

The Rev. Charles Grandison Finney was a leader in the Second Great Awakening whose preaching helped popularize reform movements in the North, including the anti-slavery struggle (Oneida County History Center, Utica, NY).

An excellent speaker, Finney's warm, compelling mannerisms and mesmerizing oratory attracted converts wherever he spoke. His well-organized, thoughtful and logical presentations were magnified by his physical presence and compelling delivery. "He was tall and spare," wrote historian Richard L. Manzelmann, "a handsome and commanding figure in appearance. He had a voice that could reach, penetrate and stir, and a tongue that could shape words and images easily. He was master of the appropriate gesture; in fact his whole body expressed his preaching. It was especially his eyes, often remarked on, that could pierce the individual and compel the masses. He had the uncommon ability to control and sustain the attention of his congregations for hours on end. He had, in short, what we call 'charisma.'"[6] One observer commented that "I have heard many celebrated pulpit orators in various parts of the world. Taken all in all, I never heard the superior of Charles G. Finney."[7]

"If Northampton, Massachusetts, was the birthplace of the First Great Awakening with Jonathan Edwards in the 18th century," wrote Manzelmann, "Oneida County [NY] was the birthplace of what has been called the Second Great Awakening with the Rev. Charles Grandison Finney. If the First Great Awakening influenced the founding of the nation, the Second Great Awakening helped to determine the great reform movements of the 19th century and influenced dramatically the great debate on slavery that ended in the Civil War."[8] "Mankind will not act until they are excited," wrote Finney. "It is the business of the church to reform the world, to put away every sin."[9] Yet Finney was only one of a number of important evangelists, well described in Bernard Weisberger's book *They Gathered at the River*,[10] who moved American religion away from predestinarianism to a broader conception of the importance of social reform as an important ingredient in salvation.

Clifford S. Griffin concluded in *The Ferment of Reform, 1830–1860* that "the dominant force behind reform in the 1830s was a tremendous evangelical religious revival generated by one of the greatest preachers of his day, the Reverend Charles Grandison Finney."[11] Although beginning as a religious revivalism, the effects of Finney's preaching reached much further than the congregations he addressed. This reorientation of Protestantism to "doing good" led directly to a melding of religious activism with social causes as documented in Griffin's fine book, *Their Brother's Keepers: Moral Stewardship in the United States, 1800–1860*, and Timothy Smith's *Revivalism and Social Reform*.[12] This infusion of religious zeal led to increasing memberships in such religious organizations as the Bible Society, the American Home Missionary Society, the Tract Society, the Education Society, the Sunday School Union, and the Sabbatarian movement. Since the Second Great Awakening challenged people to positive action, thousands of Northerners began looking for a cause to support. Some became involved in the temperance movement, some gravitated toward the growing women's rights movement, but the vast majority, in the tens of thousands, adopted the anti-slavery movement as their cause. To Southerners, the slavery issue was based on economics and a defense of their social institutions. Increasingly, Northerners now viewed it as a moral issue relevant to the salvation of their immortal souls. Slavery was immoral. It had to be eliminated, and it had to be eliminated now. New recruits poured into the anti-slavery movement at exactly the time that Southerners were becoming much more defensive about Northern attacks on their way of life.

America's "Peculiar Institution"

Sometimes referred to as America's "Peculiar Institution," the practice of slave labor dated back to the early colonial period. Owners of large tracts of land in the New World could only benefit from that land if it were made profitable. Encouraging farmers to move into the area would yield taxes, but the most profitable enterprise was growing commercial crops such as tobacco, rice, indigo, and later cotton for sale to Great Britain. To accomplish this, the key ingredient other than land was labor, lots of labor.

Slavery had existed in the world since ancient times, and during the colonial period was practiced in South and Central America and Africa, among other places. One estimate suggests that during the two centuries from 1610 to 1810 some 400,000 slaves had been imported into the areas of North America that would become the United States. This amounted to about 5.4 percent of the total number of slaves imported into the

Western Hemisphere during that time, the vast majority going to the Caribbean and Central and South America.[13]

Life on plantations in America could be brutal. Conditions, and the lives of the workers, were totally dependent on the owner. Working hours were long, often dawn to dusk during the planting and harvesting seasons, with very few holidays. Christmas Day, Easter Day, and sometimes the owner's birthday were usually the only times a slave might look forward to having off each year, unless some special occasion arose. According to testimony from a number of observers quoted by Theodore Weld in his 1832 work *American Slavery As It Is*, the labor required of slaves was debilitating. One person observed that in Florida "during the cotton-picking season they usually labor in the field during the whole of the daylight, and then spend a good part of the night in ginning and baling. The labor required is very frequently excessive, and speedily impairs the constitution." Slaves were given a daily target for the number of pounds of cotton they were to pick and if it was not reached the slave could be whipped or otherwise punished. Weld's witnesses described slave housing as being of log or clapboard construction, "often they had no floor, some of them have two apartments, commonly but one; each of these apartments contains a family. Sometimes these families consisted of a man and his wife and children, while in other instances persons of both sexes, were thrown together without any regard to family relationship." One of the witnesses described slave quarters as "seldom affording a comfortable shelter from wind or rain; their size varies from 8 to 10, to 10 by 12, feet, and six or eight feet high; sometimes there is a hole cut for a window, but I never saw a sash, or glass in any."[14]

Clothing consisted of "two suits of clothes a year, viz. one pair of trowsers with a shirt … for summer, and for winters, one pair of trowsers, and a jacket of Negro cloth, with a beige shirt and a pair of shoes. Some allowed hats, and some did not; and they were generally, I believe, allowed one blanket in two years. Garments of similar materials were allowed the women."[15] A native of Maryland observed that "their clothing is often made by themselves after night, though sometimes assisted by the old women, who are no longer able to do out-door work; consequently it is harsh and uncomfortable. And I have very frequently seen those who had not attained the age of twelve years go naked."[16] The average slave diet, according to a statement made by Robert Turnbill, a South Carolina slave owner, "consists, from March until August, of corn ground into grits, or meal, made into what is called hominy, or baked into corn bread. The other six months they are fed upon the sweet potato. Meat, when given, is only by way of indulgence or favor."[17] This was generally confirmed by an article appearing in the *Maryland Journal and Baltimore Advertiser* on May 30, 1788, which claimed that "a single peck of corn a week, or the like measure of rice, is the ordinary quantity of provision for a hard-working slave; to which a small quantity of meat is occasionally, though rarely, added."[18] Weld then compared these unfavorably to "the common allowance of food in the penitentiaries [which] is equivalent to one pound of meat, one pound of bread, and one pound of vegetables per day. It varies a little from this in some of them, but it is generally equivalent to it."[19] A combination of the working conditions, poor housing, and lack of essential dietary nutrients conspired to weaken the slave's health and make him more susceptible to disease and other ailments. The average life expectancy of a slave was about 22 years, compared with 43 for the balance of the population. Half of all those born into slavery died during the first year after birth, a rate twice as high as white babies, and the death rate continued to be twice that for white children through age fourteen.

A black family and their small cabin at St. Helena Island, near Beaufort, South Carolina, in 1863. Judging from other descriptions, this was most likely better constructed than most (Library of Congress).

Slaves were deprived of any freedom, denied any opportunity for education and cultural expression, and had no recourse to law if mistreated. Slaves who acquired proficiencies as blacksmiths, butchers, carpenters, cooks, drivers, furniture makers, masons, silversmiths, tailors, weavers, or some other skilled occupation were often rented out with the profit going to the owner. In some cases an owner would share a small portion of the payment with the slave as an encouragement for the slave to do good work. Physical abuse on the plantations was commonplace. Owners could not be held responsible if a slave was physically abused, even if the person died as a result. Slave marriages were not recognized by law. Families could be split at any time, with spouses or children sold to another owner anywhere. Some scholars estimate that about 20 percent of slave marriages were dissolved by the sale of a spouse, while the rate that children were forcibly removed from parents through sale is estimated to have been even higher. When sales did not separate families, about a third of the married couples were separated because they had different owners and could only visit one another with the permission of their owners. So prevalent was this that marriage vows for slaves were changed to "until death or distance do us part."

Studies have shown that most people value social status and recognition. The same was true in plantation society. Within the slave population on the plantation there was a distinct social structure, much as there was a hierarchy of social class in free society. At the bottom of the social order were the common field hands, but even among them there might be some social distinction based on the price paid for a slave or some particular ability the person might have. From there, status increased as skill level and access to the owner's home increased. Slaves who were musicians or had some other skill gained status from those abilities. Those who were trusted to supervise other slaves ranked higher, as did skilled artisans who were sometimes allowed off the plantation, and domestics who had an easier work load and access to the owner's home. Occasionally an owner would free one or more slaves in his will, usually domestics who were close enough to be personally known by the owner and to develop at least some kind of bond of appreciation for their loyalty and good work. Similarly, those slaves who toiled in the cities usually had a higher status and a somewhat less brutal life.[20]

Although slaves led a very hard life everywhere, in general conditions tended to be worse in the Deep South (the Carolinas, Georgia and the states bordering the Gulf of Mexico) where the large cotton plantations required backbreaking work. As cotton agriculture spread through the Deep South, the demand for labor increased but Congress had passed a law in 1808 making the further importation of slaves illegal. Smuggling did occur, but as the slave population increased in the Upper South (Maryland, Delaware, Virginia, Kentucky and Tennessee) owners began to sell excess slaves to planters in the Deep South in need of labor. The expression being "sold down the river" became widespread, referring to slaves in the Upper South being literally sold down the Mississippi River to new owners in the Deep South, a fate that not only separated families but also meant a much harder life for the person going "down the river." In more modern times the phrase came to mean anyone who was betrayed by someone.

Of 11,133,084 people in the South in 1860, 7,033,973 were free and 4,097,111 slave (36.8 percent). Despite popular depictions of massive plantations like those portrayed in the movie *Gone with the Wind*, there were

Life on Southern plantations could be brutal as evidenced by the lash marks on the back of Gordon, who escaped from the John and Bridget Lyon plantation in St. Landry Parish, Louisiana. This photograph was taken in Baton Rouge in March 1863. Gordon, whose name may have been Peter Gordon, later joined the U.S. Colored Troops and survived the war (National Portrait Gallery, Smithsonian Institution).

only eleven people in the entire South in 1860 who owned more than 500 slaves, 243 people owned between 200 and 499 slaves, and less than 8,000 other people owned 50 to 199 slaves. Fully half of all slave owners possessed fewer than five. The massive plantation was not the norm. Most slave owners were small but prosperous farmers who owned only a few slaves and often worked in the fields alongside them. Among slave owners, only slightly more than 8,000 in the entire South could qualify as planters, fewer still being members of the rich planter class that dominated Southern politics. The ownership of slaves was also uneven geographically. By 1860, 47 percent of the population in the Deep South consisted of slaves, 29 percent of the population in the Upper South, and 13 percent in the Border States (Delaware, Maryland, Kentucky and Missouri that bordered on the free states). Similarly, the percentage of slaves per state varied considerably between these regions as the following table based on the 1860 federal census suggests.[21]

State	Percent	State	Percent
Mississippi	49	Virginia	26
South Carolina	46	Tennessee	25
Georgia	37	Kentucky	23
Alabama	35	Arkansas	20
Florida	34	Missouri	13
Louisiana	29	Maryland	12
Texas	28	Delaware	3
North Carolina	28		

The argument is sometimes made that slavery was not profitable and would have died out naturally without a painful civil war. In 1860, the South contained about 30 percent of the nation's free population, but 60 percent of the nation's "wealthiest men." In the South, the per capita income was almost twice that of the North and greater than any European nation except England. Cotton was the single largest U.S. export and accounted for almost 60 percent of all the cotton grown in the world. From 7.1 percent of U.S. exports in 1800, cotton rose steadily to 32.0 percent in 1820, 51.6 percent in 1840, and 57.5 percent in 1860. Clearly, by 1860 cotton was well entrenched as the mainstay of American exports and the basis for both the economy and class structure of the South.[22] With commercial cotton agriculture holding such a position of prominence, slavery was integral to the national economic system as well as the Southern "way of life."

The Rise of the Anti-Slavery Movement

There had always been sentiment against slavery in the North, and there were Southerners opposed to slavery during the colonial and early national periods as well. The existence of slavery had been a divisive issue at the Constitutional Convention, requiring compromises to gain enough votes for ratification. In the process, political leaders generally sidestepped the central moral issue in order to promote unity. In the end, the word "slavery" did not appear in the Constitution. Yet, despite the preference among most to avoid the confrontational issue, the anti-slavery movement began to grow. Quakers in Philadelphia formed in 1775 the Society for the Relief of Free Negroes Unlawfully Held in Bondage, in 1789 Benjamin Franklin founded the Pennsylvania Abolition Society, and in 1794 the American Convention for Promoting the Abolition of Slavery came into existence as the first national antislavery society. Between 1777 and 1804 Connecticut,

Massachusetts, New Hampshire, New Jersey, New York, Pennsylvania, Rhode Island, and Vermont all enacted laws eliminating slavery within their boundaries.

As early as 1790, petitions were sent to the First Congress demanding an end to slavery. Congress abolished the importation of slaves effective January 1, 1808, and in December of 1816 a group of prominent Americans including the *Star Spangled Banner* author Francis Scott Key, Chief Justice John Marshall, Congressman Daniel Webster, Speaker of the House Henry Clay, President James Monroe, and future President Andrew Jackson established the Society for the Colonization of Free People of Color of America, simply known as the American Colonization Society. The organization attracted clergy, philanthropists, and other people opposed to slavery, but who earnestly believed that people of African descent would never be accepted on anything approaching an equal legal footing by white Americans. Rather than have the elimination of slavery lead to a permanent national racial division, the Society proposed that "repatriation" to Africa would provide those of African descent with a better opportunity for equal treatment and successful lives. The organization eventually grew to include 218 local affiliated societies numbering thousands of members. Though not a member of the group, another prominent supporter of the colonization idea was Illinois lawyer Abraham Lincoln.

One option for resettlement was Haiti, a nation created as the first black-led republic in the Western Hemisphere through a successful revolution by its population against France, which had controlled it as a colony. The other option was Liberia, a region in West Africa purchased by the Society in 1822 with the idea of resettling free black people from America to an area where they could establish their own government. Its capital was named Monrovia in honor of President James Monroe. In 1819 the Society received a grant of $100,000 from the U.S. Congress, and over the years it occasionally received funds from Maryland, Missouri, New Jersey, Pennsylvania, and Virginia, but most of its funding came from individual donations. In the succeeding years, an estimated 13,000 free Africans relocated to Liberia until, in 1847, it declared itself to be an independent nation. Although this may not seem very progressive today, people involved in the colonization effort saw themselves as philanthropists who, as friends of the African population, were raising funds to purchase the freedom of slaves and resettle them in these black-controlled regions. The Society began to lose momentum and support by the mid–1840s after the rise of the Abolitionist movement which stressed the right of people of African heritage to equal civil and political rights within America.

The controversy over the Missouri Compromise in 1820 began to excite feelings on both sides, and in the following year Benjamin Lundy launched publication of *The Genius of Universal Emancipation* in Ohio. A vocal anti-slavery newspaper, its articles were republished by other periodicals. With the rise in anti-slavery feeling in the North, attitudes in both North and South began to stiffen during the 1820s. Gradually, over the following forty years, anti-slavery activities in the North increased, the South became more defensive and less tolerant of dissent, and the two sections of the nation drifted apart as emotionalism increased on both sides.

In 1822 a planned slave uprising to be led by a free African, Denmark Vesey, in Charleston, South Carolina, was betrayed to authorities and several presumed leaders arrested. With a large percentage of the population being slaves, in places along the coastal areas of South Carolina as much as 90 percent, one of the worst fears of planters and other white residents was a slave uprising. Although there was scant evidence of any real plot, fears were aroused and word of the supposed plan spread widely throughout the state and the South. In its wake, the state legislature took steps to prevent any reoccurrence. Since Vesey had been a free African, laws were enacted making it illegal to free slaves without the specific approval of the state legislature and then only on the condition that they leave the state within thirty days. Other laws made it illegal to teach Africans to read and write, because if they were literate they could read incendiary literature, become incited with dangerous ideas, and plan revolt. Still other legislation limited the movement of Africans and imposed other restrictions.

At the end of the decade of the 1820s, the slavery issue took a new and dramatic turn. In 1829, David Walker, a free African living in Massachusetts, published *Walker's Appeal in Four Articles* calling on slaves to revolt and kill their masters. Two years later, in Boston, William Lloyd Garrison, a co-founder of the American Anti-Slavery Society, began publishing *The Liberator*. In his first issue dated January 1, 1831, he explained his purpose: "I am aware that many object to the severity of my language; but is there not cause for severity? I will be as harsh as truth, and as uncompromising as justice. On this subject, I do not wish to think, or to speak, or to write, with moderation. No! no! Tell a man whose house is on fire to give a moderate alarm; tell him to moderately rescue his wife from the hands of the ravisher; tell the mother to gradually extricate her babe from the fire into which it has fallen;—but urge me not to use moderation in a cause like the present."[23]

Garrison was a leader in a movement called "abolitionism." The anti-slavery movement was not monolithic. There was a wide spectrum of people who were against slavery. Some who were more conservative could generally be termed "gradualists." These included members of the American Colonization Society who wanted to purchase the freedom of slaves and resettle them abroad. There were also proposals that the federal government gradually purchase the freedom of slaves over time until none remained. Another was to enact a law that anyone born after a certain date would be free, so that once all of the slaves in existence died the institution would expire. Toward the other end of the spectrum were the "immediatists" who were not willing to wait and wanted an immediate elimination of slavery. At the far end of the continuum, on the radical fringe of the movement, were the "abolitionists." The abolitionists demanded the immediate, uncompensated emancipation of all slaves. The abolitionists were insistent, direct, and spared no words in their condemnation of slavery, as well as the South itself, eliciting from Southerners a quick and equally unequivocal defensive response.

William Lloyd Garrison, editor of *The Liberator*, is generally considered to be the most influential abolitionist of the antebellum era (Library of Congress).

With William Lloyd Garrison, David Walker, and other abolitionists calling for everything from immediate emancipation to slave uprisings, the South was on edge. Its worst fears came true in 1831 when Nat Turner led a slave insurrection in Southampton County, Virginia, that killed 57 white men, women and children before being subdued. In its wake, dozens of Africans were killed, many of them completely innocent. No one knows how many actually suffered this fate, but with the entire area aroused it did not take much to bring forth retaliation. Southerners immediately blamed Northern agitators for the revolt and enacted additional laws to prevent further outbreaks. Possession of anti-slavery newspapers and other such materials was prohibited and anti-slavery dissent was no longer tolerated. Anti-slavery people in the South either learned to keep their opinions to themselves or fled to the North.

Before Walker, Garrison and Turner, most Southerners defended the slavery system as a necessary part of their economy. Following the Turner insurrection and the rise of militant abolitionism, the South developed a sense of "nationalism" that portrayed Southerners as the legitimate heirs to the American Revolution, while characterizing Northerners as a disparate mixture of peoples seeking to overturn the Constitution for their own benefit. Along with this Southern writers increasingly defended slavery not only as an economic necessity but as a positive good, a system that benefited everyone including the slaves. Thomas R. Dew, a professor of history and politics at the College of William and Mary in Virginia, who became president of the college in 1836, argued that slavery provided a productive economy for the South and was actually good for the slaves. Unlike the "wage slavery" of Northern factory workers who were paid little, were constantly in debt to their employers, and could be terminated at any time without a means of support, Dew argued that slaves enjoyed protection against being discarded if sick, injured, infirmed, or aged. Unlike "greedy" Northern factory owners, the argument went, Southern plantation owners provided for the needs of their slaves whether they were healthy or not, or whether they were too young or too old to work. Nor did slaves have to worry about food, clothing or shelter, it was all provided for them. Dew's arguments, and those of others who arose to defend the South beginning in the 1830s, fed into the growing emotionalism of the times that gradually pushed North and South farther and farther apart, decreasing the possibility of future compromise.

Later, in 1852, Dew again rose to the defense of the South asserting that "a merrier being does not exist on the face of the globe than the Negro slave of the United States" and that it was wrong to "disturb his contentment by infusing into his mind a vain and indefinite desire for liberty—a something which he cannot comprehend, and which must inevitably dry up the very sources of his happiness." Further, he argued, "it has been contended that slavery is unfavorable to a republican spirit; but the whole history of the world proves that this is far from being the case. In the ancient republics of Greece and Rome, where the spirit of liberty glowed with the most intensity, the slaves were more numerous than the freemen. Aristotle and the great men of antiquity believed slavery necessary to keep alive the spirit of freedom. In Sparta the freeman were even forbidden to perform the offices of slaves, lest [they] might lose the spirit of independence. In modern times, too, liberty has always been more ardently desired by slaveholding communities."[24]

In *Cotton Is King*, E. N. Elliott argued that the anti-slavery movement among Northerners was simply a way for them to forget the abuses of their own industrial system. He concluded that many people in the North

> are engaged in the [antislavery] crusade to divert attention from their own plague. We all recollect … the ever-active antagonism of labor and capital.… For the time perhaps they have succeeded in hounding on the rabble in full cry after the South, and in diverting attention from themselves? But how will

they be in the end.... Will they spare the hoarded millions of the money-prices and nabobs of the North? ... Yet capitalists, ye merchant princes, ye master manufacturers, you may excite to frenzy your Jacobin clubs ... but remember! the guillotine is suspended over your own necks!!

Ye people of the North, our brothers by blood, by political associations, by a community of interest; why will ye be led away by a cruel and misguided philanthropy, or by designing demagogues? So long as you confine yourself to making or hearing abolition speeches, or forming among yourselves anti-slavery societies ... you neither injure nor benefit the slaves.... But when you attempt to circulate among them incendiary documents, intended to render them unhappy, and discontented with their lot, it becomes our duty to protect them against your machinations. This is the sole reason why most, if not all the slave States, have forbidden the slaves to be taught to read. But for your interference, most of our slaves would have been able to read the word of God for themselves, instead of being so dependent, as they now are, on that oral instruction, which is now so generally afforded them....[25]

Yet, while Elliott and other Southerners rose to the defense of their "way of life," Abolitionists were calling on people to oppose the system even if it meant civil disobedience. Angelina Grimké, the daughter of a South Carolina slaveholding family, was forced to flee north with her sister because of her anti-slavery views. Becoming a committed Quaker, she quickly established a reputation as an avid Abolitionist, attacking slavery on moral grounds. "The great fundamental principle of Abolitionists," she wrote,

is that man cannot rightfully hold his fellow man as property. Therefore, we affirm that every slaveholder is a man-stealer; a man, is a man, and as a man he has inalienable rights he cannot rightfully be reduced to slavery. Our principle is that no circumstances can ever justify a man in holding his fellow man as property. We hold that all the slaveholding laws violate the fundamental principle of the Constitution of the United States. So far from thinking that a slaveholder is bound by the immoral and unconstitutional laws of the southern states, we hold that he is solemnly bound as a man, as an American, to break them, and that immediately and openly. Every slaveholder is bound to cease to do evil now, to emancipate his slaves now.... With regard to the connection between the North and the South, I shall say but little. I deny the charge that abolitionists are endeavoring to convince their fellow citizens of the faults of another community. Not at all. We are spreading out the horrors of slavery before Northerners, in order to show them their own sin in sustaining such a system of complicated wrong and suffering. It is because we are politically, commercially, and socially connected with our southern brethren, that we urge our doctrines upon those of the free states.[26]

Originally from South Carolina, Angelina Grimké and her sister Sarah fled north where they continued to support emancipation (Library of Congress).

To Southerners, these sentiments were hardly reassuring. Yet many Northerners also believed that abolitionists went too far in promoting animosity between the sections.

As attitudes hardened in the South against the rise of more aggressive abolitionism, some Northerners also opposed what they viewed as a group of troublemakers intent on provocation. Between 1834 and 1836, mobs assaulted abolitionists and blacks in several Northern cities. In October of 1834 a mob attacked black residents in Philadelphia. In the following year William Lloyd Garrison was attacked by a Boston mob, dragged through the streets, and nearly lynched before authorities jailed him for his own protection. Other mobs struck anti-slavery meetings and black settlements in Cincinnati, Hartford (CT), and Utica (NY). In 1837 the anti-slavery newspaper publisher Elijah P. Lovejoy was killed by a proslavery mob in Alton, Illinois, that destroyed his printing presses and burned his warehouse. Tensions rose so much that between 1836 and 1844 the Postmaster General refused to deliver anti-slavery material to the South in the U.S. mail and the House of Representatives voted to routinely table any proposals or petitions dealing with the slavery issue. Proponents hoped that this would prevent any further rise in tensions.

Despite these efforts, the fervor of religious revival melded with the growing anti-slavery movement to energize opposition to the South's "peculiar institution." An example of this was an open letter circulated by the abolitionist chancellor of the Protestant University of the United States in Cincinnati, Ohio, William Wilson. He argued forcefully that slavery was a sin. "No man is born a slave or a slaveholder," he asserted. "Such unnatural and false relations only exist, by might usurping the prerogatives of right. Every man is born free of every other being but God." The moral law, he reminded readers, required that "we shall love our neighbor as ourselves. Now, how stands slavery in the light of this law of God, whether as it respects the person, the property, the character, the reputation, or the interests of the poor slave? Alas, the scene of moral turpitude and heartless villainy which here rises up, is most loathsome, shocking and heart-rending! How has such a system withstood the influence of civilization, liberty and Christianity, so long?" To eliminate the evil he instructed all good Christians to use the elective franchise. "You will vote, my dear sir, so that this thing which, like the Devil, cannot love, shall not at least be propagated by your influence; and that any candidate who is either neutral or friendly toward it, shall have leave to stay at home, and not be allowed to occupy and dishonor 'the White House.'"[27]

Yet, Southerners could also use religion to defend their cause. Thornton Stringfellow is one example of this. He wrote:

> [Slavery] is branded by one portion of the people, who take their rule of moral rectitude from the Scriptures, as a great sin; nay the greatest of sins that exist in the nation. And they hold the obligation to exterminate it, to be paramount to all others.
>
> If slavery be thus sinful, it behooves all Christians who are involved in the sin, to repent in dust and ashes, and wash their hands of it, without consulting with flesh and blood....
>
> I propose, therefore, to examine the sacred volume briefly, and if I am not greatly mistaken, I shall be able to make it appear that the institution of slavery has received, in the first place,
>
> 1st. The sanction of the Almighty in the Patriarchal age.
>
> 2d. That it was incorporated into the only National Constitution which ever emanated from God.
>
> 3d. That its legality was recognized, and its relative duties regulated, by Jesus Christ in his kingdom; and
>
> 4th. That is full of mercy....
>
> [The abolitionists'] hostility must be transferred from us to God, who established slavery by law in that kingdom over which he condescended to preside; and to Jesus, who recognized it as a relationship established in Israel by his Father, and in the Roman government by men, which he bound his followers to obey and honor.[28]

Throughout the decade of the 1830s, events multiplied quickly, increasing feelings on both sides. The New England Anti-Slavery Society began operation in 1832, the American Anti-Slavery Society opened in Philadelphia in the following year, and in 1835 the New York Anti-Slavery Society came into existence in Utica. By 1837 there were over 600 abolitionist societies in New York, Massachusetts, and Ohio alone, and by the following year the nation counted some 1,300 anti-slavery societies with an enrollment of 109,000. The escaped slave Harriet Tubman was one of a number of daring individuals who helped slaves find their way to freedom on the "Underground Railroad," while a series of appeals brought a flood of petitions to Washington, D.C., imploring Congress to eliminate slavery in the District of Columbia and take other actions against the inhuman institution. The South reacted with a gag resolution proposed by Representative Henry L. Pinckney of South Carolina to table all anti-slavery petitions sent to the House of Representatives. Another bill stated that the House had no authority to interfere with slavery in the states, while a third asserted that the House found it "inexpedient" to interfere with slavery in the District of Columbia. Fearing an escalation of the growing danger, enough moderate Northerners voted for each in an attempt to defuse the divisive issue that all three were enacted. Yet, when John C. Calhoun proposed that the United States prohibit the circulation of antislavery pamphlets through the mail the attempt failed. Through it all, North and South became more emotional, less flexible, and less able to reach common ground for compromise.

Despite these attempts to downplay the slavery question, Northern opposition continued to escalate. In 1839, wealthy New York businessmen Arthur and Lewis Tappan, assisted by James Birney, a New Yorker who was a former Alabama slaveholder, formed the Liberty Party as a political home for abolitionists and other anti-slavery activists anxious to translate their cause into political action. "An independent abolition political party is the only hope for the redemption of the slave!" Alvan Stewart wrote in a letter to the *Emancipator* in January 1840. Slavery was a political issue, supporters of the idea claimed; consequently, it could be eliminated through control of the ballot box. The new party held its first convention in Albany in 1840, nominating Birney for the presidency.[29] Consumed by their fervent abolitionism, inflamed by the excitement of the campaign, the novice politicos produced catchy lyrics they repeated at rallies throughout Upstate New York. One, sung to the tune of "America," lamented the fate of a nation soiled by the blight of slavery:

> My country, 'tis of thee,
> Dark land of slavery,
> For thee I weep;
> Land where the slave has sighed,
> And where he toiled and died
> To serve a tyrant's pride
> For thee I weep.

Liberty Party leaders were greatly disappointed when they attracted less than 1 percent of the national vote.[30] Nevertheless, despite the poor showing, they vowed to continue the crusade. Throughout the next two years a procession of prominent anti-slavery speakers toured the nation. "In this section a Liberty party convention is an abolition convention, and an Abolition convention a Liberty party convention," Gerrit Smith, a wealthy abolitionist supporter from central New York wrote to Salmon P. Chase, a prominent Senator and future Secretary of the Treasury and Supreme Court justice. The ballot box, William Goodell trumpeted in the *Friend of Man*, was "an element of reformation which God has put into the hands of abolitionists."[31]

In 1848, most of the Liberty Party followers merged with groups of anti-slavery Whigs and Democrats to form the Free Soil Party which also supported homestead laws to grant free land for settlement in the west and advocated federal support for internal improvements. By the late 1840s the anti-slavery movement was gaining traction, much to the concern of Southern leadership which feared being overwhelmed by Northern political attacks and especially resented the increasing anti-slavery attacks on its whole society.

"Manifest Destiny" Shapes America's Future

Popularized by the Jacksonian Democrats, the phrase "Manifest Destiny" referred to the idea that it was the destiny of the Unites States to spread west until it reached from ocean to ocean. While settlers moved west into what had been the Northwest Territory, many also continued on into the lands of the Louisiana Purchase, crossing the Mississippi and at least in small numbers pushing beyond into Mexico. During the early 1830s, the Mexican government was open to American settlement in Texas, even encouraging it for exactly the same reasons colonial proprietors along the Atlantic coast earlier sought to encourage people to move to England's Atlantic coast colonies. More people meant more production and that meant more financial gain. However, the Mexican government did not allow slavery so Americans were welcome, but without slaves. Some brought them anyway.

In 1836, Americans in Texas, along with many Tejanos (Mexican Texans), rebelled against the Mexican government. Some sought enforcement of the Mexican Constitution which President Antonio López de Santa Ana was accused of ignoring, while others wanted outright independence. Among the latter were Southerners who saw in the vast land of Texas an opportunity to offset the huge tracts of potential free states included in the Louisiana Purchase that lay north of the Missouri Compromise line. The vast plains of Texas, which lay south of that line, might well be divided into multiple states to offset this Northern territorial advantage and thus maintain the crucial balance of power in the U.S. Senate.

When the Texan army under General Sam Houston defeated the Mexican army at the Battle of San Jacinto and captured the Mexican leader, President Santa Ana was forced to sign a treaty granting Texas its independence. Although Texas was interested in entering the Union as a state, Northerners were unwilling to vote in favor of its admission because it would be a slave state and would give the South more votes in the Senate. As a result, Texas existed as an independent republic for eight years, recognized by the U.S., Britain and France, among others.

During this time, settlers began moving across the Great Plains into the Pacific Northwest. These were largely Northerners who moved along the "Oregon Trail" into what later became Washington and Oregon. Movement along this route began to increase by 1843, but the settlers were moving into an ambiguous area, portions of which were claimed not only by the U.S. but also by Britain and Russia. By the election of 1844, Northerners called for official U.S. annexation of Oregon, while Southerners wanted the annexation of Texas. As a campaign platform, Democrat James K. Polk of Tennessee pledged if elected to annex both Oregon and Texas in the hope of gaining enough votes from Northerners and Southerners to defeat his Whig rival, Henry Clay of Kentucky.

Clay had to be careful since the slavery issue was beginning to divide the Whigs into Southern "Cotton" Whigs and Northern "Conscience" Whigs. With a smaller party base to rely upon, he could ill afford to alienate any potential supporters by having his party endorse either a pro- or anti-slavery plank. Consequently, Clay attempted to ignore the controversial question and focus instead on a campaign based on promoting internal improvements, discussing financial issues and, to win over some anti-immigrant votes, promises to support more restrictive immigration and naturalization laws.

Undeterred by the poor showing in its initial campaign, the Liberty Party convened its second convention in Buffalo in 1843 in what was the first national political convention in American history to include blacks among its leadership positions.[32] Although resting its political hopes on a single issue, the convention released the longest platform statement of the nineteenth century. Choosing James G. Birney as its standard bearer, it again finished a far distant third in the balloting, posing no threat at all to the two major parties.

James K. Polk appealed for votes from both North and South during the 1844 presidential campaign by promising to annex both Oregon and Texas (Library of Congress).

Polk won the contest with just under 50 percent of the popular votes cast.

Popular Candidate	Popular Party	Electoral Vote	Percent	Vote
James K. Polk	Democratic	1,339,494	49.5	170
Henry Clay	Whig	1,300,004	48.1	105
James G. Birney	Liberty	62,103	2.3	0
		2,703,659	100.0	275

Ironically, the Liberty Party, Polk's most outspoken opponent, may have actually swung the election to him by drawing enough potential votes from Clay to swing New York's large electoral vote into the Democratic column.[33]

Polk's victory led directly to a renewed debate on Texas annexation. Typical of Northern objections were the arguments of Ohio Representative Joshua R. Giddings who asserted that the Southern states habitually voted as a bloc to defeat the interests of the North and that the admission of Texas as a slave state would harm Northern business interests.

By the annexation of Texas, the protection of the free labor of the North has been surrendered to the control of the slave power; our constitutional rights, and the honor of our free States, are delivered over to the keeping of slave-holders. Indeed, our people of the free States have been politically bound, hand and foot, and surrendered to the rule and government of a slave-holding oligarchy. This has been done by the party in power, under the declared policy of obtaining Texas and retaining the whole of Oregon. But having obtained Texas, a portion of the party now propose to give up a part of Oregon. Their plan is, to add territory to the South, and surrender up territory on the North, to increase their power, to decrease ours; to enlarge the area of slavery, to diminish the area of freedom.

He argued "in the most emphatic terms that the rights and the interests of the free States have been sacrificed; and will not be regained until the North shall be awakened to its interests, its honor, and to its political duties."[34] But Polk's victory on an annexation platform bound the Democrats to support the admission of Texas and it entered the Union as a slaveholding state on February 19, 1846.

Texas statehood aroused Mexico that still held hopes of regaining its former province. Disagreements on whether the border of Texas ran along the Rio Grande River, claimed by the Texans, or the Nueces River, claimed by Mexico, added to the problem which eventually led to the outbreak of the Mexican War. Gen. Zachary Taylor led a U.S. army into northern Mexico in 1846, and the following year Gen. Winfield Scott led another invasion along the coast to central Mexico culminating in the capture of Mexico City. Under the terms of the resulting Treaty of Guadalupe-Hidalgo, signed on February 2, 1848, Mexico ceded to the United States some 525,000

Representative Joshua R. Giddings of Ohio was a leader in the movement to oppose the entry of Texas into the Union (Library of Congress).

square miles of land (called the "Mexican Cession"). In return Mexico received $15 million and the United States agreed to pay off over $6.8 million in Mexican debts owed to U.S. citizens. The U.S. also agreed to honor the property rights of Mexicans who owned land in the ceded area.

The newly-acquired territory immediately became a battleground between North and South over the potential expansion of slavery. California, which had been a Mexican province, already had sufficient population to apply for statehood. Its entry, much like Missouri a quarter century earlier, would upset the carefully maintained balance of Northern and Southern states. The debate over its entrance into the Union, and by extension the debate over slavery, once again became a national issue. The dispute quickly stirred emotions on both sides when David Wilmot of Pennsylvania introduced a bill into the House of Representatives, known as the Wilmot Proviso, to prohibit slavery in the entire Mexican Cession. Northerners were generally supportive; Southerners were appalled. In the Senate, John C. Calhoun led a blistering attack on Northerners for interfering with slavery in the territories, while rancorous debates swept both houses of Congress for the next two years. By March of 1850 Calhoun was near death, too ill to address the Senate yet as concerned as ever over the nation and his beloved South. Virginia's Senator James Mason read his speech for him. "I have, Senators, believed from the first that the agitation of the subject of slavery would, if not prevented by some timely and effective measure, end in disunion.... The agitation has been permitted to proceed ... until it has reached a period when it can no longer be disguised or denied that the Union is in danger. You

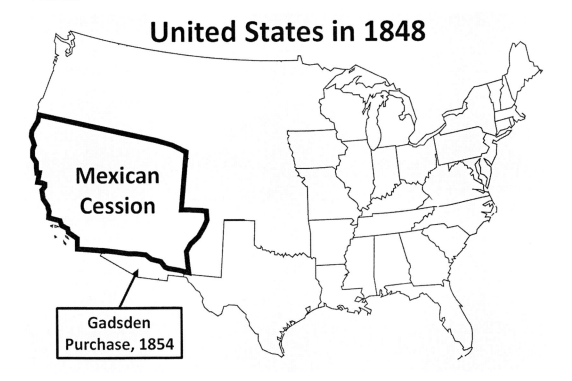

The area obtained by the United States from Mexico under the Treaty of Guadalupe-Hidalgo and the subsequent Gadsden Purchase (James S. Pula).

have thus had forced upon you the greatest and the gravest question that can ever come under your consideration: How can the Union be preserved?"[35]

Eventually, moderates were able to cobble together a compromise that at least temporarily eased tensions. California would enter the Union as a free state and the slave trade would be prohibited in the District of Columbia, two provisions that favored the North. To balance the compromise with provisions favoring the South, Congress agreed that it had no authority to interfere with the interstate slave trade, the U.S. agreed to assume the state debts of Texas from its time as a republic, the concept of "popular sovereignty" would be used to determine how future states carved from the Mexican Cession would enter the Union, and Congress agreed to pass stricter fugitive slave laws.

The idea of popular sovereignty meant that the people in a territory would decide for themselves whether they preferred to enter as a free or slave state prior to applying for admission to the Union. This was appealing to the South for two reasons. First, it gave them an opportunity to obtain more slave states than they would have had if the Missouri Compromise had been extended to the Pacific coast. Second, by allowing the people in a territory to determine its future, Congress was implicitly accepting the idea of "States' Rights" that the South had supported all along.

Southerners had been increasingly angered by abolitionist efforts to not only assist runaway slaves, but encourage them to run away, as well as by northern states that had passed personal liberty laws aimed at inhibiting efforts by Southerners to apprehend escaped slaves. Stricter fugitive slave laws were designed to force Northerners, under penalties of fine and imprisonment, to assist Southerners in recovering their property.

While Southerners were generally content with the compromise, anti-slavery Northerners viewed it with concern, going so far as to label proponents as traitors to their section. Although the compromise solved the immediate issue, it set the stage for the continuing escalation of emotional debates as the nation entered a new decade that would be fraught with crises, increasing hostility, and an ever widening divide. The words of the editor of the Columbus, Georgia, *Sentinel* regarding the aftermath of the compromise were prophetic: "It is the calm of preparation, and not of peace; a cessation, not an end to the controversy."[36]

3

The Crucial Decade

The decade of the 1850s began with the Compromise of 1850 seemingly decreasing the tensions that arose in the wake of the Mexican War, yet the very compromise itself held seeds that would blossom into a series of major controversies during the coming decade. While previously it was Southerners who felt aggrieved by Northern opposition to slavery, now the anti-slavery forces felt outraged over one portion of the compromise in particular. With Southerners already feeling defensive, Northerners began to exhibit the same emotional response. As the decade unfolded, one incident after another inflamed passions on one side or another, or sometimes both, with little or no cooling off period in between. When the decade began, most Americans, whether North or South, did not want to see the nation torn asunder. Gradually, as calmer rational thought gave way to rising emotionalism, people began to drift from the moderate middle of the political spectrum to the passionate extremes—secessionism in the South and radical abolitionism in the North. As this shift took place, opportunities for a peaceful settlement declined in proportion to the rise in emotional ferment.

The Fugitive Slave Act

In theory, the Fugitive Slave Act only restated what had long been the law of the land. Article IV, Section 2, of the original Constitution contained the following provision: "No Person held to Service or Labour in one State, under the Laws thereof, escaping into another, shall, in Consequence of any Law or Regulation therein, be discharged from such Service or Labour, but shall be delivered up on Claim of the Party to whom such Service or Labour may be due."[1] Everyone knew that the phrase "person held to Service or Labour" referred to slaves.

Although this provision of the Constitution protected slave owners against the loss of their workers, it did not stipulate a process for enforcement. The Fugitive Slave Act of 1793 provided this by specifying that the owner, or the owner's agent, could apprehend any suspected fugitive and bring him or her before an appropriate federal, state, or local court. There, upon presentation of testimony or evidence that the suspect was in fact a fugitive, the court official was required to provide written certification allowing the return of the fugitive to the state or territory from which the person had fled. The law also provided that anyone attempting to conceal or rescue a fugitive or obstructing the apprehension of a fugitive would be fined $500, then the equivalent of about twice the annual income of the average worker. President George Washington not only had signed the act into law but on two occasions used it to attempt to reclaim an escaped slave who was his servant while he resided in Philadelphia. Although Washington's efforts were not successful, slave catching grew into such a profitable enterprise that not even legally free black people were safe. Since people of African ancestry could not offer testimony in the courts, there are recorded instances of free people being sent into slavery when they could not provide proof they were legally free.

As the anti-slavery movement began to spread during the 1820s, free states increasingly attempted to circumvent the law. Eight states enacted "personal liberty" laws that required a trial by jury before accused fugitives could be sent out of state. The purpose of these was to provide sympathetic local juries with an opportunity to declare the accused to be free and thus not subject to return, even in cases where the accused was in reality a fugitive. An important test case occurred in Pennsylvania where slave catcher Edward Prigg was convicted of violating the state personal liberty law by apprehending a woman within the state and taking her to slavery in Maryland. In 1842 in Prigg *vs.* Pennsylvania Justice Joseph Story of the U.S. Supreme Court gave Northern states hope when he appeared to suggest that state laws might prohibit state authorities from cooperating with the apprehension of fugitives. Some free states immediately began to enact laws prohibiting state and local officials from assisting slave hunters or using public jails to hold those accused of being fugitives. The result was that slave owners faced mounting difficulty in locating and reclaiming fugitives. Southerners grew increasingly angry.

The Fugitive Slave Act of 1850 was designed to address Southern complaints by *forcing* Northerners to assist Southerners in recovering fugitives. Under the Act, subject to penalties of a fine of up to $1,000 and confinement of up to a year in prison, law enforcement officials were required to assist slave owners or their agents in locating, apprehending, and holding for trail any alleged fugitives. They were also authorized to deputize citizens who were then *required* to participate in a posse or in other ways assist in the location and apprehension of alleged fugitives. Once apprehended, law enforcement officials were held liable for any escapes. In court, alleged fugitives were not permitted to testify on their own behalf, but owners or their agents were permitted to testify to ownership. Even more unpalatable to anti-slavery Northerners was the provision establishing special courts to hear cases arising from the Fugitive Slave Act, with judges paid a fee of $10 if they certified the return of a slave to his or her owner, but only $5 if the judge did not certify the person as a runaway slave. To anti-slavery Northerners this was blatant bribery.

Northern anti-slavery advocates were outraged, and even those who had previously held ambiguous feelings or were unconcerned became alienated because they were now being forced to participate in upholding slavery. Gerrit Smith, a wealthy central New York financier of anti-slavery activities, teamed with the renowned African abolitionist Frederick Douglass in 1851 to craft a series of resolutions against the offending act. "Resolved," they began, "that we pour out upon the Fugitive Slave Law the fullest measure of our contempt and hate and execration; and pledge ourselves to resist it actively, as well as passively, and by all such means, as shall, in our esteem, promise the most effectual resistance." They went on to assert that people cooperating with the enforcement of the law "are to be regarded as kidnappers and land-pirates" and that "it is our duty to peril life, liberty, and property, in behalf of the fugitive slave, to as great an extent as we would peril them in behalf of ourselves." Reflecting the strong religious underpinnings of the abolitionist movement, the authors asserted "we do condemn and defy all laws, which insult Him, who is above all Constitutions, and which, aiming not to protect, but to destroy, rights, are, therefore to be regarded as no laws" and "hence our first and great work is to get rid, not of the law, but of slavery."[2]

Northerners increasingly came to believe that the government was being subverted by a "slave power conspiracy," while state and local governments in the North once again attempted to employ legislation or other methods to block enforcement of the new law. The Wisconsin Supreme Court declared the law unconstitutional, but its verdict was later overturned by the U.S. Supreme Court. Abolitionists and other anti-slavery activists announced they planned to disobey the law, while stepping up activities to assist fugitives to reach safety in Canada. Enrollment in anti-slavery societies increased and abolitionists became more aggressive in their attacks not just on the law but on the institution of slavery and on the South. The situation quickly became so critical that some Southern political leaders threatened secession and President Millard Fillmore warned that he would use the army to enforce the law if necessary.

One of the richest men in the country, Gerrit Smith lived in the small Upstate New York town of Peterboro and used his fortune to support anti-slavery activities (Library of Congress).

The controversy drove a deep wedge between North and South and between members of the major political parties. One immediate result of this was that Daniel Webster, a leading New England politician believed to be a serious candidate for president in the upcoming 1852 election, was passed over by the Whigs because his support for enforcing the Fugitive Slave Law antagonized the party's anti-slavery supporters. The Whig Party soon began to fragment between the Northern anti-slavery wing, called "Conscience Whigs," and the Southern bloc of the party which became known as "Cotton Whigs." Among Democrats, the only remaining really national political party, three factions began to emerge. Southern members remained solidly pro-slavery partisans. Among Northerners some emerged as anti-slavery advocates while the larger majority remained committed to pursuing compromise to preserve party and national unity.

Slavery Becomes a National Issue Once Again

Before the hostility stirred by the Fugitive Slave Act controversy had time to subside, another event took place that contributed further to the rising anti-slavery sentiment in the North. Harriet Beecher Stowe, a New England native, penned a novel set against the background of the Southern slavery system. Serialized in the anti-slavery *National Era* in Washington, D.C., once completed the work was re-published in book form under the title *Uncle Tom's Cabin, or, Life Among the Lowly* in 1852. The novel focused on the brutality and injustice of slavery in sometimes graphic terms unusual for that age. By mid–1853, some 1,200,000 copies had been published. Immensely popular in the North, it greatly broadened interest in and support for the anti-slavery movement. Banned in the South, the effect there was to place Southerners more on the defensive, fearing that increased abolitionist attacks might lead to attempts at adverse legislation or new slave uprisings. Amid the flood of passions accompanying the publication of *Uncle Tom's Cabin*, the slavery issue continued to command center stage in the American national dialogue.

Once again Thomas R. Dew rose to defend the South, arguing that there was nothing "in the Old or New Testament" that said

the master commits any offense in holding slaves. The children of Israel themselves were slaveholders and were not condemned for it. All the patriarchs themselves were slaveholders; Abraham had more than three hundred, Isaac had a "great store" of them; and even the patient and meek Job himself had *"a very great household."* When the children of Israel conquered the land of Canaan, they made one whole tribe "hewers of wood and drawers of water," and they were at that very time under the special guidance of Jehovah; they were permitted expressly to purchase slaves of the heathen and keep them as an inheritance for their posterity; and even the children of Israel might be enslaved for six years. When we turn to the New Testament, we find not one single passage at all calculated to disturb the conscience of an honest slaveholder. No one can read it without seeing and admiring that the meek and humble Saviour of the world in no instance meddled with the established institutions of mankind.

He went on to recall Christ was "born in the Roman world, a world in which the most galling slavery existed, a thousand times more cruel than the slavery in our own country; and yet he nowhere encourages insurrection, he nowhere fosters discontent; but exhorts *always* to implicit obedience and fidelity."[3] Dew further points out several biblical passages supporting slavery, including where the apostle Peter said, "Servants, be subject to your masters with all fear; not only to the good and gentle but to the forward. For what glory is it if when ye shall be

Harriet Beecher Stowe's *Uncle Tom's Cabin* is generally considered the most important anti-slavery novel of the antebellum era (Library of Congress).

buffeted for your faults ye take it patiently; but if when ye do will and suffer for it, yet take it patiently, this is acceptable with God.”[4]

Continuing his argument, Dew went on to assert that slaves were actually well treated by owners possessing Christian morality. “Look to the slaveholding population of our country and you everywhere find them characterized by noble and elevated sentiments, by humane and virtuous feelings. We do not find among them that cold, contracted, calculating *selfishness,* which withers and repels everything around it, and lessens or destroys all the multiplied enjoyments of social intercourse.” Yet he made a distinction between the treatment slaves received from Northerners and Southerners.

> Is it not a fact known to every man in the South that the most cruel masters are those who have been unaccustomed to slavery. It is well known that Northern gentleman who marry Southern heiresses are much severer masters than Southern gentlemen…. Every one acquainted with Southern slaves knows that the slave rejoices in the elevation and prosperity of his master; and the heart of no one is more gladdened at the successful debut of the young master or miss on the great theater of the world than that of either the young slave who has grown up with them and shared in all their sports, and even partaken of all their delicacies, or the aged one who has looked on and watched them from birth to manhood, with the kindest and most affectionate solicitude, and has ever met from them all the kind treatment and generous sympathies of feeling, tender hearts…. A merrier being does not exist on the face of the globe than the Negro slave of the United States…. Why, then, since the slave if happy, and happiness is the great object of all animated creation, should we endeavor to disturb his contentment by infusing into his mind a vain and indefinite desire for liberty—a something which he cannot comprehend, and which must inevitably dry up the very sources of his happiness.[5]

The anti-slavery response was more often than not couched in moral terms. Yet there were others who proceeded along different pathways in their attack on the peculiar institution. Called upon to speak at a July 4 commemoration in Rochester, New York, in 1852, the well-known black abolitionist Frederick Douglass used the occasion to lament the fact that the ideals of American liberty were not available to everyone. “Fellow citizens,” he began, “pardon me, and allow me to ask, why am I called upon to speak here today? What have I or those I represent to do with your national independence? Are the great principles of political freedom and of natural justice, embodied in that Declaration of Independence, extended to us?” He went on to elaborate on the decided differences between white and black residents of the United States. “I am not included within the pale of this glorious anniversary! Your high independence only reveals the immeasurable distance between us. The blessings in which you this day rejoice are not enjoyed in common. The rich inheritance of justice, liberty, prosperity, and independence bequeathed by your fathers is shared by you, not by me. The sunlight that brought life and healing to you has brought stripes and death to me. This Fourth of July is yours, not mine. You may rejoice, I must mourn.”[6] There were even a few who, like many of their pro-slavery antagonists, used economic arguments but came to opposing conclusions. One of these was Hinton Rowan Helper, ironically a North Carolinian, who used data from the 1850 census to argue that slavery degraded and impoverished white Southerners as well as the blacks they kept in bondage. House Republicans published 100,000 copies of his *The Impending Crisis of the South* for use in the 1860 presidential campaign.

Amid this growing tension the nation plunged into its quadrennial exercise in inflated rhetoric. The presidential election in 1852 featured for the first time a major candidate running for office specifically on an anti-slavery platform. The Democrats, the majority party in the country, chose to run Franklin Pierce of New Hampshire. A “dark horse,” Pierce was a relatively safe choice since he had not been a vocal anti-slavery advocate and would probably be acceptable to the South. As their candidate for vice president, the Democrats chose William King of Alabama to balance their ticket with a Southerner. Their primary platform was support for the Compromise of 1850.

Frederick Douglass, a former slave, escaped to become the foremost black abolitionist orator and editor of the influential newspaper *North Star* in Rochester, New York (Library of Congress).

The other major party, the Whigs, had been in decline for some time. Their strength in New England had begun to wane with only the central area of Kentucky and Tennessee remaining solidly Whig. In 1852 they nominated the Virginian Winfield Scott for president. The hero of the Mexican War, Scott was a popular figure, but the Whig Party was by this time generally demoralized and rent with divisions over the slavery issue. Northerners, mostly from New England where the abolitionist movement was strong, were reluctant to support a Southerner for president. These "Conscience Whigs" were even more reluctant to support the Whig platform which emphasized support for the Compromise of 1850, a pro–States' Rights position, and sought an end to Northern slavery agitation. As a result, the Whigs were deeply divided along sectional lines.

The election witnessed the entry of a new political party on the national scene, the Free Soil Party. Basing its platform on an anti-slavery plank, the party also came out in favor of "homestead" legislation and favorable immigration laws. The term "homestead legislation" referred to the enactment of laws that would make it easier and more inexpensive for settlers to obtain western lands. States in what was then the northwest favored homestead legislation to help populate the area and build its economy. Since the region drew large numbers of immigrants, especially Germans, the northwest also generally favored laws providing for short residency requirements that would allow immigrants quickly to become citizens and vote. But the key to the party platform was its stance against slavery. The party nominated John P. Hale of New Hampshire for president and George Julian of Indiana for vice president, making no attempt to balance the ticket between North and South.

Pierce won the contest with 51 percent of the popular vote to 44 percent for Scott and only 5 percent for Hale. In the Electoral College the vote was not even that close, Pierce recording 254 votes to 42 for Scott and none for Hale. Pierce proved to be a relatively weak president, with the most influential people during his administration being his Secretary of War, Jefferson Davis of Mississippi, and Senator Stephen A. Douglas of Illinois. Both supported the Compromise of 1850 and other efforts to negotiate national issues dividing the country. They would have their work cut out for them.

The Kansas-Nebraska Controversy

By the early 1850s the westward movement was in full swing, the Pacific coast had been firmly incorporated into the Union and proposals were circulating for the construction of a transcontinental railroad. This raised the question of where it was to be built since the route, and especially the eastern terminus, was sure to become economically profitable. Senator Stephen A. Douglas, chair of the Senate Committee on Territories, favored a route that would head west from Chicago in his home state of Illinois. To support this route Douglas wanted to organize the intervening land quickly into official territories under the jurisdiction of Congress. Since a portion of this territory already had sufficient population to apply for admission to the Union, the divisive questions regarding the extension of slavery and the balance of power in the Senate once again took center stage in the political debates.

Since the territory where Kansas was located had been part of the Louisiana Purchase in 1803, it was subject to the Missouri Compromise of 1820. Under that agreement, any states admitted to the Union in the future were to be "free" if they were above the southern boundary of Missouri (36°30′ north latitude) or "slave" if they were below that line. Thus, Kansas ought to be free. But Southerners vehemently opposed this. For a generation the Compromise worked well with each free state being offset with the admission of a slave state; but in 1850 California entered the Union as a free state giving the North two more votes in the U.S. Senate than the South. With no other potential slave territory ready for admission in the near future, Southerners hoped to have Kansas admitted as a slave state to restore the balance of power in the Senate. By 1854, the Kansas Territory was ready to apply for admission to the Union. With this, the old controversy over the admission of western states resurfaced with a new fury.

The issue quickly began to take on the proportions of another looming crisis. In an attempt to avert this Douglas introduced into the Senate a bill favoring the use of "popular sovereignty"—much as it had been in the Compromise of 1850—as an acceptable alternative to the debate over the slave or free status of Kansas. While seeking to resolve this important issue peacefully, Douglas was also interested in a fast resolution since he was promoting Chicago as the eastern hub of the proposed transcontinental railroad. In its final form, the bill stated that "all that part of the territory of the United States included within the following limits … is hereby, created into a temporary government by the name

Senator Stephen A. Douglas, leader the moderate Northern Democrats who sought to compromise with the South, promoted popular sovereignty as a solution to the controversy over the admission of new states (Library of Congress).

of the Territory of Nebraska; and when admitted as a State or States, the said Territory, or any portion of the same, shall be received into the Union with or without slavery, as their constitution may prescribe at the time of their admission." It also went on to affirm that "the provisions of … [the Fugitive Slave acts of 1793 and 1850] … be and the same are hereby, declared to extend to and be in full force within the limits of said Territory of Nebraska."[7]

Southerners solidly supported the measure because it overturned the Missouri Compromise line that separated free and slave states and would, thereby, give them the possibility of adding new slave states in an area from which they had previously been prohibited, and because the whole idea of popular sovereignty supported their theory of States' Rights. Moderate Northern Democrats seeking compromise rallied behind Douglas to ensure passage of the measure, but the growing anti-slavery sentiment in the North regarded this as a sellout and began referring to the principle as "squatter sovereignty." Representative Joshua Giddings and Senator Salmon P. Chase, both of Ohio, authored an emotional "Appeal of the Independent Democrats in Congress to the People of the United States" that argued strenuously against the proposal, proclaiming, "We arraign this bill as a gross violation of a sacred pledge; as a criminal betrayal of precious rights; as part and parcel of an atrocious plot to exclude from a vast unoccupied region immigrants from the Old World and free laborers from our own States, and convert it into a dreary region of despotism, inhabited by masters and slaves."[8]

Positions on the bill largely mirrored regional and political affiliation. Free-Soil and Northern Whig members of Congress cast their votes against the bill, while Southern Democrats and "Cotton" Whigs supported it. Northern Democrats tended to be split, but a personal appeal from President Franklin Pierce in favor of the bill, combined with the bloc of moderate Democrats who preferred compromise to confrontation, led to eventual passage. In the Senate the vote was in the affirmative by 35–13 while in the House it barely passed 113 to 100.[9] Northern Whigs voted unanimously against the measure while Northern Democrats split almost evenly with a slight majority in favor. Southern Democrats voted almost unanimously in favor, with only two negative votes, while Southern Whigs split with approximately two-thirds in favor. President Piece signed the bill into law on May 30, 1854.

Particularly venomous in the wake of passage was the anti-slavery reaction to the author of the compromise. The Utica (NY) *Herald* labeled Douglas a "demagogue," a "scavenger," a "second Benedict Arnold," and an "enemy of Liberty."[10] In nearby Whitesboro, a citizen's committee announcement that he would be publicly burned in effigy while a band entertained the crowd with "the rogues march and other appropriate airs on this occasion, for the Prince of Doughfaces and enemy of Liberty."[11] The next day the Utica *Morning Herald* described the event:

> Amid the hurrahing, the Court House, Academy, Furnace, Baptist, and Presbyterian bells commenced tolling. Someone with a pitchfork picked up the effigy and put it on the bier. Behind it was a sign saying "Douglas, Successor to Arnold. The Traitor's Doom." They walked up and down Main Street for a while, while the band played a "mournful dirge" … such unearthly groans were given as *told* in unison with the tolling of the bells, that the North is not wholly given up to Slavery. There is still a nucleus around which the friends of Liberty will rally and achieve a freedom from Doughfaces and Slavocratic rule worthy of the blood of our Revolutionary sires. Then, they went to the schoolhouse lot, erected a stake, and put *him* on it. In a few moments, the flames reached the object and it WITHERED as we trust the real Douglas now withers under the SCORCHING indignation of the enraged and intelligent friends of freedom everywhere.[12]

Throughout the North a tide of new anti-slavery petitions flooded Congress while popular demonstrations against the measure continued for months.

The Kansas-Nebraska Act effectively repealed the Missouri Compromise leading to further sectional conflict. Southerners began moving into Kansas from neighboring Missouri in an effort to boost the pro-slavery population prior to the upcoming elections, while others, labeled "Border Ruffians" by Northern abolitionists, merely crossed the border at election time to vote illegally in local Kansas elections. Northerners, too, began moving into Kansas to boost the free state vote potential. Ely Thayer formed the Massachusetts Emigrant Aid Society, later known as the New England Emigrant Aid Society, for the purpose of funding people who wished to move west to settle in Kansas on the condition that they vote for a free state. Another New Englander, Henry Ward Beecher, began shipping large crates of Bibles to Kansas, but when one of the boxes fell off a wagon and broke apart the contents were revealed to be not Bibles but muskets.

Violence soon erupted. Pro-slavery forces attacked the free state settlement at Lawrence on May 21, 1856, killing men and burning part of the town. Free state raiders retaliated by dragging pro-slavery men from their homes in the middle of the night at Pottawatomie Creek (May 24) and Osawatomie (August 31) and slaughtering them. These free state raiders were led by John Brown. After a history of failure as a businessman and farmer in Ohio, Brown migrated to Kansas in 1855. There, together with his five sons, he became an ardent enemy of the pro-slavery forces. Fighting quickly engulfed the territory in what the popular press referred to as "Bleeding Kansas." Over 200 people were killed in this territorial civil war in 1856 alone.

As the crisis over Kansas intensified contentious debates broke out in Congress. On May 19 and 20, 1856, Massachusetts Senator Charles Sumner rose in the Senate to denounce the advocates of slavery, and those who would strike bargains with them, in his famous "Crime Against Kansas" speech. Following a general condemnation of the "hateful embrace of Slavery" and the "depraved desire for a new Slave State, hideous offspring of such a crime, in the hope of adding to the power of Slavery in the National Government," Sumner became personal, attacking by name "senators who have raised themselves to eminence on this floor in championship of human wrong: I mean the Senator from South Carolina [Andrew P. Butler] and the Senator from Illinois [Stephen A. Douglas], who, though unlike as Don Quixote and Sancho Panza, yet, like this couple, sally forth together in the same adventure."[13] His allusion, of course, was to the famous knight errant, Don Quixote de la Mancha, the protagonist of Miguel Cervantes' popular novel *El Ingenioso Hidalgo Don Quijote de la Mancha*—better known simply as *Don Quixote*. In that tale, Don Quixote fancied himself a knight in shining armor who roamed the countryside righting wrongs. The problem was that the era of knighthood was long past. Don Quixote, supported by his loyal servant Sancho Panza, attacked windmills that he envisioned as dragons and attempted to save Dulcinea, a local tavern worker of dubious repute whom his mind pictured as a fair damsel in distress. In his speech, Sumner drew on Cervantes' work for his analogies.

Sumner continued,

> The Senator from South Carolina has read many books of chivalry, and believes himself a chivalrous knight, with sentiments of honor and courage. Of course he has chosen a mistress to whom he has made his vows, and who, though ugly to others, is always lovely to him,—though polluted in the sight of the world, is chaste in his sight: I mean the harlot Slavery. For her his tongue is always profuse in words. Let her be impeached in character, or any proposition be made to shut her out from the

extension of her wantonness, and no extravagance of manner or hardihood of assertion is then too great for this Senator. The frenzy of Don Quixote in behalf of his wench Dulcinea del Toboso is all surpassed. The asserted rights of Slavery, which shock equality of all kinds, are cloaked by a fantastic claim of equality. If the Slave States cannot enjoy what, in mockery of the great fathers of the Republic, he misnames Equality under the Constitution,—in other words, the full power in the National Territories to compel fellow-men to unpaid toil, to separate husband and wife, and to sell little children at the auction-block,—then, Sir, the chivalric Senator will conduct the State of South Carolina out of the Union! Heroic knight! Exalted Senator! A second Moses come for a second exodus!

Turning to Douglas, Sumner described the sponsor of the popular sovereignty compromise as "the squire of Slavery, its very Sancho Panza, ready to do all its humiliating offices."[14]

To Southerners in particular, to whom duels of honor had been fought over far less insults, these were fighting words. In the House of Representatives sat Preston Brooks, Senator Butler's nephew. The senator had not been present to hear Sumner's denunciation of him, but word of the verbal assault soon

Massachusetts senator Charles Sumner was a vocal leader of the anti-slavery forces in Congress. He gave a scathing speech against those who defended slavery, singling out for special criticism senators Andrew P. Butler of South Carolina and Stephen A. Douglas of Illinois (Library of Congress).

reached the House. Brooks crossed from the House chamber to the Senate where he observed Sumner at his desk. Approaching the senator, Brooks is reported to have said, "You've libeled my state and slandered my white-haired old relative, Senator Butler, and I've come to punish you for it."[15] Before Sumner could reply, Brooks proceeded to beat him over the head with a cane, knocking him senseless and breaking the walking stick in the process.

Northerners were appalled that physical violence had been perpetrated on the floor of the U.S. Senate. What else, they asked rhetorically, could one expect from these uncivilized Southerners? Brooks was universally condemned in the North where Sumner was portrayed as one more victim of Southern brutality. A movement in the House to expel him failed when every Southern Representative except one vote against the measure. In the South, the opposite was true. Brooks returned home to South Carolina a hero for standing up for the honor of his family, his state and the South. Admiring constituents donated funds to present him with new canes to replace the one he had broken over Sumner's head. The different reactions to the incident clearly illustrated the gap that had developed between North and South. Sumner went home to Massachusetts to recuperate, remaining absent from the Senate until December 1859. During that time he traveled to Europe "for his health," and was re-elected to the Senate *in absentia*. Northern newspapers periodically ran stories about the extent of his injuries and the progress of his recuperation, while Southerners felt sure that Sumner was faking, using the incident to prolong sympathy and anti–South feelings. The whole affair heightened emotionalism on both

SOUTHERN CHIVALRY _ ARGUMENT versus CLUB'S.

Titled "Southern Chivalry—Argument versus Clubs," this cartoon promotes the Northern view deploring the attack on Charles Sumner in the Senate chamber (Library of Congress).

sides and kept the issues alive for months, if not years. By that summer violence had engulfed Kansas, the battleground had spread to the floor of the U.S. Senate, and passions had been enflamed to new heights throughout the nation.

The Election of 1856

With civil war raging in Kansas, verbal and physical attacks in Congress, and the country being torn into hostile sections, the nation plunged into its next national political campaign. Once again there would be three main candidates for the presidency in the 1856 election, but the parties would be somewhat different. The Whigs had by now faded from the scene, their party fatally torn by the slavery issue. There remained only one really national party, the Democrats. They searched for a candidate that would be acceptable to both North and South, something that was not easy in view of the heightened tensions. They finally settled on James Buchanan of Pennsylvania, whose chief qualifications were that he supported compromise and had been out of the country for the past eight years serving as Minister to England. Because of his absence he had not been called upon to make any partisan statements during the recent political turmoil. He had not offended anyone, North or South. As vice president, the Democrats nominated John C. Breckinridge of Kentucky, a leading Southern politician who would certainly appeal to voters from that section. Their platform stressed support for States' Rights and the use of popular sovereignty in the territories.

A large increase in immigration in the 1840s and 1850s led to a resurgence in anti-immigrant and anti–Catholic nativism and formation of the American Party, usually referred

James Buchanan of Pennsylvania was tapped as the Democratic nominee in 1856 largely because he was not on record opposing the expansion of slavery into the territories (Library of Congress).

to as the "Know-Nothing Party." At the peak of their influence in the mid–1850s, they nominated former president Millard Fillmore of New York for president and Andrew Donelson of Tennessee for vice president. Their platform called for exclusion of Catholics and foreigners from political office and a 21-year residency for citizenship. Clearly, these proposals had nothing to do with the heated issues of the day, leading one to wonder why they were able to eventually attract so many voters.

The third party was also new to the political area, the Republican Party. Formed in Wisconsin as a local group in 1852, the Republicans included former members of the Free Soil Party, Conscience Whigs, anti-slavery Democrats, and a sizeable number of German immigrants. Their platform reflected the interests of these constituencies including opposition to slavery, support for homestead legislation, espousal of favorable immigration laws, and backing for internal improvements. The latter included such things as federal support for education, canals, and railroads, all of which many Northerners supported while Southerners, who favored a limited central government, opposed. Running their first national campaign, the Republicans offered John C. Frémont of California for president and William Dayton of New Jersey for vice president. Because of their anti-slavery stance, Republicans appealed only to Northerners as evidenced by the fact that they made no attempt whatever to balance the ticket with a Southerner.

In the end, Buchanan won relatively easily with 174 electoral votes to 114 for Frémont and 8 for Fillmore. What was surprising was that the brand new Republican Party, in its first national race, did surprisingly well winning one-third of the popular vote.

Candidate	Popular Vote	Percent	Electoral Vote
Buchanan	1,838,000	45	174
Frémont	1,341,000	33	114
Fillmore	875,000	22	8

Looking at the results, it is important to note that Buchanan became a minority president, winning only 45 percent of the vote. This reflected the nation's divisions at the time. All of Frémont's electoral votes came from New York, New England, and areas of the Midwest where abolitionism was strongest. In his inaugural address, Buchanan stressed the use of popular sovereignty and appeal to the Supreme Court to settle outstanding national issues. These conciliatory statements mollified the South enough to head off, at least momentarily, the rising crisis.

The Dred Scott Decision

The new president had barely been inaugurated when another tempest kept the slavery question before the public. Dred Scott was a slave who was taken by his owner to the free state of Illinois, and then to Wisconsin which was at that time a free territory. When his owner brought him back to the slave state of Missouri, Scott sued for his freedom arguing that residence in a free state and a free territory had made him free. The case wound its way through the courts over a period of several years. A lower state court ruled in Scott's favor in 1852, but this was later overturned by the Missouri state supreme court. This led to an appeal being filed in federal court with the case eventually coming before the Supreme Court for adjudication in 1857.

There were three major issues in the case. Was Scott a citizen entitled to sue in federal court? Was residence on free soil a valid claim to freedom? Was the Missouri Compromise constitutional? Of the nine Supreme Court justices, seven were Democrats and two Republicans, the two latter having joined the new party after their original elevation to the bench. Each justice rendered his own opinion. The one usually cited as "the Dred Scott Decision" was the opinion given by Chief Justice Roger B. Taney a States' Rights Jacksonian Democrat from Maryland. Regarding the first question Taney found that Scott was not a citizen, and thus not entitled to sue in federal court, because people of African descent were never intended to be citizens. Three justices agreed, while the two Republican justices dissented. With this finding the case should have been concluded since Scott was not eligible to sue in federal court, but the justices went on to determine the merits of the case anyway.

Taney found that Scott should not be free because he resided in Missouri at the time of the suit and Missouri allowed slavery. Five other justices agreed with this position; three dissented. By a similar majority of six to three, the Court also found that the Missouri Compromise was unconstitutional because slaves were considered property and the Fifth Amendment read, in part, "No person shall be ... deprived of life, liberty, or property, without due process of law; nor shall private property be taken for public use,

Dred Scott, seen here with his wife Harriet, sparked a nationwide emotional debate when the Supreme Court ruled against his claim of freedom (Library of Congress).

without just compensation." Clearly, the Constitution says that property cannot be taken from people without due process of law. Since the majority of justices considered slaves to be property, Scott could not be freed against the wishes of his owner. In his majority opinion, Taney wrote that

> the right of property in a slave is distinctly and expressly affirmed in the Constitution. The right to traffic in it, like an ordinary article of merchandise and property, was guaranteed to the citizens of the United States, in every state that might desire it, for twenty years. And the government in express terms is pledged to protect it in all future time if the slave escapes from his owner. This is done in plain words—too plain to be misunderstood. And no word can be found in the Constitution which gives Congress a greater power over slave property or which entitles property of that kind to less pro- tection than property of any other description.... Upon these considerations it is the opinion of the Court that the act of Congress which prohibited a citizen from holding and owning property of this kind in the territory of the United States north of the line therein mentioned is not warranted by the Constitution and is therefore void; and that neither Dred Scott himself, nor any of his family, were made free by being carried into this territory; even if they had been carried there by the owner with the intention of becoming a permanent resident.[16]

Southerners were jubilant. The Supreme Court had validated their position. Slaves were property and the right of people to own property was protected by the Constitution. "We regard the decision of the Judges of the Supreme Court in this case with the highest satisfaction," trumpeted the *Southern Enterprise* of Greenville, South Carolina. "It meets

with our hearty, cordial, unqualified approval. The highest judicial tribunal in the land has decided that the blackamoors, called, by the extreme of public courtesy, the colored population, are not citizens of the United States." The same newspaper hastened to place the decision in the con- text of the growing national divide. "This is the most fatal blow which the fanatical Abolitionists have ever received, and their malignity and venom are proportioned to their desperation. The decision of the Supreme Court ... overwhelms the mis- chief makers with confusion. It blasts their nefarious schemes as with a lightning stroke. No marvel, is it then, that they man- ifest such unseemly opposition to the august tribunal which has visited them with such a crushing overthrow."[17] The long disagreement over the expansion of slavery into the territories appeared to have been finally decided in favor of the South.

Roger B. Taney of Maryland was the chief justice of the Supreme Court who wrote the "Dred Scott Decision" (Library of Congress).

Northerners were outraged. "I speak what cannot be denied," Charles Sumner proclaimed, "when I declare that the opin- ion of the Chief Justice in the case of Dred Scott was more thoroughly abominable than anything of the kind in the history of courts. Judicial baseness reached its lowest point on that occasion. You have not forgotten that terrible decision where a most unrighteous judgment was sustained by a falsification of history. Of course, the Constitution of the United States and every principle of Liberty was falsified, but historical truth was falsified also."[18]

What the court's opinion implied was that slaves could be taken anywhere regardless of local law because slaves were property and the right to own property was guaranteed in the Constitution. The decision mobilized Northerners against slavery more than any previous occurrence. "Surely," wrote influential New York politician Roscoe Conkling, "there can be fewer great monstrosities than the proposition that one race has the right to enslave another."[19] His hometown newspaper, the Utica, New York, *Herald*, editorialized: "A new code of political ethics is pronounced: a new theory of Government has been discovered. It is not a Republic, but a Despotism we are living under. The Constitution is not a chart of freedom, but an instrument of Bondage. The object of the Government is not to protect the liberties of the People, but to further the interests of Slavery. It is not Freedom that is national, but Slavery."[20] Horace Greeley spoke for many Northerners when he editorialized in his *New York Tribune* that the decision was "entitled to just so much moral weight as would be the judgment of a majority of those congregated in an Washington barroom."[21]

If slavery was protected by the Constitution, then what was there to prevent a slave owner from bringing slaves into New York, or Ohio, or Indiana, or any other free state? If the Constitution protected the right to own slaves in Missouri, then it also protected that right in every other state. As an Illinois lawyer named Abraham Lincoln remarked, "Put this and that together, and we have another nice little niche, which we may, ere long, see filled with another Supreme Court decision, declaring that the Constitution of the United States does not permit a State to exclude slavery from its limits.… We shall lie down pleasantly dreaming that the people of Missouri are on the verge of making their State free, and we shall awake to the reality instead, that the Supreme Court has made Illinois a slave State."[22] Northerners who had heretofore been ambiguous or disinterested in the slavery issue began to join the anti-slavery ranks fearing that slavery might spread nationwide, forcing *them* to compete with slave labor.

The Dred Scott Decision was a major turning point along the road to civil war. As opposed as they were to the extension of slavery to the territories, or the very existence of slavery in the South, the thought of being forced to accept slavery in their own states, as remote as that may have been in actuality, filled Northerners with an explosive combination of fear and rage. To a growing number of people, conflict appeared inevitable. In 1858 Senator William H. Seward of New York opined that the growing division was "an irrepressible conflict between opposing and enduring forces."[23] The *New York Tribune* informed its readers that "we are not one people. We are two peoples. We are a people for Freedom and a people for Slavery. Between the two, conflict is inevitable."[24]

"Much as I abhor war," New Yorker Gerrit Smith declared, "I nevertheless believe, that there are instances when the shedding of blood is unavoidable."[25] To Joshua Giddings in Ohio, Smith wrote in 1858, "The slave will be delivered by the shedding of blood— and the signs are multiplying that his deliverance is at hand."[26] The Democratic Party split over the issue, while membership in the new anti-slavery Republican Party grew quickly from an influx of disenchanted Democrats. The swift emotional response by Northerners to the decision, coupled with the already high emotionalism south of the

Mason-Dixon Line, made any further compromise on the issue less likely, propelling the nation further toward near fatal division.

The Lincoln-Douglas Debates

Although 1858 was not a presidential election year, the political campaigns that fall drew more attention than many presidential contests. One of the more important campaigns was the race for an Illinois Senate seat pitting Democrat Stephen A. Douglas against former "Conscience" Whig and now Republican Abraham Lincoln. The campaign was important mainly because of the national profile of Douglas and his leadership of the moderate Northerners who crafted and supported the concept of "popular sovereignty." As Douglas explained it, "If the people of Kansas want a slaveholding state, let them have it, and if they want a free state they have a right to it, and it is not for the people of Illinois, or Missouri, or New York, or Kentucky, to complain, whatever the decision of Kansas may be."[27] Many people believed the election to be a referendum on Douglas and his policies.

The political battle lines were drawn early when Lincoln, at that time a relative unknown beyond the immediate confines of his Illinois district, accepted the nomination of his party in a speech made famous by his declaration "A house divided against itself cannot stand." He went on to say:

> I believe this government can not endure permanently half slave, and half free.
>
> I expressed this belief a year ago; and subsequent developments have but confirmed me.
>
> I do not expect the Union to be dissolved. I do not expect the house to fall; but I do expect it will cease to be divided. It will become all one thing, or all the other. Either the opponents of slavery will arrest the further spread of it, and put it in the course of ultimate extinction; or its advocates will push it forward till it shall become alike lawful in all the states, old, as well as new. Do you doubt it? Study the Dred Scott decision, and then see, how little, even now, remains to be done.[28]

Amid the background of continuing violence in Kansas and national debates on its future, as well as that of the nation, attempts were made to move statehood forward. In accordance with the idea of popular sovereignty, a constitution was to be submitted for a popular vote by the people in the Kansas Territory. Not surprisingly, two proposals for the new constitution emerged. Anti-slavery forces meeting in Topeka under the leadership of James H. Lane drafted a document that would make Kansas a free state. Meanwhile, the largely pro-slavery territorial legislature met under Territorial Governor Robert J. Walker at Lecompton to create a government that would give voters two options: one that guaranteed slavery and the other that provided for no more slaves in the territory than already existed. Free state advocates boycotted the obviously biased options resulting in a vote of 6,226 in favor of the first provision and 569 for the second. However, subsequent investigations found that 2,720 of the pro-slavery votes, 43.7 percent, for the Lecompton Constitution were fraudulent—cast by illegal voters or dead people.

While Governor Walker was away in Washington, D.C., Lt. Gov. Frederick Stanton put the entire constitution up for vote with options that included provisions (1) for slavery, (2) without slavery, and (3) against the entire constitution. In this instance pro-slavery forces boycotted the voting yielding only 138 votes for slavery, 24 without slavery, and 10,226 against the entire constitution. President Buchanan, who supported the Lecompton Constitution, pushed for its adoption by Congress despite the negative vote but this was blocked by a coalition of Republicans and anti-slavery Democrats. In 1858 the constitution was resubmitted with a promise to Kansas voters that if they would adopt a provision legalizing slavery they would receive an additional five million acres of land. Despite this obvious attempt at bribery, the third vote, held under federal supervision, returned 1,788 votes for slavery and 11,300 against.

With the national attention continuing to be transfixed by the Kansas crisis, the issue naturally demanded the attention of the candidates for the Illinois Senate seat. During the campaign they gave speeches throughout the state and engaged in seven face-to-face debates, the most famous being held in Freeport, Illinois. During the debate, Lincoln posed a question to Douglas: Can the residents of a territory exclude slavery prior to statehood? It was a very simple question, but it was also a trap. It was a question Douglas could not answer without subjecting himself to criticism. If he responded in the affirmative, Lincoln could criticize him for seeming to set himself above the Supreme Court which had just ruled in the Dred Scott Decision that slavery could *not* be prohibited because the Constitution gave citizens the right to own property free from government interference. But if he answered in the negative, then Lincoln could accuse him of repudiating the concept of popular sovereignty which he had previously been championing. When pressed, Douglas responded by trying to minimize the question, suggesting that its answer was already well known to his opponent.

The next question propounded to me by Mr. Lincoln is, Can the people of a Territory in any lawful way, against the wishes of any citizen of the United States, exclude slavery from their limits prior to the formation of a State constitution? I answer emphatically, as Mr. Lincoln has heard me answer a hundred times from every stump in Illinois, that in my opinion the people of a Territory can, by lawful means, exclude slavery from their limits prior to the formation of a State constitution. Mr. Lincoln knew that I had answered that question over and over again. He heard me argue the Nebraska bill on that principle all over the State in 1854, in 1855, and in 1856, and he has no excuse for pretending to be in doubt as to my position on that question. It matters not what way the Supreme Court may hereafter decide as to the abstract question whether slavery may or may not go into a Territory under the Constitution, the people have the lawful means to introduce it or exclude it as they please, for the reason that slavery cannot exist a day or an hour anywhere, unless it is supported by local police regulations. Those police regulations can only be established by the local legislature; and if the people are opposed to slavery, they will elect representatives to that body who will by unfriendly legislation effectually prevent the introduction of it into their midst. If, on the contrary, they are for it, their legislation will favor its extension. Hence, no matter what the decision of the Supreme Court may be on that abstract question, still the right of the people to make a Slave Territory or a Free Territory is perfect and complete under the Nebraska bill. I hope Mr. Lincoln deems my answer satisfactory on that point.[29]

Abraham Lincoln as he appeared at the time of the famous Senate debates in 1858 (Library of Congress).

In his answer Douglas drew closer to the anti-slavery view, but he led Southerners to question his commitment to pursuing compromise. This did not hurt him in 1858 because of course Southerners could not vote in the Illinois Senate canvass, but their growing suspicion of him would later resurface when he presented himself as a candidate for president two years later.

The speeches and debates were reported nationally keeping alive the disputes dividing the nation and bringing Lincoln's name before readers, and voters, as yet unfamiliar with him or his positions on the issues. When the final tally of votes was in Lincoln gained more popular votes but Douglas was elected Senator by a total of 54 to 41. At that time, U.S. Senators were elected by the state legislatures, not by the people directly as they are today. Since the Democrats had more representation in the state legislature, Douglas prevailed. Lincoln lost, but became much more well known nationally than before the campaign. In a portent of the near future, the Republicans swept the important elections in every northern state except Illinois and Indiana, including even President Buchanan's home state of Pennsylvania.

John Brown

Major events like the Dred Scott Decision and the fall elections in 1858 kept the divisive disagreements before the public eye denying any cooling off period as emotionalism continued to run high. Even had there been a respite it would have been brief.

Following the civil strife in Kansas, John Brown moved east where he received financial assistance from Gerrit Smith and other New York and New England abolitionists. Dubbed the "Secret Six," this conspiratorial group was dedicated to the abolitionist's mission of eliminating all slavery from the nation as soon as possible. These six—Dr. Samuel Gridley Howe, the Rev. Theodore Parker, Thomas Wentworth Higginson, George Luther Sterns, Franklin B. Sanborn and Gerrit Smith—joined together to pool their influence and money to support a new effort by Brown to effect the elimination of the national evil—by force if necessary. In the summer of 1858, Smith confirmed to Sanborn his support of Brown, stating: "For several years I have frequently given him money towards sustaining him in his conquests with the slave-power. Whenever he shall embark in another of these contests I shall again stand ready to help him; and I will begin with giving him a hundred dollars. I do not wish to know Captain Brown's plans. I hope he will keep them to himself."[30] To Thaddeus Hyatt, Smith wrote: "We must

John Brown as seen at the time of the Harpers Ferry raid in 1859 (Library of Congress).

not shrink from fighting for Liberty—and if Federal troops fight against her, we must fight against them."[31]

Believing that slavery could only be eradicated by the sword, Brown hatched a plan to seize the federal arsenal at Harpers Ferry, Virginia, distribute weapons contained in the arsenal to local slaves, and begin a rebellion designed to establish a free state in the Appalachians where slaves could move under his protection. Recruiting an "army" of 21 men, Brown slipped into Harpers Ferry one night in October 1859, captured a portion of the town, but was confronted by local militia once the alarm was raised. With a revolt in progress, President Buchanan had to act to protect the public and contain panic. He found an army officer who was home on leave across the Potomac River in Virginia, Col. Robert E. Lee, and ordered him to lead a contingent of U.S. Marines from the Washington Naval Yard out to suppress the insurrection. Another officer in Washington, Lt. James Ewell Brown "Jeb" Stuart, acted as second in command. Brown barricaded his group into a small railroad building where they were surrounded. When he refused to surrender, Lee ordered Stuart to lead an assault that quickly brought the revolt to an end. Ten of Brown's men were killed, including two of his sons, five were captured, and five others who had not been cornered in the building or surrounding town escaped.

This attempt to arm slaves, arousing long-held fears of slave rebellion, sent a shock wave throughout the South. Malevolent editorials vied with venomous oratory in Congress and throughout the South to excoriate Brown, the abolitionists, and the North in general. Captured, Brown was placed on trial for treason by the state of Virginia on October 16–18. Found guilty, he was hanged on December 2. Five of his "soldiers" met a similar fate.

On his way to the gallows, Brown slipped to the jailer a note that read, "I John Brown am now quite certain that the crimes of this guilty land will never be purged away but with Blood." Previously, in a letter to his family, he wrote, "I am worth inconceivably more to hang than for any other purpose."[32] In a sense, he was correct. While moderate Northerners were appalled by the violence, to abolitionists Brown became a martyr. The popular literary figure Henry Wadsworth Longfellow commented that Brown "will make the gallows as glorious as the cross,"[33] while Louisa May Alcott penned the following lines:

> No breath of shame can touch his shield
> Nor ages dim its shine
> Living, he made life beautiful
> Dying, made death divine.[34]

To Southerners, it was one thing to argue politics, it was quite another to arm slaves and encourage them to rebel and kill their owners. Nothing struck more fear into Southern hearts than the idea of slave rebellion, and here was proof positive that the abolitionists and their Northern allies had promoted and helped finance exactly that. Brown had planned to arm the slaves he sought to free with pikes—short spears. These were displayed in legislative hall after legislative hall throughout the South to show members what Brown had planned for the men, women, and children of the South. Southerners blamed the entire incident on the abolitionists, and by extension the so-called "Black Republicans," making no distinction between the abolitionists and general Republican support for the anti-slavery movement. They were amazed that some in the North reflected determined emotionalism in support of Brown's horrendous deed as, for example, when Henry David Thoreau, spoke of Brown, as a "man of rare common sense and directness of speech, as of action; a transcendentalist above all, a man of ideas and principles."[35] The outspoken secessionist Edmund Ruffin warned in the Richmond *Enquirer* that Northern abolitionists "designed to slaughter sleeping Southern men and their awakened wives and children."[36] Emotions on both sides were heated to the boiling point. The *Charleston Mercury* ominously predicted, "The day of compromise is passed."[37]

The Election of 1860

By 1860, the nation was more polarized than at any point in its history. Northerners, still outraged by the Supreme Court's pronouncement that slavery was legal, swelled the ranks of anti-slavery societies throughout their section. Southerners, livid over the abolitionist's support for John Brown's attempt to foment a slave rebellion, were more adamant than ever to protect their very lives against this aggression. Southerner E. N. Elliott noted in 1860 that

> there is now but one great question dividing the American people, and that, to the great danger of the stability of our government, the concord and harmony of our citizens, and the perpetuation of our liberties, divides us by a geographical line. Hence, estrangement, alienation, enmity, have arisen between the North and South.... Witness the growing distrust with which the people of the North and South begin to regard each other; the diminution of Southern travel, either for business or pleasure, in the Northern States; the efforts of each section to develop its own resources, so as virtually to render it independent of the other; the enactment of "unfriendly legislation," in several of the States, towards other States of the Union, or their citizens; the contest for the exclusive possession of the territories, the common property of the States; the anarchy and bloodshed in Kansas; ... the existence of the "underground railroad," and of a party in the North organized for the express purpose of robbing the citizens of the Southern States of their property; ... the attempt to circulate incendiary documents among the slaves in the Southern states; ... and finally, the recent attempt to excite, at Harper's Ferry, and throughout the South, an insurrection, and a civil and servile war, with all its attendant horrors.[38]

Adding fuel to the fire, as if any more incendiary material was needed, in February of 1860, when emotions were still running high on both sides of the Mason-Dixon line in the wake of the John Brown affair, Senator Jefferson Davis of Mississippi introduced a number of resolutions into Congress designed to guarantee protection to slave owners. He began by stating the basis for his proposals which echoed traditional Southern arguments:

> Resolved, That in the adoption of the Federal Constitution, the States adopting the same acted severally as free and independent sovereignties, delegating a portion of their powers to be exercised by the Federal Government for the increased security of each, against dangers domestic as well as foreign; and that any intermeddling by any one or more States, or by a combination of their citizens, with the domestic institutions of the others, on any pretext, whether political, moral, or religious, with the view to their disturbance or subversion, is in violation of the Constitution, insulting to the States so interfered with, endangers their domestic peace and tranquillity—objects for which the Constitution was formed—and, by necessary consequence, serves to weaken and destroy the Union itself.[39]

After asserting that "negro slavery, as it exists in fifteen States of this Union, composes an important portion of their domestic institutions, inherited from their ancestors, and existing at the adoption of the Constitution, by which it is recognized as constituting an important element of the apportionment of powers among the States," Davis went on to conclude that any and all attacks on the institution of slavery violated the Constitution and "the mutual and solemn pledges to protect and defend each other, given by the States, respectively, on entering into the constitutional compact which formed the Union, and are a manifest breach of faith and a violation of the most solemn obligations." He then called upon the Senate to guarantee "equality of rights and privileges" among the states, to affirm the right of people to own slaves free of any attempt by Congress or territorial legislatures to interfere with that right, to reaffirm the right of territories to enter the Union "with or without slavery, as their constitution may prescribe at the time of their admission," and that the Constitution and the Fugitive Slave Acts of 1793 and 1850 be enforced. In his concluding remarks, addressed to Vice President John C. Breckinridge who was then the presiding officer of the Senate, Davis declared that he had "presented these resolutions not for the purpose of discussing them, but with a view to get a vote upon them severally, hoping thus, by an expression of the deliberate opinion of the Senate, that we may reach some conclusion as to what is the present condition of opinion in relation to the principles there expressed."[40] Whether Davis really believed the resolutions could be voted on without debate is doubtful, but regardless of his expressed hope the proposals immediately opened yet another emotional debate which only served to reinforce the opposing points of view.

Neither side was in the mood for compromise, but for Southerners the upcoming election held particular importance. In the early years of the nation they lost control of the House of Representatives since the Northern population increasingly outnumbered that of the South. With the admission of California as a free state in 1850, the South lost control on the Senate. The admission of Minnesota (1858) and Oregon (1859) and the pending admission of Kansas, all as free states, made it obvious that the South could no longer count on protecting itself by controlling any part of Congress. What was left to it? Since the president can veto bills, and even with its majority in the Senate the North was not strong enough to override presidential vetoes, Southerners believed it was crucial that they win the presidency in 1860 if they were to have any hope of protecting their welfare.

The Democrats were still the only major national political party with an organization that stretched into every state. They met in Charleston, South Carolina, but because of the sectional discord found themselves unable to agree upon a candidate acceptable to enough delegates to gain the nomination. In frustration, with each faction unwilling to trust a candidate from the opposing section of the country, the convention adjourned. Northern Democrats reconvening in a separate convention in Baltimore to nominate Stephen A. Douglas of Illinois as president and Herschel V. Johnson of Georgia as vice president in an attempt to balance the ticket. Their platform advocated the annexation of Cuba as a slave state to help redress the balance of power in the Senate and recourse to the Supreme Court to address other issues. Southern Democrats met separately nominating John C. Breckinridge of Kentucky and James Lane of Oregon in another effort to put forth a balanced ticket, with a platform that also called for the annexation of Cuba as well as support for the expansion of slavery into the territories. Although the only major party, this division would of course result in splitting Democratic votes between two candidates lessening the chances of either in the general election.

Republicans also had difficulty picking a standard bearer from several contenders, chief among them being William H. Seward from New York and Salmon P. Chase of Ohio. Meeting in Chicago, the major contenders for the nomination were unable to claim a majority of the votes after several ballots leading the delegates to turn to Abraham Lin-

Titled "Dividing the National Map," this cartoon depicts the four presidential candidates of 1860 symbolically tearing apart the Union (Library of Congress).

coln of Illinois as a compromise candidate. Hannibal Hamlin of Maine ran as vice president, the lack of any attempt to balance the ticket with a Southerner clearly recognizing that they expected little support in that section of the country. Much as in 1856, the platform opposed the extension of slavery into the territories and supported homestead legislation, internal improvements including the proposed transcontinental railway, a protective tariff and liberal immigration laws. All of these were clearly calculated to appeal to the party's constituent groups which were all predominantly Northern-based.

To make matters even more interesting, in an attempt to forestall civil war, moderates, largely from the border states between North and South, formed the Constitutional Union Party on a platform that promised to solve the slavery controversy through Constitutional amendment. Adopting a platform condemning sectional parties, supporting preservation of the Union, and advocating compromise of all outstanding issues, the group's supporters were mostly ex–Whigs from Kentucky and Tennessee and former members of the American Party. They nominated John Bell of Tennessee and Edward Everett of Massachusetts for president and vice president, respectively.

The election proved to be one of the closest in American history. Bell, Breckinridge and Lincoln largely followed tradition by remaining home and giving few or no speeches while Douglas campaigned energetically through the country. Democratic campaigners and literature tended to make fun of Lincoln's appearance, the *Charleston Mercury* referring to him as a "horrid looking wretch,"[41] while portraying him as an uneducated country bumpkin. Southerners actively worried aloud that his election would lead to racial miscegenation. Nor was negative commentary limited to the Democrats, a Republican handbill described Douglas as being "about five feet nothing in height … [has] a red face, short legs, and a large belly … talks a great deal, very loud, always about himself."[42] Republicans mobilized thousands of people into "Wide Awake" clubs that actively promoted their candidate as "Honest Abe," a friend of the common man who would support internal improvements important to commercial interests and small farmers. None of the Republican campaigners was more active or important than Carl Schurz, a liberal German immigrant who traveled more than 22,000 miles throughout the North addressing both English- and German-speaking audiences including his famous "Doom of Slavery" speech in St. Louis where he predicted that slavery would not survive a Republican victory. While most of Lincoln's supporters echoed the candidate's view that as president he would have no Constitutional powers to eliminate slavery, Southerners quite naturally paid more attention to the radical rhetoric of Schurz and the abolitionists which aroused all their worst fears.

When the ballots were counted, Breckinridge won the south except for Kentucky, Tennessee and Virginia which went to Bell. In the North, Lincoln and Douglas went head to head, with Douglas being hurt by his support for popular sovereignty and compromise measures many Northerners were no longer willing to accept. Since the winner of each state received all of its electoral votes, and Lincoln eked out a very close victory in all of the Northern states, he won nearly all of those electoral votes even though the popular vote was quite close. Lincoln tallied 180 electoral votes to 72 for Breckinridge, 39 for Bell and only twelve for Douglas. In the popular vote, Lincoln did not win a single electoral district in any Southern state and ended with less than 40 percent of the total vote—his opponents tallied 930,000 more votes than he received—making him the most minority of presidents. When the Electoral College met it ironically fell to its presiding officer, Vice President John C. Breckinridge to certify the final vote.

Candidate	Popular Vote	Percent	Electoral Vote	Source
Lincoln	1,858,000	39.9	180	18 free states
Breckinridge	850,000	18.4	72	11 slave states
Bell	646,000	13.9	39	3 border states
Douglas	1,292,000	27.8	12	Missouri + 3 New Jersey
Total	4,646,000	100.0	303	

Lincoln, the "Black Republican," would be the new president. All that remained now was to await the Southern reaction.

4

The Crisis of the Union

The Republican victory in the 1860 election was for South Carolina the proverbial last straw. As soon as the election results were known, the state legislature met to adopt a resolution condemning the Northern attacks on slavery, the victory of what it termed a sectional political party, and stating its determination to leave the Union. On December 20, 1860, it adopted the South Carolina Ordinance of Secession.

> We, the people of the State of South Carolina in convention assembled, do declare and ordain, and it is hereby declared and ordained, that the ordinance adopted by us in convention on … [May 23, 1788]…, whereby the Constitution of the United States of America was ratified, and also all acts and parts of acts of the general assembly of this State ratifying amendments of the said Constitution, are hereby repealed; and that the union now subsisting between South Carolina and other States, under the name of the "United States of America," is hereby dissolved.[1]

On December 29 South Carolina demanded that federal troops leave Charleston harbor. The following day it seized the federal arsenal in that city. These actions, along with the Ordinance of Secession, left President James Buchanan in a position where some response was required. Buchanan opposed secession, favoring peaceful compromise. He also feared that the South had "cried wolf" too often so that Northerners failed to appreciate the real dangers of the new situation. In his response, the president proposed holding a general convention of all the states to discuss outstanding issues. Few outside the Border States expressed any serious interest.

Attempts at Compromise

With a national crisis at hand, other compromise proposals quickly emerged. Charles Francis Adams proposed admitting New Mexico as a slave state to begin redressing the balance of power in the Senate, but the bill was tabled in the House. A proposal had been introduced for the addition of a Thirteenth Amendment that would prohibit the federal government from interfering with slavery, but it failed to gain approval. Perhaps the oddest proposal came from William H. Seward who had harbored aspirations for the Republican presidential nomination that went to Lincoln in 1860. He suggested that since Lincoln was a divisive figure he should step aside in favor of Seward who would then instigate a war with another country since nothing would unite the nation faster than war against some foreign power.

Two days before South Carolina's Ordinance of Secession, Kentucky Senator John

Southern Ass-stock-crazy.

This lithograph ridiculing the South Carolina threat to leave the Union was published in New York by John T. Ruoff in 1861 (Library of Congress).

J. Crittenden, representing one of the Border States whose population reflected a division of sentiments, presented his proposal for a solution to the national emergency in the form of a resolution. "Whereas, serious and alarming dissensions have arisen between the Northern and Southern States, concerning the rights and security of the rights of the slaveholding States, and especially their rights in the common territory of the United States," his resolution began, "and whereas it is eminently desirable and proper that these dissensions, which now threaten the very existence of this Union, should be permanently quieted and settled by constitutional provisions, which shall do equal justice to all sections, and thereby restore to the people that peace and good will which ought to prevail between all the citizens of the United States," he proposed the adoption of six new amendments to the Constitution. The proposals would revive and establish the old Missouri Compromise line along 36° 30' as a permanent boundary between free and slave territory, deny to Congress any right to abolish slavery anywhere in the country or to interfere with the interstate transportation of slaves, protect slavery in the District of Columbia, extend to Congress the authority to reimburse the owners of runaway slaves for the value of any slaves who were not returned, and provide that none of these new amendments could ever be changed to allow for the Congress to abolish or otherwise interfere with slavery.[2]

Both the House and Senate rejected Crittenden's attempt. In the Senate, a move to get the proposal out of committee failed by a vote of 7 to 6. All five Republicans voted "no" along with two Democrats, while the remaining six Democrats voted "yes." As the crisis escalated, on January 16 an effort to force the bill out of committee was once again defeated with all 25 Republicans voting "nay" and all 23 Democrats voting "yea." Party lines were as deeply divided as the nation.

While the politicians failed to make any progress toward a solution, and between Lincoln's election and inauguration, six other states joined South Carolina in voting to secede: Mississippi (January 9), Florida (January 10), Alabama (January 11), Georgia (January 19), Louisiana (January 26), and Texas (February 1). All were from the Deep South where the percentage of slaves was highest and the dependence on cotton plantations to sustain the ruling political class most pronounced. On the suggestion of former president John Tyler and Virginia Governor John Letcher, a peace conference convened in Washington, D.C., from February 4 to 27. Although some 100 representatives from 21 states met at the Willard Hotel, none came from the Deep South states that had already seceded. Considerable speechifying failed to gain support for either the Crittenden proposals or seven suggested Constitutional amendments.

With the situation seemingly spiraling out of control, there was a final attempt to resurrect Crittenden's original proposals. In the Senate it again failed along strict party lines, 20 Republicans voting "no" and 19 Democrats voting "yes." The House was nearly as polarized with all 110 Republicans voting "no" while only three Democrats joined them and 80 voted "yes."

The Congressional votes plainly indicate that it was the Republicans who were not inclined to consider compromise. In part this was no doubt due to the rising emotionalism in the North due to the Dred Scott Decision, as President Buchanan had feared, and the feeling that the South was only bluffing to obtain concessions in a compromise agreement, much as they had in previous "crises" that resulted in compromise. This position was reflected in a *New-York Tribune* editorial on March 27, 1861. Edited by its founder, Horace Greeley, the *Tribune* was the leading Republican-oriented newspaper in the nation and as such serves as a good gauge for their political thought. The editorial sketched three possible alternatives that could be pursued in the secession crisis. The first was war. The second was peaceful secession. The third option, the one supported by the newspaper, was "a Fabian policy, which concedes nothing, yet employs no force in support of resisted authority, hoping to wear out the insurgent spirit and in due time re-establish the authority of the union in the revolted or seceded states by virtue of the returning sanity and loyalty of their own people."[3] The name "Fabian" referred to Quintus Fabius Maximus, a Roman politician and general whose nickname was

Horace Greeley's *New York Tribune* supported the Republican Party and often served as its messenger (Library of Congress).

"Cunctator" or "delayer." During the Second Punic War he avoided direct confrontation with a stronger Carthaginian force, choosing instead to launch raids on the enemy supply lines, communications, and reconnaissance or foraging forces. By this tactic he postponed any major confrontation, planning to win the campaign by delaying a decision while he wore down the strength of the opposing forces.

Note that one of the three choices the editorial advanced was *not* compromise. The Republican leadership believed that secession was a bluff. They did not desire either war or national schism through peaceful secession. Likewise they did not intend to see the Southern position strengthened by the concessions that would be required to achieve compromise; therefore, the tactic to be pursued was delay. In retrospect this may seem unrealistic given the circumstances, but hindsight is much clearer than foresight. Interestingly, since during this period of great national tension, Lincoln did not offer the comforting words of assurance to the nation, North and South, that he would later offer, Lincoln may also have hoped that delay could help heal the nation's conflict. To Republicans at the time, this appeared to be a viable option. There were fifteen states in which slavery was legal. Seven of these had seceded prior to Lincoln's inauguration, but eight had not. Further, Virginia actually voted *against* secession on February 4 in the same month 54 percent of voters in Tennessee cast ballots *against* convening a secession convention. Missouri and North Carolina each voted *against* secession, while Arkansas delegates met but failed to take any action. In the month before Lincoln's inauguration no additional Southern states left the Union. The tide appeared to some Northerners to be turning, time was working to their advantage. The initial emotional impact of secession seemed to have reached its peak with anti-secession voices beginning to gain strength. Delay was working, passions were ebbing, soon the tide of secession would be reversed as cooler heads prevailed. If the Fabian strategy could be successful the Union would be reunited without the necessity of any further Northern concessions.

President Buchanan's Response

While politicians debated possible compromises, or whether to compromise at all, President Buchanan was left with the task of handling the emerging crisis. On December 3, he sent a message to Congress in which he maintained that secession was illegal, but he also opined that the federal government lacked any authority to prevent states from leaving if they chose to do so. This equivocal approach pleased no one. Georgian Howell Cobb, Buchanan's Secretary of the Treasury, resigned five days later over the president's assertion that secession was illegal. On December 14, Secretary of State Lewis Cass from Michigan resigned for directly the opposite reason, Buchanan had failed to respond strongly enough to the threat of secession. Similar division occurred throughout the nation. Meanwhile, as states began to secede each appropriated federal property and demanded that United States troops leave its territory. Soon only two facilities remained in federal hands, Fort Pickens on Santa Rosa Island off the coast of Pensacola, Florida, and Fort Sumter in Charleston harbor, South Carolina.

Both of these positions were in danger, but Fort Pickens could be approached from the sea without great danger and was soon reinforced. Fort Sumter was different. It rested well within the harbor surrounded by locations from which artillery could bring it under fire or prevent any relief force from approaching. Faced with threats, the local Federal commander consolidated his forces into Fort Sumter as the most defensible position and refused all calls for him to give up the post. Meanwhile, Buchanan took his most overt action by dispatching the merchant ship *Star of the West* with supplies and reinforcements for the surrounded fort. When it arrived on January 9 South Carolina artillery batteries opened fire and it was forced to retire without completing its mission. Southerners roundly criticized the president for a provocation while Northerners condemned him for failing to retaliate for South Carolina's overt act of war. Governor Francis Pickens of South Carolina sent a letter to the president demanding the surrender of Fort Sumter, arguing that its occupation by federal forces was "not consistent with the dignity or safety of the State of South Carolina."[4] Buchanan responded to protests from both sides by doing nothing except calling for a convention of the states to discuss the issues, effectively choosing to bequeath the crisis to his successor.

Two New Presidents Are Inaugurated

Between South Carolina's secession on December 20 and Abraham Lincoln's inauguration on March 4, several other suggestions for compromise were offered but no agreements were reached. On February 18, 1861, Jefferson Davis of Mississippi was inaugurated President of the Confederacy with Alexander Stephens of Georgia as Vice President. The Confederacy's constitution, approved on February 4, generally mirrored the U.S. Constitution except for five major changes. The Southern constitution specifically declared slavery to be legal, indicated that the individual states retained their sovereignty, provided a single six-year term for the president, prohibited protective tariffs, and gave the president an "item veto" that allowed him to veto specific provisions of bills without vetoing the entire bills. Yet, the new document was not as radical as some would have liked. Delegates chose not to include a provision limiting membership in the Confederacy to only slaveholding states or to agree to reopen the international slave trade.

In his inaugural address, Davis expressed the hope that

the beginning of our career, as a Confederacy, may not be obstructed by hostile opposition to our enjoyment of the separate existence and independence we have asserted, and which, with the blessing of Providence, we intend to maintain. Our present political position has been achieved in a manner unprecedented in the history of nations. It illustrates the American idea that governments rest on the consent of the governed, and that it is the right of the people

Jefferson Davis of Mississippi, President James Buchanan's secretary of war, was elected president of the Confederacy (Library of Congress).

The inauguration of Jefferson Davis as president of the Confederate States of America took place in Montgomery, Alabama, on February 18, 1861 (Library of Congress).

to alter or abolish them at will whenever they become destructive of the ends for which they were established.

He then went on to detail the rationale and legal basis for the formation of the Confederacy.

> Sustained by the consciousness that the transition from the former Union to the present Confederacy has not proceeded from a disregard on our part of just obligations, or any, failure to perform every constitutional duty, moved by no interest or passion to invade the rights of others, anxious to cultivate peace and commerce with all nations, if we may not hope to avoid war, we may at least expect that posterity will acquit us of having needlessly engaged in it. Doubly justified by the absence of wrong on our part, and by wanton aggression on the part of others, there can be no cause to doubt that the courage and patriotism of the people of the Confederate States will be found equal to any measure of defense which their honor and security may require.[5]

The Southern states, he said, were

> an agricultural people, whose chief interest is the export of commodities required in every manufacturing country, our true policy is peace, and the freest trade which our necessities will permit. It is alike our interest and that of all those to whom we would sell, and from whom we would buy, that there should be the fewest practicable restrictions upon the interchange of these commodities. There can, however, be but little rivalry between ours and any manufacturing or navigating community, such as the Northeastern States of the American Union. It must follow, therefore, that mutual interest will invite to good will and kind offices on both parts. If, however, passion or lust of dominion should cloud the judgment or inflame the ambition of those States, we must prepare to meet the emergency and maintain, by the final arbitrament of the sword, the position which we have assumed among the nations of the earth.

After dismissing any thought of reunification with the North, Davis closed by invoking "the God of our fathers to guide and protect us in our efforts to perpetuate the principles which by his blessing they were able to vindicate, establish, and transmit to their posterity. With the continuance of his favor ever gratefully acknowledged, we may hopefully look forward to success, to peace, and to prosperity."[6] While hoping for peace, Davis made it clear that the South would maintain its independence by force if necessary.

Exactly two weeks later, on March 4, Abraham Lincoln took the oath as President of the United States. With seven Southern states having already voted to leave the Union, he faced the gravest crisis in the country's history. The entire nation waited to hear what he would say when he took to the podium for his inaugural address. Yet he also knew that the majority of slave-holding states had *not* seceded. To Horace Greely he confided that "my paramount objective is to save the Union and it is not either to save or to destroy slavery."[7] With this overarching priority in mind, he determined to use the occasion to stress the limits of the office of president, his own intention to uphold all of the laws, and to otherwise reassure Southerners that they had nothing to fear from his administration. He began,

> Apprehension seems to exist among the people of the Southern States, that by the accession of a Republican administration their property and their peace and personal security are to be endangered. There has never been any reasonable cause for such apprehension. Indeed, the most ample evidence to the contrary has all the while existed and been open to their inspection. It is found in nearly all the published speeches of him who now addresses you. I do but quote from one of those speeches when I declare that "I have no purpose, directly or indirectly, to interfere with the institution of slavery where it exists. I believe I have no lawful right to do so, and I have no inclination to do so."[8]

The new chief executive went on to assure listeners that he had no authority to interfere with "the delivering up of fugitives from service or labor" which was written into

The inauguration of Abraham Lincoln as sixteenth president of the United States, March 4, 1861 (Library of Congress).

the Constitution and the laws of the land. Then, addressing his words directly to those who would cause disunion, he made it clear he believed that "the Union of these States is perpetual. Perpetuity is implied, if not expressed, in the fundamental law of all national governments. It is safe to assert that no government proper ever had a provision in its organic law for its own termination." He based this, he said, also on the history of the documents forming the Union dating back to the Articles of Association in 1774. He had no wish to transgress the provisions of the Constitution or the laws enacted by Congress, nor to fail to support them. In this, "there needs to be no bloodshed or violence; and there shall be none, unless it be forced upon the national authority."[9]

Lincoln went on to reassure the people that life would go on as usual. "So far as possible, the people everywhere shall have that sense of perfect security which is most favorable to calm thought and reflection." There was no cause for disunion. No right guaranteed by the Constitution had been violated or denied. Yet not all questions, he explained, could be anticipated in any document. The answer to these questions was not in secession, which he equated with anarchy, but with the Supreme Court. "One section of our country believes slavery is RIGHT, and ought to be extended, while the other believes it is WRONG, and ought not to be extended. This is the only substantial dispute."[10] This question, he suggested, was easier addressed as friends than as separate countries. After a final appeal to rely on the legislative process, he concluded with a final call for peace.

> In YOUR hands, my dissatisfied fellow-countrymen, and not in MINE, is the momentous issue of civil war. The government will not assail YOU. You can have no conflict without being yourselves the aggressors. YOU have no oath registered in heaven to destroy the government, while *I* shall have the most solemn one to "preserve, protect, and defend it."
>   I am loathe to close. We are not enemies, but friends. We must not be enemies. Though passion may have strained, it must not break our bonds of affection. The mystic chords of memory, stretching from every battlefield and patriot grave to every living heart and hearthstone all over this broad land, will yet swell the chorus of the Union when again touched, as surely they will be, by the better angels of our nature.[11]

The two presidents shared a hope for peace but were equally determined to support the cause they led. Davis pledged to use force if necessary to preserve the Southern Confederacy while Lincoln was obligated by the Constitution to preserve the unity of the United States.

President Lincoln Responds to the Crisis

Faced with the same dilemma that confronted Buchanan regarding the federal troops besieged in Fort Sumter, Lincoln also chose to send the *Star of the West* with provisions to resupply the garrison. Yet he still had reason to believe that peaceful reunification might be achieved. No further states had seceded over the previous month and in fact some slave states had voted affirmatively *not* to do so. Not wishing to provoke hostilities, he sent word to the South Carolina authorities that the ship would carry only food and medical supplies. No attempt to reinforce the garrison or bring in weapons or munitions would be made. His hope in doing this was that South Carolina leaders would not oppose maintenance of the *status quo*.

In South Carolina, authorities had other ideas. Since his initial letter to President Buchanan, Governor Pickers's resolve had only hardened. He wanted the federals out and was afraid that resupply would only prolong the ability of the national troops to hold their position. With the ship on the way, he realized that if the fort did not immediately yield it might hold out indefinitely. A resupply could not be allowed. In a war full of ironies and complicated personal relationships, Fort Sumter was commanded by Major Robert Anderson, a native of Kentucky, the father-in-law of the governor of Georgia, and a former slave owner who retained pro–Southern sentiments.[12] The Southern military commander, General Pierre Gustave Toutant Beauregard,[13] had been the commandant at West Point when Anderson was assigned there as an artillery instructor. Beauregard called on Major Anderson to surrender the fort, giving him a final deadline. When Beauregard's deadline passed, he ordered artillery to open fire.

With hostilities initiated, Lincoln, acting under his authority as commander-in-chief of the nation's armed forces and the Constitutional requirement that he suppress internal rebellion, called for 75,000 troops to put down the revolt.

April 15, 1861

WHEREAS the laws of the United States have been, for some time past, and now are opposed, and the execution thereof obstructed, in the States of South Carolina, Georgia, Alabama, Florida, Mississippi, Louisiana, and Texas, by combinations too powerful to be suppressed by the ordinary course of judicial proceedings, or by the powers vested in the marshals by law: Now, therefore, I, ABRAHAM LINCOLN, President of the United States, in virtue of the power in me vested by the Constitution and the laws, have thought fit to call forth, and hereby do call forth, the militia of the several States of the Union, to the aggregate number of seventy-five thousand, in order to suppress said combinations, and to cause the laws to be duly executed.

The details for this object will be immediately communicated to the State authorities through the War Department. I appeal to all loyal citizens to favor, facilitate, and aid this effort to maintain the honor, the integrity, and the existence of our National Union, and the perpetuity of popular government; and to redress wrongs already long enough endured.

I deem it proper to say that the first service assigned to the forces hereby called forth will probably be to repossess the forts, places, and property which have been seized from the Union; and in every event, the utmost care will be observed, consistently with the objects aforesaid, to avoid any devastation, any destruction of, or interference with, property, or any disturbance of peaceful citizens in any part of the country.

And I hereby command the persons composing the combinations aforesaid to disperse, and retire peaceably to their respective abodes within twenty days from this date.

Deeming that the present condition of public affairs presents an extraordinary occasion, I do hereby, in virtue of the power in me vested by the Constitution, convene both Houses of Congress. Senators and Representatives are therefore summoned to assemble at their respective chambers, at twelve o'clock, noon, on Thursdays the fourth day of July next, then and there to consider and determine such measures as, in their wisdom, the public safety and interest may seem to demand.

Abraham Lincoln[14]

According to law, the number of troops was apportioned to each state by population, with each state to provide the required number of men. The free states generally responded quickly and affirmatively. How the slave states would respond was another matter. Eight of the Southern states had remained in the Union, and some had even taken a vote not to secede, but asking them to provide troops to be used against their fellow Southerners was another matter altogether. North Carolina had already held a popular referendum on the issue of secession which narrowly recommended keeping the state in the Union by a vote of 47,323 to 46,672. Yet when the requisition for troops arrived, Governor John Ellis would have none of it. "Your dispatch is received, and, if genuine, which its extraordinary character leads me to doubt, I have to say in reply that I regard the levy of troops made by the Administration for the purpose of subjugating the States of the South, as in violation of the Constitution and a usurpation of power. I can be no party to this wicked violation of the laws of the country, and to this war upon the liberties of a free people. You can get no troops from North Carolina."[15]

The Border States had been among the leaders in attempting to construct a viable compromise to preserve the Union. How would they respond? The pro-slavery governor of Maryland, Thomas Hicks, despite his feelings about slavery, promised to provide the requisite number of troops, but feelings were greatly divided in the state and its principal city of Baltimore. Not so Kentucky whose legislature voted to remain neutral. Governor Beriah Magoffin, sympathetic to the South, telegraphed Secretary of War Simon Cameron: "Your dispatch is received. In answer, I say emphatically that Kentucky will furnish no troops for the wicked purpose of subduing her sister Southern States."[16] Similarly, the pro-secession chief executive of Missouri, Claiborne Jackson, notified the Secretary of War that "your requisition, in my judgment, is illegal, unconstitutional, and revolutionary in its objects, inhuman and diabolical, and can not be complied with. Not one man will, of the State of Missouri, furnish or carry on such an unholy crusade."[17]

Finding themselves torn between taking up arms against other Southern states or joining them in forming a new nation, Virginia, North Carolina, Tennessee and Arkansas left the Union rather than supply troops to carry on a war against their fellow Southerners, bringing the number of Confederate states to eleven.

The Border States

The failure of all attempts at compromise, and in fact the relative minority of people seriously interested in compromise, reflects the enormity of the passionate divide that separated North from South in 1861. Particularly effected were residents of the Border States where communities and indeed individual families saw their traditional bonds torn asunder. President Lincoln's wife Mary's four brothers fought for the South, while General Ulysses S. Grant's father-in-law also supported the Confederacy. Three grandsons of the "Great Compromiser," Henry Clay, donned the blue while four others chose the gray. Thomas L. Crittenden rose to major general in the Union Army, while his brother George held a like rank in the Confederacy. Brig. Gen. William R. Terrill died leading Federal troops at Perryville; his brother James B. Terrill fell leading Confederates at Totopotomoy Creek. Pennsylvanian John Pemberton became a Confederate general, while his Tennessee in-law David G. Farragut became a Union admiral. Gen. George McClellan's cousin Henry served as a major and chief of staff for Southern Gen. Jeb Stuart. At the Battle of Front Royal in 1862, Capt. William Goldsborough of the Confederate 1st Maryland Infantry captured his brother Charles Goldsborough of the Union 1st Maryland Infantry. At First Bull Run a wounded Frederick Hubbard of the Washington Artillery of New Orleans was carried to a field hospital where he found himself lying next to his wounded brother Henry of the 1st Minnesota. At the siege of Vicksburg there were 39 units from Missouri among the contestants: 17 for the South and 22 for the North. And these are but a few examples, there were countless more.

Although allowing slavery, there was never any serious threat that Delaware would secede. The state was somewhat isolated from the South, being linked to the North by land. While it did share a border with Maryland, it was on the Eastern Shore separated from the rest of Maryland and from the South by Chesapeake Bay. Less than 2 percent of the population consisted of slaves and these resided mostly in the southern counties of the state. When the issue was considered in the state legislature the vote against secession was overwhelming.

Maryland presented a very different set of circumstances, not the least of which was geographic. Maryland shared a long border with Virginia and, more importantly, if Maryland were to secede Washington, D.C., would be surrounded by territory in rebellion, cut off from direct access to the loyal states. Maryland was deeply divided in its sympathies with Baltimore tending to be pro–South while the more rural areas generally housed a majority of pro–Union sentiment. Although the state legislature rejected the initial call for secession, it also closed rail connections into the District of Columbia and called for

The 6th Massachusetts being attacked along Pratt Street in Baltimore as depicted in *Frank Leslie's Illustrated Newspaper*, April 30, 1861.

the removal of all national troops from the state. This left the nation's capital at the mercy of rebels in Virginia or any future movement by Maryland toward secession. Northern states, led by Massachusetts and New York, immediately dispatched troops in response to Lincoln's call for protecting the capital. On April 19 the 6th Massachusetts Volunteer Infantry arrived in Baltimore on its way to Washington. Because the rail lines were not connected, the regiment was forced to detrain to march through a portion of the city to another station where it could board another train to continue its journey south. While moving through the city it was attacked by pro–South mobs triggering five days of rioting that cost the lives of several people. With Washington cut off from relief for almost a week, many of its citizens rose to the occasion with local militia turning out to protect the president and government buildings. It was not until May 13 that the arrival of more Northern troops finally secured the streets of Baltimore so that additional troops could continue on south without further delay.

While more reinforcements arrived, Lincoln acted to suppress active support of the rebellion by suspending habeas corpus—the right to be brought before a court to determine if one's detention is legal. According to Article I, Section 9, of the Constitution, "The privilege of the Writ of Habeas Corpus shall not be suspended, unless when in Cases of Rebellion or Invasion the public Safety may warrant it." Given the rebellion,

Lincoln believed ordering the arrest of those suspected of fomenting disloyalty was clearly justified. Among nearly 13,000 people eventually arrested were the mayor, police chief and city council of Baltimore. Another of those arrested was John Merryman, a member of the Maryland legislature, who was engaged in obstructing the movement of Federal troops while also recruiting men to serve the rebellion. Merryman, through his attorney, appealed to Chief Justice Roger Taney for a writ requiring that the arresting authority appear in court to justify the arrest and, failing to do so, that Merryman be released. Taney's ruling, known as Ex parte Merryman, found that the president had no constitutional authority to suspend habeas corpus and required that the prisoner be brought before the court. Lincoln, arguing that his action was legal under the constitutional requirement that the president quell internal rebellions, ignored Taney's ruling and ordered military personal to do as well. In fact, when the Maryland legislature attempted to reconvene later that fall approximately one-third of the legislators were arrested. In the end, Maryland was held in the Union by force of arms. Its people sent men to both sides during the war, about 70 percent joining the Union army and the balance the Confederate forces.

Kentucky was also greatly torn by the secession movement. On May 20 its legislature declared that the state would remain neutral and requested both sides to honor its decision by keeping their forces out—it would not secede but neither would it provide troops to the Federal government for the purpose of opposing the Southern states. The Ohio Valley was vital to east-west communications and the efficient movement of troops and supplies to where they might be needed by United States forces. Located as it was along the border between North and South covering the entire area from the Appalachian Mountains to the Mississippi River, Kentucky also occupied a critical strategic position. If it seceded it would open Ohio and Indiana to possible invasion, while if it remained loyal the critical invasion routes along the Tennessee and Cumberland Rivers would be opened to Federal movement south. Neutrality raised yet other possibilities. If the state remained neutral and the Lincoln administration honored that declaration, the North would be unable to use these natural routes of invasion to the south. This would clearly favor the South because it would be better able to concentrate its more limited forces to protect the Mississippi Valley and the Virginia front.

Lincoln clearly recognized Kentucky as particularly important to the preservation of the Union. "I think to lose Kentucky is nearly the same as to lose the whole game," he wrote. "Kentucky gone, we cannot hold Missouri, nor Maryland. These all against us, and the job on our hands is too large for us."[18] Initially the president played a waiting game fearful that if United States troops entered Kentucky the move would drive it into the Confederacy. The quandary eventually reached resolution in September when Confederate troops began fortifying Island Number Ten in the Mississippi River and the surrounding area. Since this included land in Columbus, Kentucky, Lincoln used this as justification for sending Federal forces into the state to protect it from what he called a Southern invasion. Kentucky too was thus preserved for the Union, but like Maryland its population sent men to serve both sides. So prominent were Kentuckians in the Southern forces that the Confederate government counted Kentucky among its members, allowed the state representation in the government, and placed a star on its flag for Kentucky even though the state never formally seceded.

The final Border State, Missouri, was as divided in its sympathies as Maryland and Kentucky. Missouri's pro-secession governor, Claiborne F. Jackson, called upon the state legislature to convene a special constitutional convention to consider secession, which it did. To Jackson's disappointment, the legislature voted to remain in the Union but not provide any troops to oppose the South. Not content with the result, the governor called out the state militia and opened secret correspondence with the Confederate government. Jackson planned to seize the St. Louis arsenal but the German-American militia in that city turned out to support the Union, fought a pitched battle with Southern sympathizers, and occupied the arsenal and adjacent locations before the governor could strike. Captain Nathaniel Lyon, leading another pro–Union force, surrounded the pro–South militia in "Camp Jackson" capturing the lot. Although fighting continued throughout the war, and it would be some time before the state was relatively secure, the critical arsenal and the state were kept in the Union by force.

Historian James McPherson estimates that some 170,000 residents of the Border States fought in the Union armies and 86,000 in the Confederate forces. Yet the status of those states was especially important for the resources that they contained. Men could move, they could go north or south to join the contending armies, but whoever actually controlled the land area of the states controlled their resources. For most of the war this was the North.

5

1861—War Becomes Reality

The failure of compromise led directly to the confrontation in Charleston harbor that triggered outright war between the North and the South. War caused the states to choose where they believed their best interests lay. It also required the development and selection of military leadership and strategies, immediate efforts to raise troops, concern over how to pay for it all, and the potentially critical but challenging issues involving foreign relations. The side that quickly arrived at viable answers to all of these questions would be in the best position to emerge victorious.

The Contending Sides Develop Their Strategies

At the beginning of the war the North seemingly held decided advantages in the men and materiel needed in the coming contest. Its population was significantly larger. The following data, taken from the 1860 census, painted a dismal picture for Southern aspirations.

Free States	Population	Slave States & DC	Population
California	379,994	Alabama	964,201
Connecticut	460,147	Arkansas	435,450
Illinois	1,711,951	Delaware	112,216
Indiana	1,350,428	Florida	140,424
Iowa	674,913	Georgia	1,057,286
Kansas	107,206	Kentucky	1,155,684
Maine	628,279	Louisiana	708,002
Massachusetts	1,231,066	Maryland	687,049
Michigan	749,113	Mississippi	791,305
Minnesota	172,023	Missouri	1,182,012
New Hampshire	326,073	North Carolina	992,622
New Jersey	672,035	South Carolina	703,708
New York	3,880,735	Tennessee	1,109,801
Ohio	2,339,511	Texas	604,215
Oregon	52,465	Virginia	1,596,318
Pennsylvania	2,906,215	District of Columbia	75,080
Rhode Island	174,620	Total	12,315,373
Vermont	315,098		
Wisconsin	775,881		
Total	18,907,753		

As the table indicates, the population of the Free States outnumbered that of the Slave States by 1.5 to 1. This calculation does not include the 220,195 residing in the territories most of whom, except for some of the indigenous tribes in the lower trans-Mississippi area, sided with the Union. Including these numbers would not change the relative strengths of North and South. However, much of the population of the Border States remained loyal to the Union, thus increasing the Northern advantage and correspondingly decreasing the manpower available to the South. Then, of course, the South was not about to arm slaves so the proportion of the slave state population available to bear arms was correspondingly less. If only white males from the age of 18 to 45 are considered, the primary age group that would normally be called upon to take up arms in the conflict, and if adjustments are made for the border states whose populations were split in their allegiance, the relative advantage of the North was approximately 4,265,000 to 1,347,000 or 3.2 to 1. Although many writers have stated as fact the myth that most of the West Point–trained military men "went south," in fact, according to a study by Herman Hattaway and Archer Jones, of the 824 West Point graduates on active duty only 184 became Confederate officers. There were approximately 900 graduates of the U.S. Military Academy then in civilian life with some 400 joining the Union army and 99 casting their lot with the rebels. Of about 1,300 naval officers, 322 joined the Confederacy, while of 287 graduates of the Naval Academy at Annapolis, 60 resigned to head south.[1]

Yet it was not only in manpower that the North enjoyed a marked advantage. Fighting a war, especially if it became a prolonged contest, requires horses and mules for mounted units and to pull artillery, wagons, ambulances, and other conveyances. Both men and animals required food. Animals required harnesses, in some cases saddles, and other equipment, while the humans required uniforms, blankets, tents, cooking utensils, field glasses, medical instruments, and a host of other manufactured goods without which an army cannot operate with maximum effectiveness. All of this required money—lots of it! Once all of these commodities were acquired they, along with the troops themselves, needed to be transported to the assembly points and the battlefields and in virtually all of these respects the North also enjoyed a decided advantage in railroad mileage and usefulness.

Although the South was known as the agricultural area of the nation, some two-thirds of America's farms were in the North allowing it to far out-produce the South in corn, wheat and oats. The North also had about 35 million cattle, sheep and pigs compared with about 30 million for the South, providing the Union with an ample food supply to meet the needs of both its civilian population and its armed forces. The North had double the number of horses, giving it an advantage in moving its wagons and artillery during the war. And what the North lacked it was in an excellent position to manufacture or purchase. Financially, it possessed significant advantages. The North had an established government and credit, both of which meant that it was in a better position to borrow money both at home and abroad. Its banks contained about 75 percent of the nation's deposits and 67.5 percent of the specie in circulation. The Northern war effort would be greatly aided by the fact that 85.9 percent of the factories and 92.2 percent of the nation's factory workers needed to supply the massive amounts of weapons, munitions, uniforms, tents, wagons and untold other items necessary to fight a war were located under its control. In 1860 some 92 percent of the nation's manufacturing output came from the free states. Significantly, Northern arsenals were capable of producing 5,000 muskets a day, those in the South only 300. In 1860 the North produced firearms valued at $2,270,000

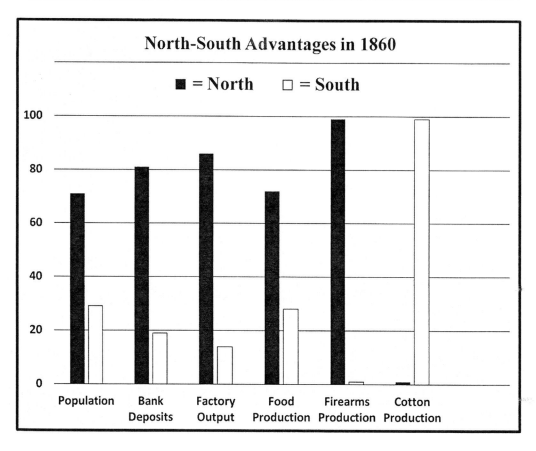

This graph illustrates the dramatic difference in resources and production available to the North and South in 1860 (James S. Pula).

compared to only $73,000 in production in the South. Clearly, in terms of manpower, provisions, finance and production, all of the key indicators favored the North.[2]

The Union also possessed the means of transporting all of these people, animals and industrial goods to where they were needed. Some 71 percent of the railroad mileage was located in the North and more importantly there were several lines linking the western states along the Mississippi River with the east coast. This rail network, originally developed to facilitate trade between the northeastern and northwestern states, provided the North with an excellent means of easily shipping men and supplies to places where they were needed. South of the Mason-Dixon Line dividing the North from the South only a single rail line connected the Mississippi with the Atlantic. Further, Southern railroads tended to be built to transport produce from plantations to the nearest river to be floated down to the sea where it could be shipped to manufacturers in the North or in Europe. As an example, in 1861 Jefferson Davis's plantation in Mississippi was 285 miles from Montgomery, Alabama. When he went to Montgomery to be sworn in as president of the Confederacy he had to travel some 600 miles by rail to reach the city. To make matters even worse, the gauge of Southern railroads differed greatly making it impossible to use the rolling stock of some lines on the tracks of another. Further, in 1860 Northern factories produced 451 locomotives while Southern facilities turned out only 19 (only 4 percent). All of this meant that the South could not shift men and supplies to where they were needed as readily as could the North.

A listing of the Southern advantages was considerably shorter. The nation's most valuable crop, cotton, was produced exclusively in the slave states with, in 1860, some five million bales in the states that would form the Confederacy and 4,000 bales in the Border States. It also produced 87 percent of the nation's tobacco crop. Cotton and tobacco, as valuable commodities, could be used to raise money for the purchase of vital supplies to at least partially offset Northern advantages in manufacturing. Its 187 million pounds of rice (plus 50,000 pounds in the Border States) could also assist in supplying its army. Further, the South was in a somewhat similar position to that of the colonists at the beginning of the American Revolution. To win, the North had physically to invade and conquer this large land area, a considerably more formidable task, as the British found out between 1775 and 1783, than holding out until the other side became exhausted. To win, the South did not have to invade and conquer, it only had to exist, to keep its armies in the field until the other side grew exhausted from attempts to subjugate the new nation.

Initially, very few people North or South believed the war would last long. One of the few who did was the Virginian Winfield Scott. He predicted it would take at least 300,000 men and two to three years just to subdue the Deep South. Nearly everyone thought he was crazy. A veteran of the War of 1812 and the general who captured Mexico City during the Mexican War, at the beginning of the Civil War Scott was commanding

general of the United States Army. At 75 years of age and overweight, he could barely ride a horse and was far too frail to lead an army in the field; but he remained loyal to the Union and devised the general plan that would forecast how the North fought the war.

Scott also realized that to win the war the North had to be aggressive. It could not simply sit back and wait. If the United States government made no attempt to assert its authority the result would mean passively allowing the South to secede. Dubbed the "Anaconda Plan" because it resembled the giant snake of that name that strangles its prey, Scott's plan called for taking advantage of the Northern economic strength by cutting the South off from overseas where it might obtain the materials it could not produce for itself. Scott planned to institute a naval blockade of the entire Southern coastline to interdict its overseas trade. The second part of the blueprint called for capturing New Orleans and the Mississippi Valley. Taking New Orleans would eliminate the largest Southern port on the gulf coast and turn it into a Northern naval base to enforce the blockade. Taking the Mississippi Valley

Winfield Scott as he appeared in 1861 (Library of Congress).

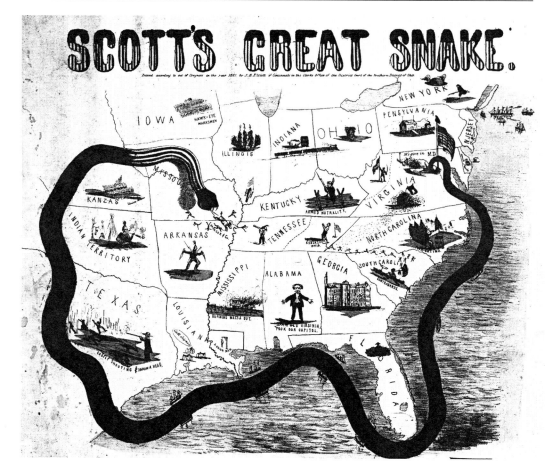

"Scott's Great Snake" illustrates how the Northern strategy was designed to economically strangle the South (Library of Congress).

would divide the South into two pieces, cutting off Texas, Arkansas and Louisiana from the rest of the South. This would not only prevent reinforcements and supplies from being sent east, but would also cut off any attempt by the South to import supplies through Mexico and then overland through Texas. Later, others would add to these goals the capture of the Confederate capital at Richmond, Virginia, both because of its iron works and other manufacturing establishments and its morale value as the Confederate capital.

With all of its disadvantages, and a Northern plan designed to take advantage of Southern economic weaknesses, how did the South ever expect to win? Militarily, the South planned to fight a defensive war. The South did not have to invade and conquer the North to win, it only had to protect its own territory. In fact, it did not even have to do all of that, it only had to keep its armies in the field to exist. Much like the British during the American Revolution, to win the North had to invade and conquer. This would be an extremely difficult thing to accomplish over thousands of miles and would require, according to military analysts, at least a three-to-one manpower advantage to accomplish. By fighting on the defensive, the South could take advantage of hills, rivers, and other natural obstacles, along with entrenchments and other fortifications. It was extremely more difficult and much more costly in human life to assault prepared defenses than it was to defend them. Military analysts at the time believed that forces assaulting prepared positions needed a five-to-one advantage to have a good chance of capturing the position. Clearly, operating on the defensive offered the South the best chance of husbanding its own manpower while making any advance painful for the North. The South hoped to make the war as expensive for the North as possible, both financially and in terms of casualties. Lincoln had received only a minority of the popular vote and ran only barely ahead of Stephen Douglas in most Northern states. There were already numerous peace societies in the North. By prolonging the war and making it as costly as possible the South reasoned that increasing dissention in the North would eventually force an end to the conflict on terms that would guarantee Southern independence.

Another factor the South planned to turn to its advantage was cotton. Often referred to as "King Cotton" or "White Gold," cotton formed the largest U.S. export. Of $334 million in exports in 1860, cotton accounted for $192 million, or 54.4 percent of the total. The South planned to use this to force diplomatic recognition of the Confederacy by Britain and France. This was referred to as "Cotton Diplomacy." Being cut off from Southern cotton would hurt the Northern economy, but the Confederate leadership believed it would be devastating to the British economy where two-thirds of British exports consisted of cotton textiles and it was estimated that up to 20 percent of the labor force was directly or indirectly involved in the textile industry. To support its textile factories, it was estimated that Great Britain needed 900 million pounds of cotton annually. The American South provided 700 million pounds (78 percent of Britain's need). The South planned to use this to its advantage as collateral for loans and credit. In the initial stages of the war the South actually did receive some £2 million in credit for cotton to be delivered at a later date. Should the Union blockade become effective and the South be unable to ship cotton to Europe, the shortage would so badly damage the British economy that, Confederate leaders reasoned, England would be willing to break the Northern blockade to obtain cotton, which the South would trade for what it needed to continue the war. If events went exceptionally well, Britain might even enter the war on the side of the South. If that happened, the North would hardly be able to fight both the South and Great Britain at the same time. So, using cotton, the South hoped to obtain recognition as an independent country from Britain and France, and use trade with these nations to supply what it could not produce for itself.[3]

Lastly, there was the Southern concept of "chivalry" that viewed warfare as a grand medieval tournament, a romantic contest in which honor and courage would prevail. The Southern emphasis on physical courage led to the belief that one rebel could lick ten Yankees before breakfast, a concept that many in the South truly believed. During the War of 1812, they pointed out, it was the New England states that threatened to sign a separate peace with Great Britain if amendments were not made to the Constitution to give them more political clout. During the Mexican War far more Southerners volunteered for service than had their Northern countrymen. Southerners interpreted this as a lack of courage, not as an opposition to acquiring more territory for the spread of slavery. Both examples appeared to them to justify the belief that when the time came Northerners would recoil from the fight. This conviction was reinforced in textbooks used in to South during the antebellum era. The North had no stomach for war. A battle or two, Southerners believed, and it would all be over.

Financing the War

Before it was over the Civil War would be the most expensive event in American history up to that time. For the North alone, the war would require $339 million just to transport troops and supplies, $727 million to feed and clothe the army, $127 million to purchase horses, $76 million to purchase arms, $8 million to feed and care for Confederate prisoners—and the list went on, and on, and on. By the end of the war the North would spend an average of $2 million per day to subdue the rebellion.[4] And this did not include the expenses incurred by the Confederate states. How would all of this be paid for?

The traditional means of raising money by selling western land and collecting tariffs would come nowhere near meeting the need for money to fund the war. Trying to solve the immense financial difficulties fell to U.S. Secretary of the Treasury Salmon P. Chase and Confederate Secretary of the Treasury Christopher Memminger. There were three primary means that governments used for raising money: taxation, issuing coin and currency, and borrowing through the sale of bonds. New taxes were added in the form of direct taxes on the states, excise taxes on the manufacture, sale and consumption of products, and a new federal income tax on every adult wage earner. In 1861 the U.S. Congress, with most Southern representatives absent, adopted the Morrill Tariff which eventually would raise rates to 47 percent. It also enacted a tax of 3 percent on incomes over $800. The following year the Internal Revenue Act provided for a graduated tax of 5 percent on incomes from $600 to $5,000, 7.5 percent on incomes from $5,001 to $10,000, and 10 percent on incomes over $10,000. Less than $2 million in taxes were collected in 1862, but during the next year, with the addition of the new taxes in force, collections rose to $41 million. Nevertheless, the $211 million collected during the war was a drop in the bucket compared to the total cost of the war.[5]

The U.S. government enacted Legal Tender Acts in 1862 and 1863 that authorized the Treasury to issue $450 million in paper money ($432 million was actually circulated). Printed with green ink, the bills came to be called "greenbacks." The problem with printing paper money was that it fueled inflation. The value of the paper money gradually decreased as it had in the American Revolution, which especially hurt those on fixed incomes and urban dwellers. People were at first reluctant to accept the paper money, so it was decided to put it into circulation by paying the troops with it. By mid–1864, a greenback was worth only 39 cents in gold, but as the North began to win the war, and public confidence increased, the value rose to 67 cents by end of war. Although this accounted for twice as much funding as taxation, it still came nowhere near the amount of money needed.

Secretary Chase favored selling bonds because more money could be raised quickly and it would not result in the inflation associated with printing paper money. Early in the war, when it appeared that the North was losing, the government had little success with the public sale of bonds. Compounding that problem was the lack of a national bank—there were some 1,600 state-chartered banks in existence with over 7,000 forms of bank notes in circulation. Because of the lack of a federal banking facility, the government had to rely on bankers and financial brokers to sell bonds at a commission. The most successful of these was Jay Cooke who ran a Philadelphia banking house that sold over $400 million in bonds at a high commission. In the South, taxation was not particularly helpful. Import and export duties raised little because of the increasing effectiveness of the blockade and because the Confederate constitution limited tariff powers. The

Direct Tax on real estate, slaves and other property raised only about $17.5 million, and the Confederate Internal Revenue Act of April 1863 providing for sales, personal income, business, professional, and trade taxes did better but provided only modest income. A "tax-in-kind" was added for farmers to pay with produce, cattle, horses, and other needed commodities. Taxation, however, proved relatively ineffective, raising only about 1 percent of Confederate wartime income.

With no established government or international credit, selling bonds proved difficult for the South. By backing the bonds with cotton, there was some stimulus to blockade running, but attempts to sell bonds in Europe met with limited success. The most important sale was the so-called "Erlanger Loan" subscribed by Emile Erlanger and Company of Paris on March 19, 1863. Sold at 90 percent of face value, the bonds raised $8,535,486. The ability of the South to sell bonds varied in general concert with its perceived fortunes in the war. After 1863, when the war clearly turned against the South, it became increasingly more difficult to sell bonds. This was not the answer to the South's problem.

The North relied mostly on the sale of bonds to fund the war. As early as July 1861 Congress adopted an Act for a National Loan which authorized the Secretary of the Treasury to borrow up to $250 million over the next year. The South, through necessity, resorted to massive printing of paper money, issuing over $1.5 billion. The paper currency was backed by cotton rather than gold, but so much was printed that it led to steady runaway inflation and a progressive devaluation of the paper money. In 1861 a Confederate dollar was worth about what a federal dollar was, 90 cents in gold. By 1863 it dropped to 29 cents, 4.6 cents in 1864, and only 1.7 cents in 1865. This resulted in serious inflation. By the beginning of 1862, less than a year after the war began, consumer prices in the South had already doubled, and by the middle of 1863 they had increased by a factor of 13. In 1862, a barrel of flour cost $18 in Raleigh, North Carolina, but by 1865 it increased to $500. A pair of shoes cost $125, a coat $350, a chicken $15, and a barrel of flour $275. By May 1865, $1 U.S. was equal to $1,200 in Confederate currency. By the end of the war inflation in the South reached about 9,000 percent, which led to corresponding weakening of morale.[6]

International Diplomacy

In large part the Southern strategy for winning the war relied upon favorable European relations. Southern cotton could be traded for European manufactured goods, especially weapons and other materiel necessary for the prosecution of the war. The two most important nations were England and France, both of which depended heavily on Southern cotton to fuel their textile industries. By 1860, about one-quarter of Southern cotton went to the North, one-quarter to continental Europe, and fully one-half to England. In 1861 public opinion in Britain about the American crisis was divided. Slavery had already been eliminated in the British Empire and most working class people tended to support the North because of its association with the anti-slavery movement. The upper class, many of whom had economic ties to the South because of the need to import cotton to feed British textile mills, was inclined to favor the Confederacy. In France a similar divide occurred with republicans and Orléanists favoring the North while supporters of the Bourbon restoration and Roman Catholics tended to line up behind the Confederacy. Emperor Napoléon III was inclined to offer official recognition and support to the South, but with the United States threatening war if he did so he was unwilling to move unless Britain agreed to a joint declaration. Thus the important relationship was that between the United States and Great Britain. It would no doubt determine whether the South would be successful in gaining at least the tacit trading support of Britain and France. Relations between the two endured a rocky beginning.

Winfield Scott's Anaconda Plan was based on economic warfare. To be successful, it required that the North blockade the South to prevent the rebels from obtaining support from overseas that would be crucial in a lengthy war. But the Southern coastline stretched some 3,350 miles from Washington, D.C., to Matamoros, Mexico, and the North had available for use only around 100 ships, some two-thirds of which were either antiquated or not intended for ocean service. Only 26 were ocean-going steamers. This presented a serious problem because international law, specifically the 1856 Declaration of Paris, required that to be lawful a blockade must be (1) formally proclaimed, (2) promptly established, (3) enforced, and (4) effective. Nations were not required to respect a blockade if it was not effective; that is, if the blockading nation did not have the resources to effectively enforce its blockade. But this was not the only problem the blockade posed.

By announcing a "blockade," Secretary of State William Seward used a word that, in international affairs, implied something done by one sovereign nation to another during time of war. The result was that, although he did not mean to do so, Seward appeared to give *de facto* recognition to the Confederacy as an independent nation. This, of course, was exactly the opposite of Lincoln's claim that secession was illegal and therefore the South was not an independent nation. What he should have said, instead of announcing a "blockade," was that the Southern ports were "closed." Under international law a nation had the right to "close" its own ports to other nations. This would have had the effect of cutting off the South from outside assistance, requiring foreign nations to observe the order, and at the same time avoiding the appearance of recognizing the Confederacy as an independent nation.

The question of "blockading" versus "closing" the ports was not simply an exercise in semantics. It had real repercussions. When Great Britain announced its neutrality on May 13, rather than be pleased that the British were not siding with the Confederacy as an independent nation the Lincoln administration was outraged because neutrality implied that there were two separate belligerent powers. One cannot be neutral between one thing, so there must be two things; that is, two nations. Of course, the British pleaded innocence merely explaining that the Lincoln administration had already recognized the Confederacy as a separate nation by proclaiming a wartime blockade, thus granting the South belligerent rights under international law.

Secretary of State William Seward erred in declaring a blockade, giving other nations a legal argument for continuing trade with the Confederacy (Library of Congress).

Although Britain never formally recognized the Confederacy, it did provide significant "unofficial" aid to the rebels during the war. British merchants traded with the South, British shipyards built vessels that were used as Southern commerce raiders to prey upon Northern shipping, and the British government looked the other way as rebel ships put in to ports within the British Empire for resupply. All of this would be an ongoing problem during the war, but never more so than later in 1861 when the United States and Britain briefly teetered on the brink of war.

Hoping to force Great Britain and France to recognize its independence and come to its aid, the Confederacy withheld cotton shipments at the beginning of the war. By doing this it hoped to cause sufficient economic distress to force the Europe nations to come to its aid. But in 1861 most British manufacturers had a stockpile of cotton that could last several months. This delayed any serious effect of the South's withholding of cotton. By 1862, new sources of cotton from Egypt and India began to replace the lost supply from the South. Also, by that time the United States was placing major orders for manufactured goods, weapons, ships, textiles, and other products with British firms that more closely tied the British economy to the North. Further, Midwestern grain was also a major export to Europe that became increasingly important when crop failures reduced European grain supplies. Taken together, these factors made it increasingly less likely that Britain, and hence France, would openly recognize the Confederacy and offer significant support.

Raising the Armies

In 1860 the United States Army numbered only some 16,000 men, most of whom were scattered in small groups throughout the western territories guarding forts and frontier settlements. One study indicates that only about 10 percent were stationed east of the Mississippi River with most of those located along the Atlantic coast or the Canadian border. With the obvious shortage of troops, immediate action was needed if the rebellion were to be quickly extinguished. Because very few people thought the war would last long there was a reluctance to expand the regular army for a short contest. American military planning had envisioned a small standing army that could be expanded as needed by reliance on the militias of the various states. With this in mind President Lincoln issued his initial call in April for 75,000 men to serve for three months, barely enough time to get the men together, organize and train them, and get them into the field before their terms of service expired. At that time President Jefferson Davis had already called on March 6 for the enlistment of 100,000 Southern volunteers to serve for one year, while on May 8 the Confederate Congress authorized the recruitment of 400,000 men and the move of the Southern capital to Richmond, Virginia. Apparently having second thoughts, on May 3 Lincoln issued, without specific authority, a further call for 42,000 volunteers for national service for a period of three years.

In 1861, with emotions running high throughout the nation, in many places North and South the initial calls for volunteers were met with a rush to the colors so large that some had to be sent home for lack of arms, uniforms and equipment. Since regiments were recruited locally the backgrounds and occupations of the men usually mirrored the areas where they were raised with farmers predominating in rural regiments and mechanics, factory workers, and artisans in those that came from urban settings. To the extent that averages mean anything, historian Bell I. Wiley found that the mean age of a Civil War soldier was just under 26, with most falling between 18 and 39. He was a white farmer about 5'8" tall, and unmarried.

Age	Union Enlistments	Occupation	Percent of Union Army
18 or Under	1,000,000	Farmer	48
17 or Under	800,000	Mechanic	24
16 or Under	200,000	Laborer	16
15 or Under	100,000	Commerce	5
14 or Under	2,000	Professional	3
13 or Under	300	Miscellaneous	4
10 or Under	25		

The typical soldier was Protestant, but large numbers of Catholics served and an estimated 7,000 Jews fought for the North and 3,000 for the South. At the beginning of the war privates received $11 per month plus a $3 clothing allowance but in June 1864 Union pay rose to $16 per month and Confederate to $18, but with the devalued Confederate dollar due to rampant inflation the rebel invariably had much less actual buying power even when he did get paid, which was not often. When the North began recruiting black troops they were initially paid only $10 per month without any clothing allowance.

Reflecting the substantial immigration in the antebellum years, the armies contained sizeable numbers of men who were born outside the United States or, in the North, were of African ancestry. Data for the Union forces is much more complete than for the Confederacy because of the destruction of many of the Southern records toward the end of the war. Based on existing documentation, about one-quarter of all white troops serving the Union were of foreign birth. Estimates vary, but generally accepted numbers based on a study of some 2.2 million Union records include the following.[7]

Place of Birth	Approximate Number	Percentage
United States (whites)	1,290,000	58.6
Germany	216,000	9.8
African Ancestry	210,000	9.5
Ireland	200,000	9.1
The Netherlands	90,000	4.1
Canada	50,000	2.3
England	50,000	2.3
France or French Canada	40,000	1.8
Scandinavia	20,000	0.9
Italy	7,000	0.3
Jewish Ancestry	7,000	0.3
Mexico	6,000	0.3
Poland	5,000	0.2
Indigenous Americans	4,000	0.2
Other	5,000	0.2
Total	2,200,000	100.0

Of course, the above table reflects place of birth and not, with the exception of Africans, ancestry. If one includes those born in the United States of German, Irish, or other ancestries then the "ethnic" backgrounds of Union troops is magnified all the more. German historian Wilhelm Kaufmann, for example, concluded in *Die Deutschen im amerikanischen Bürgerkriege*[8] that 216,000 men born in the German states fought for the

Union, but added another 300,000 Federal soldiers who were sons of German parents and still another 234,000 of more remote German descent. This amounts to a total of 750,000 men of German ancestry or more than a third of all those who served in the Union cause. Although the foreign-born appeared across the entire spectrum of Union units, there were also regiments raised in heavily immigrant areas that took on the personality of their respective group. New York, for example, fielded the "Cameron Highlanders," the "Garibaldi Guard," the "Gardes Lafayette," the "Polish Legion," and numerous Irish and German units.

Replicating the much smaller immigration in the South, the Confederate forces, as near as can be determined, contained only about 9 percent foreign-born with the Irish being the largest (estimated 40,000) group followed by Germans, French and Mexicans. A number of Cherokee, Chickasaw, Choctaw, Creek and other indigenous people also cast their lot with the Confederacy. Among the "foreign" units were an Irish brigade, several German regiments, a Polish Brigade[9] and a European brigade of mixed nationalities from Louisiana, and some 13,000 Hispanics in several regiments from different states.

Waging War in 1861

Postwar analysis revealed that the structure of the Union and Confederate armies was quite similar, no doubt because they came from the same traditions, their leaders mostly graduated from the same national military academy, and they made use of the same textbooks and military treatises. The only slight difference was in the percentage of cavalry employed. The Union armies consisted of about 80 percent infantry, 14 percent cavalry and 6 percent artillery. Confederate forces contained 75 percent infantry, 20 percent cavalry, and 5 percent artillery. It is generally believed that the South enjoyed an advantage in the quality of its cavalry units at least during the first half of the war while the North possessed a superiority in its artillery.

The structure of the armies on both sides was the same. An "army" (such as the Army of the Potomac or the Army of Northern Virginia) was comprised of two or more divisions, a division of two or more brigades, and a brigade of two or more regiments. The basic units of organization were regiments (infantry and cavalry) or batteries (artillery). When it quickly became apparent that more troops would be needed, and for a longer term of service, the states were called upon to fill progressively larger quotas. In this way the vast majority of men who fought in the war, in both armies, served in state organized "volunteer" regiments. These were normally raised locally with the commanding officer, the colonel, being appointed by the governor of the state. Although exact procedures varied somewhat, the other field officers were usually appointed. A standard infantry regiment consisted of ten companies of approximately 100 men each giving the full regiment a complement of some 1,000 soldiers. The line officers—captains and lieutenants—were sometimes elected by the men in their companies, sometimes appointed based on the number of men they recruited, and sometimes appointed by the colonel with the approval of the governor.[10]

Led by a colonel, the other two field officers were a lieutenant colonel and a major. Usually each of the latter commanded a wing (or battalion) of the regiment when formed in battle order. A captain led each of the ten companies assisted by a first lieutenant and a second lieutenant with each company containing, when full, 97 enlisted men of all ranks. In a typical battle line two companies were advanced as skirmishers with the other eight drawn up in a double line with the colors at the center of the regiment. The colors were the heart of the regiment. They were entrusted to a color guard of non-commissioned officers generally selected for their reliability. It was a very dangerous position since much of the enemy's fire might be directed toward the colors. In the noise and confusion of combat, soldiers could maintain their place by aligning on the colors and would be aware of orders to charge or withdraw by the movement of the colors. In the Confederate army each regiment usually carried a single color although some companies brought along banners from home. Confederate regimental colors were issued by central depots

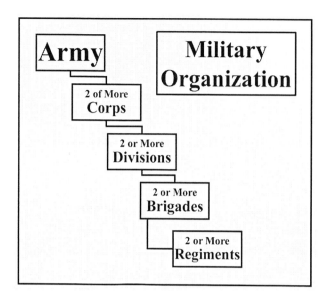

The graph indicates the organization of the armies fielded by the United States and the Confederacy (James S. Pula).

of specified pattern. The red flag with the crossed blue stripes enclosing stars that is typically referred to today as the "Confederate" flag or the "Stars and Bars" was neither; it was the battle flag issued to the Army of Northern Virginia. The Confederate national flag, the real "Stars and Bars," was of various designs roughly mirroring the United States flag but with three red-white-red stripes on some and briefly a white background on others. Union regiments normally carried two colors: the national color and a "state" color which was variously either issued by the state or donated by local citizens groups and could thus vary wildly in design. The colors represented not only the regiment but the folks back home who had entrusted its defense and theirs to their hometown volunteers. One of the bravest acts a soldier could undertake was to capture an enemy color, an action which was often rewarded in the Union forces with the Medal of Honor.

A fortunate regiment would have as its officers men who had some military experience, but more often even colonels could be appointed because of political connections or some other factor without any previous military experience at all. The result was a volunteer force that was especially uneven with some regiments having the benefit of experienced officers while most did not. This problem was especially evident in the North. Officers in the regular army who remained loyal to the United States were generally not inclined to resign their commissions to accept promotion in the volunteer forces because advancement in the regular army during peacetime was painfully slow and with the rebellion expected to be short-lived they did not want to risk their long-term careers for temporary advancement. Therefore, at least during the first few months, the most trained and experienced Northern officers were reluctant to join the volunteer forces and remained lieutenants and captains in the regular army. This was not so for Southerners who resigned to go South. They were immediately offered commissions as majors,

Top: The Sumter Light Guards, which became Company K of the 4th Georgia Volunteer Infantry, are seen here in April 1861. The flag, which is no doubt added to the original photograph, depicts the original Confederate "Stars and Bars." *Bottom:* Soldiers of the 63rd New York Infantry pose in front of their regimental colors. Each Union regiment carried a national color and a state color, the latter often donated by people from the area where it was recruited. Note that both colors have been decorated with the names of the engagements the regiment fought in, which means this was taken at the end of the war with newly issued banners. Note also the Irish harp on the state color identifying this as a predominantly Irish regiment (both photographs, Library of Congress).

colonels, and even generals in the service of the Southern states. The result was that, at least initially, the South made better use of its trained military personnel than did the North and this may have contributed to early southern successes.

The use of volunteer forces raised by the states had two unforeseen results during the war. The first was the effect on recruitment, once it became clear that the war would become prolonged. As battles multiplied so did casualties. The size of regiments which marched off to war were soon whittled down to half their initial number of men, or less, through the effects of disease and combat. How would these losses be replaced? In the North, some regiments sent officers home occasionally to recruit replacements, but this practice varied considerably between units and states. In some cases state governors found it more expedient to make political friends by appointing more colonels to new regiments than to allow recruiting for existing regiments. The result was that as the war progressed Union brigades and divisions often contained several small regiments of veterans and one or two large regiments of new recruits. This did not make for good use of the experienced talent. The same was true, but to a lesser extent, in the South where there was more of an effort to recruit new troops to replace those lost in veteran regiments. The result was that by mid-war rebel regiments tended to be larger than corresponding Union units and to contain a greater mixture of veterans and recruits. At Gettysburg, for example, the average size of the Confederate infantry regiment was around 350 men while that of the Union was only about 250. Confederate brigades, then, could usually count on being larger and having a more balanced fighting ability between regiments than could the Union.

The other unanticipated consequence was the very uneven sacrifice that communities made. Since regiments were raised locally but were deployed by the national government, one unit might be assigned to guard a fortress while another was assigned to active duty in an army in the field where it engaged in multiple battles. The latter would normally suffer many more casualties meaning that the community where it was raised would suffer disproportionally to others. Even when regiments were both assigned to the same army differences in positioning could lead to great disparity. Looking again to Gettysburg as an example, the 5th Wisconsin was assigned to the Sixth Corps which was not heavily engaged. The regiment brought 439 men to the field, suffering no losses. The 26th Wisconsin was assigned to the Eleventh Corps that was heavily engaged resulting in a regimental loss of 217 out of 446, or 48.7 percent. The impact on a small community when a high percentage of men died of disease or combat or came home as cripples cannot be understated. The long-term result of this was the adoption of a policy in the armed forces in succeeding wars of mixing recruits up; that is, not assigning people from the same community to serve together but instead assigning recruits irrespective of where they came from.

Although weaponry varied in manufacture and caliber, the standard Civil War infantry weapon was the .58 caliber rifled musket. Prior to the war most armies were armed with smoothbore muskets which was also the standard infantry weapon of the American Revolution, the War of 1812 and the Mexican War. The term "smoothbore" meant that the inside of the barrel containing the explosive charge and projectile was smooth. Given the fact that the musket ball did not usually fit snugly in the barrel, when fired there was a tendency for some of the force of the explosive charge to be lost, thereby limiting the range, and for the ball to jiggle slightly as it left the barrel, thereby limiting accuracy. The effective accurate range for a trained soldier with a smoothbore was about

80 to 100 yards although "lucky" shots could kill at greater range. So notoriously inaccurate were the weapons that the British manual of arms for loading and firing the Brown Bess musket of the American Revolution did not even contain a command to "aim." By pointing all the weapons in the same general direction and firing all at once (volley firing) the belief was that something would most likely be hit.

Between 1847 and 1849 Claude-Etienne Minié, a French Army officer, invented what came to be called the minié ball for the rifled musket. Instead of the smooth inside, the rifled musket contained grooves on the inside much like the grooves seen on the outside of a modern screw. The minié ball was not really a ball but a conoidal bullet with a hollowed-out end at the rear. When fired the thin walls of the hollow end expanded to engage the rifling and impart a twirling motion to the bullet. This served two purposes. By expanding the end of the bullet to exactly fit the size of the barrel less explosive force was lost causing the bullet to have greater velocity and travel farther. By imparting the spinning motion and keeping the bullet on a straight trajectory out of the barrel the result was greatly increased accuracy. The combination of the rifled musket and minié ball increased the overall accuracy of the weapon to about 250 yards and its range to some 1,000 yards. Clearly this innovation carried the potential to greatly increase the deadliness of opposing battle lines that continued to use the traditional Napoleonic formations.

A trained soldier could fire a maximum of three aimed shots per minute. In 1861 there were other guns available including early versions of repeating weapons. Although they generally had a somewhat shorter range they offered significantly more firepower to the average infantryman than the single-shot musket. Ambrose Burnside, who became a prominent Union general in the war, won a contest at West Point in 1857 with a breech-loading weapon that used a single brass cartridge containing both the explosive charge and projectile. While not strictly a repeating rifle it had a mechanism which ejected the spent cartridge and allowed for easily inserting a new one so that the rate of fire was greatly increased. In 1860 Benjamin Henry patented the Henry rifle which used a lever-action breech-loading device with a sixteen-shot magazine containing copper-coated cartridges. The weapon could be fired as quickly as the soldier could work the lever and aim. Another weapon patented in 1860 was the Sharps or Spencer rifle invented by Christian Spencer, an employee of Sharps. By lowering the trigger guard the soldier could in the same motion eject the old cartridge and insert a new .52 caliber metallic cartridge. Equipped with a seven-shot magazine, the soldier could fire these off as fast as his hand could go up and down on the mechanism. With extra magazines in his cartridge box, a trained soldier could easily fire twenty or more aimed shots per minute. The advantages in firepower of any of these weapons over the muzzle-loading rifled musket were obvious. At the outbreak of the war Brig. Gen. James Ripley, head of the United States army ordnance office, declined to purchase repeating weapons to arm infantry regiments because of their relative cost—$20 for the average rifled musket and $36 for a repeating rifle. When repeating weapons were offered to the Confederacy, Brig. Gen. Robert E. Lee, then acting as military advisor to President Jefferson Davis, declined the offer on the grounds that such a weapon would encourage poor fire discipline.

Field artillery batteries were normally commanded by a captain and were divided into two-gun sections with a lieutenant, or in some cases a sergeant, in charge of each section. In the Union army a battery normally included six guns while those in the Confederate army most often had four. As with muskets, there were two general types of field guns, smoothbore and rifled. The most common smoothbore was the 12-pounder Napoleon with the "12" referring to the weight of the solid shot that it fired. The Napoleon was very popular as well as versatile. As a smoothbore its range was more limited than the rifled guns, about 1,200 yards, and less accurate at longer ranges, but it could fire solid shot, shell, spherical case, and canister and was the gun of choice for close-in defense against infantry. Solid shot, as the name implies, was a solid metallic ball that was normally fired at distant targets, especially enemy artillery, with the aim of hitting and destroying it. Shell was a hollow ball filled with explosive that when fired exploded near the target sending shards of jagged metal into anything nearby. Spherical case was also hollow but had a thinner casing and was filled with small metal balls for use as an antipersonnel weapon. For the Napoleon spherical case contained 78 balls that spread out as "shrapnel" when the shell exploded. Canister resembled a very large shotgun shell filled with small metal balls. When fired the shell disintegrated so that the contents spread out in a killing field much like the shotgun shell. When used effectively, canister was exceptionally deadly against charging infantry. The typical Union battery carried into action for its six pieces 288 solid shot, 96 shells, 288 spherical case shells, and 96 rounds of canister.

The favored rifled field gun was the 3-inch Ordnance Rifle named for the diameter of the bore. Firing a 9.5 pound projectile it was accurate to 1,830 yards. Valued for its durability and accuracy, the rifled gun could fire shot, shell, and canister, but usually gunners refrained from using canister except in emergencies since a few discharges of the metal projectiles tended to ruin the rifling in the barrel. For long-range work it was

A drawing of a 12-pounder Napoleon, the standard smoothbore artillery piece of the war, by newspaper correspondent Edwin Forbes in 1863 (Library of Congress).

excellent, yet when firing shell or spherical case accuracy depended a great deal, for both Napoleons and 3-inch rifles, on judging the correct distance to the target since the fuses had to be cut to a specific length to explode at a given range. Each piece, whether Napoleon or rifle, had a crew of twelve—eight to fire the weapon and four to handle the horses and equipment. The Union very early attempted to standardize all of the pieces in a battery to make resupply of ammunition easier while the Confederates, most often from necessity since it was harder for them to manufacture or import artillery, mixed pieces in the same battery creating some problems of resupply. No doubt this, and the generally poorer quality of its shell and gunpowder, contributed to the superiority of Union artillery during the war.

Once in the field the standard combat formation remained the traditional battle line. Regiments normally formed in a double line with two companies in reserve. Brigades kept a regiment in reserve and divisions kept a brigade or multiple regiments in reserve. Of course good commanders attempted to place their troops in good defensive positions behind fences, woods, embankments, of other features offering some protection. The better the protection the better the chance to repel an attack. If all other considerations such as terrain and defensive protection were equal, there were essentially four ways of attacking the enemy. The most prevalent was a head on frontal attack. This was usually the most costly and stood the least chance of success, especially if the enemy enjoyed any kind of defensive protection. The preferred method would be an attack from the rear where the enemy was virtually unprepared, but this was exceptionally difficult to achieve except against the most incompetent of commanders. The other two were the enfilade attack and the flank attack. If an attacker could place his troops diagonally across the front and flank of an enemy all of the attacker's troops could fire on the defender while it was difficult for the defenders farther away from the attack to bring their weapons to bear on the attackers. Better yet was the flank attack, similar to the famous "Crossing the T" maneuver in naval warfare when the attacker's battle line is perpendicular to that of the defender and aligned across its end so that all of the attackers could fire directly down the defender's line while only those at the very end of the defender's line can fire back. Other movements used to bring troops into action were the envelopment and the double envelopment. In the former the attacker attempts to move around the flank of an enemy in an attempt to gain the defender's rear, or at least an exposed flank. The double envelopment simply meant that the attacker tried to turn both flanks at the same time.

Combat, of course, meant casualties. But before the armies even engaged the factor that would cost more lives than any during the war began to ravage the growing camps North and South—disease. Both of these required medical personnel, but there were precious few in the regular army at the time. In 1860 the regular army enrolled only 30 surgeons and 83 assistant surgeons. Following secession, there remained only 98 surgeons of all ranks, but by 1865 there would be a need in the Union armies alone for almost 13,000. Few civilian physicians wanted to give up established practices to go off to war at a fraction of the income and for an undetermined time. Some naturally did out of patriotism or local peer pressure, but as the armies expanded exponentially it became difficult and in many cases impossible to find trained surgeons to serve the troops. In some cases anyone with some form of medical knowledge, no matter how minute, was pressed into service—medical students, veterinarians, and even occasionally the local barber. As the Wisconsin Surgeon General quipped, "neither in civil nor military practice,

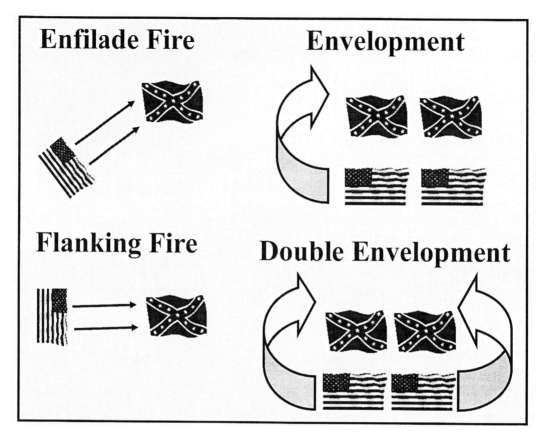

The graph illustrates the standard infantry assault tactics preferred by the offense which sought to create enfilading or flanking fire and to maneuver around the flanks of the enemy (envelopment) (James S. Pula).

any more than in any other avocations of life, is scholarship the measure of practical ability."[11] In the crisis, almost anyone would do and they could learn on the job. Surgeon Charles S. Tripler, Medical Director of the Army of the Potomac in 1861–62, confirmed that "for the most part, physicians taken suddenly from civil life, with little knowledge of their duties, had to be taught them from the very alphabet."[12]

Each volunteer regiment was entitled to enroll one surgeon and one assistant surgeon with the colonel responsible for their recruitment. Surgeons were usually accorded the rank of major with a salary of $169 per month while assistant surgeons were mustered as captains or lieutenants at $115.50 or $105.50, respectively, per month. No matter how many there were, or how well trained, they had their work cut out for them as the thousands of men suddenly living in close quarters with one another, in mostly temporary camps with very poor sanitation, were subject to a variety of diseases that spread very quickly. In an age of limited medical knowledge, dysentery, measles, smallpox, typhoid fever and other maladies became significant killers. Union records reveal that out of about 2,600,000 soldiers enrolled during the war, surgeons treated some 400,000 combat wounds and 6,000,000 cases of disease. At this rate, each soldier was sick enough to seek treatment almost 2.3 times! During the first year of the war the Federal sick rate was 69 officers/1,000 and 106 enlisted men/1,000 while the mortality rate was 53/1,000 including

44 by disease and nine by all other causes including battle. It has been estimated that death from disease claimed about 2.01 percent of the U.S. Army and 3.81 percent of the Confederate Army.[13]

In addition to diseases and poor sanitation, irregular and unhealthy diets were also major contributing factors to the high instances of illness and death. Normal field rations included beans, salt pork, pickled beef (which the troops referred to as "embalmed beef") and hardtack (described by one soldier as "a little softer than cast iron"[14]). There was no provision for fresh vegetables other than what the troops could forage from the local countryside. Almost everything was fried, including the hardtack which many soldiers fried in the grease of their meat to make it soft enough to eat. Under these conditions diarrhea and dysentery were ever-present dangers. In 1861, when the war was yet young, Union records reveal 640 cases per 1,000 which skyrocketed to 995 cases per 1,000 the following year. Based on 5,825,480 cases in Union army records, the leading causes of death by disease were chronic diarrhea (27,558), typhoid (27,050), acute dysentery (4,084), malaria (4,059), chronic dysentery (3,229), acute diarrhea (2,923), and typhus (850). In 1861 one of every twelve Union soldiers were treated for venereal disease, with the rate for the war being 8.2 percent. About 15 percent of soldiers died of disease during the Civil War as opposed to 8 percent in World War I, 4 percent in World War II, and 2 percent in Korea.[15]

For those who lived long enough to see combat the medical services were little better. Musicians were customarily detailed as stretcher bearers. Whatever wounded they could reach were taken to regimental or brigade field hospitals that were set up as close behind the battle lines as possible. There a triage occurred with the most seriously wounded receiving some initial care before being sent back to the division or corps hospitals that were normally located in barns or other large buildings a relatively safe distance from the front. Eventually, if the patient survived and could be moved he was evacuated to a General Hospital established as a permanent facility in a larger city. Again looking at Union records, 35.1 percent of the wounds surgeons treated were in the arms, 35.7 percent in the legs, 18.4 percent in the trunk, and 10.7 percent in head. Of course this is somewhat misleading because serious wounds in the head and trunk usually resulted in death before the victim could be removed to a hospital. Wounds where balls were embedded in the flesh or organs were normally probed with an unsterilized finger, the bullet extracted if possible, and the wound bound with cloth. The cloth was to be kept moist to keep down the swelling while pain was relieved with opiates, quinine, or liquor. The smart soldier removed the bandage and washed the wound frequently which seems to have helped some to survive.[16]

If a wound resulted in a broken bone in the arm, leg, foot or joint the standard treatment was amputation. "We operated in old blood-stained and often pus-stained coats, the veterans of a hundred fights," Surgeon William W. Keen later recalled. "We used undisinfected instruments from undisinfected plush-lined cases, and still worse used marine sponges which had been used in prior pus cases and had been only washed in tap water. If a sponge or an instrument fell on the floor it was washed and squeezed in a basin of tap water and used as if it were clean."[17] Visiting the Eleventh Corps hospital at Gettysburg, General Carl Schurz wrote:

> There stood the surgeons, their sleeves rolled up to their elbows, their bare arms as well as their linen aprons smeared with blood, their knives not seldom held between their teeth.... As a wounded man was lifted on the table, often shrieking with pain as the attendants handled him, the surgeon quickly

examined the wound and resolved upon cutting off the injured limb. Some ether was administered and the body put in position in a moment. The surgeon snatched his knife from between his teeth…, wiped it rapidly once or twice across his bloodstained apron, and the cutting began. The operation accomplished, the surgeon would look around with a deep sigh, and then—"Next!"[18]

Naturally mortality rates from amputations were high with about 26 percent succumbing to the trauma and unhygienic conditions. Generally speaking, the farther from the trunk the better the chances of survival. Mortality for amputations of the foot was 6 percent, ankle 25 percent, below the knee 33 percent, above the knee 54 percent, and the hip 83 percent. Penetrating wounds of the intestine were 99.9 percent fatal, penetrating wounds of the head or abdomen killed 90 percent, penetrating wounds of the chest 60 percent, spinal wounds 56 percent, wounds in the abdomen 49 percent, and wounds to the head and chest 28 percent; although, again, most of those with serious wounds to the head and chest did not survive long enough to reach even a field hospital. The chances of a wounded soldier surviving was only about 7 to 1. In the Korean War it was 50 to 1 and in Vietnam 99 to 1.[19]

War means death, and the Civil War was going to be the most deadly conflict in American history.

The War Unfolds

Much of the first half of 1861 was devoted to raising and providing at least rudimentary military training to soldiers both North and South. In the west, where the Northern strategy envisioned a push down the Mississippi Valley, the major operations took place in and around Missouri as the two sides continued to contend for possession of that key state. Much of the early fighting took the shape of bushwhacking between individuals and small groups, but both sides also attempted to secure the state and the surrounding area for their side.

Following the seizure of the St. Louis arsenal Nathaniel Lyon was quickly promoted to brigadier general on May 17 and, on the last day of the month, given command of the Department of the West encompassing the entire state of Missouri. Lyon pursued the pro–South Missouri State Guard commanded by Gen. Sterling Price, capturing Jefferson City. Lyon continued his advance to Springfield with an army of some 5,400, but, in the meantime, Gen. Benjamin McCulloch arrived with additional rebel troops raising Price's strength to about 12,000. At Wilson's Creek on August 10 the Union force was soundly defeated and Lyon killed. Price followed up his victory with the capture of Lexington in September. Yet Southern successes were short-lived. Gen. John C. Frémont, who had played a prominent part in California during the Mexican War, arrived with an army of 38,000 troops that forced Price to flee before his advance. To consolidate Federal control Frémont declared a state of martial law and issued a proclamation declaring that "the property, real and personal, of all persons in the State of Missouri who shall take up arms against the United States, and who shall be directly proven to have taken active part with their enemies in the field, is declared to be confiscated to the public use; and their slaves, if any they have, are hereby declared free."[20] Not yet willing to endorse the provision of freeing slaves, Lincoln acted quickly to rescind the proclamation and replace its author with Gen. David Hunter.[21] Meanwhile, Confederate forces were consolidated under the overall command of Gen. Albert Sidney Johnston.[22] His command, initially with about

40,000 troops, encompassed all of the territory west of the Allegheny Mountains. But his troops were spread out over a very wide area with about 10,000 remaining in Missouri under the immediate command of Price.

Beyond Missouri, some 25,000 Federal troops began to concentrate in Cairo, Illinois, under the command of Gen. Ulysses S. Grant, who briefly entered Missouri to attack Confederate troops in Belmont.[23] A second, much larger Union force of approximately 80,000 converged on Bowling Green, Kentucky, under Gen. Don Carlos Buell[24] who was assigned to command the Department of the Ohio with the expectation that he would occupy Kentucky and later advance into Tennessee where there was a strong pro–Union sentiment in the eastern portion of the state. To counter these Federal moves, Johnston assembled about 50,000 rebel troops in southern Kentucky positioned to oppose any Federal advance. While these were organized and drilled, other troops, assisted by local slave labor, began constructing fortifications along the Mississippi, Tennessee and Cumberland Rivers, natural arteries for potential invasion of the South, and other critical strategic points, while Price attempted to protect Confederate interests west of the Mississippi River.

Events in the west were certainly important, but the eyes of the nation were focused on the opposing capitals in Washington and Richmond, especially since the newspapers that could afford to send correspondents into the field were largely employed by the major eastern press. Naturally their focus was on the east and what was then perceived to be the "main" armies gathering around Washington, D.C., and in northern Virginia. There, with Gen. Winfield Scott physically unable to take the field, a commander was needed to lead the Union army into Virginia. The man chosen was Irwin McDowell of Ohio.[25] His army of about 30,000 men was largely comprised of ninety-day volunteers who lacked training and, in some cases, suitable weapons. Both Scott and McDowell wanted to spend time drilling and otherwise preparing the troops to take the field, but pressure from the press and politicians for an early drive "On to Richmond" forced McDowell to move before he believed his army was ready.

To the south of Washington Gen. P. G. T. Beauregard,[26] "the Hero of Fort Sumter," led some 20,000 Southern troops in and around Manassas Junction, an important railroad depot. Acting separately from Beauregard was a second rebel force in Virginia's Shenandoah Valley led by Gen. Joseph E. Johnston.[27] His force of about 11,000 was charged with protecting this likely invasion route and the rich fertile valley lands that would play a large part in feeding Southern forces operating in Virginia throughout most of the war.

The opposing sides were roughly equivalent in training, or the lack thereof. Weaponry

Gen. Pierre G. T. Beauregard led the largest Confederate force in Virginia (Library of Congress).

was not standardized which led to serious supply problems, especially in combat where available ammunition had to be matched with regiments that may be moving about throughout the day. Uniforms also lacked standardization. While we think of the North as wearing blue and the South either gray or butternut, such was not the case at the beginning of the conflict when militia units usually wore their normal state uniforms when they marched off to war. Georgians, for example, wore their standard blue state attire, while some New York regiments wore gray. All of this would be very confusing in the excitement and stress of combat, nor would the colors the units carried always help in identifying them. The original national flag of the Confederacy had three horizontal stripes of alternating red-white-red and a blue canton in the upper left with a white star for every Confederate state. When hanging from a staff, especially if there were no wind to stir it, the rebel banner was quite indistinguishable from the United States flag from a distance.

Goaded by Congress and the press, McDowell began his movement south on July 16. Irish-born Gen. Robert Patterson was sent with 18,000 troops to capture Harpers Ferry and keep an eye Johnston's force to prevent it from moving to support Beauregard, but the 69-year-old general, a veteran of the War of 1812 and the Mexican War, failed miserably in his assignment. When it became apparent that a major Union invasion was developing under McDowell, Johnston very adeptly left a few soldiers to make it appear that he was still in camp before Patterson while he marched the bulk of his men to a rail head, placed them aboard trains, and sped them off toward Manassas Junction.

McDowell led some 30,000 men south in three columns with the intent of making a diversionary attack with two forces along the rebel lines at Bull Run, a small creek flowing north and east of Manassas Junction, while sending the third on a flanking move to envelop the Confederate right. This was designed to force Beauregard to abandon his position and retreat behind the Rappahannock River, the next major defensive obstacle on the route to Richmond. While the columns labored south in the sweltering summer heat, Beauregard positioned his 22,000 men defensively behind Bull Run as McDowell suspected. After an inconclusive thrust at the rebel right across Blackburn's Ford, McDowell determined to try the Confederate left instead. Around the same time Beauregard, after receiving some initial reinforcements from Johnston, planned to attack the Union left. If both movements had advanced as planned, the odd result would have been that the two armies would essentially exchange positions with the Confederates closer to Washington and the Federals closer to Richmond!

McDowell launched his advance in the

Gen. Irwin McDowell led United States forces for the 1861 invasion of Virginia (Library of Congress).

early morning hours of July 21. Although it began at 2:30 a.m., confusion among the inexperienced troops clogged the roadways so that the actual attack did not materialize until hours later. When it finally broke, Beauregard was eating breakfast. Although he quickly issued orders for a counterattack, staff work suffered from the same inexperience that plagued McDowell's advance so that nothing developed as planned. The immediate threat was met by Capt. Edward Porter Alexander who made use of the first semaphore "wig-wag" signal, used in the Civil War, to warn the rebel commander at the spot of the Union attack to "look out for your left, your position is turned."[28] In response to this warning, the Confederate line, which was being driven back, reorganized on Matthews Hill. They consisted of three brigades led by Col. Nathan "Shanks" Evans, Col. Francis S. Bartow, and Brig. Gen. Barnard Bee. This force repelled an attack by the lead Union brigade under Brig. Gen. Ambrose Burnside, but another Federal brigade led by Col. William T. Sherman hit the rebels in the flank and the Confederate line fell back in some disorder.

While the early fighting raged, the last of Johnston's reinforcements arrived by rail from the Shenandoah Valley and were immediately marched to the sound of the guns. Rather than continue the assault immediately, McDowell chose to pause to let his artillery fire on the new line the rebels were forming on Henry House Hill. This provided time for the arrival of a brigade under Brig. Gen. Thomas J. Jackson, the Hampton Legion under Col. Wade Hampton, and a cavalry force under Col. James Ewell Brown

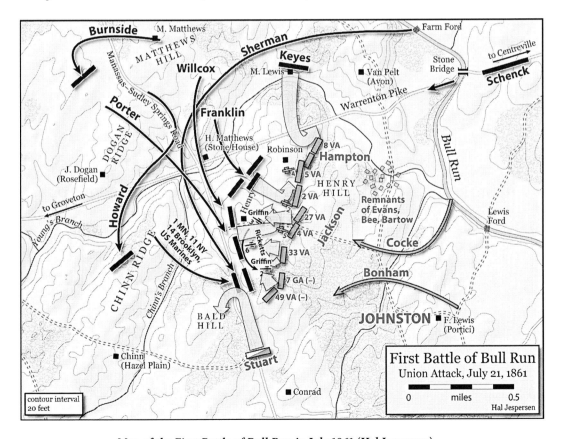

Map of the First Battle of Bull Run in July 1861 (Hal Jespersen).

"Jeb" Stuart. Jackson placed his infantry on the reverse slope of the hill where his men received some protection against direct Federal fire. Following a spirited artillery duel that favored the rebels, McDowell launched his attack shredding the Confederate lines until they were on the verge of breaking. With his troops being shot down all around him, Gen. Bee spotted Jackson's Virginia brigade standing in line behind and to his left. Desperate for help, he called upon Jackson for support, then uttered words which were to become instantly famous, forming the basis for one of the most recognizable nicknames of the war. Turning to his men, Bee is said to have exclaimed "Look at Jackson's Brigade! It stands there like a stone wall."[29] Versions of the statement vary as does its meaning. Usually taken as a compliment to the discipline and firmness of Jackson's command, other Southerners later claimed Bee was mad that Jackson was not moving to his support and therefore the statement was not intended as a compliment. Bee was mortally wounded soon thereafter, so we shall never know. The important points are that the Virginians held and "Stonewall" Jackson became a household name both North and South.

When the 33rd Virginia approached the battlefield soon after the Bee-Jackson incident, its men outfitted in standard blue state militia uniforms, Major William Barry commanding the Federal artillery mistook them for Union reinforcements, especially since their colors hung limply from its staff looking much like the United States national flag. Barry ordered his guns not to fire on the troops, an error that became all too clear when the Virginians sent a deadly volley into the guns and the 11th New York which was in support. Surprised by this killing fire and a sudden flank attack by Stuart's cavalry, the Union line began to disintegrate.

It had been a close encounter, very close, but once the Union troops began to retreat their inexperience turned what should have been an orderly withdrawal into a chaotic rout. One of the Union cavalrymen trying to screen the disorganized federal retreat was Lt. Manning Kimmel of the 2nd U.S. Cavalry, West Point class of 1857. A native of Missouri, following the battle he resigned to take a staff position in the Confederate army. His son, Husband Kimmel, was the admiral in charge of the U.S. Pacific Fleet when it was attacked by Japan at Pearl Harbor in 1941.

Citizens who had come out from Washington with picnic lunches to witness the demise of the rebellion were caught up in the disorderly panic. Hundreds were taken prisoner, soldiers and civilians alike, including New York Congressman Alfred Ely who was taken by the 8th South Carolina and rewarded with a six-month visit to Libby Prison. The precipitate race to safety did not end until the troops reached the relative safety of the nation's capital. The Confederates, almost as disorganized in victory as the Federals were in defeat, did not aggressively follow.

In the wake of the fighting casualty lists began to appear in newspapers on both sides of the conflict. Losses were shocking.

	Union	Confederate
Killed	460	387
Wounded	1,124	1,582
Captured & Missing	1,312	13
Total	2,896	1,982

It had been the most costly battle ever fought by American troops in the history of the United States up to that time. Shock muted celebrations in the South and combined with defeat to depress many in the North.

The Consequences of Combat

How do we evaluate the results of a battle? There are at least three important factors to consider: tactical, strategic, and political. The term "tactical" refers to the movements and results of the operations on the battlefield. "Strategic" indicates the results in terms of the operations that were planned and the goals for the overall campaign. "Political" of course relates to the effect of a battle on political considerations, but here the term includes not only politics *per se* but such related issues as finances, recruiting, foreign affairs and the civilian or military decisions or actions taken as a result of a victory or defeat. In the case of the First Battle of Bull Run described above the evaluation is fairly straightforward. Tactically, although both armies fought stubbornly and were handled with reasonable control, the eventual disintegration of McDowell's organization once defeat loomed must clearly give a strong nod to the South. Strategically the same is true. The objective of McDowell's force was to invade Virginia successfully and inflict a crippling defeat on rebel forces that would hasten the end of the rebellion. Another issue was to utilize 90-day under-trained recruits before their service was ended, an issue of great concern to Lincoln. The objective of Beauregard and Johnston was to defend Virginia and defeat any attempted Northern invasion. There is no doubt that McDowell did not succeed and the Beauregard/Johnston combination did.

Politically the consequences of the engagement were sobering, the number of casualties was shocking to both sides. While grieving for their dead, Southerners were convinced that they were correct about the superiority of their *élan* and valor over their Northern opponents. It was only a matter of time, they convinced themselves, before the war was over and their independence assured—after all, the goal they sought was not defeating the North but defending Southern secession. This was unfortunate for their cause since it led to a false sense of security. Believing that it was winning, or had already won, the South largely rested on its laurels. Johnston wanted to pursue the defeated Federals before they could recover, but President Davis overruled him. The Confederate Congress also suffered from some overconfidence. It did enact a "War Tax" in August that placed duties on property valued at $500, slaves, and some luxury items, but these were inadequate to support the continuing Southern war effort. It proved to be the proverbial "drop in the bucket," yielding only some $17.5 million (in Confederate dollars), far less than needed. More important, it took the self-defeating action of withholding cotton from shipment to Europe at a time when the Union blockade was mostly in name only. On the belief that by causing a financial crisis in England it could force British recognition, the South thus lost a significant opportunity to build up credits that it could have used to purchase what it needed to offset the Northern financial and manufacturing advantages.

In the North surprise at the defeat was followed by shock over the casualties. It also brought a general sense of realization that the war would be longer than most believed the previous week. Congress had already authorized the enlistment of 500,000 troops for three years on July 4. Now, with many of the dead of the recent battle still to be buried, Congress went on record stating that the purpose of the war was to preserve the union and not to interfere with Southern rights. To raise money for an anticipated longer war, Congress enacted the Revenue Act of 1861 on August 5 requiring a tax to be "levied, collected, and paid, upon the annual income of every person residing in the United States, whether such income is derived from any kind of property, or from any profession, trade, employment, or vocation carried on in the United States or elsewhere, or from any other source whatever."[30] The amount assessed was a flat 3 percent on all incomes of $800 or more. Congress also increased some of the existing tariffs and instituted a tax on real estate that was to be apportioned among the states, but oddly based on population rather than land. Considerable opposition arose from farmers and other landowners over the real estate tax which they believed unfairly cast the burden of supporting the government on their shoulders. Thaddeus Stevens, chair of the House Ways and Means Committee, agreed that the

> bill is a most unpleasant one. But we perceive no way in which we can avoid it and sustain the government. The rebels, who are now destroying or attempting to destroy this Government, have thrust upon the country many disagreeable things. It is unpleasant to send your sons and your brethren to be slaughtered in this unholy war. It is unpleasant to send the tax gatherer to the door of the farmers, the mechanics, and the capitalists of the country to collect taxes for defraying the expenses of this war. But these things must come, or this Government must soon be buried in its grave. When we have to choose between these disagreeable duties; when the annihilation of this Government is the alternative on one side, no loyal man can hesitate which to choose.[31]

The bill passed.

On the following day, August 6, the president signed into law a Confiscation Act which allowed the United States government to confiscate any property used in support of the rebellion. Specifically, it ordered owners of any property who

> knowingly use or employ, or consent to the use or employment of same as aforesaid, all such property is hereby declared to be lawful subject of prize and capture wherever found; and it shall be the duty of the President of the United States to cause the same to be seized, confiscated, and condemned.... And be it further enacted, That whenever hereafter, during the present insurrection against the Government of the United States, any person claimed to be held to labor or service under the law of any State, shall be required or permitted by the person to whom such labor or service is claimed to be due, or by the lawful agent of such person, to take up arms against the United States, or shall be required or permitted by the person to whom such labor or service is claimed to be due, or his lawful agent, to work or to be employed in or upon any fort, navy yard, dock, armory, ship, entrenchment, or in any military or naval service whatsoever, against the Government and lawful authority of the United States, then, and in every such case, the person to whom such labor or service is claimed to be due shall forfeit his claim to such labor, any law of the State or of the United States to the contrary notwithstanding. And whenever thereafter the person claiming such labor or service shall seek to enforce his claim, it shall be a full and sufficient answer to such claim that the person whose service or labor is claimed had been employed in hostile service against the Government of the United States, contrary to the provisions of this act.[32]

The act did not specifically state that slaves so confiscated were to be free, which left much to the discretion of the local military commanders. Some considered the "contrabands," as slaves in Union custody came to be known, to still be property, while others went so far as to declare the people free. At least in 1861, Lincoln was quick to rescind any declarations issued by military commanders freeing confiscated slaves, no doubt for fear of alienating loyal slaveholders. Later, however, the Confiscation Act provided a legal basis for Lincoln's Emancipation Proclamation.

The stunning defeat at Bull Run also led to political investigation and a change in Northern military leadership. To scrutinize military operations—some would say in a politically partisan manner—radicals led by Rep. Thaddeus Stevens of Pennsylvania and Sen. Benjamin F. Wade of Ohio established the Congressional Committee on the Conduct of the War. Meanwhile, seeking a replacement for McDowell, Lincoln settled on George

B. McClellan[33] who had won one of the few early Union victories when he bested troops under Gen. Robert E. Lee at the Battle of Rich Mountain in western Virginia. Well known in the army, and well connected politically to Gen. Winfield Scott and Secretary of the Treasury Salmon P. Chase, Lincoln appointed McClellan to replace McDowell. When Scott retired on November 1, McClellan was also named commander of all the Federal armies. Exceptionally adept at organization, he brought order out of the relative chaos of defeat, reorganized the army and instituted a detailed program of instruction for the troops. In the process he quickly won the respect of his troops, officers and men alike, who believed that he was looking out for their welfare. Of course not everyone came to love McClellan, but his influence became so strong that his shadow would be cast over what came to be the Army of the Potomac long after his eventual departure from command.

International Threats

International affairs were exceptionally important for both sides during the war, especially in the early stages when uncertainty prevailed over how the European powers, and especially Britain, would react. A substantial factor in Southern planning was obtaining support from England and France to offset the economic and manufacturing advantages enjoyed by the North. The Lincoln government, in turn, had as its most important foreign affairs goal keeping the European nations from providing the support that Richmond sought. The most important link in this international tug-of-war was England because France, though disposed to support the South, did not wish to risk openly doing so without a joint agreement with Britain.

In August President Davis selected two men experienced in foreign affairs, John Slidell of Louisiana and James Mason of Virginia, to represent the Confederacy in England and France. The two ministers evaded the Union blockade, made it safely to Havana, and there boarded the British mail packet *Trent* bound for England. On November 8 the USS *San Jacinto*, Captain Charles Wilkes commanding, approached the *Trent* in international waters demanding that she heave to for inspection. Union sailors quickly found the two ministers and their secretaries who they removed from the British ship as contraband of war, then allowed the *Trent* to proceed on its way. Although public opinion in the North initially rejoiced over Wilkes's success, the mood in England was quite different. There both the government and the general public were outraged by what they considered a blatant violation of British neutrality and an insult to the nation's honor. Queen Victoria's government demanded an official apology and the immediate release of the prisoners, while at the same time dispatching 11,000 troops to Canada in December in a move to signal clearly the seriousness of its objections.

What was especially ironic about this entire situation was the way in which the positions of the United States and Great Britain had changed from their earlier policies on international trade in time of war. A half-century earlier one of the causes of the War of 1812 between the U.S. and Great Britain was the British practice of stopping U.S. merchant ships at sea. The British would demand papers from everyone aboard and if anyone could not provide absolute proof of American citizenship he could be "impressed" into the Royal Navy. On some occasions, even U.S. citizens were forced to serve in the British Navy. The U.S. had vigorously protested this policy of "impressment," arguing that a neutral ship traveling from one neutral port to another could not legally be stopped, searched, and its cargo or personnel seized. The British countered with the "Doctrine of Continuous Voyage," arguing that regardless of where the ship originated or its destination, what was important was where the cargo was destined. If an American ship was carrying cargo to a neutral port and from that port it was then shipped to France or to one of Napoleon's allies, then Britain was within its right to prevent cargoes from reaching Napoleon's forces. Similarly, when the British forcibly removed Americans from their ships and impressed them into the Royal Navy they argued that the men in question were British subjects and therefore required to serve. The rights of neutrals on the high seas was one of the primary reasons for the War of 1812 between Britain and the United States. In 1861 the positions of the two nations were exactly reversed with the British asserting the right of neutral shipping on the high seas and the Americans arguing that they had every right to stop neutral shipping to determine if it carried "contraband of war."

As concern over a possible war with England rose, Lincoln recognized that the U.S. was in no position to risk a war with Britain while the Civil War was tearing the nation apart, so he sought a way to accommodate the British without losing support at home by seeming to give in to their threats. In a cabinet meeting Charles Sumner proposed that the ministers be released to satisfy the primary British concern, while at the same time reaffirming America's traditional support for the rights of neutrals. To do this, Lincoln, at Sumner's suggestion, explained that Captain Wilkes had erred in "impressing" the Southerners from the *Trent*, that to be legal under international law he should have taken the entire vessel into port for legal authorities to decide if it had violated international law. With this ingenious interpretation Lincoln could free the diplomats on a legal "technicality." Thus, he could defuse the situation with Britain while at the same time supporting American interpretations of the law and "needling" the British about their change in attitude when the violated vessel was their own. With the release of the Southerners, tensions receded and the crisis passed. There was no apology, save the assertion that Wilkes had acted improperly. The British did not press the case further and the crisis dissipated as quickly as it arose.

While the crisis with England drew the attention of Washington, another international difficulty arose to the south. Napoléon III was more inclined to direct support for the Confederacy than was the British government but did not want to act unilaterally for fear of becoming involved in a war with Britain should its policy change. In July 1861 President Benito Juárez suspended Mexico's interest payments on its foreign debt, a move that most effected its major creditors—France, Britain, and Spain. With initial endorsement from Britain and Spain, Napoléon III landed French forces at Veracruz ostensibly to collect debts. When it quickly became apparent that France planned to seize all of Mexico, Britain and Spain withdrew from the agreement while Napoléon III declared creation of the Second Mexican Empire. In 1864 the Archduke Maximilian I, a member of the ruling Habsburg family in Austria, arrived to assume the position of Emperor of Mexico.

The Lincoln administration protested this French action as a violation of the Monroe Doctrine and expressed support for all Latin American republics, but realistically could do little to opposed French actions while fully engaged in subduing the rebellion. Fighting between the French and Juárez's forces continued throughout the American Civil War. On April 4, 1864, Congress expressed official concern in a joint resolution stating that "the Congress of the United States are unwilling, by silence, to leave the nations of the

Left: **Capt. Charles Wilkes of the USS *San Jacinto* sparked an international incident when he captured two Confederate ministers and their secretaries heading to Europe.** *Right:* **Emperor Napoléon III of France attempted to take advantage of the Civil War to reestablish an empire in Mexico (both photographs, Library of Congress).**

world under the impression that they are indifferent spectators of the deplorable events now transpiring in the Republic of Mexico; and they therefore think fit to declare that it does not accord with the policy of the United States to acknowledge a monarchical government, erected on the ruins of any republican government in America, under the auspices of any European power."[34]

Once the Civil War ended, the United States government took steps to address the situation in Mexico. In 1865 President Andrew Johnson ordered General Grant to send 50,000 troops under Gen. Philip Sheridan to the Mexican border. Sheridan also shipped some 60,000 muskets to Juárez and the U.S. allowed the Mexican president's agents to sell American citizens almost $18 million in bonds which it could then use to purchase needed supplies. With the war turning against French forces Napoléon began to withdraw his troops at the end of May 1866. Maximilian chose to remain in an attempt to solidify his position as emperor. Defeated and captured by Juárez, he was executed on June 19, 1867.

* * *

The year 1861 closed with the dawning realization that the war would not be short, but it would be costly. The North could take solace from the fact that, however tenuous, the Border States had been kept in the Union, the Europeans had thus far been kept relatively neutral, and their armies in the west had emerged from the first months of the conflict occupying more territory than they had when it commenced. Southerners could take heart that they had met the first major attempt by the Union to invade their territory and drive on the capital at Richmond and had thrown it back, proof positive many believed that the Southern soldier was indeed superior. Both sides made preparations for continuing the war in the spring once the first budding flowers signaled the beginning of the new campaigning season.

6

1862—The Year
of Missed Opportunities

The second calendar year of the war began with considerable uncertainly, but much hope. Southerners were encouraged by their success at First Bull Run and several smaller actions both east and west. To be sure, the North has been successful in keeping the Border States in the Union, but many of their residents were heading South to joint what they hoped and expected would be armies of liberation that would redeem their states from Northern occupation. Northerners, on the other hand, shocked by the loss at Bull Run, confidently enrolled and trained even larger armies in the expectation that they would make short work of the rebels once the new campaigning season began.

Spring

THE WEST

The Anaconda Plan aside, from a military standpoint, to win United States forces had to physically invade and conquer the rebelling states. In the western theater, the main advance was planned to be along the Mississippi River to deny its use to the Confederacy and to cut the rebellion into two parts. Southern leaders knew this so they planned a defensive line that would bar entry along the most logical invasion routes—the Mississippi, Cumberland and Tennessee Rivers. These three arteries not only provided obvious entry points into the Confederacy, they offered relatively easy supply lines that could bring reinforcements, ammunition, provisions, and other supplies to any army as it advanced into hostile territory. To protect these vulnerable entrances the South fortified Island Number Ten on the east bank of the Mississippi just upriver from New Madrid, Missouri, Fort Henry along the Tennessee River just south of the Kentucky-Tennessee line, and Fort Donelson some dozen miles east on the Cumberland River. This would be the South's main line of defense along its northern boundary in the western theater of operations.

Given the length of the open territory along the Kentucky-Tennessee border, added to the need to defend the Mississippi and the gulf seaports of New Orleans, Mobile, and Pensacola, the South had to apportion its limited forces over widely separated areas. In early 1862, Gen. Leonidas Polk commanded 16,000 troops, but 4,000 were distributed in a number of small garrisons with his main force of 12,000 at Columbus, Kentucky, guarding the upper Mississippi River. Gen. Lloyd Tilghman commanded about 5,000 troops in garrison at Forts Henry and Donelson, while Gen. William Hardee led another 22,000, but these were scattered among several posts with the largest concentrations of about 15,700 near Bowling Green, Kentucky. Numbering in total some 43,000, all of these were under the overall command of Gen. Albert Sidney Johnston who was considered by many at the time to be the best general officer the South possessed.[1]

Marshaling its forces for the invasion, the North split its western command into three different departments with two, the Departments of the Ohio and the Missouri, being the areas from which the major thrusts south would be made. Gen. Don Carlos Buell commanded some 45,000 men in the Department of the Ohio with his major concentration centered along the Louisville & Nashville Railroad about half way between Louisville and Bowling Green. An Ohio native, Buell's initial orders for the campaign were to move south into east Tennessee taking

Albert Sidney Johnston, considered by many to be the best general officer in the Confederacy, commanded in the west (Library of Congress).

Nashville if possible and occupying an area critical to the Confederacy.

Command of the Department of the Missouri went to Gen. Henry Halleck.[2] One of his subordinate officers was Gen. Ulysses S. Grant[3] who commanded a force of about 15,000 troops. Anxious to move despite his relatively small numbers, Grant proposed to advance on Fort Henry but Halleck feared a reverse given the diminutive size of Grant's command. Halleck finally agreed after Grant secured the cooperation of seven gunboats under the command of Commodore Andrew Foote, whose willingness to cooperate with Grant gave the army access to the fleet's firepower and control of the river for use as a supply line.

The garrison of Fort Henry included between 3,000 and 3,400 men under Brig. Gen. Lloyd Tilghman, a Marylander who graduated from West Point in 1836. As colonel of the 3rd Kentucky, he was promoted to brigadier general and tapped because of his engineering expertise to build what became Forts Henry and Donelson to protect these natural avenues into the Confederacy. Grant planned to attack the former by landing two divi-

Nicknamed "Old Brains," Henry Wager Halleck commanded all of the armies of the United States in 1862 (Library of Congress).

sions of troops above the fort and marching overland to attack it in a combined assault coordinated with a bombardment by Foote's fleet. Selection of the site for the fort, which was done before Tilghman was assigned as engineer, was very poor since it was located in low-lying, marshy land. To make matters worse, most of the rebel defenders were armed with obsolete muskets and as Grant approached the rains began to fall so heavily

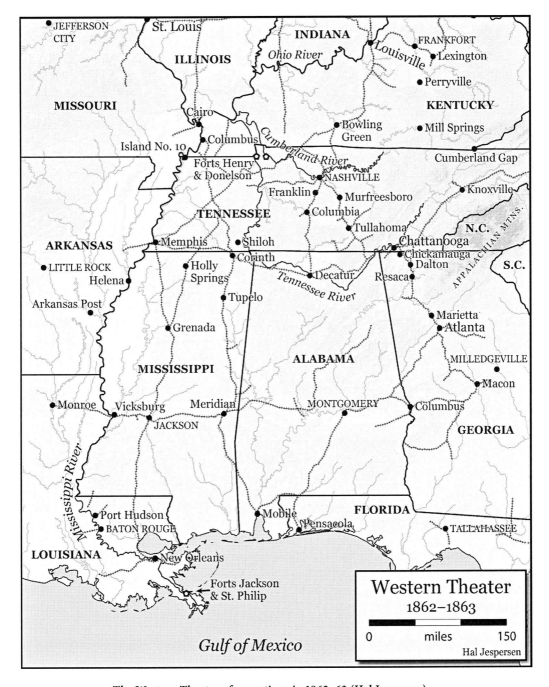

The Western Theater of operations in 1862–63 (Hal Jespersen).

that the river rose and flooded a portion of the works. On February 6 Foote's gunboats opened fire. Tilghman held out as long as he could, allowing many of his troops to escape, then, with artillery rounds nearly exhausted, finally hauled down his flag in surrender. By then all but about 120 of his men had escaped since the rain that inundated the ground around the fort also held up Grant's infantry under Gen. John A. McClernand long enough so that they were unable to close the trap. Foote reported losses of about forty men, while Tilghman lost around fifteen killed, twenty wounded, and 94 prisoners. In terms of casualties this was a small affair, but its consequences were far beyond this measure. Loss of Fort Henry opened the Cumberland River as a Union invasion route at very little cost, while also gaining praise for Grant as the commander of the invading forces.

With the fall of Fort Henry, Confederate Gen. Albert Sidney Johnston was placed in a difficult position. Charged with defending the entire Confederate border west of the Appalachian Mountain chain, he had spread his forces out to cover a number of potential Union targets while maintaining larger concentrations at Columbus and Bowling Green that could be used to parry any Union thrust along the Mississippi or into central and eastern Tennessee. The loss of Fort Henry punctured the main Confederate defense line, so should Johnston attempt to re-take the lost position? Should he reinforce Fort Donelson? Should he retire to a more southerly position? What he chose was in essence a compromise that effectively relinquished the initiative to Grant. He elected to reinforce Fort Donelson with 12,000 troops under Brig. Gen. John B. Floyd[4] while at the same time retiring the balance of his troops at Bowling Green south to Nashville. Under his command in Fort Donelson he had 17,000 well-entrenched troops that enjoyed considerable advantages over the imperfect defenses of Fort Henry. Located about 100 feet above the river, Fort Donelson had much more formidable fortifications fronted by trenches and an abatis. The fort contained a dozen large guns some of which were sited to deliver a plunging fire at anything on the river, along with some smaller artillery including a howitzer and a large ten-inch Columbiad.

Grant lost little time pursuing after the fall of Fort Henry, but did have to await the redeployment of Foote's gunboats onto the Cumberland River and the cessation of the rain which turned the area into a muddy quagmire. He began shifting his infantry east on February 12 covering the twelve miles to Fort Donelson by the 13th. At the same time, reinforcements raised his strength to some 25,000 troops. After some initial skirmishing and Union probing attacks on the 13th, Foote brought his gunboats forward on the following day to engage the defenses but was roughly handled with the fleet suffering some serious damage and its commander being slightly wounded before he withdrew. Despite this success, by that evening Floyd called a conference of his senior commanders convinced that the fort could not be held. The meeting ended in a plan to launch an attack early in the morning in the hope of breaking through Grant's encircling army. If successful, the fort would be abandoned with the army marching off to safety.

Floyd selected Gen. Gideon Pillow to lead the breakout.[5] The attack stepped off at dawn, catching Grant by surprise. In fact, Grant was absent having gone to visit with Foote to discuss the engagement of the previous day and plan future operations. In some heavy fighting, Pillow managed to drive back a portion of the Union forces under Gen. McClernand opening an escape route toward Nashville, but inexplicably halted allowing Union reinforcements from Gen. Lew Wallace to arrive. Grant, returning from his visit to Foote, ordered Gen. Charles F. Smith to attack the Confederate trenches opposite the left of the Union line, the point farthest from Pillow's attack. Smith's assault broke the rebel line. With that, the Confederates retired back into their inner defenses, losing the opportunity to break the siege and save a large part of their army. At another conference that evening, Floyd determined that surrender was inevitable. Fearing that he would be prosecuted for his actions while U.S. Secretary of War, Floyd turned over command to Pillow and made his own escape. Pillow, who also feared Northern retribution, quickly turned the command over the Brig. Gen. Simon Bolivar Buckner and escaped the tightening noose. Infuriated, Brig. Gen. Nathan Bedford Forrest led several hundred of his cavalry in a daring breakout. They would be the only Confederates, aside from the two generals, who escaped Grant's encirclement.

Buckner, the new commander at Fort Donelson, was a West Point graduate from Kentucky who had served in the Mexican War and was well acquainted with Grant. The two had served together in the prewar army. In fact, when a despondent, destitute Grant resigned from the army it was Buckner who lent him the money to head back home where he could be reunited with his family. Perhaps because of this previous relationship Buckner hoped for lenient terms from his prewar friend. If he did he was sadly mistaken. In response to Buckner's proposal that a ceasefire be granted to allow time for representatives to discuss surrender terms, Grant replied succinctly and bluntly, "No terms except unconditional and immediate surrender can be accepted."[6] An astonished Buckner had little choice but to accept, commenting that the victor's behavior had been "unchivalric." Despite this, Buckner later served as a pallbearer at Grant's funeral in 1885. His son was killed in action while commanding U.S. troops in the invasion of Okinawa during World War II.

Union losses were 2,832. Confederate losses are estimated at between 1,500 and 2,000 casualties along with 12,000 to 15,000 prisoners. Grant's exceptional campaign quickly broke the main Confederate defensive line opening both the Tennessee and Cumberland valleys into the heartland of the western Confederacy, severed the only major railroad connecting the eastern and western portions of the Confederacy, and forced the rebel evacuation of Nashville.

To counter Grant's rapid and extraordinary advance and restore the Confederate defensive line Gen. Albert Sidney Johnston gathered a force of about 40,000 men around Corinth, Mississippi, by drawing in 10,000 men from defenses along the gulf coast under Gen. Braxton Bragg, a like number under Gen. Pierre G. T. Beauregard positioned near Jackson, Mississippi, as support for rebel positions along the Mississippi, and 5,000 under Brig. Gen. Daniel Ruggles from northern Alabama. In doing so he weakened those defenses, but the collapse of the defenses along the Cum-

Gen. Simon Bolivar Buckner, a prewar friend of U.S. Grant's, was forced to accept "unconditional surrender" as the only choice given him by the Union commander (Library of Congress).

berland and Tennessee Rivers called for desperate measures to protect an otherwise clear path into the Confederacy's western interior.

While Johnston attempted to draw in as many troops as he could and organize them to oppose the Union invasion, Grant bided his time with his troops encamped at Pittsburgh Landing along the Tennessee River awaiting the arrival of Gen. Don Carlos Buell's Army of the Ohio with some 50,000 men under orders to join him. Buell had been held up for about ten days by flooding of the Duck River. With the Federals seemingly content to remain in camp, Johnston ordered his army into motion, determined to attack Grant before Buell could reinforce him. Surprise was a key element in the plan. With new reinforcements swelling his ranks to about 47,000 men that he dubbed the Army of Mississippi, Johnston placed his command in motion on April 3. Once again heavy rain intervened, this time to postpone the planned assault for about two days. When finally in position, Johnston planned to drive in the Union left, cut off Grant's command from its supports along the river, then destroy it in detail.

Since Federal pickets had not uncovered the rebel approach, Grant was not expecting an attack. In fact, on April 5 Brig. Gen. William T. Sherman had sent a message to Grant at nearby Savannah where Grant was staying assuring him that there was nothing to fear. Sherman, the ranking officer in Pittsburgh Landing at the time, failed to maintain active patrolling beyond his own picket lines to gather intelligence of any enemy activity. When Johnston's attack burst from the woods near Shiloh Church on the early morning of April 6 Sherman's position was completely unprepared. The division under Brig. Gen. Benjamin Prentiss facing the center of the assault broke after brief resistance, fell back, but eventually rallied. The attack also smashed into Sherman's division and began to drive it back in heavy fighting, along with the divisions of Brig. Gens. William H. L. Wallace and John A. McClernand.

Once the initial contact occurred in the dense woods, the alignment of the attacking troops was quickly broken into smaller segments as some advanced faster than others or simply lost contact due to the woods and other obstructions. A contributing factor to the increasing confusion in the Confederate ranks was the configuration Johnston's chose for his attack. Instead of assigning his generals to command successive assault waves where they might exercise control over an attack all along the line, he chose, perhaps because of the dense woods, to divide the attack into three segments with Polk commanding the left, Bragg the center, and Hardee the right with a reserve held back under Brig. Gen. John C. Breckinridge, a former United States Senator and presidential candidate against Lincoln in 1860. By doing this it placed each of the three generals in charge not only of a single attack wave but also then required them to lead reinforcements forward from their second line as well. This was

Ulysses S. Grant failed in every civilian occupation he tried, but excelled commanding troops in the field (Library of Congress).

asking a lot and the inevitable breakdowns occurred as different portions of the attack made disjointed advances and supports arrived at varying times and locations. The result was that much of the impetus of the original surprise waned as Confederate confusion set in and Union resistance stiffened.

When he became aware of the engagement Grant, who had been injured when is

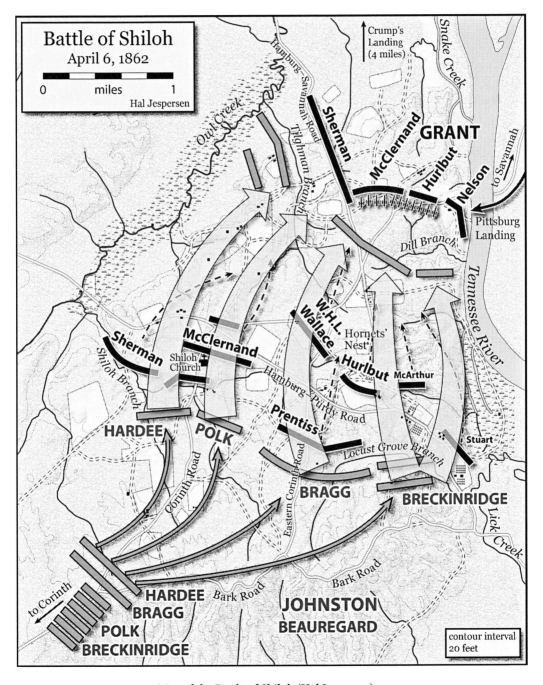

Map of the Battle of Shiloh (Hal Jespersen).

horse fell on him and was able to get about only on crutches, hurried to the scene of the action on a steamboat. While he was trying to rally troops near Pittsburgh Landing and form a defensive line, two fortuitous events helped save the Union army from a disastrous defeat. First, Johnston was wounded in the foot, an injury that at first did not appear critical but had apparently severed an artery and he bled to death. This added further confusion to the attack because of the time needed to inform the key leaders of the change in command and the fact that the new commanding officer, Beauregard, did not appear to be completely informed about the current situation or Johnston's plans. The other important event was that valuable time was gained by the stubborn resistance of Prentiss and Wallace in a position later labeled the "Hornet's Nest." Charge after charge was made against the position, some estimates ranging as high as eight different assaults, all of which were repelled at great loss to both sides. As Union troops on each flank were driven back, the Hornet's Nest took enfilade fire from both flanks as well as the front, eventually becoming virtually encircled. Still it held. Wallace was mortally wounded. Ammunition became short. Eventually Confederate Gen. Daniel Ruggles managed to have about 60 guns manhandled forward to fire directly into the stubborn position. After some seven hours of dogged defiance Prentiss finally surrendered the survivors having bought Grant the time he needed to reform a solid defense line nearer the river.

Under the cover of fire from the gunboats *Lexington* and *Tyler* in the river and some artillery positioned to fire on the Confederate positions, Grant struggled to form his troops on the new line. His efforts received a needed boost with the arrival of a brigade of troops from Buell's army during the late afternoon. It filed into place where directed to stabilize Grant's left. A final Confederate assault was thrown back, then Beauregard decided to call an end to the day's slaughter around 6:00 p.m. bringing a merciful relief. Against a backdrop of the cries of the wounded and shouted orders to form, Sherman approached his commander. "Well, Grant, we've had the devil's own day, haven't we?" "Yes," came the reply with remarkable calm. "Yes. Lick 'em tomorrow, though."[7]

In the Confederate camp Beauregard congratulated himself, convinced he had won a great victory, and so he wired to Jefferson Davis. Although intelligence reached him that Buell was nearby, he preferred to reject it since other reports had Buell miles away, some reporting him heading in a different direction altogether. He chose wrong. Gen. Lew Wallace's[8] division arrived to strengthen Grant shortly after 7:00 p.m. Buell's army filed in overnight with much of it being available by daylight on April 7 giving Grant some 45,000 men against, when casualties are deducted, Beauregard's perhaps no more than 30,000 at most, although reports reaching him from the various commands indicated a total closer to 20,000. Unaware of the odds now against him, Beauregard planned to continue the attack in the morning with the aim of driving Grant into the river. Before he could move, Grant launched his own sharp counterattack.

Rolling forward at 7:30 a.m., the Federals swiftly retook most of the ground lost, faltered under a rebel counterattack, recovered, then pushed forward again. Fighting surged around Shiloh Church, the name ironically meaning "Place of Peace," but by early afternoon Beauregard realized that no reinforcements would be reaching him and he began to disengage his troops for a painful retreat back to Corinth. One of the rebels left behind as a captive was Private Henry Stanley of the 6th Arkansas. Stanley would later become world famous as a journalist and explorer when he found David Livingstone in Africa in 1871. Livingstone's own son was killed fighting in a Massachusetts regiment at Gettysburg in the following year.

There was no pursuit, Grant citing the exhaustion of his own army as the reason for allowing the rebels to retire unmolested. Some skirmishing occurred on the following day when Grant pushed Sherman forward and he encountered some of Brig. Gen. Nathan Bedford Forrest's cavalry screening the rear of Beauregard's army, but the Battle of Shiloh was over. Tactically, labeling it a draw was not far from the truth since the two armies seemingly bled each other into exhaustion. Strategically, it must be recorded as a Northern victory since the Johnston/Beauregard goal of destroying Grant's army had not been achieved. Grant held the field; it was the Confederates who withdrew. The door was now completely open into the Confederate heartland.

Politically, if the casualties of First Bull Run stunned the nation, those of Shiloh plunged it into a state of shock on both sides of the Mason-Dixon line. The generally accepted return of Thomas L. Livermore, author of *Numbers and Losses in the Civil War in America 1861–65*,[9] counting both Grant and Buell together, recorded the following:

	North	South
Effectives	62,682	40,335
Killed	1,754	1,723
Wounded	8,408	8,012
Missing	2,885	959
Total	13,047	10,694
Percent Lost	20.8	26.5

During the entire Mexican War American battle deaths numbered 1,733. In two days at Shiloh each side lost as many. It was a bloodbath the likes of which the nation had never experienced. If taken together, "American" losses during those roughly 36 hours numbered twice the combat deaths during the Mexican War, the country's most recent conflict. The appalling losses convinced any who did not already believe it that the war was going to last much longer and cost more in blood and treasure than most initially believed.

Grant had held against a major surprise attack, but at a heavy price. Yet the price paid by the South was in some respects greater. The butchery began a long, steady reduction of Confederate manpower that the South could ill afford in a lengthy conflict. More than a quarter of the men Johnston led to Pittsburgh Landing were lost, a large percentage lost for good to active service through death or disabling wounds. With a smaller manpower pool to draw from, the South could not afford to trade combatants at this rate and survive. Yet Grant did not escape censure, especially in the newspapers, for being surprised. Not a few suggested he had been drunk, though clearly that was not the case. Calls for his removal began to flood the press and the White House. Lincoln rejected them, but Halleck took the opportunity to shunt Grant aside, naming him to the mostly inconsequential post of second in command that gave him "title" but took from him all authority. He was not restored to command until Halleck was called east to direct all of the Federal armies. Meanwhile, Halleck assumed control in the field, plodded slowly south and occupied Corinth. Another force captured Memphis further destroying any chance the South might have had for a unified defense of the line between the Mississippi and the Appalachians.

If the news from Tennessee was bad for the Confederacy that spring it would be overshadowed by catastrophe before the end of April. New Orleans near the mouth of the Mississippi was the largest seaport on the gulf coast. Essential to the Southern economy, by 1860 72 percent of all receipts through the port derived from the cotton and sugar trade. That year's census reported a population of 168,675, making it the fifth largest city in the nation and the largest urban, banking, brokerage, and market center in the entire South. With the outbreak of the rebellion, New Orleans had the potential of playing a major role in the export of Southern cotton to establish credits that could be used to purchase needed supplies in Europe and to import those supplies when they arrived. Close to both Cuba and Mexico it could also be used by swift "blockade runners" timing their runs to avoid the as yet very thin Union blockade by arriving during the darkness of night. Maintaining control of New Orleans clearly should have been a priority of the Southern government, as capturing it was with the Lincoln administration. Yet, when the invasion force arrived off the coast there were only an estimated 3,000 ill-trained militia on hand to defend the city.

Admiral David. G. Farragut struck a serious blow to the Confederacy when his fleet pushed into the Mississippi Delta to capture New Orleans (Library of Congress).

Union naval forces arrived under the command of Adm. David G. Farragut.[10] Aboard Farragut's fleet was an invasion force of some 15,000 men under Maj. Gen. Benjamin Butler.[11] The primary defenses of the port, under the overall leadership of Brig. Gen. Mansfield Lovell,[12] were Forts St. Philip and Jackson sited to command the entrance of the Mississippi below the city. Lovell scattered his meager force among several small fortifications covering water access into the Mississippi delta, but the primary defenses were the two main forts located on either side of the river, which had been blockaded at that point by sunken hulks, and a chain floating atop barges that stretched across the water at Fort Jackson. Between them the forts contained about 500 men and nearly 80 guns that could contest any ships coming upriver. These defenses were backed by the Confederate ram *Manassas*, two incomplete vessels (*Louisiana* and *Mississippi*), a number of smaller ships and some fire barges that could be set alight and floated into enemy ships.

On December 3, 1861, Federal troops went ashore on Ship Island on the approaches to Lake Pontchartrain where they established a base of operations for Butler's army. With this in place, Farragut's fleet of two dozen ships and another 19 mortar vessels opened fire on the main forts hoping to silence their guns so as to open the way upriver for his wooden ships. After a week of bombardment which appeared to have little effect, at 2:00 a.m. on April 24 Farragut ordered his ships to run past the forts under cover of darkness. The daring move succeeded. Union vessels then fought a brief engagement with Confederate ships which were quickly silenced. Farragut continued on to New Orleans where he landed a small force to accept the surrender of the city, but met hostile crowds and the refusal of civilian authorities to capitulate even though Lovell had withdrawn his forces to the north of the city. After reducing some fortifications above the city, Farragut returned on April 29 to accept the surrender of the city. In exchange for the most important Confederate port on the gulf coast he had lost only 36 men killed and another 135 wounded.

Butler's army occupied the city on May 1 after surrounding Forts Jackson and St. Philip and forcing their capitulation on April 28. Although the rebel defenders were overpowered fairly easily, the women of New Orleans were not so simply subdued. They quickly took to hurling insults at Federal troops, providing false information, and some even making it a point to "accidentally" empty their chamber pots from upper floors of a building while Union troops were passing below. Outraged by the behavior, Butler issued General Orders No. 28:

HDQRS. DEPARTMENT OF THE GULF
New Orleans, May 15, 1862
   As the officers and soldiers of the United States have been subject to repeated insults from the women (calling themselves ladies) of New Orleans in return for the most scrupulous non-interference and courtesy on our part, it is ordered that hereafter when any female shall by word, gesture, or movement insult or show contempt for any officer or soldier of the United States she shall be regarded and held liable to be treated as a woman of the town plying her avocation.
                    By command of Major-General Butler,
                    Geo. C. Strong,
                    Assistant Adjutant-General and Chief of Staff[13]

In short, women who insulted United States forces would be treated as prostitutes. If Butler was angered by the conduct of Southern women in the Crescent City, Southerners were outraged by Butler's order. Ceramic chamber pots appeared with his image emblazoned at the bottom of the receptacle, rewards were offered for his capture, and he was referred to throughout the Confederacy as "Beast Butler," or sometimes "Spoons," a reference to the Southern belief that he and his troops helped themselves to the citizens' silverware and other valuables. Butler further enraged Southern sensitivities by creating the "Corps D'Afrique," three regiments of Louisiana Native Guards, recruited mostly from former free black militia units supplemented with freed slaves, and with black officers as well, to bolster his army and enforce occupation edicts against the former city rulers.

Lovell was assigned to command a corps during the Corinth campaign, which he did competently, but the fallout from the loss of New Orleans dogged him, as did suspicions of his loyalty due to his years in New York. He eventually demanded a court of inquiry which cleared him of any responsibility for the loss of the city, but he never held another active command after that, serving only as a volunteer on the staff of Gen. Joseph E. Johnston in the summer of 1864. Butler, despite his reputation, treated the citizens of New Orleans fairly dur-

Benjamin Butler's troops occupied New Orleans, but he earned the resolute hatred of Southerners for his supposed insults to the city's female population. Outraged, they placed a bounty on his head (Library of Congress).

ing the balance of his time in command, being credited by some for providing food and other assistance without which the poor of the city might well have succumbed to malnutrition. He also instituted a system of refuse control that greatly reduced the deadly effects of the annual yellow fever epidemic. He was replaced in December 1862 and in the following year assigned to command the Department of Virginia and North Carolina which later became the Department of the James including the Army of the James.

Tactically, strategically, and politically the fall of New Orleans was a Southern disaster. It denied the use of its port to a Confederacy whose very existence depended on foreign imports while at the same time providing the United States navy with an excellent port from which to support the blockade of the remaining Southern gulf coast. It also opened a wide doorway for the invasion of the Mississippi Valley from the south, while forcing the Confederacy, its manpower resources already stretched thin, to guard yet another front along its southern coast and in the areas surrounding New Orleans from which a further invasion might be launched at any time. The fall of New Orleans was an exceptionally painful loss to the South.

THE EAST

George B. McClellan had a considerable aptitude for organization. Over the winter of 1861–62 he put these skills to good use organizing and drilling a new Federal army to replace the disorganized and poorly trained one defeated along the banks of Bull Run the previous July. Since many of those units had enlisted for three months their service had long since elapsed, the regiments mustered out, and the men went home. Some of the others enlisted for a year, but by the late spring of 1862 they would have but a short time remaining in their terms of service. It had been necessary to recruit a new army to quell the rebellion and the task of whipping this new assortment of farmers, clerks and mechanics into a disciplined army fell to McClellan. The general appeared to excel in this role. Morale among the troops soared as the training made them feel more prepared and McClellan's attention to their food, pay, equipment and other factors affecting their welfare convinced the men that he had their best interests at heart. The army quickly rose to over 100,000 men, the largest force the United States had ever fielded at that point. But beyond the army McClellan also oversaw the construction of an immense system of defenses surrounding the nation's capital whose purpose was to secure his crucial city and eliminate the fear that a Confederate army might seize Washington. His energy seemingly without limit, his work in all of these tasks was exemplary.

Given the inglorious end to the first campaign in Virginia, it was understandable that McClellan would want to proceed in an orderly manner, making sure that the troops were well trained, the officers reviewed for their competence, and the organization of the force such as to promote success. Yet these reasonable factors fed into an overly conservative nature to produce in the general a continuing desire for more time. Adding to McClellan's desire for more time was the information he received from the newly appointed head of his intelligence service, Alan Pinkerton.[14] In this capacity one of his responsibilities was estimating the strength of the opposing forces, which he continually miscalculated by wide margins leading McClellan to believe the rebel forces were considerably stronger than his own. This, coupled with the general's natural tendency to slow, methodical work, began to cause increasing concern in the White House and the

War Department as month after month passed with no forward movement in sight. McClellan compounded the administration's feeling of frustration with an excessive concern for security that led him to refuse to reveal any of his plans even to the president.

As winter began to give way to spring concern continued to grow along with frustration that McClellan appeared in no hurry to advance. With no prospect for movement

Right: George Brinton McClellan replaced Irwin McDowell as commander of Union troops in the Army of the Potomac. He came to the position with excellent credentials, including having bested rebels under Robert E. Lee in western Virginia. *Below:* This cartoon, published in *Frank Leslie's Illustrated Newspaper* on February 1, 1862, was titled "Masterly Inactivity or Six Months on the Potomac." It portrays the two large armies peering at each other across the Potomac River with nothing more deadly than a snowball fight (both photographs, Library of Congress).

in sight, Lincoln issued two orders in January requiring McClellan to move and directing, at least in the most general terms, how the movement should be made. McClellan ignored his commander-in-chief. Completely frustrated, the president is said to have remarked, "If General McClellan does not want to use the army, I would like to borrow it for a time."[15]

With the newly christened Army of the Potomac essentially immobile, the opening moves in the spring campaign in the East occurred in the Shenandoah Valley, a strategically important agricultural region that the South counted upon to feed its armies. In early March Gen. Nathaniel P. Banks[16] led a Union force into the northern Shenandoah Valley threatening this Confederate granary. To meet this menace, and also divert Federal attention away from any movement against Richmond, President Jefferson Davis, on the recommendation of his military advisor, Gen. Robert E. Lee, ordered Gen. Thomas J. Jackson to the Valley to defend against the anticipated Federal attempt to seize the valuable agricultural region. Although Jackson suffered a reverse at the First Battle of Kernstown on March 23, he successfully outmaneuvered his opponents to the extent that Washington ordered Gen. John C. Frémont into the Valley from the west with some 15,000 troops and Gen. Irvin McDowell with another 30,000 from the east. Soon these were reinforced further with 9,000 men under Brig. Gen. James Shields and 6,000 under Gen. Ludwig Blenker. With their arrival, some 68,000 Federal troops faced only 18,000 men under Jackson, but the Northern commands were not yet unified. This dispersal gave Jackson an opportunity to attack individual portions of the Federal force. Recognizing this immediately, Jackson pushed his men relentlessly to take advantage of the momentary disunity in the Union command. Over 39 days he marched his men some 600 miles, fought five major engagements—McDowell, Front Royal, Winchester, Cross Keys, and Port Republic—and defeated four separate armies in what is generally considered one of the most brilliant military campaigns in history.

Tactically and strategically, Jackson's campaign was a glowing success for rebel arms. Politically, it engendered such fear for the safety of Washington, D.C., an easy march east from the northern entrance to the Valley, that troops intended for the Army of the Potomac were withdrawn to protect the capital, thereby weakening any movement south that McClellan might eventually make. Further, to protect the capital the administration brought Gen. John Pope east to assume command of the new Army of Virginia that would include three army corps comprised of the various commands that had faced Jackson in the Valley along with those sent as reinforcements from the Army of the Potomac.

Thomas Jonathan Jackson was a former professor at the Virginia Military Institute who waged a brilliant campaign against great odds in the Shenandoah Valley in 1862 (Library of Congress).

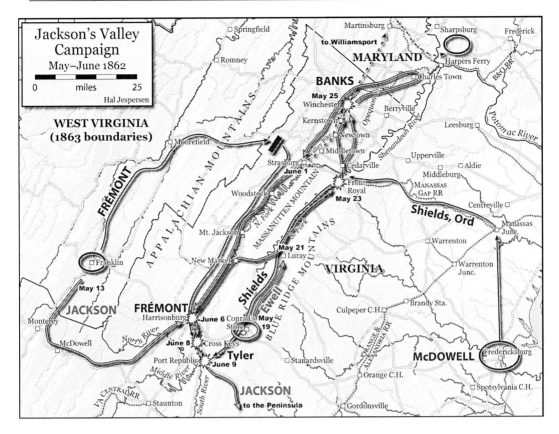

Jackson's Valley Campaign, 1862 (Hal Jespersen).

THE EFFECT

As the first full year of the war came to an end in the spring of 1862 the South, despite its public euphoria over the success of Jackson's Valley Campaign, was already beginning to feel the pinch of the limited manpower available to defend its extended border with the North. The loss of Forts Henry and Donelson, the capture of the strategically vital port of New Orleans, along with the staggering losses of Shiloh and the growing threat in Virginia, convinced the Confederate Congress of the need for more drastic measures to address the manpower shortage. To this end, on April 16 it enacted a conscription law that applied to all white males between the ages of 18 and 35 except for certain specified categories such as politicians, printers, editors, teachers, and workers in some industries considered essential to the war effort who were exempted. One provision stipulated that a man who was drafted could purchase an exemption for $300, while another provided one exemption for every plantation with twenty or more slaves. The amount required for exemption was beyond the means of all but the more affluent, while a plantation owner could exempt himself or, more likely, since the average owner was over the age of 35 he could use the exemption for a son. Both of these provoked considerable ire, and in some cases outright resistance, among the largely small farmers in the South who quickly surmised that the war would be fought by the poor while the rich could remain safely at home. Further, when workers planned a strike the Confederate government threatened the workers with wholesale induction into the army if they did not immediately return to work. One loophole the poor could sometimes use was a provision that allowed the governors of Southern states to certify those enrolled in their state militias as exempt from the draft. Georgia and North Carolina in particular made use of this to keep thousands of men at home, secure from the draft, while Southern armies were forced to meet their opponents at a numerical disadvantage in most major engagements.

In the North, Congress, feeling the pressure of the increasing financial burden of the war, with its precious metal reserves dwindling, adopted the Legal Tender Act on February 25 authorizing the printing of paper currency to pay wartime bills. This was a major departure from previous monetary policy because the law allowed the printing *without* sufficient gold or silver reserves to back the new currency. Printed with green ink, they became known as "Greenbacks." By the end of the war $432 million had been printed. This led to some inflation and fluctuations in value as well as considerable unhappiness from people reluctant to accept the new currency. Following the war the United States Supreme Court found in 1870 that the act had been unconstitutional. The majority opinion was written by Chief Justice Salmon P. Chase. Ironically, Chase had been Lincoln's Secretary of the Treasury, the very man who had pushed for the legislation. When President Grant appointed two new justices to fill vacancies on the court, the decision was soon reversed and the issuance of paper money beyond the amount of gold and silver reserves was then found to be constitutional.

With the rebel states no longer represented in Congress, Republicans took the opportunity to prohibit generals from returning escaped slaves to their owners (March), abolish slavery in the District of Columbia with each owner being compensated $300 for each freed person (April), and prohibit slavery in all federal territories without compensation (June). Congress also established the Department of Agriculture and proceeded to enact other priorities previously blocked by the South. These included the Pacific Railway Act authorizing a transcontinental railroad, the Homestead Act, and the Morrill Land Grant Act. The homestead legislation provided a head of family, including immigrants, 160 acres, the title of which became the settler's after five years of residence and payment of a registration fee of $10. The Morrill statute gave to states 30,000 acres of land for each senator and representative to endow an agricultural college. It formed the basis for the nation's 68 land grant colleges.

Summer

THE WEST

Following Shiloh, Gen. Henry Halleck came south in person to command the united Armies of the Tennessee, Ohio, and Mississippi under the respective commands of Gens. George H. Thomas,[17] Don Carlos Buell, and John Pope.[18] All three were professional military officers. Halleck chose Thomas to replace Grant whom he had come to dislike personally, and possibly considered a growing rival, with Grant moved to the relatively powerless supernumerary position of second in command. Buell continued in command of the force he led at Shiloh. Pope commanded the Army of the Mississippi.

Acting slowly and methodically, Halleck led his force of 110,000 south with his sights set on the important rail junction of Corinth in northern Mississippi. Meanwhile, Beauregard attempted to rally the survivors of Shiloh at Corinth which he recognized as an important strategic location. With his army of 30,000 he set to work fortifying the town while calling desperately for reinforcements. Given time for these to arrive by a sluggish Halleck advance that took nearly a month to move twenty miles, Beauregard's force eventually more than doubled to 66,000. Nevertheless, Beauregard found himself considerably outnumbered and with only partially constructed defenses when Halleck at last opened a bombardment of the town on May 25. Beauregard evacuated during the night of May 29–30. Halleck pursued only half-heartedly with a portion of his force, choosing instead to consolidate his position even further rather than to continue the invasion.

Meanwhile, the Confederates accumulated a small fleet of eight ironclad rams and gunboats on the Mississippi River just north of Memphis for the purpose of denying the North the use of the river as an avenue of invasion. Opposed to them were five Federal ironclads and two rams. On June 6 the rebel force moved to confront the Federals. In a haphazard battle during which there was very little coordination on either side, the various ships for the most part acting independently, seven of the Confederate vessels were wrecked or captured against a loss of only one Northern ship seriously damaged. Northern losses were reported as either one or four wounded compared to slightly less than 200 Confederate casualties. With the destruction of its defensive fleet, Memphis surrendered later the same day.

Tactically and strategically, both Corinth and Memphis were Union victories; the first opening the interior of the Deep South to imminent invasion and the latter opening the Mississippi to invasion all the way south to Vicksburg. Yet, given the hesitating nature of Halleck, the balance of the summer passed with no further serious effort by the Federals to discomfort the Confederates following these significant victories. Politically, both were also Union triumphs resulting in faltering Confederate morale in the affected regions.

Possessed of a forceful personality, Secretary of War Edwin Stanton was often at odds with Union generals but supported Lincoln loyally throughout the war (Library of Congress).

THE EAST

Gen. George McClellan had the entire winter to reorganize the United States army, recruit new troops, train his men, and plan for the 1862 campaign. Nevertheless, as the spring wore on disagreement continued to plague the general's planning and ruffle relations with Secretary of War Edwin Stanton and the president. The government officials, fearing for the safety of the capital if the army were not between it and the Confederate forces in Virginia, wanted McClellan to advance overland with Richmond as his objective. McClellan wanted to pursue a bold plan by which he would move his army south by ship to the York Peninsula, land there, and then move quickly on Richmond. The advantages of this plan were threefold: use of the York Peninsula provided a secure supply line since the Union navy controlled the waters, he would have to cover less than half the distance to reach Richmond after landing on the peninsula than he would from Washington, and, assuming he could make the move undetected, it would take Confederate Gen. Joseph E. Johnston a week or more to gather his forces and march them to Richmond before they could oppose McClellan. The keys to success appeared to be secrecy and speed. If he could keep the transfer secret as long as possible it would increase Confederate reaction time. If he could make the move quickly, then push rapidly down the peninsula he ought to be in front of the rebel capital before Johnston's army arrived to defend it.

In the early spring Johnston withdrew his army from its position in northern Virginia to camps along the Rappahannock River. With this, the administration in Washington finally relented and approved McClellan's plan provided that he left sufficient troops in the fortifications around the capital to ensure its safety. He began the move on March 17

Gen. John Bankhead Magruder was greatly outnumbered by Union troops on the York Peninsula, but used various stratagems to fool McClellan into thinking his force was much larger than it was (Library of Congress).

but immediately ran into his first problem. He had planned to move the troops up the James River to land them closer to Richmond but the appearance of the rebel ironclad CSS *Virginia* (the ex–Union ship *Merrimack*) at Norfolk meant that safety would require Federal troops to land at Fortress Monroe on the eastern tip of the peninsula. The campaign would begin farther from Richmond than envisioned, but this was not thought to be a decisive change.

After some delay to arrange everything to his liking, McClellan began his advance with about 50,000 troops on April 4, but halted twenty-four hours later when he ran into field-works along the Warwick River thrown up by Maj. Gen. John Bankhead Magruder[19] who had only some 11,000 men to oppose McClellan. Without sufficient troops to even man all of his defenses, Magruder very cleverly enlisted trickery as his ally. To cover his lack of troops he ordered men to erect bonfires at night in places where there were no troops knowing that Federal scouts would count the number of fires as a means of estimating Confederate strength. Lacking sufficient artillery, he had his men erect artillery emplacements and arm them with tree trunks trimmed to give the appearance of artillery muzzles. During the day he had troops parade through fields he knew came under Federal observation, bands playing loudly, to give the appearance that reinforcements were arriving. Once in "camp," they would quietly be withdrawn, formed out of sight, then parade again through the open country to create what appeared from a distance to be the continuous arrival of new regiments.

McClellan was completely fooled, as was his chief of intelligence operations, Allan Pinkerton, with both convinced that they faced a force of not less than 100,000 defenders. Instead of attacking with his large numerical advantage McClellan settled in for a formal siege losing valuable time during which he could have been pressing on down the peninsula toward Richmond. While McClellan's men dug siege trenches for the next ten days Magruder began to receive some reinforcement from the Richmond defenses and small groups drawn in from outpost duty raising his force to 35,000. Meanwhile, McClellan's force rose to more than 120,000 as the rest of his force continued to arrive. Except for some minor probing attacks, McClellan contented himself bringing up heavy siege artillery, a cumbersome and laborious process. By the end of the month Johnston arrived in person to take command of a force now numbering 57,000.

Johnston[20] was one of the best trained and most experienced officers in the Confederacy. He was promoted to general to rank from July 1861, but this placed him fourth on the seniority list behind Adjutant and Inspector General Samuel Cooper, Albert Sidney Johnston, and Robert E. Lee. Johnston felt shortchanged since he had been the ranking officer of the four when they served in the United States army. He protested what he considered a slight, pressing his case with President Jefferson Davis with whom he continued to feud when he received no satisfaction. This disagreement would color Davis's opinion of Johnston throughout the war to the detriment of Johnston's future appointments and the Confederate cause.

Believing that McClellan was about to open massed artillery fire, no doubt as a prelude to a major assault, Johnston had his artillery begin their own barrage on the evening of May 3 as a cover while he stealthily withdrew his forces leaving the fortifications effectively empty. Once again McClellan was completely fooled. Pushing forward, his leading elements caught up with Johnston's rear guard at Williamsburg where a sharp fight took place costing Johnston 1,682 men to McClellan's 2,283. Johnston continued his withdrawal with minimal difficulty while McClellan claimed he had won a major victory over greatly superior forces, at the same time continuing a lengthy string of appeals for more troops to offset what he still believed was a great Confederate numerical advantage. Lincoln resisted since troops were necessary in the Shenandoah Valley to oppose Jackson's force and he chose to retain another force between Richmond and Washington to screen the capital. About the only positive result thus far in the campaign was

Joseph E. Johnston was the original commander of what became the Army of Northern Virginia until seriously wounded at Seven Pines (Library of Congress).

the destruction of the CSS *Virginia* which the rebels burned when they abandoned Norfolk to concentrate their forces for the defense of Richmond.

With the withdrawal of rebel troops from Norfolk navigation of the James River was potentially opened to Federal forces all the way to Richmond itself. On May 18 Federal naval vessels steamed upriver to test the defenses but were met with vigorous opposition from a makeshift force of Confederate naval and army personnel at Drewry's Bluff that stopped them only seven miles from the city. Johnston continued the withdrawal of his 60,000 men into the outer defenses of Richmond. With McClellan advancing slowly and methodically north of the Chickahominy River, Johnston dug in behind that natural barrier, his position stretching from near Mechanicsville northeast of Richmond south along the river. When McClellan ordered Maj. Gen. Erasmus Keyes to cross his Fourth Corps to the south side of the Chickahominy and advance along the line of the Richmond & York River Railroad, Johnston bent the right flank of his line under Maj. Gen. James Longstreet back to the crossroads at Seven Pines to remain between the Federals and Richmond.

By ordering Keyes to move south of the river McClellan divided his force with the smaller portion south of the river isolated from easy support by the rest of the army. Johnston immediately seized on this opportunity to defeat a portion of McClellan's host. Maj. Gen. Samuel P. Heintzelman's Third Corps arrived to bolster Keyes, but this raised the Federal force to only 33,000 while Johnston planned to throw 51,000 men against the position on May 31. Conduct of the attack was delegated to Maj. Gen. James Longstreet.[21] Johnston's plan was complex involving a holding action to distract the Federals north of the river while south of the river the main attack force included six brigades under Longstreet, four under Maj. Gen. Daniel Harvey Hill of South Carolina, three brigades under Maj. Gen. Benjamin Huger also of South Carolina, with a division under Brig. Gen. William H. C. Whiting of Mississippi acting as a reserve. With this many commands in motion over a limited road network coordination was essential. Unfortunately, Johnston apparently neglected to make it clear that Longstreet was in overall command of the maneuvering and he issued only verbal orders to him which were either faulty or misunderstood because when the movements began Longstreet's troops ended up on the same roads as other commands throwing off the timing and largely preventing a coordinated attack. In the intense, but disjointed fighting that followed the Federals were pushed back steadily and nearly overwhelmed but for the timely arrival of a division of reinforcements sent by Brig. Gen. Edwin V. Sumner whose Second Corps was north of the river. Hearing the fighting, he sent the reinforcement south on his own initiative over the only remaining bridge across the rain-swollen river just in time to blunt the final Confederate advance.

Late that afternoon Johnston was struck in the shoulder and chest as he attempted to survey the scene of battle, knocking him out of the fight. Command devolved on Maj. Gen. Gustavus W. Smith of Kentucky. The following morning Longstreet was to continue the assault, but instead advanced only two brigades which were easily thrown back. When the proverbial smoke cleared, the Confederate attempt to destroy a relatively isolated portion of the Union army had failed costing them 6,134 casualties (980 killed, 4,749 wounded, 405 captured or missing) as against 5,031 for the North (790 killed, 3,594 wounded, 647 captured or missing). In the wake of the engagement McClellan moved most of his army south of the river within about six miles of Richmond, some of the soldiers reporting that they could clearly hear the church bells ringing in the city. But there

Robert E. Lee replaced Johnston in command of an army he would lead for the rest of the war (Library of Congress).

he ground to a relative halt, giving up the important element of initiative while he seemingly awaited events. On the Confederate side, President Davis acted quickly to replace the wounded Johnston, to whom he had taken a personal dislike, with his own military advisor, Gen. Robert E. Lee.[22] The new army commander spent about three weeks reorganizing his forces and waiting for the arrival of reinforcements including Gen. Stonewall Jackson's troops that he recalled from the Shenandoah Valley. In the meantime he dispatched Brig. Gen. Jeb Stuart's cavalry on a reconnaissance to obtain information on

McClellan's dispositions.[23] On June 12 Stuart led 1,200 cavalry on the reconnaissance, but instead of simply feeling McClellan's flank he determined to ride completely around the massive Union force. Over the course of four days Stuart covered some 100 miles pursued hotly by Union cavalry under the command of Brig. Gen. Philip St. George Cooke, his father-in-law. Aside from embarrassing both McClellan and his own wife's father, Stuart brought in important intelligence that helped shape Lee's decisions and gained fame for the raid's daring success.

By June 23, his army swollen to 92,000, Lee determined to take the initiative in what would come to be called the Seven Days' Battles. While Lee planned, McClellan moved most of his army south of the Chickahominy. By June 25 only Brig. Gen. Fitz John Porter's Fifth Corps remained north of the river. On that day McClellan launched a series of local attacks to drive back the rebel picket lines south of the river, which he did. With McClellan's attention directed south of the river, Lee planned essentially to reprise Johnston's attempt to isolate and defeat a part of McClellan's command, this time aiming at Porter's corps north of the river on June 26. Success of the plan hinged on Jackson who was to strike Porter's right flank and Maj. Gen. Ambrose Powell Hill who was to move forward against Porter's position when he heard the guns announcing Jackson's attack rolling forward. Once successful, the initial advance would be followed up by units under Longstreet and Daniel Harvey Hill. The plan began to unravel early when Jackson was unaccountably some six hours late in arriving in position to begin his advance. With Confederate coordination lost, Porter held fast inflicting losses of 1,484 against only 361 among the defenders. Lee achieved none of his objectives.

Although his army had the best of the fighting on June 26, McClellan determined to change his base of supply to the James River which would provide a closer and more secure supply route. With Porter still north of the river, Lee determined to try once more to crush his force. Lee threw 57,000 troops into the effort against Porter, reinforced to 34,000, at Gaines's Mill. Once again Jackson was slow to come into action, but repeated attacks drove Porter back and threatened his safety until a division of reinforcements arrived under Brig. Gen. Henry W. Slocum to stabilize his line. Lee won a tactical victory, but at great expense. Federal losses were counted at 6,837 against Confederate casualties of 8,751. That night McClellan withdrew Porter south of the river. Oddly, despite having inflicted serious losses on the rebels while only engaging a small portion of his strength, that night McClellan decided to begin moving his army south, away from Richmond, to Harrison Landing on the James River, the location of his new supply base, incomprehensibly yielding the initiative completely to his adversary.

Minor skirmishing occurred on June 28 as McClellan's army began to withdraw. Lee pursued, still hoping to attack a portion of the Union army to advantage, a distinct possibility as McClellan's forces retired along separate roads. The armies clashed again at Savage's Station on June 29 costing the Federals another 1,590 men and the rebels 626. McClellan continued his withdrawal toward the James. With the blue columns spread out along the roads, Lee again issued orders for an attack at White Oak Swamp on June 30. Once again poor coordination foiled Lee's original plan when only 45,000 troops were brought to bear on 40,000 Federals. Casualties on each side were roughly equivalent: Union losses were reported as 3,797 and Confederate as 3,673. McClellan, who was not present on the field for any of the previous days' encounters, having located his headquarters on a gunboat in the James River, opted to continue withdrawing his army.

By July 1 the divisions of the Union army, for the first time in the campaign, were

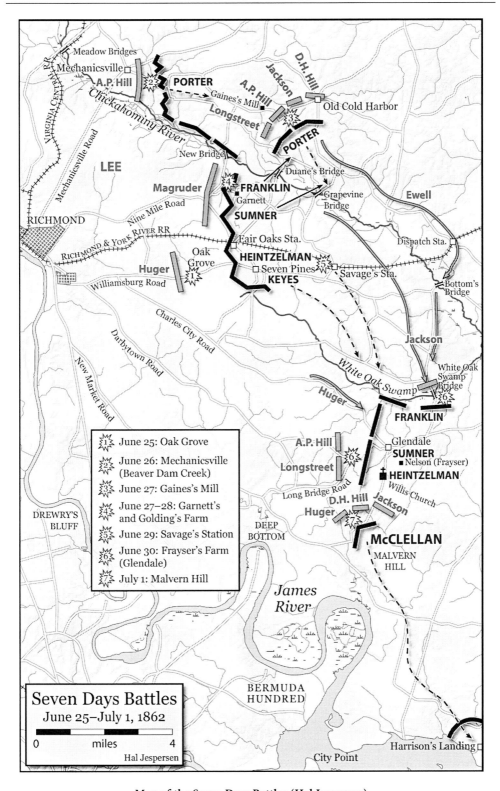

Map of the Seven Days Battles (Hal Jespersen).

deployed in a single locality within easy supporting distance of each other. They occupied a strong position along the forward slopes of Malvern Hill arranged about a massive artillery deployment of some 250 guns. Both infantry and artillery enjoyed clear fields of fire in front with reserves close at hand behind the main lines. Despite the obvious strength of the position, Lee decided on a frontal assault. The results were a Confederate disaster. Union artillery and infantry raked the approaching columns. Lee lost 5,355 casualties opposed to the Union's 3,214. Although some of his officers urged a counterattack, McClellan, who was once again absent from the scene of action, decided to remain in place.

The Seven Days Battles were over. Strategically they must be recorded as Confederate victories. By keeping the pressure on McClellan, Lee seemingly unnerved him resulting in the continued withdrawal of Union forces even after tactical battlefields victories. McClellan's drive to capture Richmond, which had every opportunity for success three months earlier, ended in failure. When it became apparent to Lincoln that McClellan planned no further activity along the James, he ordered the general to remove his army back to Washington. Casualties for the campaign were significant:

	North	South
Effectives	120,000	92,000
Killed	1,734	3,494
Wounded	8,062	15,758
Captured & Missing	6,053	952
Total	15,849	20,204
Percent	13.2	22.0

The threat to Richmond was over, but the continuing attacks against dug-in Union positions cost the South heavily. McClellan's losses were 21.6 percent less than Lee's. Political support for McClellan waned in the wake of a campaign where he appeared indecisive and at times detached from his army, more interested in arguing for reinforcements and pointing fingers than actually leading the army in person. While support within the army remained high, outside it calls for his removal rose. In the South, hope rose despite the horrific casualties. Lee appears to have taken away two messages from the campaign on the peninsula. The first was that his aggressive offensives had successfully rolled back a larger Union army, saving the capital. This reinforced his own predilection for offensive action. The second lesson was that the recurring control problems cried out for a different, more centralized organization for better control of the army in the field. He quickly reorganized his army, now styled the Army of Northern Virginia, into a division and corps structure with the two corps given to Maj. Gen. James Longstreet and Maj. Gen. Thomas J. Jackson. This done, he determined to take the offensive again.

THE RESULT

The summer campaigns resulted in a long series of Confederate victories that buoyed Southern hopes. In the North, reactions ranged from frustration to depression to despair. In the extreme, the failures led to a growing and increasingly public anti-war movement. The losses also prompted the president and Congress to take further action to suppress the rebellion which they recognized would take considerably more men and financing than even their raised expectations at the beginning of the year. On July 1 Lincoln issued a proclamation calling on Northern governors to furnish 300,000 more troops apportioned among their states based on population. He followed this with another call on August 4 for an additional 300,000 men to serve for nine months with any shortage in recruiting to be made up by a draft from among the respective states' militias.

In the same month, Congress enacted a Confiscation Act authorizing the seizure of property from those in rebellion against the country. To pay for the geometrically expanding cost of the war, Congress also adopted the Revenue Act on July 1 establishing the position of Commissioner of Internal Revenue and imposing excise taxes on such luxury items as billiard tables, carriages, jewelry, liquor, pianos, playing cards, telegrams, tobacco, and yachts, but also common items including, among others, feathers, gunpowder, iron, leather, medicine, newspaper advertisements, and professional licenses. It also imposed taxes on inheritances, interest on banking, corporate income, and value added taxes on some manufactured goods. The legislation enacted the first progressive individual income tax: personal incomes between $600 and $10,000 during the course of a year would be assessed a 3 percent tax, individuals with income over $10,000 would be liable to pay 5 percent. In 1864 the rates were adjusted to 5 percent for incomes between $600 and $5,000, 7.5 percent for those between $5,000 and $10,000, and 10 percent for those above $10,000. Revenue jumped from the $20 million raised in 1864 to $61 million when the new scale was implemented in 1865. Overall the North raised 21 percent of its wartime expenses through taxes as opposed to just 5 percent for the South.

Autumn

THE WEST

In July 1862 Gen. Henry Halleck was called to Washington to assume command of all the United States armies. With his departure, the western armies were divided between Grant with about 67,000 troops distributed among several key locations in western Tennessee and Buell with 56,000 men spread out from northern Alabama to southern Kentucky and throughout central Tennessee. Despite their successes of the spring, the Union forces were in no condition to renew a strong offensive as autumn approached.

Gen. Braxton Bragg replaced Beauregard in command of Confederate forces on June 27. He began to concentrate his scattered forces around Chattanooga with the intention of moving north in the hope that an invasion of Kentucky would force the relocation of Union forces northward to oppose his move and thus roll back the occupation of key territory essential to the Southern cause. At the same time, Bragg ordered Maj. Gen. Edmund Kirby Smith,[24] commanding 10,000 rebels at Knoxville, to move north to clear the Cumberland Gap of Union forces. Bragg's plan was for Smith then to move west, joining up with Bragg's main force for the move through east Tennessee into Kentucky. Preceded by several successful cavalry raids led by Col. John Hunt Morgan, Smith fell on 6,500 untested Federal troops at Richmond, Kentucky, on August 29–30, inflicting 5,353 casualties with a loss of only 451. With no other organized opposition. Smith occupied Lexington and Covington.

While Smith was dispatching the Federals at Richmond, Bragg began his move north. In response, Buell retired through Murfreesboro to Bowling Green but found his line of supply and communication north to Louisville cut. Grant reacted by sending a division to defend Louisville, but Buell eventually managed to get his army to Louisville where he received significant, through raw, reinforcements. He moved south again on

October 1 with some 60,000 men. They ran into Bragg's force near Perryville, Kentucky, numbering only some 22,500. It was not until fighting actually broke out on October 8 that Bragg apparently finally realized that he was facing a significant numerical disadvantage and he seemed not to have even been aware that a major engagement was in process until past midday. Buell was similarly confused, bringing less than two-thirds of his troops into action. Casualties were as follows:

	North	South
Effectives	36,940	16,000
Killed	845	510
Wounded	2,851	2,635
Captured & Missing	515	251
Total	4,211	3,396
Percent	11.4	21.2

Bragg withdrew overnight, abandoning the battlefield and moving back into Tennessee. His invasion ended in failure, as did an attack on Maj. Gen. William S. Rosecrans at Corinth by Confederate forces under Maj. Gen. Earl Van Dorn on October 3–4. Rosecrans's successful defense cost 2,520 casualties (11.0 percent) while Van Dorn lost a crippling 4,233 (19.2 percent). Tactically, both engagements were clear Union victories. Strategically, although the Union advance into the central Confederacy was stopped, it was only temporary.

Bragg concentrated his remaining 38,000 men around Murfreesboro, Tennessee,

Left: A favorite of Jefferson Davis, Braxton Bragg was named to command the major Confederate field army in the west. *Right:* William S. Rosecrans was appointed commander of the Army of the Cumberland (both photographs, Library of Congress).

where he attempted to reorganize his force into the newly created Army of Tennessee. Meanwhile, Richmond sent Gen. Joseph E. Johnston, recovered from his wounds suffered on the York Peninsula, west to provide badly needed overall command and coordination of all the Confederate forces in the west. Unhappy with Buell's halting performance, Washington replaced him with Gen. William S. Rosecrans[25] who would lead the Army of the Cumberland.. Rosecrans consolidated his new command of 47,000 around Nashville.

On the final day of the year the two forces met outside Murfreesboro next to Stones River. Coincidentally, Rosecrans and Bragg each planned to attack the right flank of the other, with Bragg landing the first blow. The Confederate attack drove in the Federal line, swinging it back like a hinge until it was at a right angle from the original line and eventually almost surrounded, its back to the river with only a small opening to the north as an escape route. By nightfall, Bragg was convinced of victory. Rosecrans held a council of war which was divided, but determined to stay and fight it out. Desultory fighting continued over the first two days of the new year until reinforcements and supplies reached Rosecrans on January 3 and troops under Maj. Gen. George H. Thomas managed to capture a portion of the rebel line in a daring counterattack. That night Bragg gave up and began withdrawing his army to Tullahoma, Tennessee. The Battle of Stones River was a slugfest, each army seemingly unwilling to give up the contest. Casualties were as severe as the fighting:

	North	South
Effectives	41,400	35,000
Killed	1,677	1,294
Wounded	7,543	7,945
Captured & Missing	3,686	2,500
Total	12,906	11,739
Percent	31.2	33.5

While Stones River could rightly be considered a tactical draw, the strategic result was much the same as Perryville. Bragg was forced farther south while Rosecrans reclaimed more territory relinquished at the beginning of Bragg's invasion. The only cheerful news for the South at the end of the year was the initial repulse of a Federal attempt on Vicksburg. In December forces led by Grant and Sherman began an advance on the strategic city of Vicksburg on the Mississippi River. Grant was temporarily frustrated by rebel attacks on his communications and the capture of a major supply base, but Sherman moved 32,000 troops south along the river landing his men north of the city on December 27–28. The following day he ordered an assault on the Confederate positions at Chickasaw Bluffs but was easily repulsed losing 1,776 (5.6 percent) against only 207 rebel casualties (1.5 percent). This minor victory hardly offset the serious losses sustained by Bragg during his invasion and subsequent retreat. Confederate manpower in the west had been further drained without any lasting positive result.

THE EAST

When informed that Stonewall Jackson's troops had left the Shenandoah Valley for Richmond, and in light of the fighting taking place on the peninsula, on June 26 Lincoln formed the Army of Virginia out of the disparate Union commands that had fought in the valley. The purpose was to have a consolidated force capable either of interposing itself in front of a Southern movement toward Washington or moving south to cooperate

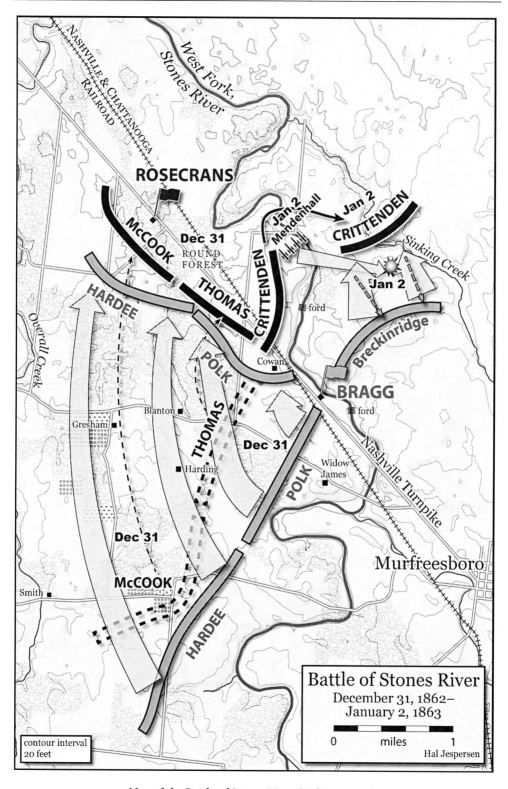

Map of the Battle of Stones River (Hal Jespersen).

in the operations around Richmond as might be needed. Placed under the command of Maj. Gen. John Pope, its 50,000 men were divided into three corps. When Confederate cavalry captured and burned the huge Federal supply base at Manassas Junction, Pope began moving his army east toward this centrally located position. While this was taking place Lee, convinced that McClellan was not going to renew his campaign any time soon and worried about the possibility of Pope moving on him from the north, determined to take the initiative. He dispatched Jackson north to contain Pope, followed soon thereafter by another division under Maj. Gen. Ambrose Powell Hill. Portions of the two forces clashed at Cedar Mountain on August 9 with about 8,000 troops under Maj. Gen. Nathaniel Banks being bested by Jackson with almost 17,000. A tactical Confederate victory, they lost 1,338 compared to Banks's 2,353. Strategically, Pope was able to extract his army and continue east.

When it became obvious to Lee that McClellan's troops were being withdrawn from the peninsula, he put the rest of his Army of Northern Virginia into motion north in the hope of crushing Pope before the two Union armies could be consolidated. Despite his best efforts he was unable to prevent Pope from placing his army securely across the Rappahannock River. After several attempts to find a route across the river, each time being frustrated by Pope's army, Lee finally cast the dice by ordering Jackson on a wide flanking movement north along the river, then east through Thoroughfare Gap to gain Pope's flank and rear. Marching fast, Jackson suddenly appeared at Manassas Junction, far in rear of Pope's army, on August 27. Pope reacted quickly, moving to the junction only to find Jackson gone. On the evening of August 28 his vanguard under Brig. Gen. John Gibbon ran into a portion of Jackson's command under Maj. Gen. Richard Ewell in position at Groveton. In the brief but fierce fight that followed Ewell was seriously wounded, later forcing amputation of his leg, and lost 1,250 out of 6,200 engaged while Gibbon lost 1,150 of 2,100. Jackson settled into a defensive position along an incomplete railroad embankment north of Groveton while Pope hurriedly assembled his troops for an effort to defeat Jackson before the rest of Lee's forces came up.

While this was happening, the Second and Sixth Corps of McClellan's Army of the Potomac began arriving in Washington. Lincoln ordered McClellan to remain in the city to move his troops forward as fast as possible to support Pope. Instead, McClellan dawdled, manufacturing reasons why he needed more time. When the lead elements finally did move off toward the fighting, they moved slowly and meticulously with McClellan in no hurry to move them along. On the very day that Pope and Lee were locked in mortal combat at Second Bull Run, McClellan suggested to the president that he ought to "leave Pope to get out of his scrape, and at once use all our means to make the capital perfectly safe."[26] Translation: McClellan did not want to give up control of any of his own troops even if it meant a Federal defeat.

On August 29 Pope launched a series of assaults on Jackson's position. In heavy fighting along the railroad embankment, his First Corps under Maj. Gen. Franz Sigel managed to drive in Jackson's left flank, but Maj. Gen. Philip Kearny leading the First Division of the Third Corps from McClellan's army failed to obey orders to support Sigel and the attack ground to a halt. Similarly, Maj. Gen. Fitz John Porter leading the Fifth Corps also disobeyed a direct order from Pope to attack later in the day. Another McClellan loyalist, Brig. Gen. Samuel D. Sturgis, was heard to utter the now-famous comment "I don't care for John Pope one pinch of owl dung."[27] Gen. Kearny was killed at Chantilly a few days later and Porter was eventually court martialed and removed from command

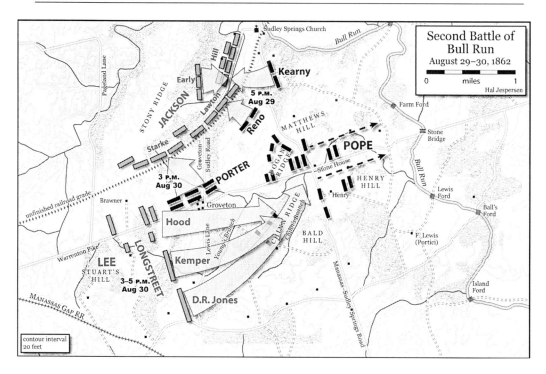

Map of the Battle of Second Bull Run (Hal Jespersen).

for his behavior at the Second Battle of Bull Run, but this would be much too late to save Pope and his embattled army.

Pope renewed the attack on Jackson the following day, ignoring reports that Longstreet had arrived with the balance of Lee's army. After Pope's strike against Jackson had run its course, Lee launched a crippling assault on Pope's thinly held left flank, breaking through and successively chewing up reinforcements sent in piecemeal in vain attempts to stop the decisive thrust by Longstreet's command. One of those killed that day was Massachusetts Col. Fletcher Webster, son of the famous senator. By nightfall only a stubborn rear guard action allowed Pope time to lead his beaten command to safety around Centreville. Tactically, once again, the South emerged victorious, although Lee's strategic goal of destroying Pope's army before it united with McClellan's was foiled. Still attempting to achieve this end, Lee sent Jackson on another wide flanking move to try to cut Pope off from Washington. Instead, Pope met him at Chantilly on September 1 in another brief but deadly encounter that blunted Lee's attempt. Losses were again high:

	North	South
Effectives	77,000	55,000
Killed	1,724	1,481
Wounded	8,372	7,627
Captured & Missing	5,958	89
Total	16,054	9,197
Percent	20.8	16.7

With yet another defeat, Lincoln was now placed in the position of deciding how to proceed. The obvious decision was to merge the Army of Virginia into the Army of the Potomac, which was immediately done. The more difficult decision was who to trust with the command. Pope had little support among the troops, with some openly scorning him. But it was also clear that McClellan had purposely delayed sending assistance to Pope that might have prevented Pope's defeat. An obvious third alternative was to bring in someone from outside, but the campaign continued and Lincoln could not afford the time necessary for someone else to assume the command. With the original Army of the Potomac still overwhelmingly loyal to McClellan, Lincoln could see no immediate alternative other than appointing the flawed popular candidate. Pope was sent off to command troops in Minnesota engaged in suppressing an Indian uprising. He would never hold another significant Union command.

One reason Lincoln had to act quickly was Lee who chose not to rest on his laurels. Only two days after the final clash at Chantilly, Lee began moving north into Maryland. He had several reasons for doing so. First, as Pope withdrew close to Washington Lee had virtually no opportunity to attack him to any advantage, especially with the balance of the Army of the Potomac on hand. Second, Maryland had a large pro–South

Lincoln brought John Pope in from the west to head the new Army of Virginia, but his bombastic address to his troops alienated many and McClellan loyalists were reluctant to support a rival to their hero (Library of Congress).

population which might be encouraged to assist his forces if reassured by the presence of rebel troops, and possibly even enlist in his army. Third, the lush autumn crops of Maryland and southern Pennsylvania, along with their livestock and other provisions as yet untouched by war, could provide ready supplies for his army that the heavily foraged countryside in Virginia could not. Fourth, by moving into a position where he might menace a number of prime targets such as Harrisburg, Baltimore, and Washington, he hoped to lure the Army of the Potomac out into the open where he would have a chance to deal it a crippling blow. Fifth, if he could invade the North and win a victory on its soil, coupled with the long string of Federal defeats in the east that summer it might encourage the anti-war movement going into the fall elections in the North. Although not stated, a further benefit, assuming a successful invasion, might convince England and France to finally conclude that the South would win and to accord it the recognition and aid which had always been the cornerstone of Confederate international diplomacy.

Lee began his next campaign on September 3, only two days after Chantilly, when the Army of Northern Virginia began crossing the Potomac River into Maryland. Assuming that it would take some time for the Federals to be ready to take the field again, Lee divided his forces into several infantry concentrations to facilitate movement and obtaining provisions with the cavalry operating more or less independently under Stuart. One of his immediate goals was the capture of Harpers Ferry. To this end, and to inform his subordinates of his expectations for the campaign, on September 9 Lee issued Special

Order No. 191 that directed Jackson to seize Harpers Ferry while Longstreet moved north to Hagerstown. Jackson was to follow Longstreet once his objective fell. In the short term Lee's army would be dangerously dispersed, but with McClellan in charge and the Union army reeling from a long series of defeats in the Valley, on the Peninsula, and in the Second Bull Run campaign Lee felt confident that time was on his side.

For once, McClellan moved expeditiously. Organization was his forte. He quickly incorporated Pope's former command into the Army of the Potomac, its three corps becoming the First, Eleventh, and Twelfth Corps. He then divided the infantry corps into three "wings," the First and Ninth Corps under Major General Ambrose Burnside, the Second and Twelfth Corps under Major General Edwin V. Sumner, and the Sixth and part of the Fourth Corps under Major General William Franklin. The Eleventh Corps was designated a reserve force to be retained for the defense of Washington. He began leading his army out of the vicinity of Washington on September 7, but there the promptness appeared to end. He did not reach Frederick, Maryland, a distance of less than fifty miles, until September 12. That day soldiers from the 27th Indiana Infantry came across some cigars rolled in a paper laying in the grass as they were setting up camp. The paper turned out to be a copy of Special Order No. 191 giving the disposition, timetable, and future movements of Lee's entire army. It was the intelligence windfall of the war. Even McClellan recognized this, commenting to a Brig. Gen. John Gibbon, "Here is a paper with which if I cannot whip Bobbie Lee, I will be willing to go home." Still, he waited eighteen more hours before finally moving.

Lee's army was shielded by the Blue Ridge Mountains so McClellan ordered one wing of his army to march on Turner's Gap and another on Crampton's Gap, two passes that would give him access to Lee's scattered command with the opportunity to defeat it in detail. Once word reached Lee that McClellan was closer than anticipated and moving toward the protective Blue Ridge, Lee immediately ordered his army to concentrate. While the orders went out, McClellan's leading elements pushed through Crampton's Gap with little trouble and fought their way through Turner's Gap in the Battle of South Mountain, both on September 14. These successes placed McClellan west of the mountains in position to administer a serious beating to Lee's still scattered army. Fortunately for Lee, McClellan again reverted to the slowness that had by then become his defining attribute. Marching deliberately, he had his entire army within a mile or two of Antietam Creek just east of the town of Sharpsburg along the Potomac River. He spent the entire day consolidating and moving a few units cautiously forward.

Lee was not that cautious, in more than one way. First, he drew in his troops as quickly as he could. Harpers Ferry fell to Jackson on the 15th and Lee ordered him to bring his entire force north as quickly as he could disarm the captured Federals and provide for their guard. The other way that he was not cautious was in his decision-making. Faced with the better part of 87,000 Union troops, Lee had with him on the morning of September 16 only some 19,000 men under Longstreet. His safest move would have been to cross the Potomac at Sharpsburg and use the river to shield him until he could reunite his army. Instead, he chose to keep his army north of the river, determined to fight McClellan where he was. This decision was fraught with danger. Lee would have only about half of the men available to him that McClellan had even when his army was reunited, assuming that happened before McClellan attacked. If the blue wave surged forward on the 16th he would be outnumbered by as much as four and one-half to one. Even if he could unify his command, he would be fighting in a pocket with his back to the river. If he suffered defeat he might well lose his entire army if the river rose or if he could not somehow manage an orderly retreat. In any case, even if his infantry managed to ford the river his wagons, supplies, and artillery would most likely be lost.

Fortunately for Lee he was fighting McClellan who frittered away the entire day to no discernable purpose. Instead of advancing he spent the day positioning troops, yet still he managed to fracture the careful organization into wings that he had implemented by positioning the First Corps on the very far right of his line and the Ninth on the extreme left even though they were both supposed to be under the immediate command of Burnside. He planned to strike at dawn on September 17, contemplating a three-pronged attack. The First Corps, supported by the Twelfth, would attack the Confederate left. The Ninth Corps was to assault the rebel right. When these attacks went home, McClellan assumed that Lee would send troops from his reserve and the center to reinforce the threatened flanks. Then, when the time appeared right, McClellan would launch his knockout punch at the depleted center of Lee's line, breaking through and destroying the Army of Northern Virginia.

The best laid plan, of course, does not always materialize as scripted. The First Corps smashed into Jackson's defensive line, followed by the Twelfth precipitating vicious fighting that in fact drew in Lee's thin reserve as well as reinforcements from his center, exactly as McClellan had hoped. But Burnside did not advance. The value of a simultaneous attack on the two rebel flanks was lost. McClellan committed the Second and Fifth Corps in the center to an assault that came perilously close to breaking Lee's center anyway. At one point almost nothing stood between the attackers and Lee's headquarters except for a thin line of infantry battling for its life in a sunken road and an artillery battery that contained Lee's own son. Since Burnside had not attacked, Lee was able to shift troops from his right to finally plug the developing gap in his center. McClellan could have, and should have, thrown in his reserve at this moment to complete the victory, but he did not. He retained the large Sixth Corps and most of the Fifth giving Lee the breather he desperately needed. Only later in the afternoon did Burnside finally cross the Antietam. When he did his troops quickly drove in the remaining thin line. Lee had no more reserves, McClellan was on the verge of victory, although he apparently did not know it. The arrival of reinforcements under Maj. Gen. Ambrose Powell Hill snatched away that last hope. Ironically, Hill and McClellan has been roommates at West point and even courted the same girl who eventually married McClellan. Now, Hill arrived just in the proverbial "nick of time" with the last of Jackson's troops from Harpers Ferry and drove Burnside back. The slaughter had been horrific, the worst single day in American military history, but Lee's army survived.

Strangely, Lee did not take the opportunity to escape across the Potomac during the night but stubbornly determined to hold his ground the following day. Although McClellan had on hand more fresh troops than Lee had in his entire battered army, McClellan chose not to attack on September 18. Instead, a brief truce allowed both sides to carry off as many of their wounded as they could reach. That night Lee finally evacuated under the cover of night, unchallenged by McClellan who allowed him to escape without further damage. The butcher's bill was worse than anything before.

	North	*South*	
Effectives	87,000	40,000	
Killed	2,108	1,546	
Wounded	9,540	7,752	*continued on p. 150*

	North	*South*
Captured & Missing	753	1,018
Total	12,401	10,312
Percent	14.3	25.8

The Northern percentage is misleading since much of McClellan's army was never committed. Counting only those troops actually used, the percentage of casualties would be much closer to 21.8 percent. Tactically, Antietam was a draw as the two armies fought themselves to a bloody standstill. Strategically, it was a Northern victory since it halted Lee's planned invasion and forced his army to retreat back into Virginia. Politically, the repercussions were disastrous for the South. Renewed hope in the North was reflected in the election that fall when the anti-war movement polled much less than expected. Internationally, news of the Confederate retreat from Antietam convinced British leaders to wait longer before extending diplomatic recognition to the Confederacy since it was now not entirely sure that the South would win. Lastly, President Lincoln had been contemplating a bold move for some time, but advisors convinced him to wait until a Union victory so his action would not be viewed as the dying gasp of a defeated nation, but rather as coming from a position of strength. With the repulse of Lee's invasion Lincoln declared Antietam a great Northern victory and announced his plan to issue an executive order that would become known as the Emancipation Proclamation. It would change the entire nature of the war.

Despite the success of the Antietam campaign, Lincoln became increasingly frustrated with McClellan's failure to pursue Lee or to follow him vigorously into Virginia to bring him to battle again before he had a chance to recover. When still no hint of action was evident by the end of the month, Lincoln traveled to meet with McClellan at his headquarters in the field on October 2. Lincoln returned to Washington in the belief that McClellan would finally move, but when another month passed with no further action the president removed McClellan from command on November 7. His replacement was Maj. Gen. Ambrose P. Burnside.[28] After initially turning down the proffered command of the Army of the Potomac, he was eventually convinced to do it by other officers who feared that if Burnside did not take the command it would be offered to Joseph Hooker whom they disliked.

Knowing full well that McClellan incurred the displeasure of the president for his failure to act decisively, Burnside felt compelled to begin an immediate offensive campaign even though winter rapidly approached. To do so he adopted the orthodox approach by shifting the army to Fredericksburg, roughly equidistant between Washington and Richmond along the direct overland route. He planned to move fast, meet pontoons at Falmouth on the north side of the Rappahannock River across from Fredericksburg, cross into that city, then push on south forcing Lee to come out and fight in the open or fall back into the defenses of Richmond. The first portion of his plan unfolded well. The First and Ninth Corps arrived at Falmouth before Longstreet's advance corps of Lee's army made it to Fredericksburg. Jackson was still in the Shenandoah Valley and would not arrive until late November. Unfortunately for Burnside, the pontoons he expected were not there and they would not be for some time. Although some officers urged him to force a crossing since there was no serious opposition, he demurred, preferring to await the arrival of the pontoons. By the time the pontoons were available, Longstreet had arrived making a crossing under fire much more problematic.

The pontoons did not arrive until November 25. By the time Burnside felt ready to move on December 11 two more weeks had elapsed and Lee's entire army was on hand. Although Burnside outnumbered Lee by about 114,000 to 72,500, all of the advantages of position favored the latter. Burnside would have to force a crossing of a wide, deep river in the face of direct opposition from troops in town and, if successful, then be confronted by an army dug in along the range of heights behind the town. Regardless, Burnside determined to proceed, ordering his troops to fight their way across the river on December 11–12. Engineers attempting to construct the pontoon bridges came under fire from rebel sharpshooters in town. Burnside attempted to silence them by opening artillery fire on the town, but with little effect since the sharpshooters were largely hidden in basements and behind other cover. Finally, volunteers from Massachusetts and Michigan rowed across the river in pontoons while the artillery attempted to suppress the sharpshooters. The infantry made it across the river, gradually cleared out the rebels, and the bridges were completed so that additional troops could cross on the 12th and 13th.

Lincoln met with McClellan at the general's headquarters in an unsuccessful attempt to encourage him to take the initiative (Library of Congress).

By the morning of December 13, Longstreet was entrenched along Marye's Heights behind the town and Jackson was in place south of the town fronting Prospect Hill. Burnside ordered Maj. Gen. William B. Franklin to launch his First and Sixth Corps against Jackson. Led by a division of the First Corps under Maj. Gen. George Gordon Meade, the attack broke through Jackson's line but was not sufficiently supported and finally driven back by reinforcements when it grew short of ammunition. The assault had been promising, but Burnside chose to change his focus to Marye's Heights, arguably what should have appeared to anyone as the strongest portion of the Confederate defenses. With the Second and Ninth Corps under Maj. Gen. Edwin V. Sumner and the Third and Fifth Corps under Maj. Gen. Joseph Hooker all in position in and about the town, Burnside ordered a frontal assault.

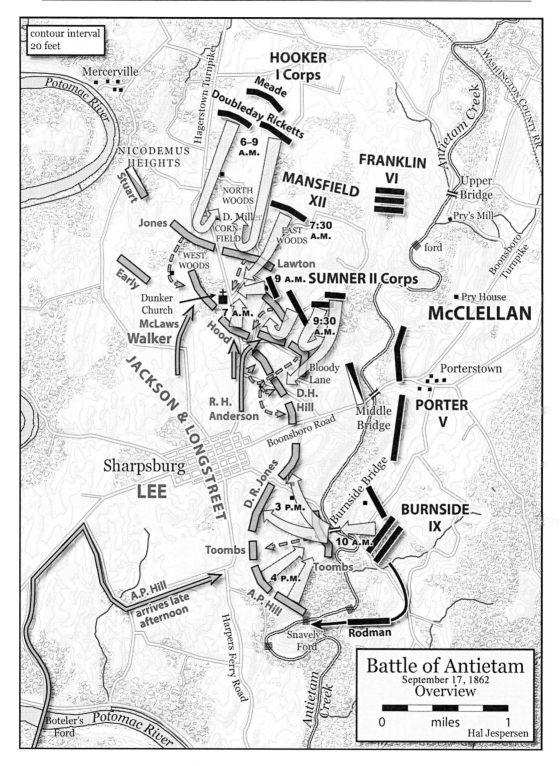

Map of the Battle of Antietam (Hal Jespersen).

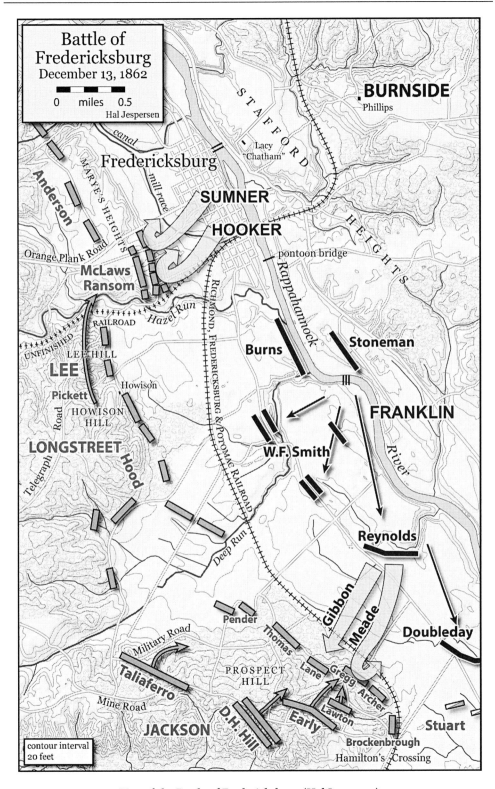

Map of the Battle of Fredericksburg (Hal Jespersen).

Lincoln appointed Ambrose P. Burnside to replace McClellan and infuse some aggression into the army. His distinctive facial foliage led to the term "sideburns" in a play on his name (National Archives and Records Administration).

The troops had to cross a 200 yard wide field, negotiate a canal and ditch under fire, then charge across another 600 yard open space and finally up the slope of the hill into masses infantry fire from behind a four-foot stone wall along the side of a sunken road. Behind this exceptional defensive position Lee crowned the heights with massed artillery under Lt. Col. Edward Porter Alexander. The attempt was tantamount to suicide. The first attack miraculously made it to within about 125 yards of the stone wall before floundering completely, its individual units reporting casualties between 25 and 50 percent. Despite repeated calls from some of his officers to stop the senseless slaughter, Burnside insisted on renewed attacks. In all, fourteen waves went forward, each to meet with similar destruction. By the end of the day, between 6,000 and 8,000 of Burnside's men lay dead or wounded. Confederate losses around Marye's Heights were estimated as only 1,200. Burnside planned to renew the pointless attacks again the following morning, but was eventually talked out of the madness by his subordinates. One of the units that suffered most severely was the Irish Brigade which repeatedly charged the heart of the Confederate position behind the stone wall. When it was all over, of about 1,200 men it took into action, it lost 545, some 45 percent. In 1963, President John F. Kennedy presented the colors of the 69th New York (1st Regiment, Irish Brigade) as a gift to the Irish People in a speech before the Irish Parliament.

During the cold December afternoon the suffering of the wounded between the lines was intense, their cries for help pitiful in the extreme. Behind the stone wall, hunkered down in Brig. Gen. Joseph B. Kershaw's brigade, Sergeant Richard Kirkland of the 2nd South Carolina could stand it no longer. Gathering up a number of canteens of water, he slipped across the stone wall and began ministering to the Federal wounded despite the obvious personal danger. When Federal soldiers understood what he was doing they withheld their fire. As night closed in temperatures fell even more, increasing the agony of those who survived. Many did not, dying from untended wounds or freezing to death during the night.

The armies both held their positions on December 14. In the afternoon Burnside requested a truce to remove his wounded. Lee agreed. For those who survived the deadly fire and the freezing temperatures relief was finally at hand. While stretcher bearers worked, Burnside's advisors convinced him that any further attempt at the heights was folly. It had been one of the most lopsided major victories of the war.

	North	*South*
Effectives	114,000	72,500
Killed	1,284	608
Wounded	9,600	4,116
Captured & Missing	1,769	653
Total	12,653	5,377
Percent	11.1	7.4

Unwilling to accept defeat, Burnside tried a different tactic in January sending part of his army on a flanking move west along the Rappahannock with the goal of crossing upriver and coming in behind Lee's position at Fredericksburg. No sooner had the troops been put in motion on January 20 than rain storms soaked the dirt roads into a muddy quagmire. Everything bogged down, especially wheeled vehicles like wagons and artillery. Amused Confederates across the river held up signs reading "Burnside Stuck in the Mud." Nevertheless, he persisted for three days until finally calling a halt to yet another dismal failure. Tactical and strategic success went to the South, as did the political victory. Fredericksburg brought renewed hope to the South while provoking dismay and outrage in the North. Morale in the Army of the Potomac fell to its nadir during the war. The bimonthly muster for the end of December 1863, was the only time during the entire war that the Northern desertion rate exceeded that of the South. Lincoln relieved Burnside of command on January 26.

THE RESULT

During the year President Lincoln had gradually come to the conclusion that he should issue a presidential order eliminating slavery. Since the Constitution required that the president defend the nation against invasion or internal rebellion, he believed that under the authority given to him as commander-in-chief of the armed forces in time of war, and the provisions of the recently adopted Confiscation Act, he had the legal right to confiscate property belonging to people in rebellion against the country. However, when he broached the idea to his cabinet, some argued that to issue such an executive order after the long string of Northern defeats on the eastern battlefields would look like a move of desperation. They urged him to wait for a Northern victory so the directive would look as if it were issued from a position of strength rather than weakness. When the September 1862 Southern invasion of the North was turned back at the Battle of Antietam, forcing the rebels to retreat into Virginia, Lincoln used the occasion to declare it a Union victory and issue the Emancipation Proclamation.

The Proclamation stated that on January 1, 1863, "all persons held as slaves within any state or designated part of a state, the people whereof shall then be in rebellion against the United States, shall be then, thenceforward, and forever, free; and the Executive Government of the United States, including the military and naval authority thereof, will recognize and maintain the freedom of such persons, and will do no act or acts to repress such persons, or any of them, in any efforts they may make for their actual freedom."[29] Immediately it came under attack by critics who complained that it did not apply to slaves in slave states that had not seceded—Delaware, Maryland, Kentucky, and Missouri—or even in areas like New Orleans that were then under Federal control, and that it could not be enforced in areas in rebellion since they were controlled by the Confederate army. In England, the London *Spectator* commented wryly that "the principle is not that

Francis B. Carpenter's painting of Lincoln reading the first draft of his Emancipation Proclamation to his cabinet. Left to right: Secretary of War Edwin Stanton, Secretary of the Treasury Salmon Chase, Lincoln, Secretary of the Navy Gideon Welles, Secretary of the Interior Caleb B. Smith (standing), Secretary of State William Seward (sitting), Postmaster General Montgomery Blair, and Attorney General Edward Bates (Library of Congress).

a human being cannot justly own another, but that he cannot own another unless he is loyal to the United States."[30] Even today critics often claim that Lincoln really freed no one, asserting this as evidence that he really did not intend to eliminate slavery but only to calm the growing demands among his abolitionist political supporters. This argument ignores the reality of the times.[31]

Some scholars have argued that Lincoln dared not antagonize the slaveholders in the Border States for fear they might be driven into the arms of the Confederacy, thus weakening the Federal government's chances in the war. This was no doubt a consideration, but there was another more fundamental reason that Lincoln chose to word his proclamation as he did. It was less than five years since the Supreme Court had decreed in the Dred Scott decision that slaves were property protected by the Constitution. The same chief justice, Roger Taney, still held that position so there was every reason to believe that attempting to free the slaves of people loyal to the Union would again be declared unconstitutional. But by relying on the argument that the Constitution required him to quell rebellions and that the Confiscation Act allowed him to seize the property of those in rebellion, Lincoln believed that his action had at least a good chance of being deemed constitutional when it inevitably came under review by the nation's highest court. Clearly, Lincoln was attempting to do as much as he could within the limits imposed by previous judicial actions.

While revisionist historians have argued that Lincoln's record on emancipation was not one of consistent support, the president was not above the requirements of the Constitution and had to abide by the interpretations of the Supreme Court. Following the

Proclamation, Lincoln supported a Constitutional amendment to eliminate slavery. When it failed to gain Congressional approval in 1864, he exerted considerable political pressure on individual members of Congress until it finally received the required vote in February 1865.

Lincoln's proclamation made emancipation a central objective of the war, holding out the promise of freedom for over four million people. While this outraged the South and angered anti-war Democrats and Copperheads in the North, it energized the anti-slavery factions and had important international consequences. Great Britain had already prohibited slavery in its empire and the British laboring class was largely anti-slavery. The Emancipation Proclamation gained the support of many Britons and is usually considered one factor that convinced the British government against open intervention in the Civil War.

The long string of Federal defeats, seemingly each with more butchery than the previous, seriously eroded Northern morale. Anti-war feelings spread. Membership in peace societies increased as did the size of the Copperhead movement. Often portrayed in newspaper cartoons by a copperhead snake, the name actually came from the copper penny supporters wore around their necks. Most favored the Union but strongly opposed the war which they blamed on abolitionist agitation. They resisted support for the war, including recruitment, fought strongly against the election of Republicans, and demanded immediate peace and a resolution of the nation's divisions through compromise. In a few cases Copperheads went so far as to cooperate with Confederate agents. Their recognized leader was Clement L. Vallandigham, an Ohio native who was elected to the House of Representatives in 1858, supported the presidential candidacy of Stephen A. Douglas in 1860, and supported States' Rights including the right of the Southern states to secede. Other prominent leaders included Wilber F. Storey, editor of the *Chicago Tribune*, and John Mullaly, editor of the *Metropolitan Record*, a New York Irish paper.

As the fall elections neared, Republican concerns grew. Confederate sympathizers in the Border States and lower Midwest organized against Republicans running for state and national office. Rising taxes, inflation, anger over presidential suspension of habeas corpus early in the war, and most of all the horrific cost of the war in human life that resulted in a long series of defeats all conspired to drive votes from the Republican camp to the Democratic. "Peace Democrats," sometimes labeled "Butternuts" to emphasize what Republicans perceived as their Southern sympathies, believed war was undermining the economy, civil liberties and the rights of the individual states. While the Emancipation Proclamation energized anti-slavery voters, it appalled others. Likewise, the threat that states might resort to conscription to address increasing difficulties in recruitment drove some to question continued support for the president's party.

When the results were tallied Republican fears were justified, though not to the extent of the more pessimistic estimates. In the House of Representatives they lost 22 seats. Counting independents and minority party candidates, the Democrats picked up a total of 28 seats. Much to Lincoln's relief, Republicans still held a majority when coupled with the Unionists, pro-war Democrats who allied with the Republicans. In the Senate the Republicans actually gained three seats giving them a clear majority of 66 percent without even counting the Unionists. Republicans lost the governorships in New Jersey and New York, as well as control of the state legislatures in Illinois, Indiana, and New Jersey. Democrats were jubilant. George Templeton Strong, a New York Republican attorney who assisted in founding the United States Sanitary Commission, called it "a national calamity ... like a great, sweeping revolution of public sentiment, like a general aban-donment of the loyal, generous spirit of patriotism that broke out so nobly and unex-pectedly in April, 1861." He attributed it to the people being "impatient, dissatisfied, disgusted, disappointed ... suffering from the necessary evils of war and from irritation at our slow progress."[32] Others noted that voting was much lower than it could have been because soldiers away from home were unable to cast their votes. Reasoning that those who volunteered would be more likely to support the war, the president, and his party, the result of this revelation was the institution of the absentee ballot for the 1864 elec-tion.

To assist in organizing this new voting bloc Republicans created the Union League with its initial home in Philadelphia. The group formed local clubs to distribute campaign literature, raise money to support the United States Sanitary Commission, and promote the recruitment of both white and black volunteers for the army. Later, in the postwar South, it would continue to strongly support Republican policies and assist those of African ancestry during the Reconstruction.

*   *   *

Northerners and Southerners alike were appalled by the casualties of 1862. The war was proving much more vicious, much more deadly, much more lasting than anyone expected just a year before. And still there was no end in sight. Although Southerners mourned the ever-increasing list of their dead, morale remained largely intact due to the highly publicized victories in the east, notably by the Army of Northern Virginia and its commanding officer, Robert E. Lee, both of which were well on their way to becoming the stuff of which legends were made. Beneath this veneer of optimist there were nonethe-less reasons for concern. The best opportunity the South would ever have for gaining European recognition had been lost among the carnage along Antietam Creek. Shiloh, the surrender of Forts Henry and Donelson, and the bloody battlefields of Virginia had taken a heavy toll of Southern dead and prisoners of war, losses the South was having trouble replacing. And the economics of the differing prewar production systems inex-orably drove the South one more year closer to financial and material exhaustion.

Northern morale was at a low ebb in the wake of the bloodbath at Fredericksburg. In the east, where most of the major newspapers were located and the attention of the nation focused, the Union armies had suffered a continuous series of disastrous defeats broken only by the horrendous casualties of Antietam where Lee's invasion ended. Yet despite popular perceptions of defeat, the North profited from significant achievements during the year. The Emancipation Proclamation energized the flagging spirits of anti-slavery forces in the North and opened the way for the eventual enlistment of soldiers of African descent in the Union army. The capture of Island No. Ten opened the invasion route south along the Mississippi River as did the taking of Forts Henry and Donelson on the Cumberland and Tennessee Rivers. The Confederate defensive perimeter in the west was shattered opening the Deep South to invasion, much of Tennessee was in Union hands while an attempted Confederate counteroffensive failed at Shiloh. Most important of all, New Orleans was securely in Union hands, denying the gulf's largest seaport to the South and making it available to Northern troops and the blockading fleet whose efforts to restrict Southern imports were beginning to be felt. The Anaconda had wrapped around its prey, poised to apply its life extinguishing compression.

7

1863—The Tide Begins to Turn

The dawn of the year 1863 found the North reeling from the most recent bloodbath at Fredericksburg. Desertions from the Army of the Potomac were up, civilian morale was down, and the press and politicians were clamoring for heads to roll. Since most of the major newspapers which could afford to send correspondents to accompany the armies were in the east, the impression the reading public received was largely that of the fate of the eastern campaigns. Certainly those in the west followed their own troops and were painfully aware of the cost in blood their men were paying, but the general sense of whether the North was winning or losing was to a large extent a reflection of what happened in the east filtered through the few correspondents who fed the constant flow of stories to their tabloids. The messages they received were those of frustration and loss. This was unfortunate for the public's morale because substantial progress had been made in the west toward subduing the rebellion. Federal troops had penetrated deeply into the central Confederacy, east-west railroad transportation in the South had been disrupted, New Orleans had been seized, and the Mississippi Valley's defenses had been breached opening the river to Union invasion from both north and south.

In the South, grief over the terrible losses of the 1862 campaigns was as real as it was in the North. Many consoled themselves in the belief that their sacrifice had not been in vain. Time after time massive Northern armies had invaded Virginia attempting to capture the Confederate capital at Richmond, each time only to meet with defeat before the prowess of smaller Southern forces. It was easy to believe the old saying that one rebel could lick ten Yankees any day. It was reassuring to know that Southern manhood had prevailed, and that it was in the capable hands of generals who seemed impervious to anything the North might try. But in the South public opinion was largely formed by the coverage of Lee's Army of Northern Virginia in its struggles against the Union general *du jour*. To the west the picture was not nearly so bright. But that directly affected only a small percentage of the population; primarily those in Vicksburg who were beginning to worry about their personal safety with Union armies threatening to move on their city, or the population of other smaller towns in the path of the next Northern move.

Spring

THE WEST

Union strategy in the west at the beginning of 1863 concentrated on the capture of the one major remaining rebel stronghold along the Mississippi River—Vicksburg. Confederate strategy was to deny the North that goal. In Confederate hands it blocked Union

John C. Pemberton, a native Pennsylvanian, was entrusted with the Southern defense of Vicksburg (Library of Congress).

attempts to seize the Mississippi Valley and the entire length of the Mississippi River in the Confederacy, keeping open a crucial east-west link to the surplus produce and livestock of the western states, as well as a route to import crucial material and supplies shipped to the South via Mexico. Capture of the length of the Mississippi River would cut the Confederacy in half. Vicksburg was well suited to defense. Located on a high bluff overlooking the river, excellent for artillery trained to control the waterway, to the north it was bounded by thick swamps through which it would be all but impossible to move an army with its artillery, supply wagons, and other impedimenta. A railroad connected it eastward to Jackson, Mississippi, through which it could be readily reinforced or resupplied. Hills to the east also provided some outlying defensive positions. The only avenue that remained relatively open to an enemy advance might be from the south, and even there defenses closer to the city formed serious obstacles. By mid-spring, command of the city rested in the hands of a covering army led by Lt. Gen. John C. Pemberton.[1] In October of 1862 he was given command of the Department of Mississippi, Tennessee, and East Louisiana. That gave him several months to study the geography of the area and plan its defenses. One of his major priorities was trying to gather enough troops for the task.

After Sherman's failure at Chickasaw Bluffs and the successful Confederate efforts to frustrate Grant's early move south the previous winter, Grant was determined to maintain the initiative with an early continuance of his move south to the citadel on the bluffs. Although unusually heavy rain with its resulting muddy roads and swollen rivers and swamps provided new obstacles to his planning, Grant tried a number of different initiatives including attempting to cut a canal across the peninsula opposite Vicksburg, a natural creation of the winding river. The purpose was to bypass Vicksburg so that he could land troops south of the city, avoiding the swampy area north of town that had frustrated Sherman and placing his troops in position to invest the city. Other attempts envisioned destroying levees to flood the Yazoo Pass so that Federal ships could navigate the river, attempting a naval passage of Steele's Bayou, and sending Maj. Gen. James

McPherson's corps on a circular 400-mile march through the Louisiana bayous, all of which either failed or were eventually abandoned.

While these frustrations were mounting, Grant addressed another challenge internal to the Union command. Maj. Gen. John McClernand, a native Kentucky lawyer who served in Congress for several terms from his adopted home in Illinois. With the outbreak of war Lincoln made him a brigadier general to assuage McClernand's Democratic constituency. Promoted to major general in March 1862, he failed to execute Grant's orders that would have cut off the Confederate retreat from Fort Henry; but, nevertheless issued press releases claiming for his own troops, and in the process himself, credit for Grant's victory. Needless to say, he and Grant were not on the best of terms thereafter. In October Halleck approved McClernand's plan to raise a separate command for a movement against Vicksburg, which was obviously the political general's attempt to remove himself from Grant's oversight. Styled the Army of the Mississippi, Grant was very much worried that this force, operating independently, would frustrate efforts to conduct a concerted, organized campaign against the rebel stronghold. On January 12 Grant succeeded in incorporating McClernand's force into his own Army of the Tennessee so that the wayward politico was once again under his command.

On March 29 Grant ordered McClernand to create a road from Milliken's Bend, north of Vicksburg, to Hard Times Plantation on the west side of the river south of the city. It was no mean feat necessitating the construction of numerous bridges, filling in depressions and swamps, and building corduroy roads over a distance of seventy miles. Grant's purpose was to move his army south of the city where he planned to cross to the east side of the Mississippi to approach his objective from below.

To do this he needed naval support, not just for the ferrying of troops across the river, but for their protection while exposed on the waters and during the initial landings on the eastern shore when they would be exposed and few in number. The guns of Rear Admiral David Dixon Porter's fleet could protect both of these vulnerable times, but getting them in position required them to run the gauntlet of fire from Vicksburg's guns which were perfectly capable of destroying the exposed fleet as it sailed past their positions. Nevertheless, Grant issued orders for the dangerous attempt. Porter selected the moonless night of April 16–17 to make the attempt with seven gunboats and three transports loaded with supplies. The Confederates quickly spotted the move and opened fire. One of the transports was destroyed, but the others miraculously made it through with only superficial damage and few casualties. Porter had apparently noticed that Vicksburg's guns were aiming high. Reasoning that the gun emplacements might not allow the rebels to depress their pieces sufficiently, he ordered his fleet to proceed closer to the eastern shore thereby avoiding the worst of the barrage. On the evening of April 22–23 another five out of six transports successfully ran the passage, giving Grant the naval force and the ships he needed to move his army across to the eastern shore of the Mississippi.

To divert Confederate attention from his move, Grant ordered Sherman to make a feint toward Snyder's Bluff north of Vicksburg and sent Col. Benjamin H. Grierson with a force of 1,700 cavalry on a massive raid from La Grange, Tennessee, south into Mississippi, eventually joining Federal troops in Baton Rouge on May 2. Grierson succeeded beyond all reasonable expectations in confusing Confederate authorities as to his ultimate destination and mission with the result that rebel forces were shifted about to counter what were thought to be his plans, thus moving them out of position to immediately oppose Grant's bold landing south of Vicksburg. On April 30, 17,000 Union troops began

Gen. John A. McClernand, an attorney and politician in civilian life, was a political appointment whose attempts to garner newspaper headlines far outreached any accomplishments (Library of Congress).

landing at Bruinsburg south of Grand Gulf. When the move was completed, Grant would have about 44,000 men to confront Pemberton's 32,000 and another force of some 6,000 men 45 miles farther east at Jackson, Mississippi. Instead of moving directly north, Grant chose to move east, capturing Port Gibson on May 1 and continuing on toward Jackson where he planned to dispatch any Confederate force gathering there so it would be unable to march to Vicksburg's relief. The seizure of Port Gibson forced the evacuation of Grand Gulf, solidifying Union control of the Mississippi River north to Vicksburg.

When he realized that Grant was across the river with a major force, Pemberton sent orders to Brig. Gen. John Gregg at Jackson to concentrate all available troops at Raymond about twenty miles southwest of Jackson and directly in what appeared to be the path of Grant's advance. There Gregg met a portion of Grant's army on May 12, the Seventeenth Corps

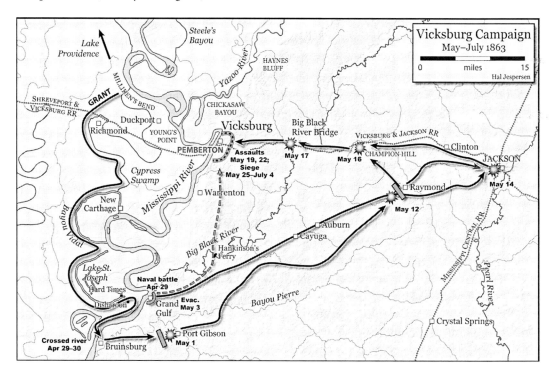

Grant's campaign against Vicksburg was one of the most successful Union movements of the war (Hal Jespersen).

under Maj. Gen. James McPherson. Although enjoying a temporary numerical advantage early in the fight, as McPherson's brigades came into action Gregg found himself outnumbered by more than three-to-one and was eventually forced to retire. Federal losses amounted to 446 (68 killed, 341 wounded, 37 missing) while Gregg suffered at least 820 (100 killed, 305 wounded, 415 captured), although some sources suggest the toll was much higher since local militia were not necessarily counted in the Confederate reports. Grant pushed on toward the state capital. In the meantime, Joseph E. Johnston was rushing to Jackson, having been ordered by the Confederate government on May 9 to assume command of the Confederate forces operating in the west. He arrived on May 13, only the day before the arrival of Grant's army. With no hope of successful resistance, Johnston immediately ordered Gregg to fight a rear-guard action to cover the evacuation of the city.

Against only brief resistance, Grant's troops entered Jackson on May 14. After destroying the railroads and anything else that might be of use to the rebel war effort, Grant turned his army west toward Vicksburg. Johnston retreated north where he soon assembled a force of about 15,000 but made no further effort to impede Grant's march. Although he sent orders to Pemberton to march east to confront the Federals, Pemberton, on the advice of his subordinates, deemed it too risky. Nevertheless, when Johnston repeated the order via a second courier, Pemberton put his force in motion. Although Pemberton again had second thoughts and began to retrace his steps, the two armies collided at Champion's Hill on May 16. Pemberton, with a force of 22,000, assumed a blocking position across the road to Vicksburg where Grant attacked him with two corps under McClernand and McPherson. Mistakes hampered both sides. McClernand failed to push his men vigorously forward allowing Pemberton to withdraw after a sharp fight with McPherson. On the Confederate side, Maj. Gen. William W. Loring disobeyed Pemberton's order to attack. Then, when ordered to cover the withdrawal, somehow managed to become separated from the rest of the army and wandered off depriving Pemberton of that portion of his command for the defense of Vicksburg. Of 29,373 men engaged, Federal losses were 2,441 (410 killed, 1,844 wounded, 187 missing; 8.3 percent) while Pemberton's 22,000 lost 3,851 (381 killed, 1,018 wounded, 1,670 captured and missing; 17.5 percent).

Pushing forward, the Thirteenth Corps under McClernand ran into Pemberton's rear guard under Brig. Gen. John S. Bowen at the Big Black River the following morning, putting them to flight with little difficulty although the rebels were able to fire the bridges to frustrate any immediate pursuit. McClernand reported losses of 276 while Confederate casualties remain largely unknown except for 1,751 that Union records reported as captured along with 18 guns. Pemberton's remaining men, more disorganized than not, streamed into the Vicksburg defenses throughout the day. When all were accounted for, including those left behind when Pemberton advanced part of his force to meet Grant, about 20,000 remained to hold the crucial city against Grant's army that had been reinforced to 49,000. Hoping to take advantage of the disorderly retreat and presumed low morale after their defeats, Grant ordered an assault on the Confederate works on May 19, but resistance was unexpectedly strong and it failed. A second attempt on May 22 was repulsed with heavy losses. Counting both assaults, Confederate casualties are estimated at only 500 to 600 while Grant suffered 659 killed, 3,327 wounded, 155 missing for a total of 4,141. In his memoirs, Grant later said there were only two assaults he ever regretted ordering. One was the continued attack on May 22 where he ordered in a second wave after the first met heavy resistance. He blamed this largely on McClernand's assurances that his men were making progress and could take the rebel positions. When McClernand issued another one of his unauthorized press releases praising his troops and their part in the attack, Grant had had enough and relieved him of command. With this, Grant settled down to what promised to be a lengthy siege, something he had hoped to avoid.

The East

At the beginning of 1863 the Army of the Potomac suffered yet another reverse with the failure of Burnside's "Mud March" in January, the last act in that officer's attempt to defeat Robert E. Lee. Morale in the army was at its nadir, something had to be done. The result was another installment of "musical generals" as Burnside's seat was taken by a new contestant for fame and glory—Maj. Gen. Joseph Hooker.[2]

Although his combat record was solid, Hooker emerged during the recent campaign as a leading critic of Burnside, a fact that soon made it to the target's ears. Following the "Mud March," Burnside submitted a demand to the president for the relief of several officers he believed to be disloyal or lacking competence. Hooker headed the list. Instead, under intense political and public pressure, Lincoln relieved Burnside. The choice of a replacement was no easy decision, especially since one of the next ranking officers with the army was none other than Hooker, who also enjoyed strong political support from Secretary of the Treasury Salmon P. Chase and a number of influential Republican leaders in Congress. Two officers, Generals Edwin V. Sumner and William B. Franklin refused to serve under Hooker and were reassigned, paving the way for his appointment. Nevertheless, Lincoln was clearly not convinced about the appointment since he chose to send the new commanding officer one of the strangest letters that a president ever sent to someone to whom he had just entrusted the fate of the nation.

> General:—I have placed you at the head of the Army of the Potomac. Of course, I have done this upon what appeared to me to be sufficient reasons, and yet I think it best for you to know that there are some things in regard to which I am not satisfied with you. I believe you are a brave and skilful soldier, which, of course, I like. I also believe you do not mix politics with your profession, in which you are right. You have confidence in yourself, which is a valuable, if not indispensable, quality. You are ambitious, which, if within reasonable bounds, does good rather than harm; but I think that during General Burnside's command of the army you have taken counsel of your ambition and thwarted him as much as you could, in which you did a great wrong to the country, and to a most meritorious and honorable brother officer. I have heard in such way as to believe it, of your recently saying that both the army and the government needed a dictator. Of course, it was not for this, but in spite of it, that I have given you the command. Only those generals who win successes can set up as dictators. What I now ask of you is military success, and I will risk the dictatorship. The government will support you to the utmost of its ability, which is neither more nor less than it has done and will do for all commanders. I much fear that the spirit which you have aided to infuse into the army of criticizing their commander and withholding confidence from him, will now turn on you. I shall assist you as far as I can to put it down. Neither you nor Napoleon, if he were alive again, could get any good out of an army while such a spirit prevails in it.
>
>   And now, beware of rashness—beware of rashness; but with energy and sleepless vigilance go forward and give us victories.
>
> Yours very truly,
A. Lincoln[3]

Despite Lincoln's misgivings, Hooker proved a particularly gifted administrator moving immediately to address the many problems besetting his army, not the least of which was its flagging morale. He reorganized the quartermaster and commissary departments ensuring that veteran troops received new uniforms, more and better provisions including fresh vegetables became available, new equipment was provided to those whose original issues had worn out, foul weather gear was distributed, and back pay soon arrived. New hospitals were established for the sick and wounded and sanitary facilities were improved to reduce debilitating diseases while a new furlough system aided the recovery of morale. Officers suspected of being deficient were ordered before an examining board to determine whether they ought to remain in the service, and for those who did remain Hooker instituted a "Tactical School" based on Casey's *Infantry Tactics* with field officers required to attend. To promote unit pride he ordered that regiments record the names of their engagements on their colors, instituted a system of corps and division badges for easy recognition, and implemented a system of recognizable corps and division flags. These reforms, combined with President Lincoln announcing an amnesty for all deserters who returned to their units by April 1, led to an improvement in morale and a corresponding decline in the desertion rate. In another significant move, he created a Bureau of Military Information, the first centralized military intelligence organization, under the leadership of Col. George H. Sharpe. "In truth," Maj. Gen. Oliver Otis Howard remarked, "during February, March, and April, the old cheerful, hopeful, trustful spirit which had carried us through so many dark days, through so many bloody fields and trying defeats, returned to the Army of the Potomac."[4]

Gen. Joseph Hooker enjoyed a good repute as a military leader, but his reputation was tarnished by constant criticism of his superiors (Library of Congress).

With his army restored to fighting order, and an influx of reinforcements, by the end of April Hooker could count on 123,000 troops for the next campaign. His opponent, Robert E. Lee, likewise spent the brief respite in early spring to add to his depleted force, rest, and bring in new supplies of food, ammunition, and other material, at least as much as the Confederacy could at this point supply. The South, already suffering from shortages of critical supplies and provisions, found it difficult to provide for all of the army's needs. Having been in place near Fredericksburg for several months, Lee's commissaries experienced increasing difficulty locating sufficient provisions to feed the troops. He considered relocating to the Shenandoah Valley to feed his army, but feared that if Hooker chose not to follow him the way to Richmond would be wide open. In an attempt to ease the shortages, Lee sent Longstreet to southern Virginia with two divisions to bring in supplies from neighborhoods thus far spared the locust-like foraging of armies moving through their towns and over their fields. By mid–April, Lee had only about 61,000 men occupying essentially the same positions they did above and below Fredericksburg that they held since the previous December, keeping an eye

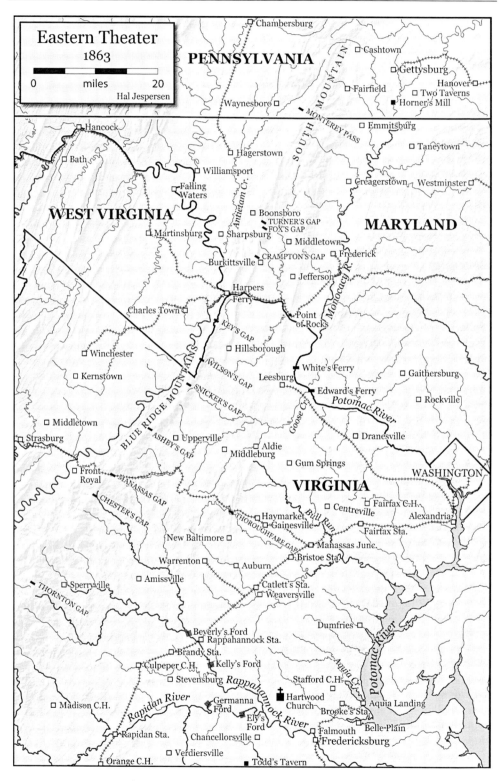

The Eastern Theater of operations (Hal Jespersen).

on the Federal army still holding the town of Fredericksburg with most of it encamped on the opposite side of the Rappahannock River.

Hooker, having witnessed in person the bloody futility of attacking the heights above Fredericksburg, decided on a reprise of the plan that Burnside had originally proposed for his ill-fated "Mud March." Leaving some of his troops in town to hold Lee's attention, Hooker planned to lead three corps off toward the west, beyond sight of the Confederates, to cross the Rappahannock upriver and circle in behind Lee's position. If successful, Lee would be caught between the two Union wings, forced to hastily withdraw south or come out from his prepared positions to engage Hooker's larger army in the open field. At the same time he planned to dispatch his cavalry force under Brig. Gen. George Stoneman on a wide flanking sweep to the west to circle in far behind Lee's position to cut off the Rebel supply and communication lines, further confusing the Confederate leadership and isolating Lee's army from intelligence and assistance from Richmond. Injudiciously, a self-satisfied Hooker is said to have remarked, "My plans are perfect, and when I start to carry them out, may God have mercy on General Lee, for I will have none."[5]

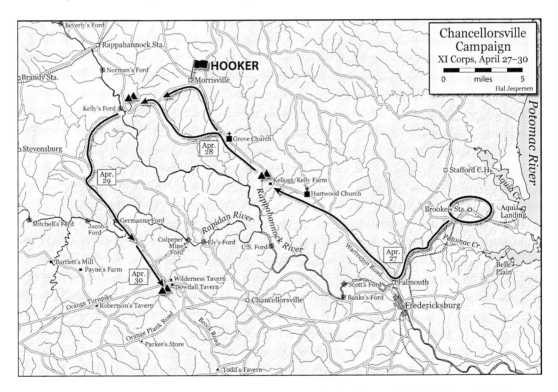

Hooker planned to swing part of his army west to come in behind Lee at Fredericksburg (Hal Jespersen).

Incessant rain and its attending mud intervened to delay Stoneman's cavalry, much as it had Burnside in January. But by the end of April the weather began to clear. Hooker set his infantry in motion on the 27th, moving west with the Fifth, Eleventh, and Twelfth Corps, roughly 42,000 men. Over the next three days they crossed the Rappahannock on a pontoon bridge at Kelly's Ford, turned south, then crossed the Rapidan River at

Germanna Ford to arrive in the vicinity of a house near a small crossroads with the over-stated name of Chancellorsville. Entirely satisfied that his plans were unfolding exactly as he envisioned, Hooker issued General Orders No. 47 to congratulate his men on their accomplishments.

> It is with heartfelt satisfaction the commanding general announces to the army that the operations of the last three days have determined that our enemy must either ingloriously fly, or come out from behind his defenses and give us battle on our own ground, where certain destruction awaits him.
>
> The operations of the Fifth, Eleventh, and Twelfth Corps have been a succession of splendid achievements.
>
> By command of Major-General Hooker:
S. Williams,
Assistant Adjutant General[6]

Although Lee was initially caught napping, he did not long remain unaware that Hooker's army was in motion. But the reports were confusing. Clearly preparations were being made for something in his immediate front as troops appeared to be repositioning in and around Fredericksburg, as well as on the far bank of the Rappahannock. Yet at the same time vague reports reached him of blue-clad troops on the march off to the west. Was this a feint to distract his attention from a renewal of the previous December's attacks on Marye's Heights or the lower lands to the south of town? Or were the preparations he was seeing in and around the town preparations for a move somewhere else? Or perhaps a feint in themselves? Which of these options was Hooker pursuing? Or was there yet something else? By April 29 Lee was becoming convinced that Hooker was intending to turn his flank, sending President Jefferson Davis on that same day a message in which he speculated that Hooker's intention was to turn the Confederate left. He requested reinforcements to meet the challenge, while at the same time ordering one division west to investigate and block the Orange Turnpike, the main road connecting the "Wilderness" area around Chancellorsville with Lee's rear at Fredericksburg. Led by Maj. Gen. Richard H. Anderson of South Carolina, the division dug in near Tabernacle Church about three miles short of the crossroads. By the following day Lee had received additional intelligence from his cavalry scouts under Maj. Gen. Jeb Stuart which, together with the relative inactivity of the Federals around Fredericksburg, convinced him that Anderson would be facing Hooker's main effort. With this, he left only some 9,000 men under Maj. Gen. Jubal Early to hold the defenses outside town while as quietly as possible removing the balance of his men and sending the rest to join Anderson's thin screening force.

Early morning on May 1 found Hooker prepared to seize the initiative. He ordered an advance along the Orange Plank Road toward Fredericksburg by the Fifth and Twelfth Corps with the Eleventh in support. They were to be joined by the newly arrived Second Corps in reserve with the Third Corps due to begin arriving at any time. Shortly the two forces engaged. The battle swayed back and forth, with some Federal units having to briefly withdraw because they had moved forward faster than those on their flank. Without waiting for further reports, Hooker, against the advice of his generals, ordered his units to retire to their original positions. By doing this he surrendered the initiative while making some of his own officers and men question whether this was to be another unhappy ending to all of the optimism with which the movement began. By way of explanation he sent a message that evening to his corps commanders: "The major general commanding trusts that a suspension in the attack to-day will embolden the enemy to attack him."[7]

That evening Lee was planning exactly what Hooker sought. During the twilight he met with Stonewall Jackson near the junction of the Plank Road and the Furnace Road. Relying on intelligence from local citizens and soldiers who lived in the area, the two developed a plan to outflank Hooker's position. To accomplish this, Jackson was to lead the bulk of the Confederate forces, some 33,000 men, south along a dirt road leading through Catharine Furnace, then turn west along a newly cut trail through the dense wilderness area, finally turning north once they were clear of the Federal flank. On arrival at their destination, Jackson planned to deploy his men to hit Hooker in the flank and rear with as many men as he could bring into action. While the Confederate leaders planned, within the Union lines officers did some minor rearranging of units and the men bedded down for the night, everyone assuming that the next day would bring a renewal of the conflict.

As dawn broke on May 2, the Federal position began with the Fifth Corps anchored on the Rappahannock, followed on the right by the Second, Twelfth, Third and Eleventh Corps, in that order. Holding the far right was Maj. Gen. Oliver Otis Howard[8] commanding the Eleventh Corps. About 43 percent of its men were enlisted in regiments that were predominantly German, either by birth or by ancestry, which unfortunately set them apart from much of the rest of the army because of the prevailing nativist prejudice against immigrants rampant at the time. They did not appreciate Howard's appointment to replace the popular German Franz Sigel, or the fact that he displaced another German, Carl Schurz, who was in temporary command. Howard's excessive Christian zeal further alienated many, Germans and "Americans" alike. The marriage between commander and men was not altogether a happy one.

The three division commanders were Brig. Gen. Charles Devens, Brig. Gen. Adolf von Steinwehr, and Maj. Gen. Carl Schurz.[9] The corps was deployed along the Orange Turnpike from the Dowdall tavern, about a mile west of Chancellorsville, west for another mile into the wilderness where it turned perpendicularly to the north forming a right angle to protect the open flank. Although there was a full brigade in reserve, and each of the divisions had two or three regiments held slightly behind the line in reserve, the far right flank was exceptionally weak. Only two regiments actually faced west along with two guns from one of the artillery batteries. There were no entrenchments. Where the line ended there was a gap of two miles north to the Rapidan River that was completely unguarded. Hooker rode over to inspect the Eleventh Corps line early in the morning. His chief of staff asked Howard to make some small adjustments to his line and later sent him a positive order:

May 2, 1863, 9:30 a.m.
  I am directed by the Major General commanding to say, that the disposition you have made of your Corps, has been with a view to a front attack by the enemy. If he should throw himself on your flank, he wishes you to examine the ground and determine upon the position you will take in that event, in order that you may be prepared for him in whatever direction he advances. He suggests that you have heavy reserves well in hand to meet this contingency. The right of your line does not appear to be strong enough. No artificial defenses worth naming have been thrown up; and there appears to be a scarcity of troops at that point, and not, in the General's opinion, as favorably posted as might be. We have good reason to suppose that the enemy is moving to our right. Please advance your pickets, for purposes of observation, as far as may be safe, in order to obtain timely information of their approach."

James Van Alen
B.G. and A.D.[10]

During the morning Maj. Gen. Daniel Sickles,[11] commanding the Third Corps, observed from his headquarters a line of Confederate troops and wagons heading off toward the west or southwest. Sickles was aggressive and personally brave. When the rebel move was observed he quickly asked permission to advance his corps to attack the Confederates while they were strung out in line of march. Hooker appears to have been less inclined to do so but eventually acquiesced to Sickles's requests.

As the morning progressed, reports began to arrive at division and Eleventh Corps headquarters that rebel troops had been seen marching across the front of their position toward the west which, of course, is where the Union flank rested. Reports arrived first from von Steinwehr's division on the corps' left, then progressively Schurz in the center and Devens on the right. It was clear to almost everyone that the gray infantry was moving west and that the Union right flank, protected by only two guns and two regiments, was not in a defensible condition. Nevertheless, Howard, who appears to have concluded that the Confederates were retreating toward their supply base at Gordonsville, ignored both the reports of his own officers and the order from Hooker to tend to his exposed flank.

By the time the Third Corps advanced most of Jackson's column had passed. The Federals met a rear guard and some limited fighting erupted. Sickles called on Howard for reinforcements in case the fight escalated, but Howard was reluctant to weaken his own force. Eventually Hooker ordered Howard to comply and the latter dispatched his only reserve brigade to Sickles's assistance, choosing to accompany it in person as did the division commander, von Steinwehr, rather than remain with his corps. Before departing, he ordered the corps to prepare dinner since he anticipated an early start in the morning in pursuit of the "retreating" rebels. His actions left his corps in a largely untenable position, with no reserve force at hand, and without its commanding officer in the minutes leading up to Jackson's assault on his weak right flank. He only returned to his headquarters a precious few minutes before the tidal wave broke.

Around 5:30 p.m. Jackson had his men deployed on the Eleventh Corps flank, some 33,000 men poised to descend on 9,500 defenders with no serious entrenchments who had been ordered to stand down for dinner. Sometime around 6:00 p.m., or perhaps a few minutes before, Jackson ordered his host forward. The result was predictable. In naval warfare the classical maneuver that every admiral longed for but few achieved was "crossing the T"; that is, placing your ships in line ahead of or behind and enemy so that all of the guns of your ships could bear on the enemy but only the forward or rear guns of the enemy could bear on you. Long lines of Confederate infantry overlapped the two regiments holding the end of the line on both flanks, creating exactly this configuration but on land. Taking the Federal line in front, flank, and sometimes the rear with a devastating crossfire, Jackson's men were in a position to roll up the entire defensive line. The initial brigade that was hit fought briefly, then retreated, in the process making it difficult for the next unit it line to change front to face the attack. Brigade after brigade, like a series of individual dominoes, found itself outflanked with each Union brigade in turn forced to fight several rebel brigades because of the nature of the attack. Devens held out briefly. Schurz, with a few minutes to prepare, put up a spirited defense behind which some of Devens' men rallied, but with both flanks turned was forced to retire. The corps made another stand at some rifle pits at the left flank where the reserve brigade should have been, but had been withdrawn to support Sickles. This position also held for a while until it too was turned on both flanks. A mile of dense wilderness separated the corps from its nearest supports. None reached it at all during this unequal fight.

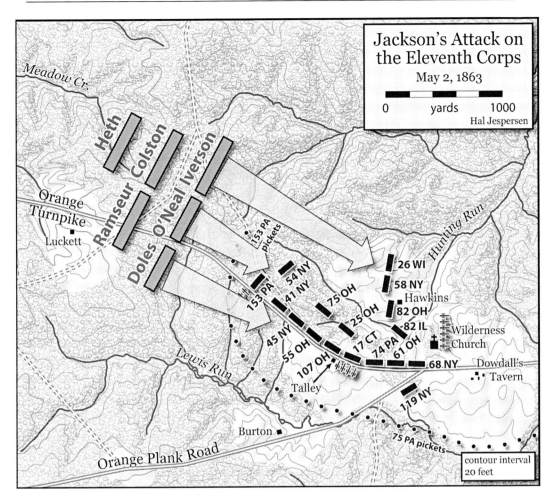

Jackson's attack on the Union right rolled up the flank despite determined resistance by the soldiers (Hal Jespersen).

Finally, it retired to some breastworks dug by the Twelfth Corps the previous day where most of it rallied to be joined by some regiments from other corps and this last line fronting Chancellorsville held as night descended to end the fighting.

May 2 was a resounding Federal defeat caused primarily by Howard's failure to prepare his corps for defense and his failure to heed the numerous warnings and direct orders that he was given. Nevertheless, May 2 was not the end of the engagement. On the following day he had available to him under his immediate command more than 75,000 men. Opposing him were little more than 40,000 Confederates. Not only did Hooker outnumber his opponent, he had both flanks firmly anchored on the Rapidan and Rappahannock Rivers with sufficient troops to secure his entire defensive perimeter. Despite these advantages, Hooker once more chose to remain on the defensive despite the fact that he held a position from which he could readily attack Lee's overmatched right flank. Instead, Lee continued to operate on the offensive, capturing the substantial breastworks constructed by the Twelfth Corps and driving Hooker's men from their advanced positions. May 4 was essentially a repeat of the previous day with Hooker remaining on the defensive, calling for Maj. Gen. John Sedgwick, commanding the Sixth Corps at Fredericksburg, to attack the rebels in his front and drive through to unite with the rest of the army under Hooker's direct command. This time, judging correctly that Hooker did not intend an advance, Lee sent a portion of his command east to confront Sedgwick's Sixth Corps inching its way west from Fredericksburg. Jackson having been mortally wounded the previous evening, Lee left Stuart with 25,000 troops to contain Hooker's 75,000. "Fighting Joe" obliged by remaining idle. Finally, when the rains began on May 5, fearing that the river at his back would rise to prevent any escape, Hooker ordered his army to retreat back across the rivers to safety. The retreat began in great haste, under a drenching rain, on the morning of May 6.

Tactically, the Battle of Chancellorsville was certainly a Confederate victory. Lee, after some initial confusion on Federal intentions, seized the initiative and consistently kept it, defeating Hooker's design to clamp him in a vice between two Northern pincers. Strategically, it must also be recorded in the Southern column. Lee completely frustrated Hooker's grand design for the campaign. Politically, the results would reverberate through both capitals, in Washington and Richmond, and set the groundwork for the next great eastern campaign. In the short run, it would naturally provide yet another boost to the antiwar, anti–Lincoln forces in the North.

Losses in the campaign were once again frightfully heavy on both sides.

	North	South
Effectives	123,000	61,000
Killed	1,606	1,665
Wounded	9,672	9,081
Missing	5,919	2,018
Total	17,197	12,764
Percent Lost	14.0	20.9

Noah Brooks was with President Lincoln when a telegram arrived announcing Hooker's retreat from Chancellorsville. Brooks noted that the president looked "ashen" as he read its contents, his demeanor "piteous. Never, as long as I knew him, did he seem to be so broken up, so dispirited, and so ghostlike. Clasping his hands behind his back, he walked up and down the room, saying, 'My God, my God, what will the country say! What will the country say!'"[12]

The Effect

The spring campaigns of 1863 largely renewed the previous trend in the two theaters of operation. In the west, Grant continued to hold the initiative, moving resignedly south with his sights set on the major prize, reducing Vicksburg. In the process he accomplished one of the most masterful marches of the war, bypassing the city, landing below it, and crushing Confederate potential for interfering with his movement on Vicksburg before the rebels could mount any serious defense. The advent of summer found him with a vice-like grip on the city, prepared for a lengthy siege. In the east, yet another Federal general promised much but accomplished little except ever-lengthening additions to the unprecedented human toll.

Politically, the most important event of the spring was the final issuing of the Emancipation Proclamation and the beginning of its enforcement in areas seized by the Union army. Yet that was not the only development. Another important political event was the transformation of the western counties of Virginia into a new state. There was a traditional political divide between the backcountry area and the coastal area throughout the South during the colonial era when those divorced from immediate contact with the lowland centers of political power felt ignored. This was exacerbated by the social and economic differences between the two regions. In the coastal area society, the economy, and politics were all dominated by a wealthy planter class supported by commercial agriculture requiring large amounts of slave labor. In the backcountry the average person was a subsistence farmer; society usually revolved around small towns or ethnic/religious affiliation and there was little political influence except on a very local level. The percentage of slaves was minimal in these western counties of the state. These differences were clearly reflected in Richmond on April 17, 1861, when the representatives of the backcountry areas voted 30–17 against the Ordinance of Session, with two abstentions. With the adoption of the Ordinance, 425 disaffected representatives from 25 Virginia counties met in Wheeling on May 13 to discuss options.

Ten days later the statewide referendum on secession voted to confirm Virginia's plan to leave the Union, but the western counties voted 34,677 to 19,121 *against* secession. On June 11, a second gathering in Wheeling declared the secession convention and vote to be illegal, as well as arguing that those government officials who favored secession had effectively relinquished their offices and ought to be replaced. On June 19, the meeting adopted a plan for a "Restored Government of Virginia" and elected a new governor. The end result was that two governments now claimed to represent the state, one in Wheeling and one in Richmond. Although representatives broached the idea of joining the Union as a new state to be named Kanawha, there were Constitutional difficulties that first had to be overcome. Article IV, Section 3, clearly stated that "no new State shall be formed or erected within the Jurisdiction of any other State; nor any State be formed by the Junction of two or more States, or parts of States, without the Consent of the Legislatures of the States concerned as well as of the Congress." Virginia, of course, did not consent. But was it now legally a state? Having voted for secession and declared itself to be out of the Union, was it not true that it had abrogated any claim to the Constitutional protections afforded to states? The other interesting complication is that President Lincoln claimed that secession was illegal. The states had not left the Union, he maintained, they were only in rebellion. If that was true, then Virginia had to consent to any reduction in its territory. But Congress argued that although secession was illegal, the South had done it, had left the Union and was now not entitled to the perquisites reserved for states.

In a canvass taken in the western counties in October 1861, 18,408 people voted in favor of creating a new state while only 781 opposed the proposition. However, opponents questioned the legality of the vote since most of the legal voting residents of the counties did not participate, and in fact the majority of votes came only from people who cast them in an around Wheeling since the balance of the counties were at least loosely occupied by Virginia state troops. In November a meeting clearly under Union control drafted a state constitution. Further organization took place during 1862 leading to a formal application for admission to statehood submitted to Congress on December 31. Congress approved the admission on March 26, 1863, and on April 20 Lincoln approved the measure to take effect June 20. With this, West Virginia came into existence as the 35th state, a result of secession from secession.

Politics aside, the continuing war required from both sides more money and more men, while legal issues began to arise questioning the nature of the conflict itself. On

February 25 the Federal Congress addressed the first issue with passage of the National Banking Act. Lacking a central national bank, the North found it difficult to raise the funds necessary to prosecute the war and the confusing system of state and private banks, which issued an estimated 10,000 different types of currency, made finance all the more difficult. To solve this problem Congress enacted a tax of 2 percent on currency issued by state and private banks which quickly led to their removal from circulation. At the same time it created a system of "national" banks by which banks that purchased 33 percent of their capital in government bonds could then issue their own loans for up to 90 percent of the value of those bonds using them as collateral. This proved popular and led to a flood of new "national" banks because they could then in effect accrue double interest on the same money: interest from the federal government on the bonds and from those who borrowed money based on the notes they issued with the bonds as security. This also largely solved the problem the government was experiencing in obtaining loans through the sale of bonds. This was by far the primary means the North used to finance its war effort.

To address manpower needs, Congress adopted the tool the Confederacy had resorted to the previous year, enacting the Conscription Act on March 3. Under the law, all males between the ages of 18 and 45 were eligible to be drafted for compulsory service in the armed forces. Calls for more troops would continue to be apportioned by state. What was controversial about the new law was its provisions for exemptions. Politicians, railroad engineers, and other people occupying positions deemed essential to the war effort were not eligible for conscription, while there were also provisions allowing people to purchase the service of substitutes should they be called to service or to buy an outright exemption for $300. Since the average unskilled factory worker in the North in 1863 commanded a wage of about $120 per year, the sum required for exemption was far beyond the normal means of the average worker, much less the average farmer or farm laborer. This created considerable opposition which rallied around the slogan "Rich Man's War, Poor Man's Fight." Among those who purchased substitutes were John D. Rockefeller and Grover Cleveland. This became an issue when Cleveland ran for the presidency in 1880, until it was found that his opponent James G. Blaine had also hired a substitute.

Voluntary enlistments would of course reduce the number required to be conscripted. By 1862, as the ready supply of volunteers began to dry up, counties, states, and later the federal government began offering bounties to men who would voluntarily enlist. One of the results of the draft was not so much the total number conscripted, but the fact that it spurred voluntary enlistments. Those who were drafted received no bounty at all, while those who volunteered did, and this could reach as high as $200 or even $300. Rather than take the chance of awaiting the draft and getting nothing but the $13 monthly salary of a private, many men were encouraged to volunteer to receive the substantial bounty payment. The practice of paying bounties for enlistment also led to a profitable scam, at least for those who were successful. This was "bounty jumping." A person could enlist in one state and collect a bounty, sneak off before his unit left for the war, then enlist in another state and claim the bounty there also. This could be repeated as many times as the nerves, and luck, of the individual held. Then, with money in hand the perpetrator could escape to the vast expanse of the American west to evade prosecution, or to Canada. It has been estimated that some 50,000 men, whether bounty jumpers or not, fled west or to Canada to avoid the draft.

In fact, the Northern draft actually resulted more in voluntary enlistments than it

Rekruten Verlangt

für das

26. Regiment

Wisc. Volunteers!!

Ver. Staaten Bounty: **$402** für ehrenhaft aus dem Dienst entlassene Veteranen!

$302 für Neue Rekruten!

27 Dollars und eine Monats-Löhnung im Voraus werden bezahlt, wenn die Mannschaft in den Dienst gemustert wird. Löhnung und Beköstigung beginnt vom Tage der Anwerbung.

Jeder Deutscher sollte sich diesem Regimente anschließen.

Rekrutirungs-Office: Vier Thüren oberhalb der Stadt-Halle, an Ostwasserstraße, 7. Ward, Milwaukee.

Druck der „See-Botin."

Recruitment posters for volunteer regiments often emphasized the bounties paid to those who enlisted, money not available to men drafted. This poster for the 26th Wisconsin Infantry was aimed at German immigrants and their sons in the Milwaukee area. Recruited in the early fall of 1862, it offers a bounty of $402 for every veteran who enlists and $302 for new recruits (Wisconsin Historical Society).

did conscripts. Federal data reveal that between 1863 and 1865, 776,829 men had their names called for service. Of these, only 46,347 were actually induced into the service. Data from the Provost Marshal General's Office for the drafts of 1863 and 1864 reveal the following[13]:

Number	Category	Percentage	
776,829	Names Drawn	100.0	
522,187	Examined	67.2	
161,244	Failed to Report	20.8	
93,389	Discharged	12.0	*continued on p. 176*

Number	Category	Percentage
159,403	Physical Exemptions	20.5
156,106	Other Exemptions	20.1
86,724	Paid $300 Commutation Fee	11.2
73,607	Provided Substitute	9.5
46,347	Held to Personal Service	6.0

Aside from the draft, one of the legal issues that rose to the fore in spring of 1863 was a series of actions based on the Northern blockade and the resulting seizure of ships on the high seas. Several of these were consolidated into a single ruling on March 10 by the Supreme Court in the "Prize Cases." The issue was whether the president had the constitutional authority to order the blockade and the seizure of ships without any Congressional declaration of war. In a vote of 5–4, the court ruled that Lincoln did have the requisite authority because several states were in fact in rebellion against the government by virtue of the firing on Fort Sumter and Jefferson Davis's approval of Confederate privateering. It further ruled that a "belligerent," for the purposes of international law, need not be a recognized nation; therefore, in the words of Supreme Court Justice Robert Cooper Grier, "the President was bound to meet [Southern aggression] in the shape it presented itself, without waiting for Congress to baptize it with a name."[14]

Another legal issue arose that spring when, in April, Maj. Gen. Ambrose Burnside,

Clement L. Vallandigham, an Ohio anti-war Democrat, was the leader of the Copperhead faction opposing the Lincoln administration (Library of Congress).

acting as commander of the Department of Ohio, arrested Clement L. Vallandigham who he charged with making disloyal public statements and aiding the rebellion. The former Democratic member of the House of Representatives was tried in a military court, convicted, and sent to prison. Vallandigham filed a writ asking for a review of the case by the Supreme Court, but the court found in Ex Parte Vallandigham in 1864 that it did not have the authority to review the finding of a military court. In the meantime, Lincoln commuted the sentence to banishment to the South, but Vallandigham managed to make his way from the South to Canada from where he continued to issue statements and political tracts.

For the Confederate Congress, the spring of 1863 brought the same financial difficulties its Northern counterpart was wrestling to address along with dangerously rising inflation and a critical shortage of basic food. Because of its massive printing of paper money—

by the end of the war it would reach more than $1.5 billion—the value of a Confederate dollar which was about 90 cents in 1861 had already dipped to a mere 29 cents, and would decline further to less than 1.7 cents by spring of 1865. Morale declined with the drop in the value of money and the attending high inflation which hurt everyone, but especially the lower economic class and those on fixed incomes. In March and April the scarcities, coupled with the high cost of existing food and the salt needed to preserve meat, led mobs in several cities in Alabama, Georgia, and North Carolina to attack food storage warehouses and in some cases loot the shops of local merchants to obtain food for their families. In Richmond, thousands of women took to the streets on April 2 where they broke into warehouses containing food and ransacked stores for food, clothing, shoes, and other necessities. The local militia had to be called up to put down the disturbance.

Richmond responded to the challenge in April with its own internal revenue act. The legislation enacted a progressive income tax, a 10 percent tax on the profits of whole-sale businesses, and an 8 percent tax on a list of products and professional licenses. Given the shortage of provisions for both civilians and soldiers alike, one stipulation of the law placed a 10 percent tax on agricultural produce which was to be paid in kind. One very unpopular part of the law exempted some of the more profitable plantation lands from the taxes which only reinforced the idea that the poor were being made to bear the burden of a war to benefit the rich. Throughout the war the Confederacy was left with the equally painful choices of either deploying badly needed manpower to try to collect taxes or simply foregoing the collection which only worsened its financial crisis.

The one monetary achievement the South enjoyed that spring was the successful sale of $15 million in bonds, backed by cotton, to the banking firm of Emile Erlanger & Company in Paris. Even here, the bonds were heavily discounted. The bank purchased them at a 23 percent discount and also received a 5 percent commission for selling them; thus, the discount in practical terms was 28 percent. In the end, the $15 million sale yielded only about $6 million to the Confederate treasury. With the continuing lack of hard money in the South, the printing presses never ceased rolling, fueling runaway inflation that reached an estimated 6,000 percent by the end of the war.

The other major legislation by the Confederate Congress in the spring of 1863 was in response to the Emancipation Proclamation and the beginning of organized Federal attempts to recruit soldiers of African ancestry from among both the free population of the North and slaves who escaped to Union lines. On May 1, the Southern Congress adopted a resolution, portions of which read as follows:

Sec. 4. That every white person, being a commissioned officer, or acting as such, who, during the present war, shall command negroes or mulattoes in arms against the confederate States, or who shall arm, train, organize, or prepare negroes or mulattoes for military service against the confederate States, or who shall voluntarily aid negroes or mulattoes in any military enterprise, attack, or conflict in such service, shall be deemed as inciting servile insurrection, and shall, if captured, be put to death, or be otherwise punished at the discretion of the court.

Sec 5. Every person, being a commissioned officer, or acting as such in the service of the enemy, who shall, during the present war, excite, attempt to excite or cause to be excited servile insurrection, or who shall incite or cause to be incited a slave to rebel, shall, if captured, be put to death, or be otherwise punished at the discretion of the court.

Sec. 7. All negroes and mulattoes who shall be engaged in war or taken in arms against the confederate States, or shall give aid or comfort to the enemies of the Confederate States, shall, when captured in the Confederate States, be delivered to the authorities of the State or States in which they shall be captured, to be dealt with according to the present or future laws of such State or States.[15]

The intent was clearly to stop the recruitment and training of African soldiers and the encouragement of slave rebellions in the belief that freedom was at hand. Its actual effect on the Northern war effort or the enlistment of African troops proved negligible.

Summer

THE WEST

The most important issue to be decided in the west in the summer of 1863 was the fate of Vicksburg. Jefferson Davis acknowledged this when he wrote that "Vicksburg is the nail head that holds the South's two halves together," while Abraham Lincoln recognized its importance proclaiming that "Vicksburg is the key. The war can never be brought to a close until the key is in our pocket."[16] Given this importance, once Grant settled into a siege of the city those in Washington feared that Gen. Braxton Bragg, commanding the Army of Tennessee, around 45,000 men in the hills of central Tennessee, might either send troops to oppose Grant or perhaps even march his entire army to Vicksburg's relief. To prevent this, Halleck ordered Maj. Gen. William S. Rosecrans to put his 55,000-man Army of the Cumberland in motion, make contact with Bragg, and prevent him from detaching any troops to assist Pemberton and Johnston in Mississippi. Though at first reluctant to move, Rosecrans finally did so on June 24. When he did, he completely outmaneuvered Bragg who found himself abandoning successive positions at Shelbyville and Tullahoma, finally taking up positions around Lookout Mountain outside Chattanooga. In his especially well-conducted campaign, Rosecrans had driven Bragg from middle Tennessee at the loss of less than 600 men, while at the same time preventing him from detaching any of his troops to assist in the relief of Vicksburg.

While Rosecrans held Bragg's attention, Grant sent a division to hold the Big Black River to protect his rear from forces Johnston was hastily gathering at Canton for a possible relief effort. On June 10 the Ninth Corps was added to Grant's command allowing him to use this force to block any attempt by Johnston. A rebel attempt west of the Mississippi to cut Grant's supply line failed when Southerners were unable to overrun the garrison of largely black troops at Milliken's Bend on June 7. Attempts by Johnston and Pemberton to communicate via messenger were often interrupted by the capture of the couriers. On at least one occasion Johnston's staff entrusted an important message to Pemberton to the care of a Union spy who immediately delivered it to Grant. As early as June 15 Johnston informed President Davis that he thought any attempt to relieve Vicksburg would be fruitless.

On June 25 and again on July 1 Grant exploded mines in an attempt to breach the Confederate defensive works, but neither produced an opening significant enough to exploit. Aside from these efforts, the siege continued day after day with Federal bombardments. Within the city, food supplies dwindled. The constant bombardment of the city drove people into caves carved in the hills and cliffs. Malnutrition began to take a toll on health among both civilians and soldiers alike. By the end of June estimates are that as much as half of Pemberton's command were in no shape to so much as attempt a breakout and people were reduced to eating rats, vermin, and shoe leather. On July 3 Pemberton finally sent a flag of truce to Grant to discuss terms of a surrender. The formal capitulation came the following day, July 4. Johnston, by then at Jackson, withdrew east on July 16. By any definition the tactical, strategic, and political results of the campaign and siege were major Union successes. Losses in killed and wounded for the entire campaign numbered 10,142 Federals and 9,091 rebels. To this should be added 29,495 Confederates who Pemberton surrendered along with 237 guns. It was the second complete Confederate army that Grant had surrounded and captured in its entirety. It would not be the last.

The loss of Vicksburg effectively cut the Confederacy into two pieces, depriving the east of the manpower reserves and the vital agricultural and livestock production west of the river. The damage to Southern morale was almost as great. From their positions in Tennessee, the Mississippi Valley, and New Orleans, the entire heartland of the remaining western Confederacy was open to invasion whenever and wherever the North chose. Pemberton, a Northerner, came under suspicion for surrendering on the North's national holiday and never held another major field command. When the news came, Lincoln happily announced that "the Father of Waters again goes unvexed to the sea." He then wrote to Grant: "I do not remember that you and I ever met personally. I write this now as a grateful acknowledgment for the almost inestimable service you have done the country. I wish to say a word further.... When you got below [Vicksburg], and took Port Gibson, Grand Gulf, and vicinity, I thought you should go down the river and join Gen. Banks; and when you turned Northward East of the Big Black, I feared it was a mistake. I now wish to make the personal acknowledgment that you were right, and I was wrong."[17] The president had finally found himself a general.

THE EAST

The summer of 1863 found the main armies in the east in all too familiar positions. The Army of the Potomac was attempting to recover from yet another major defeat, perhaps this time the most shocking of all given the size, strength, and initial successful movements of the Union host. On the other side of the opposing picket lines Lee was once again planning how best to retain the initiative. In view of the mounting losses in the west, some military and political figures in the South proposed moving part of the Army of Northern Virginia to the western theater to bolster the sagging fortunes of the Confederacy's armies in that theater. A few even suggested sending Lee himself west to restore Southern defenses and drive the invaders out of the South. Lee, wedded emotionally to his home state, would never agree to move west himself, but he did fear the reduction of his own command to provide reinforcements to the west. With this in mind he began devising a plan that would make immediate use of his own army, thereby precluding its reduction, while at the same time offering some hope of relief to the hard-pressed rebel armies in the west.

Lee proposed nothing less than a second invasion of the North, essentially a reprise of the original plan frustrated by the heavy losses at Antietam. The purposes of the movement remained largely the same. Lee reasoned, as before, that he could obtain much needed supplies and recruits in Maryland, provide encouragement for the Northern anti-war effort, influence European nations to greater support and perhaps even recognition for the Confederacy, and lastly, a new wrinkle, to relieve the siege of Vicksburg by forcing Washington to withdraw troops from the west to oppose a successful Southern invasion in the east.

To prepare for the invasion Lee had first to reorganize and reinforce his army. The loss of Stonewall Jackson left Lee with only one tested corps commander, Maj. Gen. James

Longstreet. Rather than simply appoint a replacement for Jackson, Lee chose a reorganization of his army into three corps rather than two in the hopes of creating more flexibility while still maintaining a more powerful force structure than each of the individual Union corps. To achieve general symmetry, Lee moved some of his units about to roughly balance the size of the commands. Maj. Gen. Richard H. Anderson's division was transferred from Longstreet's command to the new Third Corps along with Hill's old division which had been under Jackson's command. To these was added a newly-created division under Maj. Gen. Henry Heth of Virginia containing the brigades of Col. J. M. Brockenbrough and Brig. Gen. James J. Archer from Maryland along with a brigade transferred from North Carolina under Brig. Gen. J. Johnston Pettigrew and a Mississippi brigade under Brig. Gen. Joseph R. Davis, the president's nephew.

Gen. James Longstreet was Lee's senior and most trusted corps commander as the Gettysburg Campaign began (Library of Congress).

To lead the two new corps Lee arranged the promotion of Richard S. Ewell[18] to lieutenant general to head the Second Corps and similarly supported the promotion of Ambrose Powell Hill[19] to the same rank to command the Third Corps. Thus, as the new campaign began, the Army of Northern Virginia was in the hands of an experienced, successful commanding officer and three equally experienced and successful subordinates responsible for the three infantry corps. The cavalry continued to function under its veteran leader, Maj. Gen. Jeb Stuart.

Lee's plan was much like the operation he undertook in September 1862, beginning only farther south than that effort. To guard against any surprise move south by Hooker, Lee left Hill's corps at Fredericksburg to keep up the subterfuge that his army was still there and to block the way south. Hill would follow once it was apparent that Hooker did not intend to move on Richmond. Beginning on June 3, Lee started to shift Ewell's and Longstreet's corps west to the Shenandoah Valley, then north using the Blue Ridge Mountains to screen their movement into Maryland. From there they would continue north into Pennsylvania taking a position from which the army could menace Harrisburg, Philadelphia, Baltimore, and Washington. This would require the North to divide its forces to cover these politically sensitive locations and, under pressure from the public, press, and politicians, compel the Army of the Potomac to come out into the open where Lee hoped to once again administer a thrashing.

Smarting from his recent defeat, Joseph Hooker was also obliged to adapt to changes in his own army. By the end of May about 27,000 men, over 20 percent of Hooker's army, who had originally enlisted for two years would be free to head home to be mustered out of the service. By the time the new campaign began his available force had shrunk to no more than 90,000 men, while Lee's, after bringing in reinforcements from farther south, had grown to 75,000. But before the campaign began, Hooker had to determine both his own plan and anticipate what Lee might do. When he became aware from his pickets on June 5 that rebel forces appeared to be on the move, Hooker ordered Maj. Gen. John Sedgwick with his Sixth Corps to probe the lines in front of him at Fredericksburg. The move led to an immediate, yet minor, firefight that incorrectly convinced Hooker that Lee's army was still there in force.

In response to his scouts' reports of a Confederate movement west, Hooker also dispatched a large cavalry force under Brig. Gen. Alfred Pleasonton, supported by infantry, to move west to discover what was happening. For once, it was the Federals who caught the rebels napping. Stuart had drawn in his command near Brandy Station for a massive review before leading the cavalrymen north to screen's Lee's movement. This was probably not a good idea on the eve of the campaign, with troops already in motion, and especially as near to the front lines as the review took place. But Stuart enjoyed the opportunity to show off his command to the local population and, of course, the Union horsemen had yet to prove their mettle against Stuart's proficient command. In this case, overconfidence coupled with minimal security precautions proved Stuart's undoing. On the early morning of June 9, Pleasonton moved his command forward in two large pincers, crossing the Rappahannock River at Beverly's Ford and Kelly's Ford, respectively, north and south of Stuart's position. His advance caught Stuart's men completely by surprise. In an engagement that rolled back and forth for ten hours, Stuart finally forced Pleasonton to withdraw. Losses are generally believed to have been about 523 for the Confederates and 936 (including 486 captured) for the Union. Despite this disparity, the spirited engagement is said by most historians to mark a turning point where Federal cavalry came increasingly to be as effective as its Southern counterpart. The surprise also proved an embarrassment to Stuart, with some historians arguing that it adversely effected his decision-making and conduct on the movement north.

Following the Battle of Brandy Station, Hooker eventually became convinced that Lee did in fact have his army on the move. When this became apparent, he suggested an audacious move. Rather than pursue Lee, he proposed taking advantage of Lee's absence to move the Army of the Potomac south, break through the remaining screen of Confederate troops, then continue south to occupy Richmond before Lee could arrive to save it. Horrified at the thought of Washington being left without Hooker's army to protect it, both Lincoln and Halleck promptly and bluntly vetoed the idea. On June 13 Hooker finally ordered his army to begin the pursuit. The following day, with information that the Federals were withdrawing from Fredericksburg, Hill distributed orders for his own corps to follow in the footsteps of Ewell and Longstreet.

Meanwhile, Ewell, leading the advance down the Shenandoah toward Harpers Ferry, had arrived near Winchester. The Union commander there, Maj. Gen. Robert H. Milroy, asked for directions from Halleck, who responded with "suggestions" but no firm orders. By the time the general-in-chief finally ordered an evacuation on June 14 it was too late. Ewell skillfully maneuvered his command to surround Milroy's force and opened fire on the cornered Federals the same day. Although Milroy ordered a breakout, and succeeded in escaping himself, his command of some 7,000 suffered a severe beating. Ewell reported losses of 269 compared to Milroy who suffered 4,443 casualties including 3,358 captured. Cavalry fights took place at Aldie, Middleburg, and Upperville as Stuart screened the

Confederate march north, while Hooker remained slow to respond. By June 24, Ewell was already in southern Pennsylvania, Longstreet (accompanied by Lee) in Maryland, and Hill was completing his own crossing of the Potomac into Maryland as well. Hooker's army remained completely below the Potomac, except for the Eleventh Corps that began crossing into Maryland far to the east of the Catoctin Mountains that same day. The rest were strung out along Virginia's dirt roads as far south as the Second Corps that was then only a little west of Manassas Junction, still south of Bull Run.

On the same day, June 24, Stuart set a large portion of his cavalry force in motion. In the nineteenth century cavalry were the "eyes and ears" of an army. Stuart was considered the best cavalryman the South had, yet his role in the Gettysburg Campaign became one of the enduring controversies. His original orders from Lee read: "If you find that [Hooker] is moving northward, and that two brigades can guard the Blue Ridge and take care of your rear, you can move with the other three into Maryland and take position on General Ewell's right, place yourself in communication with him, guard his flank and keep him informed of the enemy's movements." The order told Stuart, "You will, however, be able to judge whether you can pass around their army without hindrance, doing them all the damage you can, and cross the river east of the mountains. In either case, after crossing the river, you must move on and feel the right of Ewell's troops, collecting information, provisions, &c."[20] With Hooker's army now on the move north, Stuart exercised the option given him to "pass around" the Union army. No doubt he envisioned a reprise of his successful ride around McClellan on the Peninsula and his embarrassment of Pope during the Second Bull Run Campaign.

What Stuart had not counted on was that Hooker now had his troops moving quickly north. After moving behind most of the marching blue infantry columns he reached Dranesville on the Potomac River only a few miles west of Washington. With Hooker's entire army now between him and Ewell, Stuart had only two realistic options, to retrace his steps or to continue north hoping to get ahead of Hooker and cross to the west to meet Ewell. The first was really not an option since it would require from two to three days to accomplish and still place him far south of Lee's army. He chose to continue moving north through Rockville and Westminster, Maryland, and on into Pennsylvania. He reached Hanover east of Gettysburg on June 30 where he skirmished with Federal cavalry. From there he continued north to York, expecting to find Ewell there, but when he was not Stuart turned west to Carlisle where he had another small skirmish on July 1. The result of this protracted movement around the Union army was that Stuart was unable to reunite with Lee's army at Gettysburg until the afternoon of July 2.

Many writers have concluded that Stuart's ride was an attempt to regain the prestige he believed he had lost by the surprise at Brandy Station and that his actions deprived Lee of the critical "eyes and ears" function that his men should have provided in the days leading up to the confrontation at Gettysburg. However, a review of the surviving written orders from Lee to Stuart suggest that Lee was aware that Stuart might try to ride around the blue host and that he left that decision up to Stuart. Further, Stuart's decision did *not*, as many authors contend, deprive Lee of badly needed cavalry for scouting and communication tasks. In Stuart's report on the campaign he wrote: "I submitted to the commanding general the plan of leaving a brigade or so in my present front, and passing through Hopewell, or some other gap in Bull Run Mountain, attaining the enemy's rear, and passing between his main body and Washington, to cross into Maryland and join our army north of the Potomac."[21] This seems to be confirmed by Lee's own report in which he stated that "in the exercise of the discretion given him when Longstreet and Hill marched into Maryland, General Stuart determined to pass around the rear of the Federal army with three brigades, and cross the Potomac between it and Washington, believing that he would be able by that route to place himself on our right flank in time to keep us properly advised of the enemy's movements."[22] Further, Stuart in fact left about one-half of his available force of 9,600 cavalry behind for Lee's use. He took with him three brigades. He left four brigades behind containing 13 regiments and two batteries. These were all available to Lee had he chosen to use them.

Meanwhile, Hooker was wrestling with his own problems. Charged with protecting Washington and confronting Lee's army, which Lincoln had correctly informed Hooker was to be his main objective and not Richmond, Hooker believed he was not only outnumbered by Lee's army but given orders that could only stretch his available forces even thinner if required to cover all of the objectives given him. Hooker sought reinforcements from Halleck, but the general-in-chief decided not to place other Union troops already located in the general area under his command. On June 26 Hooker suggested abandoning Harpers Ferry which he believed to be threatened and which he also felt he did not have sufficient force to relieve and still face Lee in pitched battle. On the following morning he telegraphed Halleck, "That there may be no misunderstanding as to my force, I would respectfully state that, including the portions of General Heintzelman's command, and General Schenck's, now with me, my whole force of enlisted men for duty will not exceed 105,000. Fourteen batteries of the Artillery Reserve have been sent to Washington. Of General Abercrombie's force, one brigade has just been sent home from expiration of service, and the others go shortly. One brigade of General Crawford's force has not reported with it. I state these facts that there may not be expected of me more than I have material to do with."[23]

Halleck responded to Hooker's suggestion that Harpers Ferry be abandoned on June 27 noting that the fortifications there "have always been regarded as an important point to be held by us, and much expense and labor incurred in fortifying them. I cannot approve their abandonment, except in case of absolute necessity."[24] Angered by what he believed to be a deliberate refusal to provide him with the required flexibility of action and the reinforcements he needed, Hooker sent the following telegram.

> SANDY HOOK, June 27, 1863–1 p.m.
> Maj. Gen. H. W. HALLECK,
> General-in-Chief:
>   My original instructions require me to cover Harper's Ferry and Washington. I have now imposed upon me, in addition, an enemy in my front of more than my number. I beg to be understood, respectfully, but firmly, that I am unable to comply with this condition with the means at my disposal, and earnestly request that I may at once be relieved from the position I occupy.
>   JOSEPH HOOKER,
>   Major-General[25]

This was all the justification that Halleck, who disliked Hooker anyway, needed to quickly accept the proffered resignation.

Less than 72 hours before the opening of the next major engagement the Army of the Potomac was once again in need of a new commanding officer. The choice fell on Maj. Gen. George Gordon Meade.[26] With Meade's elevation, Maj. Gen. George Sykes assumed command of the Fifth Corps.

By the evening of June 30, Lee's infantry was camped in various locations between Heidlersburg north of Gettysburg to Chambersburg west of that town. Meade's forces were similarly dispersed. The First and Eleventh Corps were several miles south of Gettysburg, the former just above the Mason-Dixon line and the latter just south at Emmitsburg, Maryland. The Twelfth and Third Corps were similarly astraddle the state line several miles to the east while the Second, Fifth, and Sixth Corps were all at least a day's march farther to the southeast at Uniontown, Union Mills, and Manchester, respectively, all in Maryland. Upon assuming command, Meade, with his headquarters at Taneytown, Maryland, issued orders to bring the scattered troops together, which they were then in the process of doing, with the intention of occupying a defensive position behind Pipe Creek until Lee's movements and objectives clarified. Lee, once he became aware on June 28 that the Army of the Potomac was much closer than he expected, also began to concentrate his force, ordering Ewell back from his advanced position south

Maj. Gen. George Gordon Meade took command of the Army of the Potomac only three days before one of the most important engagements of the war (National Archives and Records Administration).

of the Susquehanna River near Harrisburg. The initial point of concentration was to be around Cashtown some eight miles west of Gettysburg.

Late on June 30, Brig. Gen. J. Johnston Pettigrew's advance encountered cavalry pickets on the road from Cashtown to Gettysburg. Early on July 1 Hill sent two brigades of Heth's division toward Gettysburg in a reconnaissance in force to ascertain what was there, although none of Hill's general officers believed there was anything in front of them other than a few militia. What Heth ran into was two brigades of Union cavalry under Brig. Gen. John Buford[27] who, anticipating a Confederate advance once his pickets spotted Pettigrew's troops the previous evening, placed his force to cover the roads into Gettysburg from the west and north. This stretched his small command to the point where he deployed barely a heavy skirmish line, but the main roads into town were guarded.

Buford had an excellent eye for terrain and quickly understood the defensive advantages of the ridges west of Gettysburg. With Heth's approach, Buford sent word back to the closest Union infantry, the First Corps, and determined to fight a delaying action until support could arrive. Heth, thinking he was opposed only by some local militia, received a rude awakening when Buford's men opened fire with their carbines and field guns. Surprised by the rebuke, Heth brought up the rest of his division, deployed, and sent in another attack. Buford brought in most of the men of his other brigade that had been deployed north of town and, though slowly driven back, forced Heth to call for reinforcements from the following division of Maj. Gen. William Dorsey Pender. When both rebel divisions came on line they would outnumber Buford's thin screen by some

14,000 infantry to 2,800 cavalrymen. Buford's horsemen had the advantage of rapid-firing breech-loading carbines, but they remained heavily outnumbered, especially when deductions are made for those detached as horse holders (usually one man in four).

Maj. Gen. John Reynolds, a Pennsylvanian by birth and 1837 graduate of the Military Academy, commanded the First Corps encamped several miles south of Gettysburg. He had also been named a "wing commander" by Meade, placing him in charge not only of his own corps but also of the Third Corps under Maj. Gen. Daniel Sickles and the Eleventh Corps led by Maj. Gen. Oliver O. Howard. When news of the fighting arrived,

Maj. Gen. John Reynolds determined to contest the Confederate advance on Gettysburg (U.S. Army Heritage and Education Center).

Reynolds quickly ordered his corps forward, sending orders to Howard at Emmitsburg to rush to Gettysburg as quickly as possible. The First Corps arrived just as the rebels were about to push forward their next assault. The regiments went immediately into action as they arrived on the field. Although Brig. Gen. Joseph R. Davis's brigade enjoyed some success pushing back the initial Union infantry it met, Brig. Gen. Lysander Cutler's brigade launched a spirited counterattack that caught many of the rebels in a railroad cut where they were unable to resist effectively and a large number were forced to surrender while the balance retreated. Just to the south of Davis, Brig. Gen. James J. Archer's brigade pushed into the McPherson (or Herbst) woods where it was met by a withering fire from Brig. Gen. Solomon Meredith's "Iron Brigade" which succeeded in encircling some of Archer's command, including the general himself, and forcing them to surrender. Archer was further mortified to find that he had been captured by troops under the command of Maj. Gen. Abner Doubleday, a close friend from their cadet days at West Point. "Good morning Archer! How

Gen. Oliver O. Howard's laxity in preparing his corps led to disaster on May 2 (National Archives and Records Administration).

are you? I am glad to see you!" intoned the Federal as the prisoner approached in the firm grasp of a burly sergeant. "Well, I am not glad to see you, by a damn sight!" Archer angrily shot back.[28]

About this time Reynolds was killed by a bullet to the head as he directed his men into position. Command of the field fell to Maj. Gen. Abner Doubleday[29] who resisted

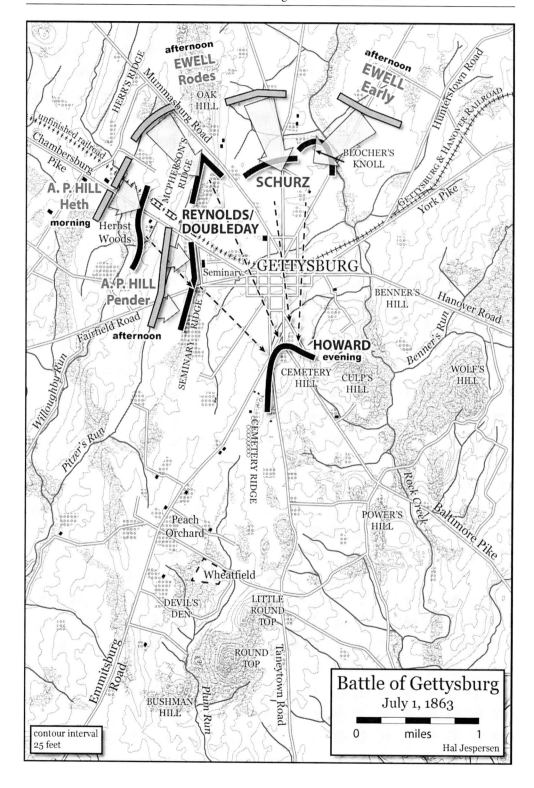

The Battle of Gettysburg, July 1, 1863 (Hal Jespersen).

stubbornly, but as Pettigrew's and Brockenbrough's brigades lent weight to Heth's attack the First Corps was gradually pushed back toward Seminary Ridge, the last remaining natural barrier between the Confederates and Gettysburg.

A little before noon the leading elements of the Eleventh Corps began arriving with Howard, as the senior officer on the field, assuming command. Doubleday continued to direct the First Corps while Howard turned command of the Eleventh Corps over to Maj. Gen. Carl Schurz. With information that Doubleday was being hard pressed and in danger of being flanked to the right, Howard ordered the first two of his divisions to arrive to hurry through town and deploy in support of the First Corps' right flank on Seminary Ridge. His final division under Brig. Gen. Adolf von Steinwehr he ordered to Cemetery Hill, a high prominence at the southern end of town, which he quickly perceived to be of great importance should the army have to abandoned its advanced positions west and north of town.

Schurz led his own division, now under Brig. Gen. Alexander Schimmelfennig, through town amidst the cheers of townspeople who offered them water, bread, sandwiches, and anything else they had on hand. Some grabbed a piece of bread to carry with them, or stopped a few seconds to quench their thirsts from a dipper of water. They had been on the road since early morning, the last two hours without any breaks and the final couple of miles into Gettysburg at the double-quick. They were near exhaustion, but they plodded on. As they exited town Schurz placed them in position on the right of the First Corps, and none too soon. Maj. Gen. Robert E. Rodes' division of Ewell's corps had arrived on Oak Hill, the northern extension of Seminary Ridge, and in the valley below to its east. Rodes was ideally positioned to drive into the exposed right flank of the First Corps. Although a gap still existed between the First Corps and Schurz's arriving Eleventh Corps troops, the German general aggressively opened fire with the single battery he had and sent skirmishers forward while the balance of his division arrived. In an effort to dislodge the First Corps Rodes ordered Col. Edward O'Neal's Alabama brigade to attack its flank along the eastern slope of Seminary Ridge. To carry out the order O'Neal had to turn his flank to Schurz's arriving troops. The 45th New York found itself ideally positioned to pour a destructive flanking fire into O'Neal's ranks as they passed, while Capt. Hubert Dilger's Battery I, 1st Ohio Light Artillery, swept the rebels with shell and canister. The rebel attack failed disastrously, a large number of prisoners being marched to the reach by the victorious Federals.

Although Schurz's arrival stabilized the Union position, rebel reinforcements continued to arrive. Schurz received a second Eleventh Corps division under Brig. Gen. Francis Barlow which he placed on his own right to extend the Union defensive line east across the northern face of town to Rock Creek. More than balancing this in manpower many times over, the Confederates were strengthened by the arrival of Pender's division of Hill's corps and Early's division of Ewell's corps. When it is recalled that Confederate divisions numbered considerably more than similar Union units, it is clear that the Southern troops, more numerous to begin with, were growing steadily stronger in relation to the Union defenders.

By mid-afternoon Early's division was forming for the attack, its position on and beyond the Federal right flank. When news of Early's approach reached Schurz he planned to meet the threat by holding a line north of town that ran roughly from the right flank of the First Corps along the Mummasburg Road on Seminary Ridge across the plain through a complex of buildings known as the alms house to Rock Creek. With Federal cavalry east of that stream Schurz had a fairly contracted line that could be held by the available infantry and artillery with its right flank guarded by the cavalry east of the creek. Unfortunately for his plan, Brig. Gen. Francis Barlow, commanding his other division north of town, disobeyed orders on where to form his men and instead advanced them north to a small rise known as Blocher's Knoll. Barlow believed that the slight rise would provide him with a better defensive position, but in reality it isolated his command several hundred yards beyond Schurz's line and with both of his flanks "up in the air." When Early's attack began, supported by one of Rodes' brigades on his right, Barlow's men were seriously outnumbered and attacked not only from their front but from both flanks at the same time. The men fought desperately, but Barlow was seriously wounded and the command was forced to retire to avoid being surrounded.

With Barlow's defeat, Schurz sent in his reserve under Col. Włodzimierz Krzyżanowski to assist, but it was too late. Barlow's and Krzyżanowski's men fell back to the alms house where they rallied until once again outflanked, then fell back to the edge of town where they made another stand. At roughly the same time that the right flank of the Eleventh Corps was being driven back, Pender's division began an attack on the left flank of the First Corps, driving it in also. With both flanks turned, Howard, still in command of the field, sent orders to Doubleday and Schurz to retire to the position he had selected on Cemetery Hill as a rallying point. The disengagement was not easy. The left flank division of the First Corps was able to skirt the southern edge of town and arrive at the designated point relatively intact. For the rest of the First and all of the Eleventh Corps the escape had to be made through the unfamiliar streets of town. Although generally made in good order, some of the units took wrong turns into dead end alleys or otherwise became disoriented or confused. Most made it through to Cemetery Hill, but some were surrounded and captured in town. One of those cut off was Brig. Gen. Schimmelfennig commanding the rear guard of his division. Chased by Confederates, he managed to get over a fence and hide out in a small shed behind a private home where he remained undetected by the rebels for the next three days.

As the retreating troops arrived at Cemetery Hill, Howard, Doubleday, Schurz, and the other officers began rallying them and assigning them to defensive positions, the Eleventh Corps on Cemetery Hill and the First Corps to its left along the northern part of Cemetery Ridge. Losses had been heavy, but Howard's foresight in placing his reserve and some artillery on Cemetery Hill provided a place for the men to reform fairly quickly. Behind the Confederate lines officers were experiencing some of the same problems. Some units which had been heavily engaged had suffered crippling losses, while others had expended nearly all of their ammunition and had to be resupplied before they could move forward again. Other units were somewhat scattered, especially those that had to advance through the same unfamiliar village as their Union foes. Then too, there were pockets of Federals still resisting within the town, especially a group of between 200 and 400 Eleventh Corps men cut off in and around the Eagle Hotel. These did not finally surrender until out of ammunition and hope of relief later that evening.

Throughout the engagement Howard had sent a string of messengers to Meade to apprise him of the situation and to both the Third and Twelfth Corps asking them to move to his support as quickly as possible. In Emmitsburg, Maj. Gen. Daniel Sickles leading the Third Corps responded with alacrity, placing most of his corps in motion immediately and sending the following message to Howard: "I have at this moment received a communication from an officer of the staff and also two written communications dated at one and half past one p.m. I shall move to Gettysburg immediately."[30] Sickles had about eleven miles to travel so his troops could not be of immediate help, but at least the knowledge they were on the way provided Howard with some assurance that if he could hold on a little longer help was on the way.

Closer to the battlefield, Maj. Gen. Henry W. Slocum's Twelfth Corps was only about five to six miles away at Two Taverns. Although Slocum later claimed that he received no orders to march to Gettysburg and no messages from Howard during the day, some of his officers later wrote that they clearly heard the sounds of the fight in progress at Gettysburg and the Eleventh Corps couriers reported delivering their messages to Slocum in person. Major Charles Howard, the general's brother and aide, asserted that he was "sent back to Slocum on the Baltimore Pike as all the other Staff Officers were otherwise occupied and was directed to request him to bring up his Corps as soon as possible and take position on the right, filing in to the right of Culps Hill, and to come up in person, even in advance of his troops, in order to survey the situation from the commanding eminence of Cemetery Hill."[31] The major reported that he delivered the message to Slocum in person but the general declined to move. Whatever the exact circumstances, Slocum remained in position until late in the afternoon when a messenger arrived from Meade. Because of the delay, his corps, which could have been arriving around the time that the retreat was taking place, did not put in an appearance until early evening.

One person who did arrive was Maj. Gen. Winfield Scott Hancock.[32] Well thought of by his fellow officers, Hancock was leading the Second Corps camped close to Meade's headquarters when word of the fighting at Gettysburg arrived. Uncertain of what was happening at the front, when news of Reynolds's death reached Meade he ordered Hancock to ride to Gettysburg, find out what was happening, and take command while he hastened the rest of the army forward. Hancock arrived while the retreating Federals were being rallied on Cemetery Hill; exactly when is much debated. He met with Howard, and again there are considerably different descriptions of what happened. Hancock later claimed that he informed Howard he was there under Meade's orders to take command; Howard later wrote that he never relinquished command and that Hancock only assisted him in forming and placing the troops. Whatever actually transpired, the First and Eleventh Corps were in relatively short order rallied and placed in position stretching from Culp's Hill through Cemetery Hill and onto the northern portion of Cemetery Ridge.

While the final Confederate assault was taking place, Lee arrived at Gettysburg and debated whether to continue the fight. With his army not yet concentrated, he was reluctant to initiate a major engagement without knowing the size of the force opposing him. Yet, the engagement had already begun in earnest so his decision was whether to halt his victorious troops or allow them to continue in the hope of further damaging the Federals before their reinforcements arrived. In view of the situation, Lee allowed the attack to continue but also issued some confusing directives about not bringing on a general engagement, something that was clearly already in progress. With the Federals driven back out of town to their new position, the question that now faced the Confederate command was whether to press the attack further in an attempt to seize the heights where this new position was forming.

With the Union forces seemingly in disorderly retreat, Lee sent Ewell an order to take Cemetery Hill "if practicable." Ewell hesitated, then declined to make the assault. Lee partisans later blamed Ewell for losing an exceptional opportunity to win the battle, while Ewell's supporters claimed that Lee did not issue a preemptive order to attack and Ewell had very good reasons for exercising his discretion to forego an assault. Ewell later wrote:

> On entering the town, I received a message from the commanding general to attack this [Cemetery] hill, if I could do so to advantage. I could not bring artillery to bear on it, and all the troops with me were jaded by twelve hours' marching and fighting, and I was notified that General [Edward] Johnson's division (the only one of my corps that had not been engaged) was close to the town. Cemetery Hill was not assailable from the town and I determined, with Johnson's division, to take possession of the wooded hill [Culp's Hill] to my left … commanding Cemetery Hill. Before Johnson got up, the enemy was reported moving to outflank our extreme left, and I could see what seemed to be his skirmishers in that direction.
>
>   Before this report could be investigated by Lieut. T. T. Turner, aide-de-camp of my staff, and Lieut. Robert D. Early, sent for that purpose, and Johnson placed in position, the night was far advanced.… On my return to my headquarters, after 12 o'clock at night, I sent orders to Johnson … to take possession of this [Culp's] hill.… General Johnson stated in reply that he had sent a reconnoitering party to the hill [which] on nearing the summit, was met by a superior force of the enemy.… Day was now breaking, and it was too late.[33]

Lt. Gen. Richard Ewell was blamed by many Southern writers after the war for not aggressively attacking Cemetery Hill and Culp's Hill on July 1 (Library of Congress).

What appears to have happened is that the forward units of the Twelfth Corps began arriving off to the northeast of Culp's Hill beyond the left flank of Ewell's force. He had located one brigade there as a flank guard and a second was ordered there as soon as the report came in. That left him with two brigades, at least one of which was engaged in capturing Union troops still in town and securing the village. That left precious few men to actually continue the assault. When Ewell's remaining division arrived on the field under Maj. Gen. Edward Johnson it went into camp close to Lee's headquarters where Lee told its commander to halt for the night. So in retrospect it seems that Ewell had few troops ready to resume the attack and that he further was legitimately worried about the possibility of Union troops arriving on his flank. He exercised his discretion by not ordering the assault. The one unit available in early evening to accomplish this was Johnson's relatively fresh division, but it was withheld under the personal direction of Lee.

While the Confederates resupplied, sorted out their intermingled troops, and made sure their left flank was secure, the Twelfth Corps began arriving, followed after dark by the Third Corps. With this, the position Howard had initially chosen was much more secure than it had been only a few hours before. It had been a long day, one of stubborn fighting and high casualties, but one in which Lee's army emerged once more victorious. That night Meade arrived on the field and decided to continue the fight from the strong positions his army held. Lee, unwilling to move away and risk losing the benefit of his army's triumph on July 1, decided to retain his position also. After conferring with his generals, he decided that Ewell would hold his position but launch a feint against the Union forces on Culp's Hill to distract them from what he planned to be the major attack designed to dislodge the defenders from their position. This was to be led by Lt. Gen. James Longstreet whose men would be arriving during the night. Scouts reported that the Federal defensive position along Cemetery Ridge ended short of two large hills—Big and Little Round Top—at its southern end. Lee saw this as an opportunity to strike this exposed flank and roll it up, forcing the Federals into precipitate retreat.

By the morning of July 2 most of Meade's army had arrived on the battlefield with the remainder scheduled to arrive by early afternoon. His defensive position has been likened to an upside down fishhook, the Twelfth Corps holding Culp's Hill (with some First Corps reinforcement), the Eleventh Corps on Cemetery Hill, then the First, Second, and Third Corps, in that order, stretched south along Cemetery Ridge. The Fifth Corps was arriving and going into reserve behind Cemetery Ridge, with the Sixth Corps several miles away marching hard toward the battlefield along the Baltimore Pike. Meade's plan for the day was to await a Confederate assault, but if one did not materialize he made contingency plans for offensive action.

Early that morning Lee sent one of his staff officers, Capt. Samuel R. Johnston, to reconnoiter the southern flank of Meade's defenses to make sure they were open to attack. The captain claimed that he rode south beyond the end of Meade's position, ascended Little Round Top, and claimed there were no Union troops anywhere near where he had gone. This report has perplexed historians ever since because if Johnston actually went where he claimed it would appear impossible for him not to have seen or at least heard activity in the Union camps. Regardless, Lee took this as confirmation that his plan would succeed. His design of attack called for a "double envelopment," two pincers that would attack both flanks of Meade's army. Hill's corps in the center of the Confederate line was to hold its position but temporarily place Maj. Gen. Richard H. Anderson's division at Longstreet's disposal to support the attack. Ewell was to launch a diversionary attack on Culp's Hill which could be exploited into a full assault if it proved successful. The main effort would be made by Longstreet. With two divisions of his corps present, he was to swing north up the Emmitsburg Road taking the Federal line in its flank and rolling it up. But there was a catch. One of Longstreet's brigades had not yet arrived. Already uneasy that only two of his three divisions were available on the field for the attack, Longstreet asked permission to await the arrival of the missing brigade. Lee agreed, effectively postponing the beginning of the attack until afternoon.

In the meantime, Meade was biding his time, conferring with his generals, awaiting the arrival of the balance of the Fifth and Sixth Corps. Holding the Federal left flank was Sickles's Third Corps. From his position where Cemetery Ridge leveled out and actually descended somewhat below the rising ground to the west toward the Emmitsburg Road, Sickles perceived himself in a trough. He became concerned that if Confederates seized the higher ground to his front his position might become untenable. After some deliberation, he decided to move his corps forward on his own authority without informing Meade. By moving his men forward he made the same ill-considered error that Barlow had made the previous day. His front line was now placed about a half mile forward of the rest of the army with both flanks completely unprotected and with too few troops to successfully man the extended line. Much as Barlow had done, Sickles created a vulnerable salient that could be attacked from three sides.

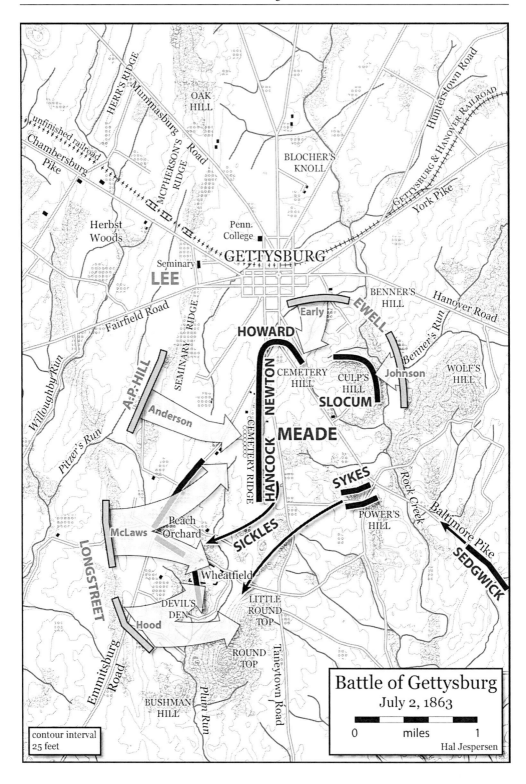

Lee's attacks on the Union line at Gettysburg, July 2, 1863 (Library of Congress).

When the commanding general became aware of this he was not happy. Although he wanted Sickles to return to the position originally assigned to him, it was too late. Longstreet's attack began *en echelon* with Maj. Gen. John Bell Hood's division moving forward onto the left flank of Sickles's position, followed at an interval by Maj. Gen. Lafayette McLaws' division to Hood's left. Resistance was again stubborn, but the rebel advance overcame the extended lines through a woods, a peach orchard, and a wheat field, threatening the gap in the Union line created by Sickles's move forward. Among the Union casualties was Sickles, his leg shattered by a shell fragment. Bravely, he insisted on sitting up with a cigar clamped in his teeth as his men carried him off the field so that his troops would know he was still alive. When surgeons amputated the leg, Sickles gave the severed bones to the Army Medical Museum in Washington, D.C., and is said to have visited his missing limb each year.

Meade quickly responded to the crisis by feeding in the Fifth Corps and elements of the First, Second and Twelfth Corps to plug the gap. At one point, Gen. Winfield Scott Hancock, noticing a large Confederate force bearing down on an undefended portion of Cemetery Ridge, found only one regiment nearby, the 1st Minnesota. Approaching its colonel, Hancock ordered him to charge. It was suicide, as anyone there could see. The lone regiment with no more than 330 men was being asked to buy time with its collective life to give other units time to arrive to stabilize the position. With little hesitation, but no doubt much trepidation, the Minnesotans rushed forward to their destiny. Fifty were killed, 173 were wounded and one was missing. Only 109 survived unscathed. The time they bought allowed reinforcements to arrive and Meade's position survived, but only barely.

While this was happening, two of Hood's brigades under Brig. Gen. Evander M. Law (4th, 15th, 44th, 47th, and 48th Alabama) and Brig. Gen. Jerome Robertson (3d Arkansas and 1st, 4th, and 5th Texas) fought their way through the rocky Devil's Den, setting their sights on the heights of Little Round Top which appeared to be unoccupied. A prominent hill at the southern end of Cemetery Ridge, Little Round Top overlooked the ridge so that in Confederate hands it could make Meade's position untenable. Meade also recognized this. As fighting erupted he dispatched his chief engineer, Maj. Gen. Gouverneur K. Warren[34] to make sure the hill was secure. Warren arrived on the strategic hill to find it empty except for a small signal corps detachment. Aghast at the approach of rebels toward this crucial position, he rushed back down the hill desperately looking for troops to occupy the height.

As Warren descended the hill, Col. Strong Vincent was ascending the back slope of the same hill through dense woods. Leading a brigade of the Fifth Corps, he placed his four regiments (20th Maine, 16th Michigan, 44th New York, and 83d Pennsylvania) at the military crest of the hill facing the south and west from where Law's and Robertson's men were approaching. Both sent their men up the steep hill, with Law striking the extreme left of Vincent's line held by the 20th Maine under Col. Joshua Lawrence Chamberlain. Thought severely pressed, the regiment held, actually advancing to force Law's men back down the hill. At the other end of the line, rebel sharpshooters killed Vincent and Robertson's men began to outflank and drive back the 16th Michigan. While this was happening, Warren ran into a column of marching infantry. Riding up to its head he found Col. Patrick O'Rourke of the 140th New York. Luck can often be important in life, including military engagements. As it happened, the two New Yorkers knew each other. O'Rourke explained that he was under orders to follow his brigade, but Warren quickly explained the situation and promised to make it right if the colonel would lead his regiment to the vital hill. O'Rourke agreed. The regiment rushed up the northeastern slope of the hill, cresting the top where O'Rourke's gaze fell on the advancing Texans. Without hesitation he ordered a charge. A minié ball found him, snuffing out his life as soon as he gave the order, but his men rushed to the attack and stabilized the wavering right flank. Additional reinforcements arrived; the position was secured.

Lee's major effort for the day appeared to come within a whisker of success, but Meade, ably assisted by Hancock and Warren, was able to shift significant reinforcements to hold Cemetery Ridge and Little Round Top. On the opposite end of his position, Culp's Hill, which had been held by the Twelfth Corps, was gradually stripped of defenders as brigades were withdrawn to reinforce the crumbling Cemetery Ridge position. By early evening, only a single brigade remained to hold a position formerly defended by an entire corps. Fortunately, that brigade was under the command of Brig. Gen. George S. Greene.[35] Although a native Rhode Islander, his brigade was solidly from the Empire State (60th, 78th, 102nd, 137th, and 149th New York). When his brigade arrived on Culp's Hill late on the evening of July 1 he immediately set his tired men to work constructing breastworks, which they continued to reinforce whenever they could during the day. Of all the Union commanders, he was the only one that conscientiously worked his troops to construct formidable entrenchments. These, together with the steep slope and wooded nature of the hill provided them with excellent defensive positions.

For some reason never adequately explained, Ewell's attack, which was supposed to take place at the same time as Longstreet's assault, did not go forward until after 7:00 p.m. when he hurled the three brigades of Maj. Gen. Edward Johnson's division at Culp's Hill. Greene called for reinforcements and the First and Eleventh Corps each responded with some of their battered, greatly reduced regiments, no more than a total of 500 men from each corps. It was enough. In the growing darkness Greene managed to hold until Johnson finally called off any further attempts. But that did not end the fighting. Almost as the attack on Greene subsided, Ewell sent two brigades from Maj. Gen. Jubal Early's division against the lynchpin of the Union line on Cemetery Hill. Five Louisiana regiments under Brig. Gen. Harry Hays and three North Carolina regiments under Col. Isaac E. Avery smashed into the greatly reduced Eleventh Corps units at the northern base of the hill. With their reserve drained off to help Greene, they had no ready support. Some regiments held, but the rebels exploited an inadvertent gap in the line to rush the batteries atop the hill. There they were met with great determination by the gunners in a hand-to-hand fight that lasted until Schurz and Krzyżanowski led reinforcements to the point of the attack. With these, and a few other Eleventh Corps units that arrived, with late support from a brigade in another corps, the rebels were pushed back down the hill and the position saved. By this time, it was pitch dark, the sun having gone down even before Early's attack began.

July 2 came to a merciful end. At his headquarters, Lee felt certain that victory had been within his grasp. If only the assaults could have been coordinated. Although losses were high and nothing tangible had been gained, Lee was certain that one more major effort would be enough to break the Federal line, bringing the much sought-after victory. Convinced that the Union center had nearly broken, he decided to make his July 3 effort there. Ewell was once again to launch a diversionary attack when Longstreet went forward. Hill would again hold his position but would provide four brigades of Brig. Gen. J. Johnston Pettigrew's division, two from Maj. Gen. Isaac R. Trimble's division, and two from

Maj. Gen. Richard H. Anderson's division as part of the attacking force. Longstreet would again direct the attack using the only fresh Confederate division under Maj. Gen. George Pickett as his striking force along with Anderson's division. A Virginian, Pickett had originally been appointed to West Point from Illinois on the recommendation Abraham Lincoln's law partner. After an artillery bombardment of more than 150 guns designed to suppress opposing artillery and scatter the defending infantry, Longstreet was to order the attack forward, aiming directly at the center of the Union line. Longstreet demurred, preferring, as he had counseled the day before, to try to turn Meade's left flank, but Lee was adamant. One more major push and the Yankees would yield.

Behind Cemetery Ridge, Meade also met with his generals that night. He asked three questions: (1) Should the army withdraw? (2) Should the army attack or remain on the defensive? (3) How long should the army wait before taking the offensive itself? Although it appears that Meade had already made up his mind, the majority opinion at the meeting was that the army should stay and should remain on the defensive. If Lee did not attack the next day, they should reconsider taking the initiative. As the meeting adjourned and the officers began to return to their commands, Meade took Brig. Gen. John Gibbon aside. Gibbon's division of the Second Corps held the center of the Union position on Cemetery Ridge. Said Meade: "If Lee attacks tomorrow it will be in your front."[36]

Daylight brought a renewal of the fighting as Johnson's division became engaged with the Twelfth Corps, now returned to its original position on Culp's Hill. Although Ewell was supposed to wait until Longstreet went forward, Federal artillery opened fire early and some of their infantry moved to take back the positions lost the evening before. The fighting became general in that area, again upsetting Confederate plans for a coordinated assault. Major fighting on this front was over by about 11:00 a.m., but Longstreet had not yet moved.

Sometime around 1:00 p.m. more than 150 Confederate guns opened on Cemetery Ridge. Shells raked the Union position, but most overshot their targets to land atop or beyond the ridge, well clear of the infantry hunkered down behind some low stone fences on the forward slope of the rise. Shells also raked Cemetery Hill, while Union artillery responded in kind resulting in the largest artillery bombardment every witnessed on the North American continent. It was obvious to everyone that this could only be a prelude to a major infantry assault. Fearing that his batteries might expend all of their ammunition before the infantry appeared, Major Thomas Osborn commanding the Eleventh Corps artillery suggested that the guns gradually reduce their fire. Brig. Gen. Henry Hunt, the army's artillery chief liked the idea and soon the counterbattery fire from the Federal artillery slackened. Within the Confederate lines the impression created was that their artillery fire was having the desired effect. When one conspicuous Federal battery limbered up and withdrew because its ammunition was exhausted, the rebels interpreted this as confirmation that they were driving the defenders away.

Finally, probably sometime around 3:00 p.m., Longstreet issued the order to advance, still reluctant to send his men into what he personally believed would be a slaughter. Recent estimates are that about 12,500 men participated in what passed into history as Pickett's Charge, a misnomer since Longstreet commanded and Pickett's division of Virginians constituted less than half of the attackers. As the men stepped off across a mile of open ground they were raked by Union artillery. Near the Emmitsburg Road they were torn apart by volleys of musketry. As the survivors closed with the Union line, men in blue on each of their flanks repositioned themselves to fire killing enfilade volleys into their ranks. A few, very few, made it across the small stone fence only to be killed or captured. The rest, those who were not killed or too seriously wounded to move, staggered back whence they came. The attack had been a disaster, a replay of the ill-considered assault on Malvern Hill the year before. Fully half of those who made the charge became casualties. Longstreet had been right.

Rain came on July 4 as each army remained in position catching its collective breath. Later that day Lee began to withdraw his wounded, his wagons, and then his infantry, his invasion of the North once more ending in failure. His ambulance train stretched 17 miles long. Meade took up a tepid pursuit on July 5. Although Lincoln and Halleck urged an aggressive pursuit to bring Lee to a stand and destroy his army, Meade contented himself with the victory achieved. In fact, Meade did have an excellent opportunity to punish or even crush Lee's army. The Confederates arrived at the Potomac to find it rain-swollen, a potential barrier to any escape. The armies skirmished several times but the only serious engagement was a Falling Waters on July 13–14 after which, the waters having indeed fallen, Lee made good his escape into Virginia. The final battle cost the Confederates another 700 captives and the life of Gen. Pettigrew who was mortally wounded commanding the rear guard.

The butcher's bill spoke to the intensity of the campaign.

	North	South
Effectives	90,000	75,000
Killed	3,155	3,903
Wounded	14,529	18,735
Missing	5,365	5,425
Total	23,049	28,063
Percent Lost	25.6	37.4

By any measure this was an enormous Federal victory. Tactically, Meade held off the strongest attacks Lee could muster, defeated them, held the ground at the end of the fight, and seriously eroded the offensive striking power of Lee's army. With the tremendous losses the South sustained during the Gettysburg campaign, it henceforth became very difficult for it to find replacements to offset the North's numerical advantage. Strategically, Lee's invasion was turned back—advantage North. Politically, the victory at Gettysburg erased forever any chance that the European nations would recognize the Confederacy. With the arrival of the news of Lee's defeat, Queen Victoria reaffirmed British neutrality on July 29. Despite the horrendous losses, and Lincoln's chagrin that Lee's army had not been completely destroyed, Northern hopes revived. This was the last time the South would ever launch a major invasion of the North.

THE EFFECT

The summer campaigns of 1863 were not yet over when one of the legislative acts taken earlier prompted events leading to riots and national headlines. The conscription act adopted earlier in the year met considerable resistance in several Northern locations. In Utica, New York, with fears of favoritism rampant, a blind man was selected to draw the named of those to be drafted from a bowl—and just to be sure he was also blindfolded. Nowhere was resistance as serious as in New York City. The Emancipation Proclamation did not meet with universal approval in the North either; in fact, complaints began to arise from some that they supported the war to preserve the Union, but would not support a war to free the slaves. Among the most vocal of these dissenters was the poorer economic class in New York City, especially its Irish immigrants. Democratic leaders, seeking to solidify their political support in the city, fed into the discontent with public statements to the effect that the city would be deluged with freed slaves who would compete with the poor of the city for jobs, housing, and services. With the exemptions granted by the conscription law, coupled with the ability of the well-to-do to purchase exemptions or substitutes, the cry of "rich man's war, poor man's fight" once more arose. Worse, since blacks were not subject to the draft the impression among those at risk was that they were being asked to put their lives on the line for people who were not going to fight for their freedom themselves. When the first drawing of names for the draft was announced to begin in July, tensions rose noticeably.

On the morning of July 13 violence erupted. At first the targets of the mobs' anger were government buildings and military recruiting offices, but attention soon turned to the city's black population along with anyone perceived to oppose the rioters. Not only were individuals attacked, but an orphanage for black children was burned to the ground. Black men found on the streets were hung, some first being tortured and others having their bodies burned once dead. In some instances the mob hurrahed for Jefferson Davis, while in others it fell upon Union officers unfortunate enough to make obvious targets in their uniforms. As the rioting spread, mobs attacked police stations, the office of the *New York Times*, and even the mayor's residence. With the situation clearly out of hand and local police forces overwhelmed, Maj. Gen. John E. Wool, commanding the Department of the East, declared a state of martial law and ordered the 65th and 74th Regiments, New York State Militia, along with part of the 20th Independent Battery, New York Volunteer Artillery, into the city. This helped to curb many of the excesses, but did not fully extinguish the uprising.

When the extent of the riots became evident, troops had to be withdrawn from the pursuit of Lee after Gettysburg to rush to New York City. These included the 7th New York State Militia, 5th New York Infantry, 9th New York Infantry, 14th New York Cavalry, 22nd New York State Militia, 26th Michigan Infantry, 27th Indiana Infantry, 47th New York Infantry, and 152nd New York Infantry. Only when they arrived was order finally restored. An exact casualty list has proven elusive but historian Adrian Cook, who has cobbled together perhaps the most complete listing, verified at least 119 deaths and 306 people injured enough to require more than casual treatment, the latter including civilians, police, and soldiers. No doubt there were many more who did not report to hospitals or other places for treatment where they might have left records, some estimates on the total number injured reach as high as 2,000. In the wake of the rioting, some whites, especially members of the Union League and a local merchants committee, raised money to assist the black victims of the violence, but one result was an exodus of much of the remaining black population from Manhattan to Brooklyn or other places leaving the island with its lowest black population since 1820. The draft was resumed in August without further violence. With the enlistment of black volunteers now widespread after the Emancipation Proclamation, New York's Union League recruited more than 2,000 which it outfitted and sent off to war with a massive parade through the city's streets.

Autumn

THE WEST

As the autumn of 1863 approached Confederate forces in the Alabama-Georgia-Tennessee tri-state area were divided into three major groups with several other smaller commands and cavalry units guarding or screening different locations. The three major concentrations were under Maj. Gen. Simon Bolivar Buckner around Loudon Tennessee guarding the East Tennessee & Georgia Railroad and the gateway into eastern Tennessee; Lt. Gen. William J. Hardee[37] along the Memphis and Charleston Railroad between Chattanooga and Cleveland, Tennessee; and Lt. Gen. Leonidas Polk[38] at Chattanooga. Buckner had had the difficult task of surrendering Fort Henry to Grant the previous year. Their combined forces numbered about 66,000 men under the overall command of Gen. Braxton Bragg.

Following the Tullahoma Campaign earlier in the year, Maj. Gen. William S. Rosecrans halted his army, resisting pressure from Halleck to continue the advance by explaining that he needing to repair a railroad and offering other excuses which Halleck did not credit. If Bragg could move, Halleck reasoned, so could Rosecrans. Finally, on August 4 he sent Rosecrans preemptory orders to move. After procrastinating another twelve days, the Union commander finally put his command in motion. With some 58,000 men under his command, Rosecrans determined to avoid a costly assault on Chattanooga or a lengthy siege by swinging south of the city in hopes of maneuvering Bragg out of his position. The tactic worked. Bragg abandoned the city on September 6 heading south into Georgia. Rosecrans pursued cautiously through the mountainous terrain, but incautiously believing that Bragg was in full retreat allowed the various parts of his army to advance separated by as much as forty miles. On September 11–12 Bragg attempted to attack an isolated portion of Rosecrans's army under Maj. Gen. George H. Thomas, but faulty staff work foiled the plan.

By August Jefferson Davis was under pressure to do something to retrieve ebbing Confederate fortunes after Gettysburg and Vicksburg. When it became apparent that Meade was not going to follow up his victory with an aggressive move toward Richmond, Davis decided to move Longstreet's corps from Virginia to reinforce Bragg in the hope of crushing Rosecrans before the North could react. Longstreet's force, having traveled by railroad through Atlanta and then north, began arriving to bolster Bragg's force as he planned his next move. Two brigades were on hand on September 18, with the rest arriving over the next two days; Longstreet himself arrived on the evening of the 19th. Without waiting for the balance of the eastern troops, Bragg, believing he had isolated another portion of Rosecrans's command, planned to launch a major attack on Maj. Gen. Thomas L. Crittenden's Twenty-First Corps on the 18th. Once again his plan was frustrated, this time by aggressive Union cavalry contesting the fords along West Chickamauga Creek which seriously delayed the infantry advance. Once again Bragg suffered frustration, blaming his subordinates for failure to carry out his orders.

With his army finally in position, Bragg attacked on September 19, opening the Battle of Chickamauga. He planned to hit the Union left with three entire corps with two divisions in reserve to exploit any breakthroughs. In often confused fighting amid the dense woods and underbrush, Bragg launched a series of piecemeal attacks all along the line. Hood's troops from Lee's army briefly broke through, but there were no troops on hand to exploit the success. Rosecrans directed reinforcements into line as they arrived

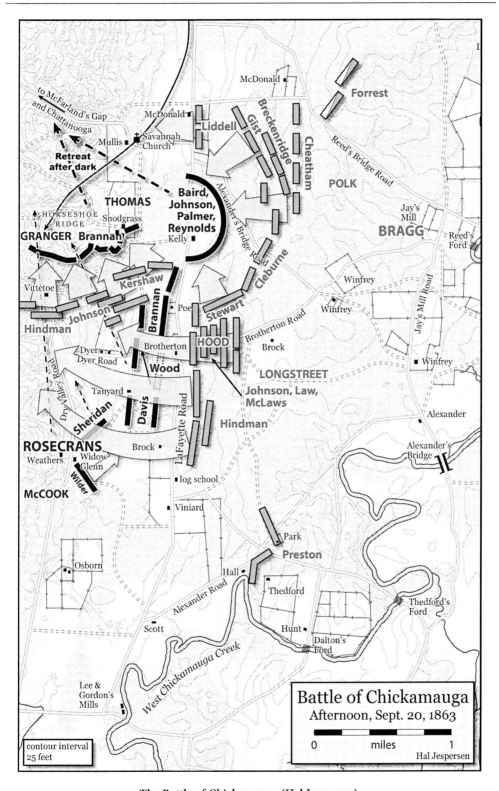

The Battle of Chickamauga (Hal Jespersen).

to prevent any serious reverse. In this bloody slugfest casualties were high but difficult to divest from the reports for the full engagement. Historian Peter Cozzens estimated anywhere from 6,000 to 9,000 for Bragg and around 7,000 for Rosecrans. That night Longstreet arrived in person. Bragg assigned him to command the left wing of his army with Polk leading the right. The plan for the following morning called for an attack *en echelon* beginning with Polk and continuing on through Longstreet.

Bragg planned to advance at dawn on September 20, but once again faulty staff work meant that orders went astray and the appointed time arrived with no sign that an attack was imminent. Instead of a 5:30 a.m. advance, nothing happened until 9:30 a.m. The delay was significant because the quiet interval allowed Maj. Gen. George H. Thomas's troops in the Fourteenth Corps to construct some defensive breastworks that would feature significantly in the fighting. Leading Bragg's attack was the "Orphan Brigade" of Kentuckians under the command of Brig. Gen. Benjamin Helm, a close friend and brother-in-law of the President of the United States. When the war began Lincoln offered him a position in the paymaster's office, but Helm declined and "went south." He fell mortally wounded leading his men forward in person. When she heard of the loss, Mary Lincoln went into mourning and invited Helm's wife to live with her in the White House raising not a few eyebrows and giving Lincoln's political enemies ammunition with which to question his sincerity in prosecuting the war. Another fatality was Sgt. Richard Kirkland, the "Angel of Marye's Heights," who braved death to bring water to Federal wounded at Fredericksburg.

Rosecrans's position was solid, but was undone by an error. Believing that Maj. Gen. James Negley's division of the Fourteenth Corps was in reserve, Gen. Thomas called for him to move up to support him. In fact, Negley was in line and any effort to obey the order would leave a gap in the Federal defenses. Negley obeyed, moving his men to support Thomas who was under attack. Brig. Gen. Thomas J. Wood moved up his division from reserve to replace Negley. All was well. But, as luck would have it, Wood had only recently been chastised for not following orders quickly enough. When an order then arrived directing him to move to another position, even though he suspected the order was an error, he dared not disobey. Clearly this was an error; headquarters had lost track of where the various commands actually were. Wood moved his men out as ordered leaving behind him a broad gap in the Federal line. Into this opening surged Longstreet's veterans. The Union defense disintegrated. Rosecrans and several other officers attempted to stem the retreating tide, but to no avail. Convinced that all was lost, Rosecrans rode back toward Chattanooga intent on rallying his defeated army once it arrived in the vicinity of the city. Behind him, Rosecrans left Thomas whose Fourteenth Corps, along with a few others, including critical reinforcement from Maj. Gen. Gordon Granger who disobeyed orders to retreat and instead rushed to his assistance, continued to resist behind the breastworks they had only completed that morning. Fighting desperately, Thomas held until nightfall, only then responding to an order from Rosecrans to retire to Chattanooga. Quite possibly Thomas saved Rosecrans's fleeing army from defeat in detail. His stubborn resistance earned him the nickname "The Rock of Chickamauga."

Casualties were, as had now become usual, high for the two-day engagement:

	North	South
Effectives	58,222	66,326
Killed	1,657	2,312
Wounded	9,756	14,674

	North	South
Missing	4,757	1,468
Total	16,170	18,454
Percent Lost	27.7	27.8

Tactically, the South emerged victorious since it held the field at the end of the engagement. Similarly, the battle must be considered a Confederate strategic victory since Rosecrans's invasion was thrown back, the Union forces being pushed out of Georgia back into southern Tennessee. But if Chickamauga was a Southern victory, it was a pyrrhic triumph. Bragg failed to aggressively follow up the victory, losing an opportunity to further damage or largely destroy Rosecrans's command. Instead, he allowed it to escape to defensive positions around Chattanooga. Losses were very heavy among Bragg's troops, men the South by the fall of 1863 could ill afford to lose. Dissention over the losses emerged in the ranks, while finger-pointing and bickering divided the Confederate command. Politically, Rosecrans's precipitate ride back to Chattanooga gave the appearance of abandoning his command, especially in light of Thomas's tenacious resistance. Rosecrans lost his position, being replaced by Thomas, while Granger also received a deserved promotion for his support of Thomas. Crittenden and Negley were relieved of command in the major Union shakeup that followed the loss.

Among the Confederates, the acrimony following the victory was more divisive than the reorganization of the Northern command following the loss. Bragg suspended Maj. Gen. Thomas C. Hindman from command and pointedly demanded from Polk an explanation for what Bragg considered his slowness to obey orders during the battle. When Polk's response was not to Bragg's liking he relieved him also. Polk then blamed Lt. Gen. Daniel Harvey Hill for his problems, Bragg determined to relieve him also. The three responded by writing to friends and officials in Richmond in attempts to undercut Bragg and secure his removal. Buckner soon joined the group of subordinates plotting against Bragg, as did Longstreet who penned a letter to Secretary of War James Seddon criticizing Bragg's planning and the general himself in no uncertain terms. On October 4, twelve of Bragg's corps and division commanders met to draft a petition to President Davis recommending Bragg's removal. At one point, Brig. Gen. Nathan Bedford Forrest, commanding Bragg's cavalry, even threatened his commanding officer with bodily harm.

The volatile situation among the Confederate high command in the west became so serious that President Davis made the long journey to personally investigate and use his authority to intervene. Longstreet bluntly told Davis that Bragg was incompetent, an opinion supported by Buckner, Hill, and Maj. Gen. Benjamin Cheatham. Despite the overwhelming disapproval of Bragg by his senior officers, Davis opted to retain him in command. Bragg quickly relieved Hill of his command, demoted Buckner, and reduced the size of Longstreet's command to only those troops he brought with him from Virginia. Relations between Bragg and Longstreet were so bad by this time that they no longer met in person but only communicated by written correspondence, and that sparingly. Given the poisonous opposition to Bragg among the officers he would have to rely on in the upcoming advance on Chattanooga, it would have been much better to have sacked him and brought in someone from outside to repair the strained relations in the high command. Instead, the dissention would be carried forth into the next phase of the fight for Chattanooga.

Bragg moved his army north to begin a siege of Chattanooga. Rosecrans, not yet having been relieved, hunkered down in the city and surrounding works, but the position was not exactly admirable. Confederates held Missionary Ridge overlooking the city to the east and northeast, as well as the massive Lookout Mountain to the south. These positions effectively controlled access into the city except from the west and northwest, but that topography contained rugged mountains, very few narrow dirt roads, and was often mired in mud during the late fall season. Further, Confederate cavalry effectively patrolled the area in position to interdict access to the city. The result was that Chattanooga was effectively cut off from necessary supplies, at least to the extent that the besieged army could not be indefinitely maintained.

Given the crisis, Lincoln immediately ordered that two corps be sent as quickly as possible from the Army of the Potomac to assist in relieving Chattanooga. The president brought Joe Hooker off the shelf to command this force. The movement began on September 25 with the Eleventh and Twelfth Corps moving to Washington from where they, their artillery and supporting materiel, boarded trains that took them west through Harpers Ferry to Benwood on the Ohio River. After crossing that waterway the trains chugged across Ohio and into Indiana where they turned south at Indianapolis. Re-crossing the Ohio at Louisville, they sped south through Nashville and Murfreesboro and on to Stevenson, Alabama, where the tracks turned northeast to Bridgeport. After only five days the leading units began to arrive in Bridgeport. In all, in only eleven and one-half days 17,500 men, ten batteries of artillery with 45 guns, 717 wagons and ambulances, over 4,400 horses and mules, and all of the two corps' baggage passed over 1,192 miles of track and arrived in fighting condition. It was the largest, most successful movement by rail in the history of warfare.

While this was taking place, Halleck ordered further reinforcement rushed to Chattanooga and issued orders creating the Military Division of the Mississippi by combining the Departments of the Cumberland, Ohio, and Tennessee under the command of Maj. Gen. Ulysses S. Grant. The new force included the Army of the Tennessee under Maj. Gen. William T. Sherman,[39] the Army of the Cumberland led by Maj. Gen. George H. Thomas, and the command brought west by Hooker and eventually assigned for operational purposes to the Army of the Cumberland.

Leaving most of the Twelfth Corps to guard the railroad line and await the arrival of Sherman's troops, Grant ordered Hooker to open a reliable supply line into Chattanooga where Thomas's troops were on the verge of starvation, reduced to eating their horses and mules for food. Reinforced by a division of the Twelfth Corps, Hooker led the Eleventh Corps across the Tennessee River and through Lookout Valley to link up with Thomas and clear the river as far as Kelly's Ford so it could be used to ferry in provisions and other supplies along what was called the "cracker line," a reference to the hardtack that was a standard ration for Union troops. Bragg attempted to stop the movement at Wauhatchie, but the squabbling among the Confederate high command no doubt contributed to the attempt by Longstreet's troops being botched when the Eleventh Corps and the division of the Twelfth fought off rebel counterattacks and secured the life-saving cracker line.

Following the opening of the supply line, Sherman arrived and Grant began positioning his troops to deal with Bragg. The Confederate commander, still seething over the attempt to oust him, unwisely approved a move by Longstreet north to Knoxville where he hoped to defeat Federal troops under Maj. Gen. Ambrose Burnside and open the way from there east into Virginia. This of course depleted Bragg's army further. Grant took advantage of it by moving Sherman and the Eleventh Corps under Howard north

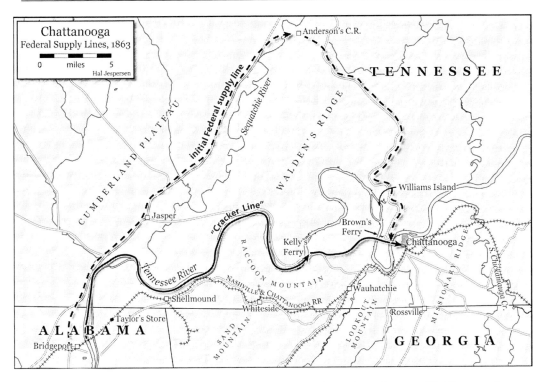

The Chattanooga area showing the "Cracker Line" opened to relieve the siege (Hal Jespersen).

of Chattanooga to operate against Bragg's right. On November 23 this force seized Orchard Knob opening Bragg's main defenses along the northern portion of Missionary Ridge to attack. To the south, Grant ordered Hooker to move against the rebel defenses around Lookout Mountain. Once the attack began, much to everyone's surprise Union troops scaled the steep edifice driving the Confederates from what had appeared to be an impregnable position in what was later referred to as the "Battle Above the Clouds." This opened Bragg's left flank on Missionary Ridge to direct assault.

On November 25 Grant ordered Thomas, in the center of the Federal line, to move forward to take rebel rifle pits at the base of Missionary Ridge. As Grant and his staff watched the blue lines moved forward, overrunning the objective, but then surprisingly continuing on up the slope toward the top of the ridge. Fearing they would be borne back in a serious repulse, Grant turned to Thomas to ask who authorized the assault on Missionary Ridge itself. Thomas, as surprised as anyone, responded that he had not. Improbably, the blue line swept on up the ridge until the rebel defenders began to withdraw. What contributed to this unlikely victory was an engineering error in placing Bragg's lines so that they were not always mutually supportive, in some cases giving the impression to defenders that they were isolated against the oncoming assault. Among the leaders of this unauthorized attack was the eighteen-year-old adjutant of the 24th Wisconsin who grabbed his regiment's colors leading the men forward and planting them atop the contested ridge. Arthur McArthur was awarded the Medal of Honor for his heroic action. Eight decades later his son Douglas would command American troops in the Pacific during World War II and then in Korea.

With the successful Union assault, Bragg's defense crumbled, a large part of his army retiring south in abject rout. Immediately following, Grant dispatched Sherman and Howard's Eleventh Corps north to save Burnside who was being threatened by Longstreet's command. Marching quickly through brutal winter weather, with shoes so worn out that some of the men had to wrap cloth around their feet rather than go barefoot, with icy winds, rain, and plunging temperatures, the force arrived within striking distance to find that Longstreet's initial assault on Knoxville had failed and rather than face this new Federal force he chose to lead his command back across the mountains into Virginia. East Tennessee, where pro–Union sentiment was high anyway, had been redeemed for the Union.

Tactically, Grant had repeatedly outmaneuvered Bragg leading to a string of Federal victories at Wauhatchie, Orchard Knob, Lookout Mountain, Missionary Ridge, and Knoxville. Strategically, the Union army saved Thomas's force in Chattanooga, drove the Confederates out of eastern Tennessee, and opened the Georgia heartland to invasion and a second possible splitting of the remaining Confederacy. Bragg's failure to close the siege of Chattanooga also eliminated the possibility of thousands of Federal prisoners that could be used to trade for the release of Southern captives taken in the disasters at Vicksburg and Gettysburg. No such relief occurred.

Casualties in the Chattanooga Campaign during the period November 23 to 25 were nowhere near as severe as some of the earlier engagements, but the losses further bled the Confederacy of irreplaceable manpower.

	North	South
Effectives	56,359	64,165
Killed	753	361
Wounded	4,722	2,160
Missing	349	4,146
Total	5,824	6,667
Percent Lost	10.3	10.4

Politically, Bragg's failure to destroy Rosecrans before the arrival of reinforcements and his subsequent precipitate withdraw south into Georgia, combined with the casualties of the Chickamauga and Chattanooga Campaigns, drew a pall over the South as morale noticeably declined and desertions from their armies increased. Davis finally relieved Bragg of command, too late to avoid the calamitous results of his flawed leadership. The president recalled Joseph E. Johnston to replace Bragg. Lincoln also found a new general. Following the successful relief of Chattanooga, he called Grant to Washington to take command of all the Union armies as general-in-chief, relieving Halleck of that title in favor of appointing him chief-of-staff. Grant would henceforth manage the Union war effort while Halleck would act as his staff assistant, distributing the orders that Grant issued.

THE EAST

With both Lee and Meade south of the Potomac as autumn began, the former encamped around Culpepper with the latter to his north across the Rappahannock River. On August 8, Lee sent a letter to President Davis offering his resignation. After thanking the president for his support, and praising the conduct of the army, he continued:

> I have been prompted by these reflections more than once since my return from Pennsylvania to propose to Your Excellency the propriety of selecting another commander for this army. I have seen and

heard of expression of discontent in the public journals at the result of the expedition. I do not know how far this feeling extends in the army. My brother officers have been too kind to report it, and so far the troops have been too generous to exhibit it. It is fair, however, to suppose that it does exist, and success is so necessary to us that nothing should be risked to secure it. I therefore, in all sincerity, request Your Excellency to take measures to supply my place. I do this with the more earnestness because no one is more aware than myself of my inability for the duties of my position. I cannot even accomplish what I myself desire. How can I fulfill the expectations of others? In addition I sensibly feel the growing failure of my bodily strength. I have not yet recovered from the attack I experienced the past spring. I am becoming more and more incapable of exertion, and am thus prevented from making the personal examinations and giving the personal supervision to the operations of the field which I feel to be necessary. I am so dull that in making use of the eyes of others I am frequently misled. Everything, therefore, points to the advantages to be derived from a new commander, and I the more anxiously urge the matter upon Your Excellency from my belief that a younger and abler man than myself can readily be attained. I know that he will have as gallant and brave an army as ever existed to second his efforts, and it would be the happiest day of my life to see at its head a worthy leader—one that would accomplish more than I could perform and all that I have wished. I hope Your Excellency will attribute my request to the true reason, the desire to serve my country, and to do all in my power to insure the success of her righteous cause.[40]

Davis declined the offer, commenting that no one could be found to take his place.

Both sides attempted to rest and recoup their strength before another confrontation. Lee was further reduced in strength by the detachment of Longstreet with two divisions to reinforce Bragg in the west, while Meade had to detach units to quell the New York City draft riots, lost a division that was sent to operate along the South Carolina coast, and also had the Eleventh and Twelfth Corps sent to help raise the siege of Chattanooga. When Lee learned of the detachments from Meade's army he attempted to take the initiative by turning the Union right flank, much as he had done at the beginning of the Second Bull Run Campaign. Meade withdrew back to Centerville, but Lee was unable to gain a favorable position for an attack despite his maneuvering. The only significant action that occurred came at Bristoe Station on October 14 when an attack by A. P. Hill was repulsed with losses more than three times those of Meade, including the death of Brig. Gen. Carnot Posey of Mississippi.

Following Hill's repulse, Meade took the initiative, gradually maneuvering so that Lee was forced to retreat beyond the Rapidan River. Although he succeeded in crossing the river with the intent of turning Lee's position to the west, rebel cavalry detected the move and Lee was able to shift his army into a strong position behind Mine Run. Meade was inclined to attack, but given the strength of Lee's position and the failure of Union scouts to locate any apparent weak spot he finally canceled the advance, deciding instead to go into winter quarters around Culpepper. Major campaigning in the east ended for the year.

THE EFFECT

On September 15 Lincoln took advantage of the Habeas Corpus Suspension Act adopted by Congress in March which gave him the authority to discontinue that Constitutional guarantee during the rebellion. Concerned about continuing opposition to the draft, he declared the suspension of habeas corpus in all cases involving, spies, traitors, prisoners of war, or anyone arrested for interfering with the draft or voluntary enlistments or acting so as to aid the Confederacy. With this in place, the mounting casualty rates attending the operations of summer and fall 1863 prompted Lincoln to issue a call for

300,000 more men on October 17. By this time, the South had no remaining pool of manpower to offset this infusion into the Union armies.

The following month the president journeyed to Gettysburg to offer "a few appropriate remarks" to help dedicate the new national cemetery. The featured speaker that November 19 was Edward Everett, a celebrated orator in an era where oratory was an art form. He was more than up to the occasion, flowing forth with classical analogies and rhetorical flourish for two hours before Lincoln, who had been invited almost as an afterthought, rose to deliver his thoughts. When he did, his comments were so short that the photographer had not even finished adjusting his equipment to memorialize the occasion when the president suddenly sat down. Nevertheless, those few moments produced a lasting impression.

> Fourscore and seven years ago our fathers brought forth on this continent a new nation, conceived in liberty and dedicated to the proposition that all men are created equal.
>
> Now we are engaged in a great civil war, testing whether that nation or any nation so conceived and so dedicated can long endure. We are met on a great battlefield of that war. We have come to dedicate a portion of that field as a final resting-place for those who here gave their lives that that nation might live. It is altogether fitting and proper that we should do this.
>
> But in a larger sense, we cannot dedicate, we cannot consecrate, we cannot hallow this ground. The brave men, living and dead who struggled here have consecrated it far above our poor power to add or detract. The world will little note nor long remember what we say here, but it can never forget what they did here. It is for us the living rather to be dedicated here to the unfinished work which they who fought here have thus far so nobly advanced. It is rather for us to be here dedicated to the great task remaining before us—that from these honored dead we take increased devotion to that cause for which they gave the last full measure of devotion—that we here highly resolve that these dead shall not have died in vain, that this nation under God shall have a new birth of freedom, and that government of the people, by the people, for the people shall not perish from the earth.[41]

In these few words Lincoln managed to solemnly recall the sacrifices made on that field while at the same time clearly defining for all time his government's wartime objectives.

Lincoln also took one more important step before the end of that long and eventful year. Sensing that the tide of war had turned, on December 8 he issued a "Proclamation of Amnesty and Reconstruction." Reasoning that the Southern states were in rebellion rather than that they had left the Union, the president argued that under these circumstances as the commander-in-chief he had the authority to determine when the rebellion was over and how the effected states would then be able to resume their natural places within the nation. Under his plan he proposed to begin healing the nation's wounds by making the restoration as painless as possible. Sometimes referred to as the "Ten Percent Plan," Lincoln proposed a blanket amnesty for all Southerners except for

> all who are, or shall have been, civil or diplomatic officers or agents of the so called Confederate government; all who have left judicial stations under the United States to aid the rebellion; all who are, or shall have been, military or naval officers of said so-called Confederate government above the rank of colonel in the army or of lieutenant in the navy; all who left seats in the United States congress to aid the rebellion; all who resigned commissions in the army or navy of the United States and afterwards aided the rebellion; and all who have engaged in any way in treating colored persons, or white persons in charge of such, otherwise than lawfully as prisoners of war, and which persons may have been found in the United States service as soldiers, seamen, or in any other capacity.[42]

These people could apply individually to the president for pardons.

When 10 percent of the 1860 voting population of an individual state took an oath of allegiance to the United States, that state could form a government and resume its position in Congress and the Union. The president's proclamation also guaranteed "restoration of all rights of property, except as to slaves, and in property cases where rights of third parties shall have intervened, and upon the condition that every such person shall take and subscribe an oath, and thenceforward keep and maintain said oath inviolate." The oath was to "be of the tenor and effect" of

I,—, do solemnly swear, in presence of Almighty God, that I will henceforth faithfully support, protect, and defend the Constitution of the United States and the Union of the States thereunder; and that I will, in like manner, abide by and faithfully support all acts of congress passed during the existing rebellion with reference to slaves, so long and so far as not repealed, modified, or held void by congress, or by decision of the supreme court; and that I will, in like manner, abide by and faithfully support all proclamations of the President made during the existing rebellion having reference to slaves, so long and so far as not modified or declared void by decision of the supreme court. So help me God.[43]

The president had struck the first blow in what would be a long, often bitter partisan struggle for control of the postwar reestablishment of political normalcy. The radicals in Congress responded in the following spring. Where the president had argued that he had the authority to determine the conditions for restoration because the Constitution gives the president the authority, and responsibility, to quell domestic uprisings, and hence the authority to use his executive police power to set the conditions for the rebellious population to regain its rights and responsibilities within the Union, Congressional leaders disagreed. They argued that although secession was illegal, the Southern states had nevertheless left the Union, been defeated in war, and were now conquered territories. The Constitution gives Congress the right to admit new states to the Union; hence, it was the prerogative of the Congress to restore the states. It was also the right of Congress to determine its own membership and decide which states and which potential representatives were qualified for membership.

The Congressional plan was outlined in the Wade-Davis Bill sponsored by Senator Benjamin Wade of Ohio and Representative Henry Winter Davis of Maryland. Under their proposal, provisional governors would be appointed to administer affairs in each of the "recovered" states. Civilian governments could be re-established when 50 percent of the adult white males had taken an oath of allegiance to the Union and the proposed new state constitutions contained provisions prohibiting slavery and repudiating all Confederate debts. The Congressional oath is sometimes referred to as the "ironclad oath" because it required not only an oath of future allegiance to the United States, but an oath that the person had always been loyal, something it would have been impossible for 50 percent of any state to do if the people were being truthful.

The first shots in this political battle had been fired, but the war would erupt only after the guns fell silent to be replaced by the heated rhetoric of political conflict.

* * *

If nothing else had gone its way during 1863 the twin Confederate disasters of July 4—Pemberton's surrender of Vicksburg and Lee's retreat from Gettysburg—combined to make this a very successful year for the United States. In those two actions alone, the Confederacy had lost some 73,000 men including about 30,000 prisoners at Vicksburg alone. But more had happened, much more. Bragg's army had been dealt a serious blow at Chattanooga, communication and transportation between the eastern and western Confederacy was severely disrupted, and the Confederate heartland lay open to invasion that would cut the fledgling nation in two once again. Even in the two major engagements the Confederacy won, Chancellorsville and Chickamauga, the South lost another 31,000 men with no discernable long-term benefit. By the end of 1863, the Confederate army consisted of 465,000 men on paper, but only some 234,000 were present for duty, only 50.3 percent of the paper total. The South was being bled of its available manpower with little hope of any significant transfusions in the future.

By the end of 1863 the anaconda was also tightening its grip on the Confederacy. With the Mississippi Valley in Union hands, precious few men were able to move east to reinforce the main Confederate armies, and virtually no supplies of any significance. Although Mobile and some other smaller gulf ports remained open, the Federal blockading squadron, safely based in New Orleans, was increasingly effective in cutting off trade to these destinations, as the Atlantic Blockading Squadron was along that coast. In 1861 only one out of every nine blockade runners were captured or destroyed, but in 1863–64 it was one of three. With far fewer ships operating in 1865 the loss rate was one of every two. By the end of the war some 1,100 blockade runners had been captured and another 300 destroyed.

On December 2 the final section of a seven and one-half ton statue measuring nineteen feet six inches in height was raised to the top of the dome of the United States Capitol building where it was emplaced as the crowning touch on the new symbol of American democracy. A 35-gun salute marked the occasion, one gun for each of the states including those in rebellion. Named the "Statue of Freedom," it featured a classical female form adorned with a helmet and flowing gown resembling the classical toga. Her right hand rested on the hilt of a sword while the left clutched a laurel wreath and the shield of the United States. Ironically, the original superintendent for the project was Captain Montgomery Meigs, now a brigadier general and Quartermaster General of the United States army. The original design called for the figure to wear a Liberty cap rather than a helmet, but the Secretary of War, under whose direction the project fell, objected that the cap had become a symbol of freedom for slaves and as such was offensive to the South. He replaced it with the helmet. The secretary was Jefferson Davis. Now, the massive figure approved by representatives of the warring sides took its place atop the Capitol dome bearing on its base the motto "E Pluribus Unum"—"From Many, One." In many respects, the war would determine whether that principle would persevere.

8

1864—Closing the Vice

At the end of December, on paper Confederate military strength stood at about 465,000 men, but only 278,000 were actually reported being with their units. Illness and growing desertion reduced the rebels' effective strength by a crippling 40.2 percent. By contrast, Union returns for the end of the same month reported a total strength of 860,737 with 611,250 actually present for duty, a comparative absence rate of 29.0 percent.

Inflation reached 300 percent in the South by the beginning of 1864. In response, the Confederate government printed more paper money, only adding to the runaway price increases. European governments began to refuse paper in payment, or to extend loans to the South, insisting on compensation in gold for military and other supplies. Northern presses added to the problem by printing counterfeit Confederate notes that flooded into the Southern marketplace. Basic food products were 28 times more expensive in the South than they had been in 1861, but average wages had risen only three to four times. Lee's army was in such desperate shape that President Davis authorized him to requisition food from the population by force if necessary, a measure that helped to meet the crisis in the army but left shortages and considerable resentment among the population, while sapping Southern morale all the more.

On the very day that Lincoln expressed his confidence in a Union victory by issuing his "Proclamation of Amnesty and Reconstruction"—December 8, 1863—Jefferson Davis delivered his annual message to the Confederate Congress in Richmond. He was not nearly as positive. Davis was honest, admitting that the war was not going well and that Southern armies had not been able to evict the invaders from their soil. Likewise, it was unlikely that England and France would recognize the Confederacy. In these trying times, he reminded his constituents that courage and confidence in ultimate victory were indispensable to achieving that end. By contrast, Lincoln, delivering his own State of the Union Address on the same day, emphasized the "improved condition of our national affairs."[1] In a *tour de force* he commented on international affairs, domestic economic policy, internal improvements, and the restoration of the Union. The comparison of Davis's stark view of the future with Lincoln's business-as-usual approach to his address reflected the relative fortunes of the two presidents as the new year, the third year of war, was about to begin.

Spring

THE WEST

The Union armies encamped in and around Chattanooga enjoyed a brief respite from active campaigning in the winter and early spring of 1864. Much of this time was taken up with a reorganization of the forces. The Eleventh and Twelfth Corps that had been shifted west from the Army of the Potomac were consolidated into the new Twentieth Corps under Hooker. Howard was transferred to command the Fourth Corps and Slocum, who refused to serve under Hooker any longer, was transferred to command the Federal garrison at Vicksburg. Similarly Schurz, who also had come to a mutual dislike with Hooker, was sent to Nashville to train new recruits and later campaigned actively for Lincoln in the fall election. Other changes were also made as some regiments mustered out or returned home for furlough after having re-enlisted as "Veteran Volunteers." The most important change was in leadership. When Grant was called east in March to assume command of all the Union armies, he left Sherman in command of the combined forces around Chattanooga with orders to march on Atlanta as soon as the weather and his arrangements permitted. Sherman's army was actually a combination of three Federal armies numbering, originally, about 98,000 men. These included the Army of the Tennessee under Maj. Gen. James B. McPherson, the Army of the Ohio led by Maj. Gen. John M. Schofield, and the Army of the Cumberland commanded by Maj. Gen. George H. Thomas, along with assorted cavalry forces. Sherman spent most of his time through the end of April preparing his men for the advance, making sure all of the troops were well rested, provisioned and supplied.

Gen. William Tecumseh Sherman led the successful Union marches through Georgia to Atlanta and Savannah, then north through the Carolinas (Library of Congress).

While Sherman prepared for a summer campaign, Maj. Gen. Nathaniel P. Banks[2] led his Army of the Gulf up Louisiana's Red River into Texas. The objective was the capture of stores of cotton that could then be shipped to New England and New York to feed the textile mills that had been largely cut off from that raw material once the war began.

The Confederate commander opposed to Banks was Maj. Gen. Richard Taylor,[3] the son of President Zachary Taylor. Outnumbered by Banks, some 14,000 to 12,000, Taylor gradually fell back toward Mansfield, Louisiana, where he suddenly turned to attack Banks on April 8, defeating him at the Battle of Sabine Crossroads and inflicting about 2,148 casualties (108 killed, 643 wounded, 1,397 captured and missing) for the loss of around 1,000 killed and wounded. Taylor's forces captured twenty guns, 156 wagons, and killed or captured about 1,000 Federal horses and mules. Banks began a retreat and dug in the following day at Pleasant Hill where the engagement resumed with the opposing forces estimated about equal. Once again Taylor's men emerged victorious with Banks resuming his retreat during the night of April 9–10. Losses at Pleasant Hill were:

	North	South
Effectives	12,247	14,300
Killed	150-	
Wounded	844	1,200
Captured & Missing	375	426
Total	1,369	1,626
Percent Lost	11.2	11.4

Left: Gen. Richard Taylor, a son of Pres. Zachary Taylor, led one of the last major Confederate forces to surrender at the end of the war.

Right: Gen. Nathaniel P. Banks had been governor of Massachusetts before the war and used his political influence to secure a generalship at the beginning of the war (both photographs, Library of Congress).

The Red River Campaign ended in a total Union failure. Tactically, Taylor clearly outmaneuvered and outfought Banks at both Sabine Crossroads and Pleasant Hill. Combining casualties for the two engagements, Banks lost 3,517 as opposed to Taylor's 2,626, not to mention all of the guns and other material Banks lost. Strategically, Taylor frustrated Banks's campaign objectives completely. Politically, the successful defense of the Red River Valley as the entrance into eastern Texas provided a ray of hope for the Confederacy amid the previous year's setbacks. The Confederate Congress voted a resolution of thanks to Taylor and his troops and rewarded the commander with promotion to lieutenant general.

Two other noteworthy events took place in the west that spring, the first being the capture of Meridian, Mississippi, by Sherman's forces in February. Meridian was an important industrial town that also contained Confederate warehouses, both of which were henceforth denied to the Southern war effort, as were the miles of railroad that Sherman destroyed. The other event was a major cavalry raid through western Kentucky and Tennessee by some 7,000 men under Maj. Gen. Nathan Bedford Forrest.[4] His purpose was to capture supplies, prisoners, and destroy Union outposts. Numerous small skirmished occurred, the most noteworthy event being Forrest's failure to trick the Federal garrison at Paducah, Kentucky, into surrendering.

After dispatching part of his force on a different mission, Forrest sent about 1,500 men to capture Fort Pillow held by about 600 men under the command of Major Lionel Booth. Booth's troops included both white and black soldiers from two artillery units. Forrest and his men arrived outside the fort on April 12. During the stiff fight that lasted from mid-morning until late afternoon Booth was killed with Maj. William F. Bradford assuming command. Bradford refused Forrest's demand for surrender, which included the threat that "should my demand be refused, I cannot be responsible for the fate of your command."[5] With this, Forrest launched an all-out assault that scaled the fortifications, broke into the interior, and sent most of the defenders retreating to the river where they hoped for protection from a Federal gunboat. From a height overlooking the river, Confederates fired into the retreating men, hitting many including some who were in the water attempting to escape. Others reportedly drowned. When the Union forces attempted to surrender, many were shot or bayonetted despite throwing down their weapons. Confederates reported 14 killed and 86 wounded. Union losses were severe: 350 killed, 60 wounded, 164 captured and missing for a total of 574 or 95.7 percent of the force on hand. An estimated 77.9 percent of the Union's black soldiers lost their lives. What came to be called the Fort Pillow Massacre appalled the Northern government. In the wake of the atrocity, Grant ordered Maj. Gen. Benjamin Butler, then responsible for negotiating prisoner exchanges, to demand that white and black soldiers be treated equally in eligibility for exchange, warning that any failure to agree would result in an end to the exchanges.

Gen. Nathan Bedford Forrest commanded Confederate troops accused of slaughtering black Union troops who attempted to surrender at Ft. Pillow. Following the war he became Grand Wizard of the Ku Klux Klan (Library of Congress).

An increasingly ugly war had crossed yet another revolting threshold.

THE EAST

Newly promoted to lieutenant general, the first person to hold this regular rank since George Washington, Ulysses S. Grant arrived in Washington, D.C., in March 1864. One of his first decisions was *not* to remain in the city, but to rely on Halleck as chief of staff as his conduit to the other commands while he accompanied the Army of the Potomac into the field. This would keep him remote from the political and journalistic pressures of the nation's capital and allow him to focus on his military duties. Meade politely offered his resignation, but Grant demurred, keeping him in command of the army while Grant provided strategic direction to Meade and all of the other commanders in the various theaters. Grant's overall strategic view of the upcoming summer campaigns was to apply pressure to both of the two most important Confederate armies. Grant, accompanying Meade's army, would advance on Lee's Army of Northern Virginia while Sherman would move on Atlanta engaging the Army of Tennessee now under the command of Lt. Gen. Joseph E. Johnston after Bragg's ouster. By coordinating these and other movements Grant planned to apply pressure on all of the major fronts at once, preventing the Confederates from moving troops about to face individual threats. Given the dwindling Southern manpower, this would presumably result in a shortage of rebel troops somewhere and a corresponding opportunity for Union success.

Chief among the objectives were Lee's and Johnston's armies. Grant realized, as did Lincoln, that the primary objective of the Army of the Potomac ought to be the Army of Northern Virginia. Taking terrain, even Richmond, would not necessarily end the war; crushing Lee's army, along with Johnston's, would. With no remaining means to resist the South would have to yield. For that reason, Grant planned to bring Lee's army to a stand out in the open where Union numbers could best be brought to bear. The last thing Grant wanted was a long and protracted siege. Better to have a fight out in the open and bring a close to the war once and for all.

Before Grant's arrival Meade had reorganized the Army of the Potomac for the upcoming campaign. Given the heavy losses at Gettysburg and the sometimes difficult communication Meade experienced with the multiple corps structure in Pennsylvania, he decided to disband the First and Third Corps. Both had suffered heavily during the fighting. Further, eliminating Sickles's Third Corps provided an excellent opportunity for Meade to rid himself of Sickles as well, a general whom he did not hold in high esteem and who engaged in intrigues against Meade after Gettysburg. Naturally, the veteran soldiers in the two corps to be eliminated were not very happy. Understandably they had grown loyal to their organizations over the hard years of fighting and were anguished to see them disappear. Meade retained the Second (Maj. Gen. Winfield Scott Hancock), Fifth (Maj. Gen. Gouverneur K. Warren), and Sixth (Maj. Gen. John Sedgwick) Corps, incorporating the regiments and brigades of the First and Third Corps into these structures. Following Grant's arrival another problem surfaced when he decided to add Burnside's Ninth Corps to the army. Burnside outranked Meade, but Grant had no intention of relieving Meade so Grant at first arranged for Burnside to retain an independent command with both he and Meade reporting directly to Grant. Eventually, when this proved awkward in practice, Grant incorporated the Ninth Corps into the Army of the Potomac with Burnside reporting to Meade despite the difference in seniority. Burnside offered no serious objection. Grant also appointed Maj. Gen. Philip Sheridan to command the Cavalry Corps. Counting the cavalry and Burnside's command, Meade would have available to him 118,700 men and 316 guns. Since Burnside was initially held back, the force actually available at the beginning of the campaign numbered 99,400.

Lee retained the same overall organization for the Army of Northern Virginia that he had the previous year. Longstreet retained the First Corps, Ewell the Second, and A. P. Hill the Third with Stuart commanding the cavalry. One of Longstreet's divisions was initially on detached service leaving Lee with 63,900 men and 274 guns at the beginning of the campaign.

In addition to the Army of the Potomac (with Burnside attached), Grant also exercised authority over Maj. Gen. Benjamin Butler's Army of the James, some 33,000 strong, located on the Bermuda Hundred peninsula between the branches of that river south of Richmond and above Petersburg. Grant planned to use this army to cut the Richmond & Petersburg Railroad and to place pressure on those two cities to prevent Lee from drawing any reinforcements from their defenses. Butler was opposed by about 14,000 Confederate defenders under Lt. Gen. P. G. T. Beauregard. Grant also had a force in the Shenandoah Valley under Maj. Gen. Franz Sigel which he expected to move south occupying a major grain producing area feeding Lee's army and preventing the rebels from moving any troops from there to reinforce Lee. The size of this force varied, at its height reaching about 48,000. It was opposed by a Confederate force initially under Maj. Gen. John C. Breckinridge numbering at its height about 23,000.

As spring came to an end and May approached, Grant issued orders for Meade to move his men into position. The next attempt to end the war would begin during the first week of the new month.

THE EFFECT

Life in the Confederacy became progressively more difficult in many ways during the spring of 1864. The more territory Federal troops occupied the less soil the South had to grow the crops necessary to feed not only its people but its army. The more railroads were captured, disrupted, or destroyed, the more difficult it was to move provisions and troops that were available to where they were most needed. The more territory the Union army occupied the more slaves were inclined to leave their work for freedom with the men in blue. And the more who left the fields, the more Southern agriculture suffered. In an attempt to plug this constant drain of agricultural labor, as well as potential labor for military purposes, President Davis issued two orders before the end of April: one required that any black member of the United States military who had been a slave and was captured must be returned to his owner, while the second required that any slave captured escaping or recaptured must likewise be turned over to her or his owner.

The drain on Confederate manpower was being keenly felt during the spring of 1864. In addition to those killed in battle, those too disabled by wounds to serve any longer, and the even larger number of those who succumbed to diseases in camp, in mid–April the Federal government issued a report stating that it had captured 146,634 rebel soldiers since the beginning of the war. When Confederate authorities attempted to round up those who were absent without leave and to enforce the draft law, protest meetings against conscription broke out in several places, especially in North Carolina. In February the Confederate Congress, facing severe manpower shortages, extended draft eligibility, which had applied to males between the ages of 18 and 45, to include those from 17 to 50. To help enforce the law, Davis suspended the right to *habeas corpus* for anyone accused of desertion, aiding the enemy, or spying. These moves greatly increased discontent, leading to a precipitate plunge in the president's popularity among civilians. During the spring Grant began a policy of refusing further prisoner exchanges since every soldier exchanged quickly reappeared in the rebel armies. This further exacerbated Confederate troop shortages.

Although Bragg had proven himself a disaster as a general officer in the west, Davis, who considered him a friend, incredibly appointed Bragg to a position of authority over all of the Confederate armies, a move that caused many in the military to question the president's judgment and left some hurt feelings as well. In early February 109 Union officers escaped from Libby Prison in Richmond, greatly embarrassing the Davis government. Although 48 were recaptured, 59 escaped to Union lines. The remaining two drowned trying to cross a river. This contributed to failing popular confidence in the government and also hastened plans to transfer prisoners to facilities farther south. Before the end of the month the first prisoners began arriving at a stockade named Camp Sumter in Georgia. It would soon become infamous for deprivation and cruelty as Andersonville.

The end of spring found the North in a much better position than the South in many respects, but it was not immune from casualties, disease, and desertion. On February 1 President Lincoln issued a call for another 500,000 men to serve for three years or the duration of the war. Later that month he agreed to a suggestion that the government compensate loyal farmers who owned slaves $300 for every slave they freed who then enlisted in the Union army. On April 8 the United States Senate endorsed a resolution to abolish slavery by a vote of 38 to 6, the first step in the eventual adoption of the Thirteenth Amendment. Later that month Congress adopted the Coinage Act of 1864, one result of which was the appearance of the phrase "In God We Trust" on the new two-cent coin. In the following year the words were extended to all gold and silver coins. Eventually, in 1956, it replaced "E Pluribus Unum" as the national slogan.

Throughout the spring there were a number of positive signs that the North was winning. In January pro–Union advocates met in Little Rock, Arkansas, and Nashville, Tennessee, to discuss how to bring their states back under the umbrella of Uncle Sam. In April a constitutional convention met in New Orleans to adopt a new state constitution that abolished slavery in anticipation of rejoining the Union. And on April 27 President Jefferson Davis dispatched Jacob Thompson to Canada on a secret mission to contact intermediaries in the North about the possibility of arranging a peace.

Summer

THE WEST

The strategy of the newly-promoted Lt. Gen. Ulysses S. Grant for 1864 was to apply pressure to all of the major fronts at the same time to take advantage of Northern numerical superiority by preventing the Confederates from shifting men back-and-forth between the East and the West as had been done when Longstreet's corps was moved west in the fall of 1862 to reinforce Bragg's army at Chickamauga and Chattanooga. In the west, the primary objective was to be Atlanta. The city itself was a vital railroad junction with warehouses and other facilities critical to the Southern war effort. Perhaps more important was Grant's belief, shared by President Lincoln, that the primary objective should be destroying the Confederate armies and not simply taking territory. By threatening Atlanta it was hoped that the defending army could be brought out into the field to confront the invaders and there, deprived of its defensive fortifications, delivered a crippling blow.

The sizes of the contending forces varied greatly during the campaign. Led by Maj. Gen. William Tecumseh Sherman, the invaders included the Army of the Tennessee (Maj. Gen. James B. McPherson; Fifteenth, Sixteenth, and Seventeenth Corps), the Army of the Ohio (Maj. Gen. John M. Schofield; Twenty-third Corps and a cavalry division under Maj. Gen. George Stoneman), and the Army of the Cumberland (Maj. Gen. George H. Thomas; Fourth, Fourteenth, and Twentieth Corps, along with a cavalry corps under Brig. Gen. Washington L. Elliott). The strength of Sherman's total force was reported as 110,123 at the end of April; 112,819 at the end of May; 106,070 at the end of June; 91,675 at the end of July, and 81,756 at the end August.[6] The Confederate forces under Gen. Joseph E. Johnston included four corps. Three were mostly infantry led by Lt. Gen. William J. Hardee, Lt. Gen. John Bell Hood, and Lt. Gen. Leonidas Polk, while the fourth was a cavalry corps under Maj. Gen. Joseph Wheeler. Johnston's Army of Tennessee reported 63,777 present on April 30, but that did not include the Army of Mississippi. On June 10 the combined forces reported 106,876 present; however a combined return for the end of the same month reported only 77,441 present. By July 31 the total present slipped to 64,762 with a slight increase by August 31 to 65,804.[7]

Sherman began his move south on May 7 and almost immediately ran into Johnston's army dug in behind entrenchments on a high hill named Rocky Face Ridge and along the valley to the east. Sherman, who did not want to risk a frontal assault on what appeared to be strong defenses, maneuvered around Johnston's flanks provoking minor actions at Buzzard Roost and Dug Gap, Georgia. Faced with this turning movement, Johnston had little choice but to fall back to another defensive position since to remain would expose his lines of communication and supply to being cut and his army isolated with Sherman between it and Atlanta. This set the script for most of the campaign with Johnston selecting excellent defensive positions, only to have Sherman flank him out of them, forcing him to retire to yet another position where the dance would begin anew.

The first major action occurred on May 14–15 when Sherman advanced against Johnston's defenses at Resaca for two days that were largely inconclusive except when Sherman eventually worked a force around the Confederate right where it crossed the Oostanaula River menacing Johnston's rear and forcing him to once again withdraw early on May 16. Together with a small rear guard action at Adairsville on May 17, losses were estimated at about 2,747 for Sherman and 2,800 for Johnston. The two-day engagement at Resaca reinforced Sherman's reluctance to order any further frontal assaults, but rather to rely on maneuver in an attempt to force Johnston out into the open where he could be attacked without the benefit of his defensive works.

Moving south, Johnston went into position at Allatoona Pass. Unwilling to risk an attack, Sherman again flanked Johnston out of his chosen defenses and made for Dallas where he hoped that by quick marching he could intercede between the rebels and Atlanta. Johnston was equal to the occasion, pushing his army forward to New Hope Church where on May 25–26 he administered a sharp rebuke to Sherman's leading corps. Estimated losses were 665 for Sherman and about 350 for Johnston. A renewal of the attempt to force Johnston's flank on May 27 at Pickett's Mill led to another rebuff with about 1,600

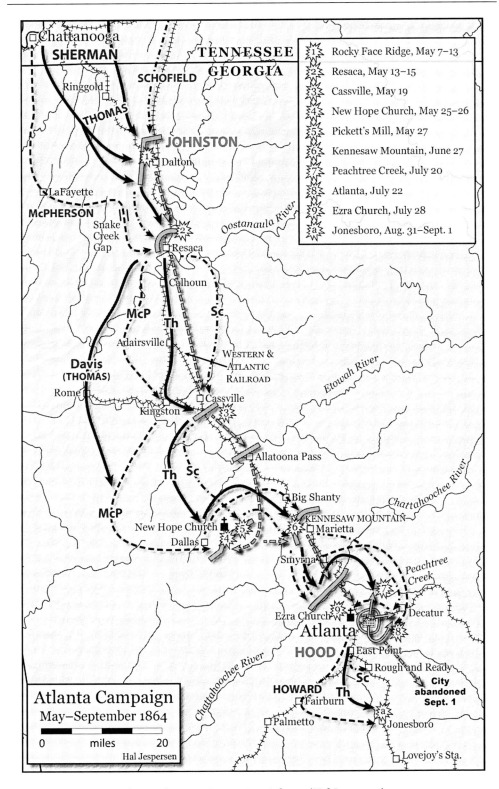

Sherman's campaign against Atlanta (Hal Jespersen).

Union casualties to 450 Confederates. The following day, May 28, Johnston, believing that Sherman's army might be overly extended because of its continual flanking moves, sent Hardee's corps against the Union Fifteenth Corps at Dallas but suffered serious losses in a costly repulse. Estimated casualties were between 1,000 and 1,500 Confederates to 380 Federals.

Johnston withdrew to Marietta where Sherman once again began his flanking movement. Johnston lost the services of Polk who was killed by a Federal artillery shell, but otherwise little developed except some skirmishing as Sherman's maneuvering finally forced Johnston to fall back once again to a very strong position at Kennesaw Mountain. On June 22 Johnston chose to attack the Union Twentieth Corps at Kolb's Farm in an attempt to catch it by surprise, but Hooker had already entrenched and the rebels suffered a damaging repulse losing around 1,000 men to 350 Federals. Perhaps frustrated by his inability to catch Johnston in open terrain, Sherman ordered an attack on June 27 that developed into his largest assault on Johnston of the campaign, losing about 3,000 men to Johnston's 1,000. Nevertheless, with his left flank endangered by a Federal penetration of his line, Johnston again fell back, this time establishing a new defensive position along the west bank of the Chattahoochee River. In early July Howard's Fourth Corps managed to cross the river on pontoon bridges, brushing aside some defending cavalry at Pace's Ferry on July 5. This once again gave Sherman the opportunity to place his army on Johnston's flank, forcing the rebels to retire to a position along Peach Tree Creek only three miles from Atlanta.

In mid–July two important events miles away had major implications for Sherman's campaign. The first was the Southern failure to cut Sherman's ever-lengthening supply line. Maj. Gen. Nathan Bedford Forrest attempted a wide circling movement to the west and northwest in an effort to get in behind Sherman's army to cut off its supplies in the hopes that this would force a halt to his advance on Atlanta. Forrest's command of about 7,000 cavalry and 2,100 infantry ran into the Sixteenth Corps under Maj. Gen. Andrew Smith with 13,000 infantry and 3,000 cavalry near Tupelo, Mississippi, on July 14–15. In the fight, Forrest suffered a serious wound forcing him to relinquish command. His force suffered 1,326 casualties including at least 215 killed compared to Smith's 674 with 69 dead. Although Sherman was later critical of Smith for not being more aggressive, Forrest's defeat preserved Sherman's supply line long enough for him to continue the Atlanta campaign to its conclusion.

The second influential event was a change in the Confederate command. Jefferson Davis had never liked Joseph Johnston, using him sparingly when no other alternative appeared readily available and relieving him quickly once he became dissatisfied over the slightest perceived problem. The Southern diarist Mary Chestnut wrote in late 1863 that Davis "detests Joe Johnston for all the trouble he has given him. And General Joe returns the compliment with compound interest. His hatred of Jeff Davis amounts to a religion."[8] Some authors have attempted to trace this mutual antagonism to prewar days, but most likely it began when Johnston chose to abandon Harpers Ferry early in the war, convinced it could not be held, while Davis wished to preserve it for Confederate use. Johnston was later angered when Davis placed him fourth on the seniority list of Confederate general officers when he believed his prior service as U.S. Quartermaster General entitled him to higher listing. Perhaps one consideration here was that Davis had supported Albert Sidney Johnston for the Quartermaster General position that had previously gone to Joseph Johnston; was it possible that ranking his original choice higher than Joseph Johnston was at least in part some revenge for his earlier choice not having been approved? Albert Sidney Johnston was in fact a long-time friend of Davis, as were Samuel Cooper and Robert E. Lee who were the other two ranked above Joseph Johnston. Of course, relations grew no better when Davis questioned Johnston's moves during the Peninsula Campaign and later appointed him to command in the west only to refuse many of his requests and then relieve him. As Johnston continued to retreat before Sherman, Davis became increasingly concerned that he planned to abandon Atlanta. When the president could get no firm commitment from Johnston that he planned to defend the city, Davis finally lost patience and replaced him with Maj. Gen. John Bell Hood[9] on July 17.

Hood had consistently urged Johnston to be more aggressive. With Johnston's removal it was clear to Hood that what the president wanted was a more aggressive approach to defending Atlanta, a belief that perfectly coincided with Hood's inclinations. Only two days after taking formal command on July 18, Hood launched a massive attack on the Army of the Cumberland at Peach Tree Creek. Committing two of his three corps under Hardee and Lt. Gen. Alexander P. Stewart to the attack, Hardee ran into stiff opposition but Stewart captured most of a Federal regiment and a four-gun battery, drove into the Federal line, and was finally only stopped by a determined counterattack. The Federals held. Tactically, the battle can be classified a draw but strategically it was certainly a Northern victory. Hood's plan to crush the Twentieth Corps failed, as did his plan to stop Sherman's inexorable march toward Atlanta. Federal losses are estimated at 1,710 with Hood's at 4,796. The long series of retreats followed by the repulse and attending losses at Peach Tree Creek began to take a toll on the morale of Hood's army as it filed back into the defensive works around Atlanta.

Gen. John Bell Hood earned a reputation in Virginia as an aggressive commander. He brought that inclination with him when he assumed command of the army defending Atlanta (National Archives and Records Administration).

Despite his failure at Peach Tree Creek, Hood determined to remain aggressive. This time he set his sights on McPherson's Army of the Tennessee, sending Hardee's corps on a circuitous fifteen mile march around the Union left to hit its flank and rear on July 22. At the same time Cheatham's corps was to occupy Sherman's front as cover for the operation, while Wheeler's cavalry was to make another attempt on Sherman's supply line. Hardee was late in arriving. The Fifteenth Corps which McPherson had in reserve easily repulsed the attempt to gain his rear, but the assault on the left flank nearly succeeded forcing McPherson to send in the Sixteenth Corps to stabilize the situation. Riding forward himself, McPherson was shot and killed by Confederate fire. McPherson's men held, but it was close.

Meanwhile, Cheatham's demonstration against the Union front actually broke through until massed artillery drove it back. Sherman lost 3,641 men while Hood lost a crippling 8,499. Once again Hood rolled the dice on an attack and lost. Tactically and strategically it was a sound Union victory with Hood wasting much of his remaining combat effectiveness.

Determined to reduce Atlanta, Sherman next ordered Howard's Army of the Tennessee to move west of the city to cut its supply line from Macon, Georgia. Hood countered by dispatching two corps under Stewart and Lt. Gen. Stephen D. Lee to attack Howard's troops at Ezra Church on July 28. Howard handily repulsed the rebel assaults inflicting 4,642 casualties for a loss of 642. But in the end he failed to cut Hood's vital supply line. Worse, at the same time he dispatched Howard, Sherman sent two cavalry forces under Maj. Gen. Edward M. McCook and Maj. Gen. George Stoneman to cut railroads south of Atlanta and, once their forces combined, to liberate thousands of starving Union prisoners at Andersonville. McCook's 2,400 men met with initial success, cutting the Atlanta & West Point Railroad and burning more than 1,000 rebel supply wagons. However, when McCook arrived at Lovejoy Station where he was to rendezvous with Stoneman the general was not there. McCook began to tear up the Macon & Western Railroad, but when after some time Stoneman did not appear he decided to retrace his steps. By this time rebel cavalry under Maj. Gen. Joseph Wheeler were in hot pursuit. Wheeler caught up with McCook at Brown's Mill where he administered a thorough beating. At a loss of about 50 men, Wheeler inflicted some 100 killed and wounded and captured 1,285 men, 1,200 horses, several wagons, two pieces of spiked artillery, and freed about 300 rebel prisoners. Meanwhile, Stoneman managed to get himself captured becoming the highest ranking Union officer to be made prisoner during the entire war.

These reverses convinced Sherman that he could not cut Atlanta's supply lines with cavalry alone. He ordered Schofield's Army of the Ohio west to extend Howard's line so as to cut the Atlanta & East Point Railroad. Schofield attacked Confederate positions at Utoy Creek on August 6 but was repelled losing about 400 men to 225 Confederates. Sherman then determined to use the bulk of his infantry to disrupt the city's supply lines. On August 25 he began to shift forces toward the Macon & Western Railroad. Hood sent Hardee with two corps including that of S. D. Lee and his own under Maj. Gen. Patrick Cleburne to prevent Sherman from cutting the last railroad link into the city. Hardee's plan was for them to attack the Fifteenth and Sixteenth Corps under Howard on August 31. The assaults by the two corps were not well coordinated due largely to Lee's being distracted by effective fire from Federal cavalry with repeating rifles. Lee finally launched a frontal assault but was easily repulsed. Casualties were estimated at 1,300 for Lee, 400 for Cleburne, and only 179 for the Federal forces involved. That night Hood, fearing an attack on Atlanta, withdrew Lee's corps into the city's defenses. As a result, on September 1 Sherman was able to overwhelm Hardee's remaining troops after a brief but stubborn resistance at Jonesborough. Union losses were reported as 1,149 while the Confederates lost an estimated 2,000.

With his last railway supply line cut and his defensive force greatly reduced, Hood evacuated Atlanta on the evening of September 1. As the rebels pulled out, Hood ordered a train with 81 cars loaded with ammunition and other military stores to be burned. The explosions were heard for miles, while the falling embers ignited other fires throughout the city. Some were easily doused, but others caused considerable damage that was later blamed on Sherman. Troops of the Twentieth Corps occupied the city the following day.

The fall of Atlanta was yet another grim blow to the Confederacy that had pinned such high hopes on defending the city. Aside from the material loss and the blow to morale, the staggering casualties suffered during the campaign were more than the South could hope to replace at this stage of the war. Using the peak strength of the opposing forces during the campaign, the following table recapitulates the losses.

	North	South
Effectives	112,819	106,876
Killed	4,423	3,044
Wounded	22,822	18,952
Captured & Missing	4,442	12,983
Total	31,687	34,979
Percent Lost	28.1	32.7

With Atlanta secured, Sherman still commanded an army of 81,000 men. Although his goal to destroy the Army of Tennessee was not completely attained, he came very close. Only about 30,000 troops remained after the evacuation of Atlanta. Added to this, on August 5 Vice Adm. David G. Farragut brought his fleet into Mobile Bay, defeating a rebel flotilla centered on the ironclad CSS *Tennessee*, bypassing the forts guarding the harbor, and seizing the last important Confederate port on the gulf coast, all with a loss of only 327 compared to an estimated Southern loss of 1,500. With Atlanta and Mobile both in Federal hands, little remained to be done to accomplish the complete subjugation of the entire western half of the Confederacy. Only Hood's remnant of the Army of Tennessee and a few smaller scattered commands remained to challenge the Northern legions.

THE EAST

The beginning of May 1864, found the Army of the Potomac reorganized but still under the command of Maj. Gen. George G. Meade. Maj. Gen. Winfield Scott Hancock's Second Corps was located between the Rappahannock and Rapidan Rivers to the south of Kelly's Ford with Maj. Gen. Philip Sheridan's cavalry command picketing the north bank of the Rapidan. Maj. Gen. Gouverneur K. Warren's Fifth Corps lay to the west camped south of Culpeper Court House while Maj. Gen. John Sedgwick led the Sixth Corps encamped north of Brandy Station. Including the artillery and engineers, this force numbered about 99,400 men. Initially comprising a separate command, Maj. Gen. Ambrose Burnside led the Ninth Corps, some 19,300 men, spread out along the Orange & Alexandria Railroad between Rappahannock Station and Manassas Junction, with a portion along the spur from Warrenton to Warrenton Junction. Together, the combined forces numbered about 118,700 men and 316 guns. Unlike his predecessors who appeared to identify occupation of real estate as the goal of their campaigns, Grant correctly identified the destruction of Lee's army as his objective. This was exactly the same approach President Lincoln had determined as the correct strategy even prior to the Gettysburg Campaign. On April 9 Grant sent an order to Meade setting the destruction of Lee's army as his purpose—"Lee's army will be your objective point. Wherever Lee goes, there you will go also."[10]

South of the line of the Rapidan and Rappahannock Rivers Maj. Gen. J. E. B. Stuart's cavalry picketed opposite Sheridan's men as well as guarding the passages over the Rappahannock east to and including Fredericksburg. Lt. Gen. Richard S. Ewell's Second Corps lay south of the Rapidan, with Lt. Gen. A. P. Hill's Third Corps camped around

Orange Court House and Lt. Gen. James Longstreet's First Corps between Gordonsville and Mechanicsburg. Including cavalry, artillery, and engineers, Gen. Robert E. Lee's Army of Northern Virginia numbered about 63,900 men and 274 guns. Lee's objective for the campaign was to defend the approaches to Richmond and, if an opportunity appeared, to attack any isolated portion of the Union army. In every previous campaign, the Federals reacted to a defeat with a retreat. Lee's purpose was to continue this scenario by forcing an end to this new Union advance.

Although greatly outnumbered, Lee could count on at least some modest reinforcements from the defenses of Richmond and Petersburg, as well as the coastal defenses of North Carolina. But these were not directly Lee's to command, he had to rely on Pres. Jefferson Davis to approve any requests that he made to draw upon these troops. These potential reinforcements were more than offset by other Union troops that Grant, as the commander-in-chief of all the Federal forces, could order about directly. Among the most immediately useful of these were 33,000 men of the Army of the James under Maj. Gen. Benjamin Butler and about 9,500 in the Department of West Virginia under Maj. Gen. Franz Sigel. Butler's assignment was to threaten Petersburg to pin rebel troops in their positions so they could not reinforce Lee and, if the opportunity arose, to capture the city. Sigel was to secure control of the rich Shenandoah Valley to prevent either troops or provisions being sent to Lee's army. Grant's strategic view for the 1864 summer campaigns was to exert pressure on the Confederacy along every front so that the rebels would not be able to shift forces from one threatened region to another. Sherman, along with some other smaller commands, was to engage Confederate forces in the west pinning them there and defeating them. At the same time Meade's army would engage Lee while Butler, Sigel, and some smaller forces would prevent significant reinforcements being sent to Lee and at the same time threaten areas the South could not afford to lose.

Grant moved south on May 4. His plan was for Meade to cross the Rapidan at Germanna and Ely's Fords, move quickly though the entangled Wilderness south of the river, then catch Lee's army out in the open south of the woodlands where the Northern numerical superiority could best be engaged against it. Although Grant expected a rapid advance through the wooded country, Meade advanced slower than anticipated then went into camp to allow his supply trains to catch up. Evening found the Second Corps camped around Chancellorsville and the Fifth about the Wilderness Tavern, both still deeply within the tangled terrain that Grant hoped to avoid. Meanwhile, Lee received early intelligence about the Federal advance and pushed his own forces forward in an attempt to engage the advance before it could clear the wooded landscape which was much better suited for defense than the rolling fields to the south. Lee ordered Ewell to advance quickly along the Orange Turnpike while Hill approached on the Plank Road. At the same time, Lee sent orders to Stuart at Fredericksburg and Longstreet at Mechanicsville to join him as rapidly as possible. Although neither army appears to have known exactly where the other was, Meade's sluggishness and Lee's quick response gave the Army of Northern Virginia an opportunity to occupy much better defensive position in the Wilderness than it would have had farther south.

As the army historian Col. Vincent J. Esposito explained, in the intertwine of woods and underbrush that was the Wilderness:

> Numbers meant little—in fact, they were frequently an encumbrance on the narrow trails. Visibility was limited, making it extremely difficult for officers to exercise effective control. Attackers could only thrash noisily and blindly forward through the underbrush, perfect targets for the concealed defenders.

In attack or retreat, formations could rarely be maintained. In this near-jungle, the Confederates had the advantages of being, on the whole, better woodsmen than their opponents and of being far more familiar with the terrain. Federal commanders were forced to rely upon maps, which soon proved thoroughly unreliable.[11]

Grant's plan to move rapidly through this dangerous region had failed.

The two armies engaged the following day when Ewell's corps ran into Warren's Fifth Corps slightly west of the Wilderness Tavern while Hill's corps fought a largely separate battle against Hancock's Second Corps to the south along the Orange Plank Road east of Parker's store. When Warren became engaged Meade ordered him to attack, but not knowing exactly what was in his front Warren wanted to wait until Sedgwick's Sixth Corps could come up to protect his flank. Meade ordered him to attack without waiting for Sedgwick resulting in a serious repulse, especially attempting to cross Saunders Field, a rare open space beyond which Ewell's troops had thrown up substantial earthworks within the edge of the woods. By the time Sedgwick arrived, Warren's men had largely broken off their assault. Nevertheless, Sedgwick pushed forward precipitating another hour of bloody fighting that gained nothing but lengthened casualty lists. With this, both sides settled in to build more fortifications while listening to the pop-pop-pop of cartridges on the dead cooked off by fires, ignited by the firefight, sweeping through the underbrush. Far more disturbing were the pained cries of the wounded as the fires reached them, burning alive those unable to move.

While Ewell and Warren slugged it out, Meade, now aware that he faced at least an entire corps, ordered Hancock to reverse his Second Corps north to come to Warren's assistance. Hancock ran into Hill's corps in the late afternoon. Another intense but inconclusive fight continued on until dark. By the time nightfall descended both sides had fought themselves to a standstill. That evening, Grant, convinced that he faced only part of Lee's army, ordered that Federal attacks be launched at dawn in the hope of overwhelming the Confederates before the rest of Lee's army arrived. Lee, expecting that Longstreet would be arriving before dawn to relieve Hill's corps, committed an error by allowing Hill's troops to rest rather than build further entrenchments overnight. Regardless of whether he planned to move Hill's corps the following morning, entrenchments were a basic precaution that whoever occupied the position—Hill or Longstreet—would certainly need if Grant continued the contest.

When dawn arrived on May 6 Longstreet had yet to arrive when Grant's attack rolled forward. Ewell, engaged by both Warren and Sedgwick had his hands full but managed to hold out, just barely. Hill's corps did not fare as well. Lacking substantial entrenchments, Hancock's advance seriously injured his command, sending its men reeling back in retreat. Just as his entire position was on the verge of collapsing, the Texas Brigade arrived at the head of Longstreet's column under the command of Brig. Gen. John Gregg. Under stress from Hill's deteriorating position, Lee became excited as Gregg's men went into line and moved forward, actually seeming to accompany them. Seeing this some of the men caught the reins of Lee's horse, threatening that they would only advance if he went to the rear. Longstreet soon arrived to assure Lee that the rest of his men were at hand and already forming for the advance. Indeed, Longstreet was correct. Not only did his men push Hancock back, but one group found an unguarded avenue to the Union rear along a railroad bed and were able to launch a surprise attack on Hancock's flank that rolled it up, forcing the Second Corps to withdraw. With success at hand, Longstreet, moving forward with his troops, was accidentally shot by Confederates only a few miles from where the same fate befell Stonewall Jackson a year earlier. Seriously wounded in the neck, he survived, but did not return to his command until October. With his incapacitation, the rebel attack ground to a halt.

Since the Union forces had been unable to advance, and casualties had been heavy, the evening of May 6 was an appropriate time for the Federal army to withdraw to lick its wounds. There is a well-known conversation often cited to illustrate the ingrained mindset of the Army of the Potomac on the one hand and Grant's thinking on the other. It seems that an officer approach the commander, concerned that he did not realize the importance of the reports they had received from the corps commanders. "General Grant, this is a crisis that cannot be looked upon too seriously. I know Lee's methods well by past experience; he will throw his whole army between us and the Rapidan, and cut us off completely from our communications." Grant hesitated not a second before snapping, "Oh, I am heartily tired of hearing about what Lee is going to do. Some of you always seem to think he is suddenly going to turn a double somersault, and land in our rear and on both of our flanks at the same time. Go back to your command, and try to think what we are going to do ourselves, instead of what Lee is going to do."[12]

The Battle of the Wilderness was a tactical draw, but could be considered a strategic Union victory since it did not end the Union movement south as Lee had hoped. Losses had been heavy on both sides during the two-day engagement in the Wilderness. In addition to Longstreet being seriously sounded, the Confederates had lost three general officers killed and mortally wounded, the Union two. Federal losses were listed as 17,666 (including 2,246 killed and 12,073 wounded; about 17.3 percent of those engaged). Confederate losses are uncertain but are generally estimated as 7,750 (about 12.7 percent),

Soldiers attempt to save wounded comrades from the approaching flames in the Wilderness in this Alfred R. Waud drawing (Library of Congress).

although some estimates place them as high as 11,400 (about 18.7 percent). Neither general displayed much brilliance in what became a simple slugfest in the confused terrain.

As Col. Vincent Esposito commented, "A year before, Hooker, commanding another Union army—just as large, and no more badly hurt—had accepted defeat and fallen back across the Rapidan."[13] On May 7 Grant began to withdraw his troops toward the northeast in seeming retreat. Federal morale dipped, but when the head of the marching column reached a crossroads it turned south instead of north. Morale soared. It was not a retreat, it was an advance.

Grant's intent was to move east around Lee's right flank with the objective of reaching Spotsylvania Court House which would place him between Lee and a direct route to Richmond. If he could do this, he might force Lee out into the open where he could be successfully attacked. Unfortunately, the Union army once again moved slowly. This, compounded by some confusion once darkness set in and a serious argument between Sheridan and Warren over whether the cavalry or infantry had the right of way on one of the roads, delayed the arrival of the infantry in the vicinity of Spotsylvania Court House until after dawn on May 8.

Lee remained in place during the day, seemingly unaware until late that Grant was moving toward the Confederate right. When he finally realized what was happening, he instructed Maj. Gen. Richard H. Anderson, temporarily commanding Longstreet's corps, on the Confederate right, to begin moving his forces toward Spotsylvania Court House at 3:00 a.m. on May 8. When Anderson could find so suitable room to camp his men away from the raging fires and the growing stench of the battlefield, he chose on his own authority to put his men in motion at 11:00 p.m. instead of waiting until 3:00 a.m. the following morning. By dawn he was within about three miles of Spotsylvania Court House where he halted his fatigued men for breakfast and a well-deserved rest. Within minutes an urgent message arrived from Stuart announcing that he was engaged with Federal infantry and needed immediate support. Anderson pushed his men on, the exhausted troops arriving just in time to halt the Federal advance on Spotsylvania Court House. By the combined circumstances of slow Federal movement and Anderson's decision to begin his march early the Army of Northern Virginia had reached Grant's objective before Union forces arrived in force to occupy the position.

As May 8 dawned, Lee's army had dug itself into entrenchments northwest of Spotsylvania Court House blocking Meade's line of advance along the Brock Road. By this time in the war, troops had become expert at fortifying a position within hours of arriving. No sooner was a halt called than the Confederates, with practiced precision, went to work digging trenches, piling logs and other hard fill, covering the obstacles with earth, cutting and placing abatis, and installing headboards to protect the men as they rose to fire over the fieldworks. In a matter of hours the men could erect very strong defenses over a large area. Warren launched an immediate attack, apparently unaware that he was facing more than cavalry, only to be sharply rebuffed. As Sedgwick's corps arrived it also went into line and became engaged, but suffered the same fate. Further troops arrived, both North and South, extending their respective positions until the Confederate defensive lines formed a large arc almost five miles long beginning near the Brock House Bridge along the Po River northeast across Laurel Hill and the Brock Road to the McCoull farm and from there southeast to and beyond Spotsylvania Court House. Anderson held the left, Early the right, with Ewell in the center holding a salient that became known as the "Mule Shoe" because of its configuration. Opposed to them were Hancock, Warren, and

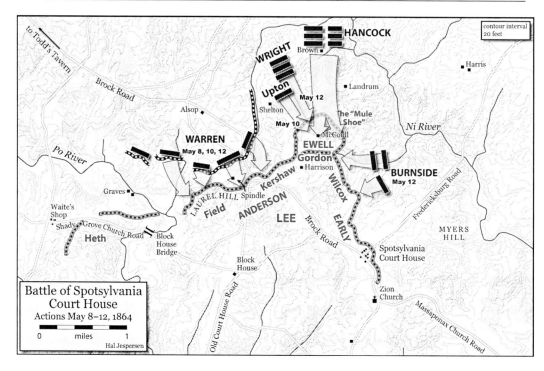

Battle of Spotsylvania Court House (Hal Jespersen).

Sedgwick on the face of the defenses held by Anderson and Ewell. On the east side of the Confederate defenses held by Early, Burnside's Ninth Corps fell into line. As the Federal troops began digging their own defensive fieldworks, Sedgwick inspected their efforts. Warned that rebel sharpshooters were active in the area he famously quipped that "they couldn't hit an elephant at this distance," only to be immediately proven wrong with a bullet through the head.[14] Meade replaced him with Maj. Gen. Horatio G. Wright.[15]

On May 10, after trading limited attacks earlier in the day, Grant ordered a major assault that went forward at 6:00 p.m. Leading it were twelve regiments numbering about 5,000 troops under Col. Emory Upton. To accomplish his mission, Upton determined to use a unique tactic. He noticed in previous battles that when attack waves went forward they slowed as men fired, reloaded, fired again, and so on. This prolonged their exposure between the lines

Col. Emory Upton devised an new and successful means of assaulting the Confederate works at Spotsylvania, but the lack of support led to ultimate failure (Library of Congress).

and hence their exposure to enemy fire. Upton ordered his men not to load their muskets but to fix bayonets and run across the intervening ground without stopping. The idea was to cover the ground as quickly as possible so the Confederates could only fire twice before the Federals would be upon them. Once they penetrated the rebel works the troops were to turn left and right to clear the way for supporting troops who would rush into the gap fully armed to exploit the breakthrough.

When the attack advanced it worked exactly as Upton hoped. His men rushed across the field, leaped over the works held by Brig. Gen. George Doles' Georgians and inflicted heavy casualties. Unfortunately for the attackers, the supports did not arrive in time. Quick reactions by Lee and Ewell moved reserves into the gap and closed it after a brief but vicious fight that was often hand-to-hand. Grant promoted Upton to brigadier general in recognition of his success in penetrating the Confederate line, acknowledging that he had used his experience to develop a new mode of attack. So impressed was Grant that he spent May 10 planning to use the same tactic on a much larger scale in an attempt to crush Lee on the following day.

Early on May 11 Grant sent a telegram to Secretary of War Edwin Stanton informing him that "The result to this time is much in our favor. Our losses have been heavy as well as those of the enemy.... I propose to fight it out on this line if it takes all summer."[16] That day he prepared to do exactly that, moving troops into position in a driving rain so they would be ready for an early morning assault. Lee, made aware of movement in the Union lines, interpreted it to mean that Grant was beginning to shift his troops east toward Fredericksburg. To prepare for his own move in pursuit, he ordered the artillery removed from the Mule Shoe to make it easier to get underway when necessary. He did not realize that he had withdrawn the artillery from exactly the position Grant planned to hit. Although Maj. Gen. Edward Johnson, holding the position, became uneasy and received permission to have the artillery returned this was not begun until early the following morning just before the Federals advanced.

Grant's troops quickly penetrated the rebel line in the heavy mist that settled in after a night of rain. Johnson, attempting to rally his troops, was captured along with Brig. Gen. George "Maryland" Steuart commanding a brigade under Johnson. Reacting quickly, Maj. Gen. John B. Gordon sent in three brigades to plug the expanding gap, while on the opposite side of the hole Maj. Gen. Robert Rodes sent in more men from his position. Additional troops fed into the melee from each side. Casualties mounted including Confederate Brig. Gen. Abner M. Perrin who was killed. Meade ordered Warren to send in his corps, but coordination was poor and only a portion of it attacked piecemeal. When the bloodbath was over the rebels had managed to halt the penetration and the Federals finally withdrew from their advanced positions. Casualties were heavy on both sides, an estimated 17,920 Federals and around 12,000 Confederates including about 3,000 rebel prisoners captured in the Mule Shoe. The aftermath on the battlefield was horrendous. Horace Porter, one of Grant's aides, later wrote that

the appalling sight presented was harrowing in the extreme. Our own killed were scattered over a large space near the "angle," while in front of the captured breastworks the enemy's dead, vastly more numerous than our own, were piled upon each other in some places four layers deep, exhibiting every ghastly phase of mutilation. Below the mass of fast-decaying corpses, the convulsive twitching of limbs and the writhing of bodies showed that there were wounded men still alive and struggling to extricate themselves from the horrid entombment. Every relief possible was afforded, but in too many cases it came too late. The place was well named the "Bloody Angle."[17]

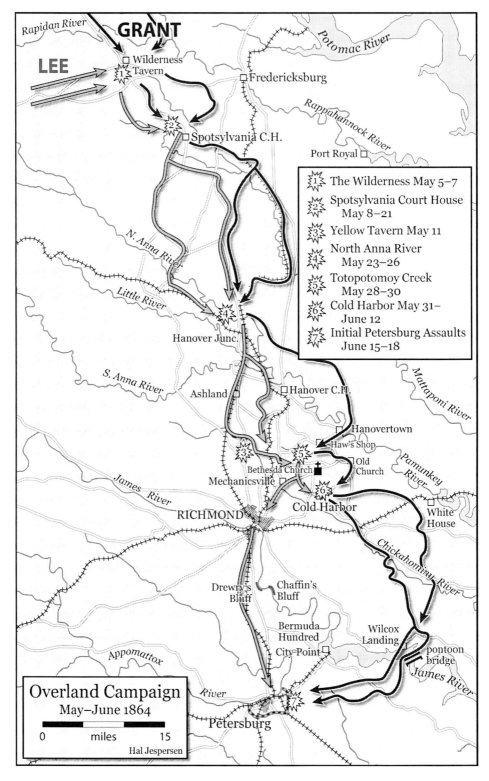

The map shows the Overland Campaign of May–June 1864, with locations including the Rapidan River, Wilderness Tavern, Fredericksburg, Spotsylvania C.H., Port Royal, Rappahannock River, Potomac River, N. Anna River, Little River, Hanover Junc., S. Anna River, Ashland, Hanover C.H., Mattaponi River, Hanovertown, Haw's Shop, Pamunkey River, Bethesda Church, Old Church, Mechanicsville, Cold Harbor, White House, RICHMOND, James River, Chickahominy River, Drewry's Bluff, Chaffin's Bluff, Bermuda Hundred, City Point, Wilcox Landing, pontoon bridge, James River, Appomattox River, Petersburg.

Legend:
1 — The Wilderness May 5–7
2 — Spotsylvania Court House May 8–21
3 — Yellow Tavern May 11
4 — North Anna River May 23–26
5 — Totopotomoy Creek May 28–30
6 — Cold Harbor May 31–June 12
7 — Initial Petersburg Assaults June 15–18

Overland Campaign
May–June 1864

0   miles   15

Hal Jespersen

The Overland Campaign of May–June 1864 (Hal Jespersen).

Northerners were heartened by the advance, but repelled by the serious casualties. Southerners became increasingly worried for the safety of Richmond despite Lee's seeming success in blunting Grant's attacks. Meanwhile, Grant had dispatched Sheridan on a massive cavalry raid that resulted in a clash with rebel horsemen at Yellow Tavern on May 11 mortally wounding Jeb Stuart causing, together with the mounting casualty lists, another round of heightened mourning in the South.

Following the major assault at Spotsylvania on May 12 the two sides felt each other's lines over the following days. After another repulse on May 19, Grant determined to maneuver Lee out of his strong defensive position. Given the need to supply his large army, Grant chose to move left, around Lee's right flank, so that he could change his base of supply to Port Royal. Aiming to place his force at Hanover Junction, Grant hoped to seize an important railroad junction to interrupt Confederate supply lines and force Lee out into the open. Yet once again Grant's army had to use more extended routes while Lee, though initially confused by Grant's maneuver, was able to use shorter interior lines to shift his army east, arriving at the junction before Grant so that when the Federals appeared they once again found rebels strongly entrenched across their line of advance. On May 24 Grant began crossing the North Anna River north of Hanover Junction, but Lee assumed a position anchored in the center on the river that resulted in Grant's forces being separated into two segments with Lee in the middle. Recognizing that this position left a portion of the Army of the Potomac isolated and vulnerable to being attacked, Grant ordered a withdrawal back across the river on the night of May 26–27 rather than run the risk.

Grant again moved left, attempting to flank Lee. Lee shifted southeast with him, going into position ahead of Grant at Totopotomoy Creek with skirmishing taking place daily between May 26 and May 30. With Lee's new position deemed too strong to assault, Grant ordered another flanking move to the southeast aiming at the road junction of Cold Harbor about 25 miles distant. Skirmishing between cavalry units, and in some cases the advance Union infantry units, continued through June 1 with rebel cavalry holding the town, being evicted, and then reoccupying it once Lee's infantry began to arrive. Additionally, reinforcements also began appearing for both sides. Grant brought in new units, largely raw heavy artillery regiments from the defenses of Washington converted into ersatz infantry. The Eighteenth Corps was also en route, some 16,000 men under Maj. Gen. William F. "Baldy" Smith, withdrawn from Butler's Army of the James. It approached the Cold Harbor area from the direction of Bethesda Church which placed it on Lee's exposed right flank. Arriving to reinforce Lee was a division of some 7,000 under Maj. Gen. Robert F. Hoke who Pres. Davis had removed from Gen. P. G. T. Beauregard's command south of the James River and rushed north. With these adjustments, Lee had at his disposal around 59,000 to oppose Grant with 108,000.

Skirmishing erupted through the day on June 1, as well as a Union attack about 6:30 p.m. Rebels repulsed it with the loss of about 2,200 Federals to 1,800 Confederates. Both Meade and Grant believed that an attack early the next morning had a good chance of succeeding. Grant ordered one for the early morning of June 2. Once again the Army of the Potomac responded sluggishly. This time it was Hancock's Second Corps that was late arriving requiring the early morning attack to be postponed until 5:00 p.m., and then until 4:30 a.m. on June 3. The unfortunate delay allowed Lee's men time to fortify their positions, shifting in reinforcements and artillery, to the point where they were nearly impregnable. To compound the problem, little pre-assault reconnaissance took place. When the attackers finally emerged out of the early morning fog Confederate fire shredded them in only fifteen to twenty minutes in a reprise of the lopsided slaughter of Fredericksburg in December 1862. In his memoirs, Grant wrote that the second assault at Vicksburg and that at Cold Harbor were the only two attacks he regretted ordering during the war. In at least the second case, what might have succeeded when originally planned, failed miserably after the lengthy delay provided the rebels with ample time to prepare their defenses.

The two armies held their positions without further major attacks until June 12 when Grant once again moved southeast in an attempt to cross the James River, aiming for Petersburg through which nearly all of the supplies supporting Lee's army had to pass. Cold Harbor cost the North an estimated 14,932 casualties to only 4,847 for the South. Many authors incorrectly state that Grant lost 12,000 to 15,000 men in twenty minutes during the attack on June 3, but these casualties included those of June 1–2 as well. Recent studies by Gordon Rhea suggest that Grant lost no more than 6,000 casualties on June 3 opposed to between 1,000 and 1,500 Confederates.

Tactically, Cold Harbor was another Confederate victory, but strategically it failed to halt Grant's inexorable march toward Richmond and Petersburg. By the time this new movement began, the "Overland Campaign," the name given by historians to the engagements of May and June 1864, had cost the Army of the Potomac some 50,000 casualties or 41 percent of its original strength. The Army of Northern Virginia lost about 32,000 or 46 percent of its beginning force. Grant had failed to bring Lee to a stand out in the open, but, unlike his predecessors, he was able to keep the initiative prohibiting Lee from maneuvering and taking the offensive himself. He had also bled Lee to the point where no large numbers of reinforcements could be found except for those few in the defenses of Richmond and Petersburg. Lee recognized very early, even before the campaign began, that if his army was forced back into the defenses of those cities it would be only a matter of time before it was defeated. Lee, acting effectively on the defensive, was still able to win tactical victories, but strategically Grant was winning the battle of position, slowly forcing Lee into the exact position he feared most.

While the bloodbath at Cold Harbor took place, Maj. Gen. Benjamin Butler, charged with threatening Petersburg, made a half-hearted attempt to do so but was easily repulsed by the few remaining defenders. On June 15 Grant began moving his own army across the James River on a lengthy pontoon bridge, a major feat of engineering expertise and a move that caught Lee by surprise. Meanwhile, Grant visited Butler in person, ordering another attempt to take Petersburg, but once again the effort came to nothing and Lee was able to shift forces south with Hill's corps beginning to arrive on the afternoon of June 18 to secure the important railroad crossroads. Another excellent opportunity to distress Lee had been lost due largely to the failure of Butler and the lack of aggressiveness by "Baldy" Smith who failed to push his advance forward. With Lee now occupying the defenses of Richmond and Petersburg, Grant had to content himself with a lengthy siege. He would have preferred to meet Lee in the open outside the defenses, but although the siege would take much longer to accomplish that, Lee, as he himself predicted, was now fused to the defenses, unable to maneuver. The end result, though prolonged, appeared to be developing as he had feared.

In a last effort to prevent the inevitable, Lee dispatched Maj. Gen. Jubal Early to assume command of 14,000 troops in the Shenandoah Valley where he was to move north eliminating Federal control of the vital grain-producing area. Much like Stonewall Jackson's Valley Campaign, Lee hoped this move would result in the withdrawal of troops from Grant's army to meet the threat, thus evening the odds and preventing the Federals from continuing their advance. Early managed to reach Winchester by July 2, then continued north to cross the Potomac River three days later. After defeating Federal troops along the banks of the Monocacy River on July 9, Early advanced directly on Washington. As Lee hoped, Stanton required that Grant dispatch troops to protect the capital. The leading elements of the Sixth Corps arrived around noon on July 11, the same day that Early reached the Federal defensive line at Silver Spring, Maryland. After some skirmishing, Early decided the fortifications were too strong to attack, especially once he became aware of the arrival of the Sixth Corps. Skirmishing took place throughout the next day, with Lincoln, who had come out to see for himself what was happening, becoming the first serving president to come under hostile fire on a battlefield. Early withdrew on the evening of July 12, re-crossing the Potomac at Leesburg two days later. Grant ordered the Sixth Corps to rejoin his army, but recognizing the need for positive action to deal with Early's force he sent Maj. Gen. Philip Sheridan to take command of Federal forces in the Shenandoah Region.

Gen. Jubal Early's raid toward Washington caused some anxiety in the capital but did not have the desired effect of weakening the siege of Richmond and Petersburg (U.S. Army Heritage and Education Center).

Recognizing that most of Lee's supplies flowed into Petersburg from the south and west before moving by rail north to Richmond, Grant determined to continue his movement south with the eventual objective of cutting these lifelines. After severing the Norfolk & Petersburg Railroad he continued extending his lines south to occupy the Jerusalem Plank Road. Toward the end of July Burnside approached Meade and Grant with an idea proposed by Lt. Col. Henry Pleasants commanding the 48th Pennsylvania. Recruited in a mining region of its state, the regiment contained a number of coal miners, including Pleasants who had been a mining engineer before the war. The proposal was to dig a long tunnel underneath the Confederate lines, pack the end with explosives, and detonate the charge to blow a major hole in the defenses. Infantry could then attack through the gap and shatter Lee's lines. As the digging progressed, the Confederates became suspicious that something was afoot. Although they attempted to countermine, none of their efforts uncovered the Union tunnel as it stretched to 511 feet in length some fifty feet below the rebel lines. After reaching its destination the mine was packed with 8,000 pounds of explosives in 320 barrels.

In preparation for the attempt, Burnside ordered Brig. Gen. Edward Ferrero's division of United States Colored Troops to undergo special assault training to prepare them to attack once the mine was exploded. Two other divisions of white troops were to be used as supports to exploit the breakthrough once it occurred. These preparations were dealt a blow when, only the day before the attack, Burnside received orders not to use the black troops in the first wave for fear that if the project failed and ended in a massacre

The Crater measured about 80 feet by 170 feet and went as deep as 30 feet destroying an entire section of Confederate defenses and the men who manned them (U.S. Army Heritage and Education Center).

public opinion might think that the black troops had been purposely used to save white lives. Because of this, when the mine exploded on July 30, working exactly as Pleasants had planned, a white division chosen by lot moved forward even though its men had not been trained or adequately briefed on what to expect. Instead of circumventing the massive crater left by the explosion as the black troops had been trained, they moved down into it and slowed down, aghast as the destruction. This gave the surviving rebels behind the front lines time to react. By the time Ferrero's division finally moved forward in support, the impetus of the attack had already waned. The battle turned into a brutal close encounter in which both sides fought with extreme bravery but the Federals were finally forced to withdraw. Part of the failure was due to the commander of the white division, Brig. Gen. James H. Ledlie, who stayed behind the lines in a bombproof shelter getting drunk rather than leading his men in person. Following the engagement he was relieved of command. Fed up with Burnside, Grant relieved him also.

The Battle of the Crater cost the North 3,798 casualties against reported Southern losses of 1,491. About half of the losses were from Ferrero's division with some Northerners asserting that rebels gave no quarter to wounded black soldiers or those who attempted to surrender. The mine experiment was Grant's last attempt to force an entry into Petersburg that summer. In three months since the campaign began he had continually moved his army south despite several bloody repulses until he had the Army of Northern Virginia pinned in the defenses of Richmond and Petersburg without sufficient strength to break the gradually closing vice on those cities and without the ability to maneuver in the open field which Lee had always relied upon to out-general his Northern opponents.

THE EFFECT

Abraham Lincoln received the nomination of his party for a second term as president at a convention held in Baltimore on June 8. It had not been a foregone conclusion. The Republicans lost Congressional seats in the 1862 elections causing some party members to fear losing the presidency if Lincoln were nominated again. Abolitionists approved of the Emancipation Proclamation, but were unhappy about the slow pace of actual emancipation. Radical Republicans were unhappy with the progress of the war and particularly Lincoln's plans for political restoration of the Union following the war. They considered the latter much too mild. A group of Radical Republicans met in Cleveland to nominate the 1856 candidate John C. Frémont, but he eventually withdrew in support of Lincoln. One group approached Lincoln's vice president, Hannibal Hamlin, with the idea of contesting the nomination, but he remained loyal to Lincoln and declined. Some sought to nominate Lt. Gen. Ulysses S. Grant, but he viewed Lincoln's re-election as crucial to winning the war and also declined. Maj. Gen. Benjamin Butler was interested, but he lacked sufficient support within the party organization and soon withdrew.

The most serious potential challenger was Salmon P. Chase, a member of Lincoln's own cabinet, who was a favorite of the dissatisfied Abolitionists and Radicals who believed Lincoln was too weak on emancipation and the use of black troops and who also opposed Lincoln's mild reconstruction plan. Chase threw his hat in the ring until pressure from fellow Ohio Republicans caused him to withdraw. Yet despite this internal conflict, some War Democrats joined with the Republicans to form a coalition styling itself the "National Union Party" to attract pro-war Democrats who might not otherwise vote for a "Republican" candidate. The group's platform supported pursuing the war until the unconditional surrender of the South, enactment of a constitutional amendment abolishing slavery, construction of a transcontinental railroad, and pensions for disabled veterans. As a running mate they chose Andrew Johnson of Tennessee, a former Senator and the military governor of Tennessee. As a Democrat, he was especially valuable in luring votes from supporters of that party. As the casualties mounted, Republicans believed they would need every vote they could get to emerge victorious in the fall canvass.

Before the political campaigning began in earnest, the Federal government continued to reflect a "business as usual" appearance as much as possible. On May 26, Congress established the Montana Territory, only seven weeks before prospectors discovered gold near Helena prompting an influx of people. On June 15 Secretary of War Edwin Stanton officially established Arlington National Cemetery by designating 200 acres of land on the Arlington, Virginia, estate of Robert E. Lee as a final resting place for Union war dead. It was selected by Union Quartermaster Gen. Montgomery C. Meigs who, grieving over the recent loss a son in the war, ordered burial details to create graves as near to the Lee mansion as possible to prevent its owner from ever using it again. On the last day of the month Pres. Lincoln signed into law a bill creating the first national park at Yosemite in California.

Over the summer a major concern both North and South was the rapidly escalating casualty lists. Grant's Overland Campaign was already exceptionally costly, while regiments that enlisted for three years in the summer and fall of 1861 were due to be discharged over the next several months further reducing his force. To feed the ongoing demand for manpower to fill the depleted ranks of the Union armies, Lincoln issued a new call for 500,000 more volunteers on July 18. In the same month, in an effort to close the means by which men were escaping induction, the president signed into law a bill eliminating the option in the conscription law for men to pay a fee to purchase an exemption.

In the South, attempts to conscript men into the rapidly diminishing Confederate military forces met with increasing resistance, while escalating desertions further thinned the ranks. To enforce conscription, as well as to silence growing anti-war agitation, the Southern Congress suspended habeas corpus between mid–February and the beginning of August. But it was not only the rebel armed forces that were feeling the pinch of diminishing resources. By the summer of 1864 the Union blockade had become much more effective resulting in further civilian shortages and greatly increasing prices. The Congress allowed people to pay their taxes in produce and livestock both to provide those commodities for the army and to ease the effects of skyrocketing inflation. Yet even when supplies were available the fragile Southern railway system, barely adequate even in peacetime, proved wholly incapable to moving men and stores to where they were needed in any reasonable timeframe, if at all.

Autumn

The West

With the fall of Atlanta Maj. Gen. William T. Sherman occupied that city with an army of about 62,000 men, having lost some troops to the expiration of their terms of service. President Lincoln declared a national day of tribute for September 5.

Southeast of the city at Palmetto, along the Atlanta & Montgomery Railroad, Lt. Gen. John Bell Hood sat camped with his 40,000-man Army of Tennessee. There he received a visit from Pres. Davis who came on the dual mission of raising Confederate morale and consulting with Hood about the management of the army once the campaign resumed. In the end, they determined that Hood ought to move north in an attempt to cut Sherman's supply lines and threaten Chattanooga. By moving west of Atlanta, Hood could expect to receive his own supplies via the Blue Mountain & Selma Railroad. With his lifeline in danger, Sherman would be forced to abandon Atlanta to move north or to operate directly against Hood. Once the Union army was out in the open Hood would presumably be able to maneuver for an opportunity to defeat a portion of it.

Sherman had other ideas. To deal with Hood he dispatched three divisions north to guard his lines as far as Chattanooga. He also sent Maj. Gen. George H. Thomas to Nashville with orders to organize all of the scattered commands in the Tennessee area. On September 29, Hood began crossing the Chattahoochee River heading north. Moving fast, he frustrated Sherman's attempts to determine his exact location through the expert leadership of his cavalry commanders. By the end of October Hood had lured Sherman as far north as Resaca, but all the while the Union general had been lobbying Grant to allow him to embark on a truly dangerous expedition. After dispatching Schofield with the Twenty-third Corps and some other reinforcement to Thomas, Sherman returned to Atlanta. On November 16 he once again left the city, but instead of pursuing Hood he headed east with 62,000 men determined to march completely across the state of Georgia to Savannah on the Atlantic coast.

Behind him Sherman left Thomas to deal with Hood who continued to move north. Although slowed by the failure of Maj. Gen. Nathan Bedford Forrest's cavalry to rendezvous with him on time, by November 26 Hood's army was at Columbia, Tennessee, along the Duck River. A portion of Thomas's command under Schofield south of the river withdrew just in time to avoid being cut off or possibly surrounded. However, Hood had a second opportunity to bag him and his troops when Forrest's cavalry and one of his infantry corps under Maj. Gen. Benjamin Franklin Cheatham went into position at Spring Hill cutting off Schofield's retreat north along the Columbia Pike. Although Hood later claimed to have ordered Cheatham to occupy the roadway to cut off Schofield, inex-

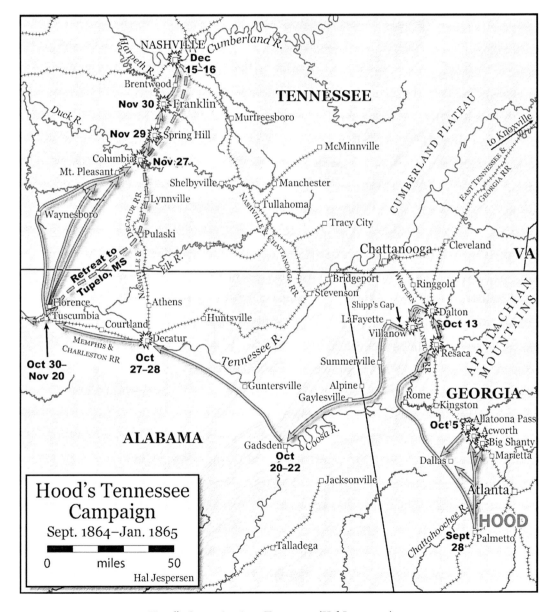

Hood's Campaign into Tennessee (Hal Jespersen).

plicably the entire Union force was able to continue north along the road within sight of the rebel campfires and within hearing of some of their conversations without being in the least interrupted. Whatever the facts of the matter, Hood lost a second clear opportunity to defeat Schofield's force before it could unite with Thomas.

Schofield arrived at Franklin on the morning of November 30 only to find that he remained vulnerable on the south side of the Harpeth River since both of the two available bridges had been burned. While engineers worked feverishly to re-plank the two bridges for the passage of the troops and their artillery and wagons, Schofield deployed his command into defensive positions which he ordered them to fortify as best they could. Franklin lay in a bend in the river, so Schofield was able to anchor each flank on the riverbank which prevented his position from being turned and allowed him to disperse his troops along the front lines while still maintaining a reasonable reserve.

When he arrived, Hood placed Cheatham's corps on his left and Lt. Gen. Alexander P. Stewart's on the right with one division of the late-arriving corps of Lt. Gen. Stephen D. Lee in reserve, a total of about 27,000 men on the field to face an equal number under Schofield. Hood, rejecting Forrest's advice to move along the river to a ford where he could bypass the strong position and cut off Schofield's retreat, instead determined to carry the Union fortifications with a frontal assault. About 4:00 p.m. six divisions containing between 19,000 and 20,000 men, more than participated in Pickett's Charge at Gettysburg, advanced across two miles of open fields toward the Union fortifications. Although the men displayed exceptional bravery, even briefly penetrating the first line of Union works in some places, they were decimated by combined artillery and musket fire that swept their ranks. Losses were crippling.

	North	South
Effectives	27,000	27,000
Killed	189	1,750
Wounded	1,033	3,800
Captured & Missing	1,104	702
Total	2,326	6,252
Percent Lost	8.7	23.2

But even these raw numbers did not tell the entire story. Hood's leadership cadre was gutted. Six general officers were killed or mortally wounded, seven more wounded, and one captured for a total loss of 14 generals, the highest of any engagement in the war. Fifty-five regimental commanders were also numbered among the casualties. Tactically and strategically it was a disastrous Southern defeat. Schofield not only survived, he was able to withdraw his entire army across the river when the bridges were finished, then march on to Nashville to unite with Thomas.

Hood followed. He found Nashville situated much as Franklin had been, the city located largely within a bend in the Cumberland River that allowed Thomas to firmly anchor his flanks on the waterway with his 55,000 men manning prepared defenses that even Hood recognized as much too strong to attack, especially with his greatly diminished numbers of only about 38,000 men. Hood went into position facing Thomas's left, the rebel numbers only enough to front about half of the Union fortifications. Despite his numerical superiority and the presence of a large number of fresh troops, Thomas bided his time making precise preparations for the forthcoming battle. After repeated inquiries about when he was going to advance, Stanton finally gave Grant permission to relieve Thomas if he did not move.

Several days of rain, sleet, snow and ice further delayed Thomas, but on December 15, the same day that Grant determined to finally relieve Thomas, the "Rock of Chickamauga" struck. His plan was to send a diversionary strike against Cheatham on the Confederate right while delivering a massive right hook to the rebel left. With the concentrated

cavalry of Maj. Gen. James H. Wilson swinging wide around Hood's left flank, massed infantry including Maj. Gen. Thomas J. Wood's Fourth Corps, Maj. Gen. Andrew J. Smith's Sixteenth Corps, and Schofield's Twenty-third Corps struck the rebel left flank. After a brief but stubborn resistance, Stewart's corps broke, its survivors streaming south along the Granny White Turnpike. The Confederate line thus unhinged, Lee's and Cheatham's corps joined in the precipitate retreat. Hood performed miracles rallying his men to form a new defensive line stretching from northwest of the Granny White house east to the Nashville & Decatur Railroad.

On the following day Thomas continued his attack. This time Cheatham's corps held the rebel left and it was his corps that broke triggering another hasty withdrawal. Covered by his cavalry, Hood retreated completely out of Tennessee to Tupelo, Mississippi, where he was finally able to halt what was left of his command for a well-deserved rest. In four short months Hood had ruined his army. On January 13 he requested that President Davis relieve him from command. The request was honored.

Gen. George H. Thomas destroyed the effectiveness of Hood's army at Nashville in December 1864 (Library of Congress).

Confederate casualties are unknown since many of the records did not survive. The following represent one estimate of losses.

	North	South
Effectives	55,000	30,000
Killed	387	1,500
Wounded	2,558	
Captured & Missing	112	4,500
Total	3,057	6,000
Percent Lost	5.6	20.0

Hood also lost over 70 guns captured. His campaign into Tennessee effectively eliminated the Army of Tennessee as an offensive fighting force. Only some 20,000 men remained, most of whom were eventually moved east to bolster Confederate forces in the Carolinas.

While Hood led the Army of Tennessee to near extinction in its namesake state, Sherman pushed his army steadily eastward across the heart of Georgia destroying railroads, factories, warehouses, and anything else that might be of use to the Confederate cause. In the process he also dealt a severe blow to Southern morale, promoting dissention among a populace that now came to understand that Federal armies could march almost anywhere they chose, whenever they chose. After being out of touch with Washington for some time, stirring concern in the administration, Sherman reappeared outside Savannah on December 10. Giving only brief thought to defense, Lt. Gen. William J. Hardee led the city's 10,000 defenders to safety across the Savannah River on a pontoon bridge. Sherman occupied the town the next day, December 21, capturing with it 25,000 bales of cotton. The same day he sent President Lincoln the following telegram: "I beg to present you as a Christmas gift the City of Savannah, with one hundred and fifty guns and plenty of ammunition, also about twenty-five thousand bales of cotton."[18] The South had once again been cut in half, a wide swath of destruction marking his "March to the Sea" with wrecked railroads, razed factories, burned warehouses, ruined commercial crops, and destroyed or confiscated material goods.

In 1865 Henry Clay Work wrote "Marching Through Georgia," a song commemorating the Union campaign. It became a hit not only with Northern veterans of the campaign, but Union veterans in general and a staple at their postwar reunions, especially when Sherman happened to be in attendance. The general came to hate the song almost as passionately as he had pursued the campaign that spawned it. He even made vain attempts to get program organizers to delete it from their repertoire, sometimes agreeing to attend only if it was not played. Yet it remained popular. When Sherman died in New York City in 1891 the funeral service was followed by a full military procession as befitting his rank and achievements. The band played "Marching Through Georgia."

THE EAST

With Grant investing Petersburg, Confederate forces in the Shenandoah Valley made another attempt to force him to release troops to protect Federal interests farther north. Early dispatched two brigades of cavalry to demand ransom from Chambersburg, Pennsylvania, and Cumberland, Maryland. Brig. Gen. John McCausland demanded $100,000 in gold or $500,000 in greenbacks from the civilian leaders of Chambersburg. When they were unable to pay he put the torch to the town destroying about two-thirds of the community. He was later overtaken by Federal cavalry under Brig. Gen. William W. Averell and defeated near Moorefield, West Virginia.

Hoping to increase Federal fears of another raid on Washington, Lee dispatched Maj. Gen. Richard H. Anderson with Maj. Gen. Joseph B. Kershaw's infantry division and Maj. Gen. Fitzhugh Lee's cavalry division to reinforce Early in the valley. This raised the rebel force to about 23,000 men. Maj. Gen. Philip Sheridan, sent to the valley to organize Union forces in response to Early, took some time to complete the initial dispositions, then began a slow movement down the valley. On September 19 the two forces met at the Third Battle of Winchester. Both armies suffered heavy losses, including Maj. Gen. Robert Rodes who was killed and Col. George S. Patton, the grandfather of the famous World War II general, killed leading the 22nd Virginia Infantry. Early was forced to retreat. Three days later Sheridan administered another sharp defeat on Early at Fisher's Hill. Skirmishing continued until October 19 with Sheridan believing that Early had been damaged to the point where he could no longer take the initiative.

Early proved this assumption wrong when he launched an attack at Cedar Creek that took the Federals by surprise. Catching many of Sheridan's men in their camps while their commander was away at Winchester, Early's men administered a sound defeat capturing 1,300 prisoners and 24 guns and driving the larger Federal force from the field. Only the heroic stand of some individual commands prevented it from turning into a complete rout. When informed of firing, Sheridan mounted his horse and, with a small guard, rushed to the battlefield an hour and a half of hard riding away. Fortunately for him, rebel troops halted to sack the Federal camps for food, clothing, and equipment which gave him a respite in which to organize a defense. When he launched a counterattack late in the afternoon Early's men put up a spirited fight until their left was turned and began to retire. Early's position then disintegrated rapidly, the men anxious to escape before their route to the rear was cut. Casualties greatly favored the South, but their estimated losses are probably incomplete and do not account for men who simply gave up after the defeat and went home. Tactically and strategically it was a major Union victory. Early's army effectively ceased to exist, its survivors eventually rejoining Lee in Petersburg. Early never held another field command.

	North	South
Effectives	31,610	21,102
Killed	644	320
Wounded	3,430	1,540
Captured & Missing	1,59	11,050
Total	5,665	2,910
Percent Lost	17.9	13.8

In the wake of his victory Sheridan reported destroying over 2,000 barns full of wheat and hay, 70 mills with wheat and flour, and took off more than 3,000 sheep to feed his troops, as well as other livestock. A cavalry sweep into Loudoun Country reported the further destruction or appropriation of 3,772 horses, 545 mules, 10,918 cattle, 12,000 sheep, 15,000 swine, 250 calves, 435,802 bushels of wheat, 77,176 bushels of corn, 20,397 tons of hay, 20,000 bushels of oats, 10,000 pounds of tobacco, 12,000 pounds of bacon, 2,500 pounds of potatoes, 1,665 pounds of cotton yarn, 874 barrels of flour, 500 tons of fodder, 450 tons of straw, 71 flour mills, 1,200 barns, eight sawmills, seven furnaces, three saltpeter works, four tanneries, a railroad depot, a woolen mill, a powder mill, and 947 miles of rails. Sheridan quipped that "a crow would have to carry its rations if it had flown across the valley."[19] The crucial food supplies of the Shenandoah Valley were lost to the Confederacy forever.

Taking advantage of his knowledge that Lee had dispatched reinforcements to Early in the valley, Grant sent Hancock with the Second and Tenth Corps to the north side of the James River to attack Richmond reasoning that the defenses there must now be weak. Hancock found the rebel lines strongly held, but skirmishing and probing attacks continued from mid–August into October to pin rebel forces in place. On August 29–30 rebels blunted a thrust at Chaffin's Farm where another clash took place exactly one month later. October 2 saw another clash at Peebles' Farm and five days later at the Darbytown and New Market Roads. Confederate losses in these meetings alone were about 5,000 compared to about 9,500 Federals. Tactically, these were all Southern victories, but strategically the result was that the continued pressure prevented Lee from sending reinforcements from Richmond south to oppose Grant's continuing efforts to cut the rebel supply lines into Petersburg.

On August 18 Grant ordered Warren to move his Fifth Corps, at the left flank of the Union position below Petersburg, to the west to cut and destroy the Weldon & Petersburg Railroad near Globe Tavern. His former positions in the trenches were taken over by the

Ninth Corps, the latter under the command of Maj. Gen. John G. Parke following the removal of Burnside. Warren reached the railroad easily and began its destruction but was hit with counter attacks on both August 19 and August 20. Both were repulsed, although the latter came close to succeeding in driving a wedge between Warren and Parke. Warren retired a short distance to a better defensive position where he again repelled a concentrated attack by Lt. Gen. A. P. Hill on August 21. Although the casualties favored the South, the railroad was permanently cut which furthered Grant's strategic objective.

	North	South
Effectives	20,000	14,500
Killed	251	211
Wounded	1,148	990
Captured & Missing	2,897	419
Total	4,296	1,620
Percent Lost	21.5	11.2

Grant then brought Hancock's Second Corps back south of the James River to reposition it on his left flank where it was to continue his movement west against the remaining Confederate supply lines.

Lt. Gen. A. P. Hill led another surprise rebel assault on Grant's advance at Ream's Station along the railroad behind the Union left flank on August 25 that overran a position of the Second Corps capturing nine guns, twelve colors, and as many as 2,000 prisoners. Total Union losses were 2,747 against 814 Confederates. Hancock had to exert every effort to stop the retreat, but the Confederates re-occupied Ream's Station and began hauling supplies overland from there west several miles to Dinwiddie Court House on the Boydton Plank Road from where they could then be shipped into Petersburg. It was a laborious and circuitous route, but it kept the supply line open. Aside from this, the only rail connection remaining into Petersburg was the South Side Railroad entering from the west beyond a crossroads named Five Forks.

While Grant and Lee settled in for a winter hiatus in the killing, Maj. Gen. Benjamin Butler led a portion of his army south on transports accompanied by a large Union fleet with the objective of capturing Fort Fisher. Located along the North Carolina coast at the mouth of the Cape Fear River, the fort guarded the approaches to Wilmington, the last major Atlantic seaport still open to Confederate blockade runners. In command of nearly sixty warships, the largest assemblage of naval power during the war, was Rear Adm. David Dixon Porter, the foster brother of Adm. Farragut. Arriving off the objective on December 23, the navy began bombarding the fort. Before an infantry assault the plan called for running a ship in close to shore loaded with 200 tons explosives in the hope that when it was detonated it might damage or cause a breach in the defensive walls. The experiment failed. Following a two-day bombardment troops went ashore north of the fort, but Butler decided to call a halt to the operation on December 27 claiming that the Confederate works were impregnable. The soldiers returned to their embarkation point without ever testing the fort's defenses. Grant had enough of Butler, relieving him of command.

THE EFFECT

By the autumn of 1864 the South was clearly under unrelenting pressure on all major fronts. Efforts to arrange an exchange of prisoners received, for the second time, a veto from Grant in August on the rationale that those who were freed would simply report back to their units and help to increase Lee's dwindling ranks. To address the growing manpower shortage Gen. Lee suggested at the beginning of September that slaves should be used as labor for his army to free white men for service under arms. By mid–September Lee's army also faced a provisions crisis, particularly acute since much of the anticipated corn crop from the Shenandoah Valley had either been destroyed or cut off from rebel lines. With food shortages everywhere, and no ready supply available to feed his army, Lee was forced to assign needed troops to dangerous raids out into the countryside, sometimes behind Union lines, to capture livestock and grain wherever they could be found.

When the Confederate Congress convened in Richmond on November 7, Pres. Davis attempted to reassure the delegates that the loss of Atlanta was not fatal. His optimism was not particularly convincing. Rumors began to circulate that Georgia, then bearing the brunt of Sherman's voracious army, might be considering suing for a separate peace with the Union government. So prevalent did this become that Davis actually conferred with Georgia's representatives to ascertain the truth. The state's leaders remained committed to the Confederacy, but when they issued a statewide call to arms for men to rally to oppose Sherman, few responded.

The crisis also spawned a number of desperate plots. In October, Confederate raiders based in Canada attacked St. Albans, Vermont, robbing money but failing in an attempt to burn the town. They escaped back across the border, causing a minor international incident. Eventually Canadian authorities returned the portion of the money they were able to seize from the raiders, but refused to extradite the men on the grounds that it was a military operation and Canada was neutral. Little damage was done in the long run except to turn some Canadians against the Confederacy which they viewed as violating their neutrality and trying to instigate a war with the United States.

In another plot a group of Confederate agents infiltrated New York City in November where they set close to twenty fires at various hotels and other locations including P. T. Barnum's famous museum. Fortunately for the city, the combustibles provided for the operation were not exceptionally powerful or reliable and the raiders did not realize that by closing the windows and doors to their hotel rooms when they left they deprived the mixture of the oxygen it needed to quickly spread the fire. Some minor fires were quickly extinguished. The conspirators mingled with the crowds in the streets before escaping by train to Albany and Buffalo where they crossed on the suspension bridge over the Niagara River into Canada. After some time, the raiders gradually made their way back to the South, but one, Robert C. Kennedy, was captured, placed on trial, and hanged in March 1865.

Confederate plots to release prisoners of war held in Camp Douglas near Chicago failed, as did attempts to seize the USS *Michigan* on Lake Erie in a plan to free rebel prisoners being held on Johnson's Island in Sandusky Bay along the Ohio coast of Lake Erie. An even more ambitious scheme to foment rebellion in the northwest to break Illinois, Indiana, and Ohio away from the Union went nowhere. In a more nefarious attempt to influence the war Dr. Luke P. Blackburn, a Southern sympathizer living in Canada, journeyed to Bermuda ostensibly to assist with a major outbreak of yellow fever since he had experience with the disease in Louisiana and Mississippi. While there he collected five trunks full of infected clothing, sheets, and other cloth items. His plan was to ship these to Halifax, Nova Scotia, from where they could be sent to several cities in the North to spark epidemics. One witness later testified that some infected shirts were even earmarked for mailing directly to Pres. Lincoln. By the time this plan developed to the point of execution the war came to an end.

Another problem still facing the North in late 1864 was the Copperhead movement. One of its activists was Lambdin P. Milligan, an attorney and farmer living in Huntington, Indiana, who supported States' Rights and frequented meetings of the anti-administration Knights of the Golden Circle. In October 1864 Milligan and three other defendants were brought before a military court charged with treason for having been part of a conspiracy to free Confederate prisoners of war, arm them, and incite further rebellion. The defendants were convicted and sentenced to death, but this was later commuted to life in prison. Milligan's attorney filed a writ of habeas corpus. The case dragged on through the courts until 1866 when the Supreme Court was asked to decide not whether Milligan was guilty of the offenses for which he was convicted, but whether the military court actually had jurisdiction for the case under the Constitution. In *Ex parte Milligan*, Chief Justice Salmon P. Chase wrote the court's majority opinion which found that the military court did not have jurisdiction since civilian courts were operating normally and there was no imminent threat of invasion or uprising.[20]

In the North, some business continued as usual. On October 13, Maryland voted to abolish slavery within its borders and on the last day of the month Nevada entered the Union as the 36th state. In the following month the quadrennial national canvass took place to determine who would lead the nation when the current four-year presidential term concluded. No president had won election to a second term since Andrew Jackson 32 years earlier and there was considerable criticism of the incumbent Abraham Lincoln. With the war dragging on amid ever-lengthening casualty lists, considerable unhappiness existed over Lincoln's handling of the war and his wartime strategy. Conservatives criticized the Emancipation Proclamation and its future impact on society, while others felt uncomfortable with the president's suspension of *habeas corpus* and other of his actions.

Sensing an opportunity to exploit public dissatisfaction, the Democrats met in Chicago August 29–31 where they nominated George B. McClellan for the presidency, hoping to use his popularity not only with the public but with his former comrades-in-arm to siphon votes away from Lincoln. This would be the first presidential election in which soldiers were allowed to vote by absentee ballot, so McClellan's military reputation was believed to be sufficient to attract support from this constituency. His running mate as vice president was George H. Pendleton, a member of the House of Representatives from Ohio. The Democratic platform criticized Lincoln for violating civil rights, issuing the Emancipation Proclamation, and other issues. It called for a ceasefire during which peace negotiations could take place to end the fratricide.

The Radicals who had attempted to wrestle the Republican nomination for John C. Frémont eventually gave up their opposition to Lincoln fearing that the continuing split would only serve to elect McClellan. During the campaign an elephant appeared in a Lincoln campaign pamphlet, the first time that this symbol was used in Republican Party material. There are differing opinions on what it originally meant, but one theory is that it derived from the phrase "seeing the elephant," Civil War slang for having been in combat. Perhaps it was an effort to conjure the image of military success as the war entered its fourth year with no immediate end in sight.

The campaign promised to be a close one with Republicans decidedly nervous about the potential outcome. Most historians believe that a deciding factor was the fall of Atlanta

Above: During the Election of 1864, McClellan attempted to portray himself as the best hope for peace. This Currier & Ives print depicts McClellan as a mediator between Abraham Lincoln and Jefferson Davis who are in the process of tearing the country apart (National Archives and Records Administration). *Below:* This 1864 pro–Lincoln cartoon shows Lincoln on the left shaking hands with a workingman represented by the square cap and saw while in the background black and white children play in freedom. This is contrasted on the right where McClellan is seen shaking hands with Jefferson Davis under a Confederate flag with slaves being auctioned off in the background (Library of Congress).

just two months before the election, coupled with Grant pinning Lee in the defenses of Richmond and Petersburg. By the November 8 canvass, the military situation had changed dramatically with renewed hope of victory apparent to many Northerners, not the least of which those in the army. In the end, it was not that close. Lincoln polled 2,218,388 popular votes to McClellan's 1,812,807, but the electoral vote was a runaway at 212 to 21 with McClellan winning only three states, Delaware, Kentucky, and his home state of New Jersey. Despite their fears, Republicans picked up fifty seats in the House of Representatives and four in the Senate. With the result of the election reaffirming Republican leadership, it became apparent to Confederate authorities that the possibility of a negotiated peace settlement based on Southern independence was most unlikely.

*   *   *

By the end of 1864 events had turned decidedly against the Confederacy. While both sides suffered through grievous battlefield casualties during the year, most people in the North felt a sense of hope that the arrival of the new year might finally bring with it victory. Few Southerners had any such hope. The crushing loss of Atlanta, the destruction of its infrastructure, the closure of nearly all of its ports, Sherman's march across Georgia with next to no opposition, the fall of Savannah, and the re-election of a president committed to forcing the South back into the Union all conspired to reduce Southern morale.

By the end of December the Federals reported 959,460 men on their enlistment rolls including 620,924 present and 338,536 absent (an absence rate of 35.3 percent). Confederate reports indicates a total of 358,692 men in its armies, 160,198 present and 198,494 absent (an absence rate of 55.3 percent).[21] Counting only those present, Federal forces outnumbered Confederate by 460,744. The North still had large numbers of men of military age upon whom to draw if needed; the South did not.

9

1865—The Union Restored

As dawn broke on January 1, 1865, the Confederacy found itself in desperate circumstances. Its premier army was tied down in the defenses of Richmond and Petersburg barely able to man the defensive lines much less take the offensive. Only the absolute minimum of supplies were trickling in from the southwest, enough to sustain the army but for how long was anyone's guess once the campaign resumed in the spring. Farther south, Sherman's army, having taken Savannah, was poised to begin moving north into the heart of secession in South Carolina with its collective eyes set on marching through the two Carolinas, as it had in Georgia, to link up with Grant at Petersburg where the two would overwhelm any remaining resistance to Federal authority. Farther west, scattered small rebel units continued to harass Northern troops, but there was no significant force that could be called upon to initiate a campaign significant enough to effect the outcome of the war. Food, reinforcements, and other supplies from the west were cut off. Virginia and the Carolinas were essentially on their own.

Faced with the reality of the situation, despite his positive public statements Pres. Jefferson Davis approved direct peace negotiations with the United States. The Hampton Roads Conference convened on February 3, 1865, aboard the steamboat *River Queen* near Ft. Monroe in Virginia. Davis sent Vice President Alexander Stephens, Senator Robert M. T. Hunter, and Assistant Secretary of War John A. Campbell to meet with Lincoln and Secretary of State William H. Seward. The South, its negotiators announced, was willing to abolish slavery in return for the United States agreeing to recognize Southern independence. The fact that Davis was willing to concede on emancipation certainly indicates the depth of desperation that the Southern president felt entering the new year. Lincoln proposed an immediate ceasefire, the dissolution of the Confederacy, and the recognition of emancipation by the Southern states. In return he was willing to discuss the possibility of Federal compensation to the owners of freed slaves and liberal treatment for Confederate civil and military officials. The important issue was of course Southern independence. That was the one non-negotiable question for each side: Davis was unwilling to yield on the subject and Lincoln was unwilling to so much as discuss it. With the sides at loggerheads over this central issue, the meeting broke up. The war would continue.

While Southern politicians desperately sought ways to forestall what increasingly appeared to be the inevitable defeat, in Washington the president and Congress engaged in political debates of another sort. In December 1863 a new Constitutional amendment was proposed that would make slavery illegal in the United States. If adopted, this would become a part of the Constitution and therefore could not be declared unconstitutional by the Supreme Court.

The Senate passed the amendment on April 8, 1864, by a vote of 38 to 6; only two Democrats, Reverdy Johnson of Maryland and James Nesmith of Oregon, voted "aye." However, just over two months later on June 15, the House failed to do so with 93 in favor and 65 against, thirteen votes short of the two-thirds vote needed for passage. The vote split largely along party lines, Republicans supporting and Democrats opposing the measure.

With this failure, Lincoln became personally involved in lobbying Representatives on behalf of the amendment, using all of the persuasion at his command, as well a liberal dose of political muscle derived from the prerogatives of his office. On January 31, 1865, the House finally approved the measure by a vote of 119–56. When adopted by the required three-fourths of all the states, the Thirteenth Amendment read:

> Section 1:
>
> Neither slavery nor involuntary servitude, except as a punishment for crime whereof the party shall have been duly convicted, shall exist within the United States, or any place subject to their jurisdiction.
>
> Section 2:
>
> Congress shall have power to enforce this article by appropriate legislation.[1]

Subduing the Carolinas

Wilmington, North Carolina, was the last major seaport open to Confederate blockade runners. Located along the Cape Fear River about twenty miles inland from the Atlantic Ocean, the approaches to the city were guarded by Fort Fisher. An expedition to reduce Fort Fisher under the command of Maj. Gen. Benjamin Butler had failed in December, prompting Lt. Gen. Grant to relieve Butler of his command. In January a second attempt began with the arrival of some 8,000 troops offshore under Maj. Gen. Alfred H. Terry, a Connecticut attorney and graduate of Yale University. A Pennsylvanian, Rear Adm. David Dixon Porter, led the accompanying naval fleet of 56 ships. The fleet began its bombardment on the evening of January 12 with troops landing in the first hours of the following morning.

The final assault took place on January 15. Sailors landed from the fleet made a direct assault on the seaward face of the fort, only to be driven back with heavy losses. To the north, four New York regiments under Col. Newton Martin Curtis raced across the sandy soil toward the northern ramparts. Met by artillery and musketry, three of the regiments were driven to ground, but on the far right the 117th New York, along with a few men from the 3rd New York, made it across the open space, chopped their way through a wooden palisade, scaled the outer walls, and established enough of a bridgehead into the fort to allow reinforcements to pour in to secure the foothold. After several hours of vicious fighting for gun emplacements and other fortifications, often hand-to-hand, the fort finally surrendered. Curtis received the Thanks of Congress and the Medal of Honor for leading the successful assault, as well as promotion to brigadier general. The last major port was now closed to the Confederacy. The road to Wilmington was open to the Union army. The city fell on February 22, opening the port for use in sending supplies and reinforcements to Sherman's army as it marched north through the Carolinas.

On February 18, 1865, *Harper's Weekly* carried this engraving of the House of Representatives when the Thirteenth Amendment was approved on January 31, 1865 (Library of Congress).

William Tecumseh Sherman led his men into South Carolina on January 16, one column aiming for Charleston and another for Columbia. Confederate forces evacuated the former on February 17, the same day that Sherman arrived outside Columbia. Maj. Gen. Wade Hampton[2] commanded the forces defending Columbia. Recognizing the impossibility of his task, he ordered his forces to evacuate the city, in the process setting fire to warehouses containing cotton and other materials to prevent them from falling into Union hands. When winds rose, the fires spread to surrounding areas, eventually consuming an estimated 80 percent of the city. Similarly, on the following night, February 18, defenders set warehouses and other facilities afire in Charleston, but the flames were

extinguished before they spread to the rest of the city. Although Southerners later blamed Sherman's troops for the conflagration that razed Columbia, it is clear that it was initially ignited by retreating Confederate troops and that at least some of the Union forces attempted to halt the spread of the flames.

The rapid progress of Sherman's troops through South Carolina, the fall of Columbia and Charleston, combined with the loss of Fort Fisher, prompted Pres. Davis, who had heretofore jealously guarded his prerogatives as military commander, to finally appoint Robert E. Lee as commander in chief of all Confederate armies. One of his first acts was to recall Joseph E. Johnston to command the remnants of the Army of Tennessee with orders to bring its survivors east where he was to take command of the forces opposing Sherman. While Southern forces under Beauregard struggled to get ahead of the fast

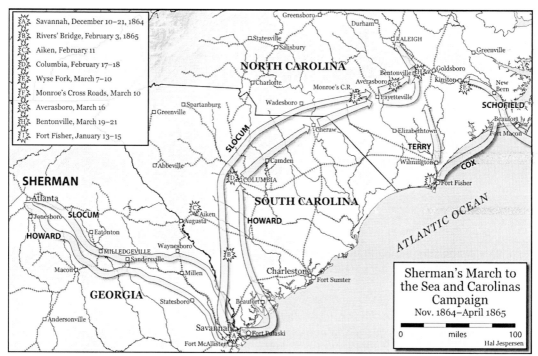

Top: Col. Newton Martin Curtis received the Medal of Honor for personally leading the assault on Ft. Fisher which closed the port of Wilmington, N.C., the last major Southern harbor open to blockade runners (Library of Congress). *Bottom:* Gen. William T. Sherman completed his "March to the Sea" in December 1864, then turned north into the Carolinas in the first month of 1865 (Hal Jespersen).

Alfred W. Waud's drawing of the burning of Columbia, South Carolina, appeared in the April 8, 1865, edition of *Harper's Weekly* (Library of Congress).

moving Federals, the men in blue crossed into North Carolina near Cheraw (SC), reaching Fayetteville by March 11.

Abraham Lincoln was inaugurated for his second term in office on March 4, 1865. His second inaugural address was relatively short, as he explained, because "at the expiration of four years, during which public declarations have been constantly called forth on every point and phase of the great contest which still absorbs the attention and engrosses the energies of the nation, little that is new could be presented." He went on to recall that at the time of his first inaugural address the nation was divided between those who sought to preserve it and those who sought to dissolve it. "Both parties deprecated war, but one of them would make war rather than let the nation survive, and the other would accept war rather than let it perish, and the war came." After clearly identifying slavery as the fundamental cause of the conflict, he stated unequivocally that it would not end until the institution of human bondage itself ceased. "Fondly do we hope, fervently do we pray, that this mighty scourge of war may speedily pass away." Looking forward to the day when the rebellion did in fact "pass away," Lincoln closed with a sentence that has endured as a part of his legacy: "With malice toward none, with charity for all, with firmness in the right as God gives us to see the right, let us strive on to finish the work we are in, to bind up the nation's wounds, to care for him who shall have borne the battle and for his widow and his orphan, to do all which may achieve and cherish a just and lasting peace among ourselves and with all nations."[3]

While Lincoln hoped for restoration of both the Union and peace, Joseph Johnston hurried east ahead of the remnant of the Army of Tennessee *en route* to join the Southern

The second inauguration of Abraham Lincoln, March 4, 1865 (Library of Congress).

forces defending North Carolina. Before Johnston arrived, Lt. Gen. William J. Hardee led a makeshift force in an attempt to impede Sherman's advance at Averasboro, North Carolina, on March 16. The clash cost 678 Federal casualties against 865 Confederates. After sunset ended the fighting Hardee withdrew. The next day Sherman continued north in two separated columns. The left, or westernmost, under the command of Maj. Gen. Henry Slocum, included the Fourteenth and Twentieth Corps. The latter advanced steadily driving back Hardee's force until darkness ended the fighting. Hardee withdrew overnight.

Johnston, arriving in person to command the Confederate forces, gathered some 21,000 troops at Bentonville in another attempt to defeat Slocum while Sherman's two columns remained separated. On March 19 Slocum attacked, driving back Hampton's cavalry, but in turn being forced back by Johnston's counterattack. Slocum, forced onto the defensive, withstood several rebel attacks until evening when Johnston withdrew somewhat to take up a better defensive position. Skirmishing occurred sporadically on March 20 as Slocum repositioned his forces. The following day he attacked, but Johnston held his position until nightfall, then retired north toward Smithfield. Each side had committed almost 17,000 troops to the fighting, with Federal losses of 1,646 being more than offset by 2,606 irreplaceable Confederate casualties. Sherman continued his march toward Raleigh.

The Siege of Richmond and Petersburg

While Sherman moved steadily northward, Grant continued his siege of Petersburg and Richmond, attempting at the same time to make sure that Lee did not escape to join Johnston in opposing Sherman. Continuing his strategy of the previous fall, Grant attempted to shift his forces south of Petersburg toward the west to cut off the remaining supply routes into the besieged cities. On February 5–7 he moved some cavalry and the Second Corps west to Hatcher's Run where a spirited Confederate counterattack was defeated killing Brig. Gen. John Pegram, the rebel commander, but not before the Federals suffered over 2,300 casualties.

With Grant's noose steadily choking off his vital supplies, Lee made one last attempt to force Grant to halt his relentless westward movement. On March 25 he ordered Maj. Gen. John B. Gordon to attack Fort Stedman only some 150 yards from the forward Confederate lines. Lee hoped that by taking the fort and breaking Grant's line he would force the Union commander to shorten his defenses to prevent disruption of his communication and supply lines. Gordon's attack achieved the crucial element of surprise. Given the short distance over which the attack took place, his troops penetrated the fort's defenses and captured the works relatively quickly, but the Federals just as promptly counterattacked under Brig. Gen. John Hartranft. With their line of retreat swept by Federal artillery fire, almost 2,000 rebels chose to surrender rather than risk the hazardous run back to their own lines. Federal casualties were reported as 2,080 while Gordon lost about 3,500. It was an expensive failure that Lee could ill afford.

If the Confederacy was in critical condition in January, by late March it needed life support. Existing returns from the Confederate armies show that on April 1, 1865, some 56 percent of all Confederate troops were absent without leave, the proportion being much higher in the Army of Northern Virginia. With only the most diehard of rebels still entertaining any hope in the triumph of their cause, in March the Southern Congress took the desperate step of authorizing the enlistment of slaves who were offered their freedom in return for service in the Confederate army. Taking this action clearly undercut the entire Southern argument that those of African descent could not learn the complicated procedures necessary to fire a musket in combat, or for that matter that they were even capable of the kind of courage the South routinely ascribed to its white warriors.

By the spring of 1865 the only major supply line open into Petersburg was the Southside Railroad, which was also the only means by which the Confederate armies in the Carolinas and Virginia could hope to be quickly redeployed to join forces. General-in-Chief Grant of course realized this. He had already warned Sherman to make sure that he prevented rebel forces from moving to join Lee, while promising that he would work to prevent the reverse. Having done this, Grant then determined to continue shifting his forces west in his attempt to isolate Lee in the defenses of Richmond and Petersburg. To accomplish this he sent Sheridan with three divisions of his cavalry force west toward the critical crossroads at Five Forks, backed up by Fifth Corps infantry under Maj. Gen. Gouverneur Warren. In response, Lee, recognizing the critical threat to his otherwise open right flank and his vital supply lines, sent some 19,000 troops to Five Forks under Maj. Gen. George Pickett. Lee ordered Pickett to "hold Five Forks at all hazards. Protect road to Ford's Depot and prevent Union forces from striking the Southside Railroad."[4]

Sheridan began his move on March 29, but the next day rebels hit his flank, slowly driving Sheridan's force back toward Dinwiddie Court House. The Fifth Corps advance

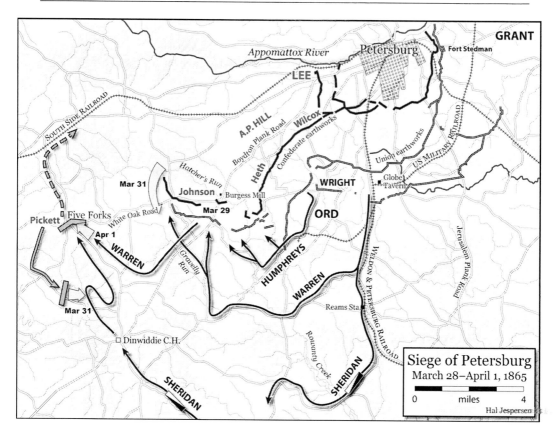

The siege of Richmond and Petersburg in the spring of 1865 (Hal Jespersen).

was similarly disrupted, but by the morning of April 1 the Federal positions had not only been stabilized but moved forward to close on the rebel position at Five Forks. Pickett, whose position was separated by about three miles from the main Confederate defensive works, was faced with defending some 1.75 miles of log and dirt entrenchments with both flanks covered only by small formations of cavalry. Despite the significance of the position, Pickett inexplicably chose to absent himself from the front to attend a shad bake some two miles away hosted by Brig. Gen. Thomas Rosser. When Sheridan, reinforced by Warren, attacked, Federal infantry quickly turned the Confederate left and began rolling up the flank. Pickett's line dissolved. Federal forces took more than a dozen Confederate colors and about 5,200 prisoners. Five Forks was in Union hands, and with it control of the vital Southside Railroad. Lee, who had ordered Pickett to hold Five Forks at all costs, realized that its loss imperiled his entire defensive position which was now stretched so thin that no adequate reserve force could be maintained. He sent a message to Pres. Davis informing him that his army would have to be withdrawn, opening the Confederate capital to occupation by Union forces.

A rising tide of Confederate deserters brought information that Lee had been forced to withdraw some troops from his defensive works to stretch his lines farther west. Convinced that the weakened defenses were vulnerable, Grant ordered a concerted assault all along the line to step off in the early hours of April 2. The Second, Sixth, Ninth, and Twenty-fourth Corps all achieved major breakthroughs completely shattering the Petersburg defenses. Only prompt action by Confederate leaders and equally swift marching allowed most of the defending troops to be withdrawn ahead of the advancing Federals. The two main forces under Lt. Gen. James Longstreet and Maj. Gen. John B. Gordon marched overnight toward Amelia Court House where they hoped to find provisions and join the rest of Lee's army.

Lee planned for the remnant of his army to move westward to Lynchburg where he hoped to receive badly needed supplies and perhaps even reinforcements from other commands. Grant, sensing that Lee was now vulnerable, pushed his army in pursuit with his cavalry surging ahead in an effort to get in front of Lee and cut off his escape route. Meanwhile, Maj. Gen. Godfrey Weitzel, a native of Cincinnati commanding the Twenty-fifth Corps, occupied Richmond on April 3. He found much of the city on fire, the flames spreading after retreating Confederates set fire to warehouses and supplies to keep them from falling into Federal hands. Weitzel's troops extinguished the blazes and established guards around the city to protect civilians and private property. Amid the fire and smoke, a young William Gorgas helped his parents save the family cow from the flames. He would later go on to a medical career highlighted by conquering the dreaded killer yellow fever.

Lincoln, who had been visiting the Federal base as City Point when Richmond fell, immediately insisted on entering the former Confederate capital. Arriving with his son Tad on April 4, he walked through the streets to an enthusiastic welcome by the former slaves who appear to have had a communications system that spread the news with amazing quickness. "No electric wire could have carried the news of the President's arrival sooner than it was circulated through Richmond," observed Admiral David D. Porter who accompanied the

Above: Gen. Philip Sheridan led Grant's flanking move that cut the last Confederate supply line into Petersburg at Five Forks. *Below:* Gen. Godfrey Weitzel led Federal troops into Richmond on April 3, 1865 (both photographs, Library of Congress).

president. "As far as the eye could see the streets were alive with negroes and poor whites rushing in our direction, and the crowd increased so fast that I had to surround the President with the sailors with fixed bayonets to keep them off.... They all wanted to shake hands with Mr. Lincoln or his coat tail or even to kneel down and kiss his boots!"[5] Lincoln visited the Confederate White House where he sat in Jefferson Davis's chair and met a delegation of self-appointed Southern leaders intent on finding a way to finally end the war. After a visit to the notorious Libby Prison where Union officers had been confined in horrible conditions, the president returned to his ship and headed back to Washington.

By April 5, the advance elements of Lee's army reached Amelia Court House where they were disappointed to find that no provisions or other supplies awaited them. With Federal troops closing off many of the potential escape routes, Lee chose to head southwest where he hoped that rations could reach his army via rail from Lynchburg, enabling him to then march south to join his force with that of Joseph Johnston. The following day, with his remaining troops strung out along the line of march—Longstreet's First Corps in the lead, followed by Lt. Gen. Richard H. Anderson (Third Corps), Ewell leading a miscellaneous force scraped from various secondary forces in Richmond, a lengthy wagon train, and Gordon's Second Corps—Grant's advancing forces caught up with the tail of the column near Sayler's Creek. Gordon, Anderson and Ewell faced their men about in an attempt to gain time for the wagon train to escape, but Federal infantry exe-

Federal officers look over the ruins of one of the burned districts in Richmond in April 1865 (Library of Congress).

cuted a textbook double envelopment encircling much of Anderson's and Ewell's commands. Six Confederate generals surrendered including Ewell and Lee's own son, Maj. Gen. George Washington Custis Lee. The various Federal commands reported 1,180 casualties with only 166 killed. Total rebel casualties were estimated at 1,500 killed and wounded along with 7,000 prisoners, the total of which was equivalent of one-quarter of Lee's entire army. Lee, seeing the disorder of those who managed to escape, wondered aloud, "My God, has the army dissolved?"[6]

Over the next three days as Southern morale fell and desertions rose, Lee struggled to keep his remaining troops ahead of Grant's encircling forces, hoping to keep open an escape route south or west. When Sheridan's cavalry occupied Jetersville, cutting off the southern route, Lee shifted westward, but Sheridan again gained the lead. Seeking to avoid further bloodshed, Grant took the initiative to communicate with Lee regarding the surrender of the rebel army.

General R.E. Lee, Commanding C.S.A.:
5 p.m., April 7th, 1865.
  The results of the last week must convince you of the hopelessness of further resistance on the part of the Army of Northern Virginia in this struggle. I feel that it is so, and regard it as my duty to shift from myself the responsibility of any further effusion of blood by asking of you the surrender of that portion of the Confederate States army known as the Army of Northern Virginia.
                                        U.S. Grant, Lieutenant-General[7]

Lee, though professing disagreement with Grant's assessment of the situation, nevertheless enquired what terms might be offered.

April 7th, 1865.
  General: I have received your note of this date. Though not entertaining the opinion you express of the hopelessness of further resistance on the part of the Army of Northern Virginia, I reciprocate your desire to avoid useless effusion of blood, and therefore, before considering your proposition, ask the terms you will offer on condition of its surrender.
                                        R. E. Lee, General[8]

The following morning Union cavalry under Brig. Gen. George Armstrong Custer captured and burned three trainloads of supplies and captured some thirty artillery pieces at Appomattox Station. Virtually no hope remained that Lee or his starving troops could avoid complete encirclement. Grant tried again.

April 8th, 1865.
General R.E. Lee, Commanding C.S.A.:
  Your note of last evening in reply to mine of the same date, asking the conditions on which I will accept the surrender of the Army of Northern Virginia, is just received. In reply I would say that, peace being my great desire, there is but one condition I would insist upon,—namely, that the men and officers surrendered shall be disqualified for taking up arms against the Government of the United States until properly exchanged. I will meet you, or will designate officers to meet any officers you may name for the same purpose, at any point agreeable to you, for the purpose of arranging definitely the terms upon which the surrender of the Army of Northern Virginia will be received.
                                        U.S. Grant, Lieutenant-General[9]

Still defiant, despite the dire circumstances, Lee continued in a state of denial about the situation of his army. Yet, after refusing to meet with Grant for the purpose of surrendering his army, he continued on in the same sentence to propose exactly that.

April 8th, 1865.

General:

　　I received at a late hour your note of to-day. In mine of yesterday I did not intend to propose the surrender of the Army of Northern Virginia, but to ask the terms of your proposition. To be frank, I do not think the emergency has arisen to call for the surrender of this army, but, as the restoration of peace should be the sole object of all, I desired to know whether your proposals would lead to that end. I cannot, therefore, meet you with a view to surrender the Army of Northern Virginia; but as far as your proposal may affect the Confederate States forces under my command, and tend to the restoration of peace, I should be pleased to meet you at 10 a.m. to-morrow on the old state road to Richmond, between the picket-lines of the two armies.

R.E. Lee, General[10]

On the morning of April 9 Lee probed the Union lines once again, seeking a weak spot through which he might lead his army to safety. The only result was adding another 700 casualties to his army's lengthy list of losses. Grant was not about to be drawn into a prolonged discussion of peace terms, especially since he clearly understood that peace was a political decision beyond his level of authority as commander of the United States army. Calling Lee's bluff, he replied:

April 9th, 1865.

General:

　　Your note of yesterday is received. I have not authority to treat on the subject of peace. The meeting proposed for 10 a.m. to-day could lead to no good. I will state, however, that I am equally desirous for peace with yourself, and the whole North entertains the same feeling. The terms upon which peace can be had are well understood. By the South laying down their arms, they would hasten that most desirable event, save thousands of human lives, and hundreds of millions of property not yet destroyed. Seriously hoping that all our difficulties may be settled without the loss of another life, I subscribe myself, etc.

U.S. Grant, Lieutenant-General[11]

With no other option remaining, Lee finally conceded.

April 9th, 1865.

General:

　　I received your note of this morning on the picket-line, whither I had come to meet you and ascertain definitely what terms were embraced in your proposal of yesterday with reference to the surrender of this army. I now ask an interview, in accordance with the offer contained in your letter of yesterday, for that purpose.

R.E. Lee, General[12]

Grant readily agreed.

April 9th, 1865.

General R. E. Lee Commanding C. S. Army:

　　Your note of this date is but this moment (11:50 a.m.) received, in consequence of my having passed from the Richmond and Lynchburg road to the Farmville and Lynchburg road. I am at this writing about four miles west of Walker's Church, and will push forward to the front for the purpose of meeting you. Notice sent to me on this road where you wish the interview to take place will meet me.

U. S. Grant, Lieutenant-General[13]

　　The two commanders eventually met at the home of Wilmer McLean in Appomattox Court House. A former resident of Manassas, Virginia, McLean's farm had been the site of some of the fighting at First Bull Run in 1861. Following the battle McLean moved to Appomattox Court House to escape the wartime violence. Now, the war that began in

Wilmer McLean's home in Appomattox Court House where Lee met Grant to surrender the Army of Northern Virginia (Library of Congress).

earnest in his backyard was to virtually end in his living room. Lee arrived in an immaculate new uniform while Grant arrived in the muddy attire of a common soldier with no particular distinguishing feature except the stars sewn onto the fabric. After brief introductions and an amiable exchange between the two principles, Grant wrote down the terms, handing them to Lee.

> Appomattox Court-House, Virginia April 9, 1865.
> General [Lee]:
>   In accordance with the substance of my letter to you of the 8th instant, I propose to receive the surrender of the army of Northern Virginia on the following terms, to wit: Rolls of all the officers and men to be made in duplicate, one copy to be given to an officer to be designated by me, the other to be retained by such officer or officers as you may designate. The officers to give their individual paroles not to take up arms against the government of the United States until properly exchanged; and each company or regimental commander to sign a like parole for the men of their commands. The arms, artillery, and public property to be parked and stacked, and turned over to the officers appointed by me to receive them. This will not embrace the side-arms of the officers nor their private horses or baggage. This done, each officer and man will be allowed to return to his home, not to be disturbed by United States authority so long as they observe their paroles and the laws in force where they may reside.
>
> U.S. Grant, Lieutenant-General[14]

Lee reviewed the terms, then asked if they might be revised to allow enlisted men to retain their horses or mules, explaining that, unlike in the Union army, the Confederate enlisted men provided their own mounts. Grant responded that while he would not change the written terms, he would instruct his officers to allow any soldier claiming to own an animal to take the horse or mule with him. He then offered to send rations to

Lee's men, asking whether 25,000 would be enough. Lee responded with appreciation, then slowly left, mounted his horse, and began the difficult ride back to officially announce the surrender to his troops.

On April 10 Lee said goodbye to his loyal men in a brief statement circulated to the various camps.

> After four years of arduous service, marked by unsurpassed courage and fortitude, the Army of Northern Virginia has been compelled to yield to overwhelming numbers and resources.
>
> I need not tell the survivors of so many hard-fought battles who have remained steadfast to the last that I have consented to this result from no distrust of them; but feeling that valor and devotion could accomplish nothing that could compensate for the loss that would have attended the continuance of the contest, I determined to avoid the useless sacrifice of those whose past services have endeared them to their countrymen. By the terms of the agreement, officers and men can return to their homes and remain until exchanged.
>
> You may take with you the satisfaction that proceeds from the consciousness of duty faithfully performed, and I earnestly pray that a merciful God will extend to you his blessing and protection. With an unceasing admiration of your constancy and devotion to your country, and a grateful remembrance of your kind and generous consideration of myself, I bid you all an affectionate farewell.
>
> R. E. Lee, General[15]

After four years of beating each other bloody, although each army naturally believed itself unexcelled in bravery and fortitude, Northern and Southern troops had come to respect each other as stubborn foes. An example is found in the memoirs of Walker B. Freeman, a soldier in the Army of Northern Virginia, who confided to his son that "there never was a greater army in the world than the Army of the Potomac, save one, which modesty forbids me to mention."[16] The son, Douglas Southall Freeman, would become the Pulitzer Prize-winning author of a four-volume biography of Robert E. Lee that is still regarded as the most definitive work on the Southern leader.

On April 12, the Army of Northern Virginia marched out of its camps to formally hand over its arms. Grant chose a volunteer general, a non–West Pointer, Maj. Gen. Joshua Lawrence Chamberlain of Maine, to receive the formal surrender. He conducted the ceremony with sensitivity, offering a formal salute as the rebels marched past. This was reciprocated by Gen. John Gordon leading the column of ex-rebels. With this, the formalities concluded. Although some cavalry and a few other men escaped, 27,805 men laid down their arms. The South's most famous army was no more.

The Confederacy Collapses

The day that Lee surrendered, Sherman turned his army toward Raleigh, North Carolina. While food was delivered to Confederate survivors of the Army of Northern Virginia and preparations made for their formal surrender, some 160 miles to the south Lt. Gen. Joseph E. Johnston struggled to keep his own force together. With his army reorganized into three corps, he was camped in the vicinity of Smithfield. Knowing that he was not strong enough to contend against Sherman's entire force, he looked for natural defensive positions and hoped that Sherman might commit an error that would provide him an opportunity to successfully attack an isolated portion of the advancing blue wave. But it did not take long for reality to overpower the urge to continued resistance. When word arrived of Lee's surrender, Johnston asked Sherman for a ceasefire on April 14. The

James Bennett's house, four miles west of Durham, North Carolina, where Johnston surrendered to Sherman on April 26, 1865 (Library of Congress).

formal capitulation came at James Bennett's house near Durham, North Carolina, on April 26, when Johnston formally surrendered some 89,270 Confederate troops spread throughout Florida, Georgia, North Carolina, and South Carolina.

With the capitulation of Lee and Johnston, aside from scattered small units, the only remaining significant formations of Confederate troops were in the Department of East Louisiana, Mississippi and Louisiana under the command of Lt. Gen. Richard Taylor, the son of former U.S. president Zachary Taylor, and the Trans-Mississippi Department under Gen. Edmund Kirby Smith. Recognizing that further resistance was futile, Taylor accepted surrender terms offered by Union Maj. Gen. Edward R. S. Canby on May 2 with the formal signing of paroles taking place six days later. Smith held out for another month before accompanying some 2,000 of his troops into Mexico rather than live under the United States government. He left his subordinate, Lt. Gen. Simon Bolivar Buckner, who surrendered Fort Donelson at the beginning of the war, to surrender on June 2, also to Canby. Other scattered smaller forces surrendered throughout May and June with the last group of any size capitulating to on June 23 when the Cherokee Brig. Gen. Stand Watie surrendered a force of Creek, Seminole, Osage and Cherokee troops in the Indian Territory.

The final meeting of the remains of the Confederate Cabinet met in Washington, Georgia, on May 4. Six days later, Jefferson Davis, attempting to flee south, was captured by United States troops near Irwinville, Georgia. When he and Vice President Alexander Stephens rode in a carriage through Augusta on their way to prison one of the bystanders who witnessed them pass was a young Woodrow Wilson. Secretary of State Judah Benjamin was the only member of the Confederate cabinet to escape, making it to Florida from where he boarded a blockade runner to Havana to take passage to England. Once there he became a noted barrister. John C. Breckinridge, former vice president of the United States and Confederate Secretary of War, also escaped to England via Florida and Cuba but soon returned across the Atlantic to Canada where elements of the wartime Southern secret service apparatus still remained. Most of the other prominent Confederate officials simply went home.

Unwilling to live under "Yankee" rule, Edmund Ruffin, the secessionist firebrand credited by some with having fired the first shot at Fort Sumter in 1861, committed suicide. Thousands of other Southerners chose exile as a less fatal alternative. Ex–Confederate generals John B. Hood and Jubal Early, along with some other Southerners, joined Breckenridge in Canada, while a few others joined Benjamin in exile. About fifty former Confederate officers joined the army of Ismail Pasha, Khedive of Egypt and Sudan. The Rev. B. R. Duval established a colony of mostly Virginians and Louisianans in British Honduras (today's Belize). Rear Admiral John Tucker established a colony in Perú where he had gained employment in the Peruvian navy, while other small settlements arose in Costa Rica, Cuba, and Venezuela.

Emperor Maximilian actively attempted to recruit ex–Confederates to Mexico with land grants and other inducements in the hope of gaining their support for his hard-pressed regime. The largest of these settlements, led by Commodore Matthew Fontaine Maury, was the New Virginia Colony centered on Carlota about half way between Veracruz and Mexico City, but smaller groups existed near Chihuahua, Cuernavaca, Monterrey, and Tampico. Ex-Confederate generals who accepted the emperor's hospitality included Hamilton Bee, Thomas C. Hindman, John B. Magruder, Sterling Price, Joseph Shelby, and Alexander Terrell. When Napoleon III withdrew French troops, many of the expatriate Southerners left also. Following Maximilian's execution in 1867, none of the land grants was recognized by the new Mexican government and the settlements quickly disappeared.

Another emperor who offered inducements was Dom Pedro II who sought to develop the commercial Brazilian cotton industry. Estimates on the number of Southerners who took the offers range from about 10,000 to 20,000, with most settling in the province of São Paulo although others moved to the southern areas of Santarém and Paraná. Most of the colonists and their descendants, known as "Confederados," were quite successful, became Brazilian citizens, and assimilated into Brazilian society while at the same time retaining a historical memory of their unique past that they preserved in the Associação Descendência Americana (American Descendants Association). In 1972, Jimmy Carter, then the governor of Georgia, visited Brazil where he and his wife Rosalynn went to see the grave of her great uncle, an original Confederado buried at Santa Bárbara d'Oeste.

The Human Toll

The Civil War cost more American lives than any war in United States history. The National Park Service estimates total casualties for both sides at 1,128,453. The usual estimate of mortality due to war-related causes is placed at 620,000, about 2 percent of the total population and 11 percent of those eligible to serve. In 2011 a demographic study of census records by J. David Hacker revealed a large percentage of the anticipated postwar population missing, leading him to conclude that a more accurate of estimate of Civil

War deaths might be about 750,000.[17] Based on surviving military records, it appears that out of every 1,000 men in uniform, 112 Northerners and 150 Southerners were wounded. A Yankee's chances of being killed in combat were one out of 18, while a rebel's were one out of eight. Of those who made it home, one in 13 returned missing at least one limb.

By far the greatest killer during the war was disease with one Northerner in eight dying from illness while one Southerner in five succumbed to one of these silent killers,

A photograph of ex–Confederate generals taken in Mexico on October 9, 1865. From the left are Isham Harris, John Magruder, Sterling Price, Joe Shelby and Thomas Hindman (Library of Congress).

For the first time, photography such as this Alexander Gardner picture of Confederate dead at Antietam brought the horrors of the battlefield to the average citizen (Library of Congress).

the two leading causes of death being diarrhea and dysentery. Poor hygiene, poor understanding of diseases and infections, and poor diet conspired to place more men in graves than were killed on the battlefield. The standard operation performed in makeshift field hospitals was the amputation which accounted for about 75 percent of surgeries. In general, the closer to the amputation was to the trunk of the body the less chance there was for survival. When the operation was at the hip, 84 percent of the patients died. For amputations of the arm, 24 percent succumbed. Surviving the actual surgery was not a guarantee of recovery since gangrene or other infections often overcame amputees days, weeks, or even months later.

"The Civil War," concluded Yale University historian David Blight, "left a culture of death, a culture of mourning, beyond anything Americans had ever experienced or imagined. It left a degree of family and social devastation unprecedented for any Western society."[18]

The Grand Review

3394

Gen. Henry Slocum and his staff lead a portion of the Army of Georgia along Pennsylvania Avenue during the Grand Review (Library of Congress).

President Andrew Johnson formally declared the rebellion to be defeated on May 10, even though isolated groups of rebels still held out into the summer. To celebrate the victory he called for a "Grand Review" of the victorious armies to be held in the nation's capital. On the beautifully sunny morning of May 23, Maj. Gen. George Gordon Meade led the Army of the Potomac, some 80,000 strong, along a Pennsylvania Avenue lined with thousands of enthusiastic citizens. The procession stretched for miles, taking six hours to pass the reviewing stand before the president, Gen. Grant, members of the Cabinet, and other dignitaries. The following day it was Gen. William T. Sherman's turn to lead his armies, 65,000 men fresh from their conquest of Joseph Johnston, before the admiring crowds. The celebrations lasted into the next week before the various volunteer units quickly began to demobilize and head home. America's most agonizing conflict was finally over … at least officially.

10

A Void of Leadership

The Union had triumphed; the United States remained united. But the end of the bloodshed on the battlefields only changed the location of continuing struggles over the same issues to the political arena.

The Assassination of Abraham Lincoln

News of Robert E. Lee's surrender raced across the North sparking public demonstrations of joy and thanksgiving. The war was not yet over, Confederate troops were still in the field, but the elimination of the South's most successful army convinced the Northern public that the end was indeed in sight. It would all be over soon. In the nation's capital jubilant crowds formed in the streets while others congregated at the White House hoping for a few words from the president. On the evening of April 11 Lincoln obliged the gathering with a brief statement in which he made an argument for his moderate plan to bring the South back into the Union quickly, with as little recrimination as possible, and with full protection for those of African ancestry.

In the crowd that night was a distraught supporter of the South depressed over the turn of events that brought an end to dreams of Southern independence. His name, John Wilkes Booth, was well known to anyone familiar with the American stage. Born in Bel Air, Maryland, in 1838, he was a member of the most prominent theatrical family of the era, the Booth family consisting of Junius Brutus Booth, Sr., and his sons Edwin, Junius Burtus, Jr., and John Wilkes. The latter began his career in 1857 and a year later joined the "Richmond Grays," a local militia unit in the Virginia capital, reportedly so that he could witness the execution of John Brown for which the unit provided security. Once the war began John Wilkes served as a Confederate agent smuggling information, drugs, and other contraband into the South, while also meeting with other Confederate operatives including those in Canada. Whether coincidental or not, he was also present in New York when rebel infiltrators attempted to set fire to the city. Now, with his cause in shambles, Booth listened intently to the president's words. Despair turned to rage as the words registered in his mind—12,000 people had sworn allegiance to the United States in Louisiana, had "held elections, organized a State government, adopted a free-state constitution, giving the benefit of public schools equally to black and white, and empowering the Legislature to confer the elective franchise upon the colored man."[1] Lincoln was advocating political equality for people of African ancestry. Something must be done.

Ford's Theater, the site of President Lincoln's assassination (Library of Congress).

Booth, who had earlier plotted to kidnap Lincoln, now turned his efforts to assassination convinced that it was the only way to avenge the South and perhaps bring an end to the president's plans for the postwar nation. Three days later he seized his opportunity when Lincoln decided to attend Ford's Theater for a performance of the popular comedy *Our American Cousin* on April 14. Contacting his small group of co-conspirators, he organized an impromptu series of attacks designed to decapitate the U.S. government. Booth assigned George Atzerodt to assassinate Vice President Andrew Johnson in his hotel, the Kirkwood House, while Lewis Powell, accompanied by David Herold, was to attack Secretary of State William Seward in his home where he was recuperating from an injury. General U.S. Grant was also to be assaulted, but he left town earlier that day so escaped the attempt. Atzerodt lost his nerve but Powell entered Seward's home, fought his way into the secretary's room, and seriously injured both him and his son before fleeing.

Booth reserved the president for himself. Entering the theater he knew so well as an actor, he easily moved through the building without arousing any suspicion from employees used to seeing him in the building. With no bodyguards present, the disgruntled actor entered the presidential box, placed a small pistol next to the president's head, and pulled the trigger. Removed across the street where a bedroom was commandeered, the mortally wounded president died the following morning, April 15, 1865.

Booth escaped by jumping from the box to the stage, fleeing across the stage and out a back door into an alley where he had asked an unsuspecting theater employee to hold his horse. Over the next few days he and David Herold made their way south through Maryland, crossed the Potomac River into Virginia, and were eventually cornered by Federal troops at a from south of Port Royal owned by Richard H. Garrett. Shot through the spine, Booth died the following morning. But that was certainly not the end of the episode or its influence. Aside from eliminating a chief executive who favored and was probably capable of delivering a speedy and relatively compassionate restoration of Southern political participation in the national government, the assassination, coupled with the public trial of conspirators that followed, produced a deep desire for revenge among many in the North, a revenge that would lead to twelve years of military occupation of the defeated rebel states.

There was certainly a conspiracy. Both circumstantial evidence and popular Northern opinion strongly suggested complicity by the defeated Southern government or its agents. Booth had clearly been not only a Southern sympathizer but active in the Confederate espionage and smuggling operations during the war. A search of his hotel room revealed coding devices used by the Confederate secret service. Mary Surratt, and her son John, who escaped, were both Southern agents and Dr. Samuel Mudd who treated Booth's injured leg was also involved in the pro–Southern ring operating in and south of Washington. At least two of the conspirators were former Confederate soldiers. Although all of this was enough to convince a large percentage of the Northern public that the Confederacy was behind the assassination, despite a recent spate of books claiming this was true no real evidence has yet surfaced to tie Jefferson Davis's government to the act. Regardless, Radical Republicans believed it implicitly, moderate Republicans and the general public mostly assumed it was true and whether true or not the belief that is was is what motivated people in the weeks, months, and years following Lincoln's death. The result was a hatred that fueled calls for revenge. In the terrible days following the killing of the president, Andrew Johnson declared that traitors must be punished and impoverished. During the years that followed the political restoration of the Union would not be swift and compassionate, it would be long and leave festering scars for decades to come.

Andrew Johnson Assumes the Presidency

Andrew Johnson took the oath of office as the seventeenth president of the United States on April 15, 1865. In general, Johnson attempted to carry out the more lenient policies toward the South envisioned by Lincoln in the Amnesty Proclamation of 1863. This stipulated that when, based on 1860 population statistics, one-tenth of the population of a seceded state swore an oath of allegiance to support the Union, that state would be restored to the Union, although there were some former leaders excluded from participation. The Lincoln Proclamation and Johnson's Amnesty Proclamation of 1865 are sometimes referred to as reflecting the period of "Presidential Reconstruction." On May 29 Johnson issued a proclamation of amnesty mostly mirroring his predecessor's with all Southerners being pardoned except those excluded by Lincoln—high-ranking Confederate civil and military officials—and Johnson's proclamation excluded persons owning taxable property valued at $20,000 or more. Those excluded from the common amnesty could apply directly to the president for an individual pardon. By fall Johnson was said to be signing some one hundred of these each day. Moreover, neither the Lincoln nor the Johnson Proclamation considered the legal status of the freedman. Kenneth Stampp, in his 1965 book, *The Era of Reconstruction, 1865 to 1877*,[2] argued that this omission and the lenient nature of restoration enunciated by the two proclamations was related to the respective goals of the presidents as each sought to use the restored Southern states to accomplish particular political objectives.

Andrew Johnson, a Southern Democrat, became president on the death of Lincoln (Library of Congress).

Congress had adjourned for the summer when Johnson issued his proclamation. Had they been in session, there would certainly have been a negative reaction to the provision in Johnson's amnesty restoring voting rights to most who had voted in 1860, not only because this would enfranchise former Confederates but because it quite obviously only extended the vote to whites. Although Johnson required Southern states to repudiate both slavery and the debts incurred by Confederate authorities and to accept the Thirteenth Amendment, little else was either demanded or sought. By the end of the year the president declared all of the Southern states "restored" and any act by Congress without Southern representation to be illegal. Congress responded that the president had acted unconstitutionally in usurping the legitimate function of the "Reconstruction" from Congress. The result was a political impasse with the president and Congress locked in a power struggle that prevented adequate Federal control in the South.

The resulting void of Federal leadership in the South during the summer of 1865 allowed the same wealthy planter class and individuals that had led the region during the antebellum and wartime years to remain in control of state governments. Under their leadership, Southern states acted quickly to find ways of keeping those of African heritage in subservient positions. South Carolina, for example, adopted a new constitution that it sent to Washington for approval so that it could reassume its place in the Union. The new instrument of government retained racial qualifications for voting and serving in the state legislature, as well as imposing severe restrictions on residents of African ancestry. In addition to political disenfranchisement, the document attempted as nearly as possible to perpetuate the inferior economic status that had existed for blacks prior to emancipation. "No person of color," one section read, "shall migrate into and reside in this state, unless, within twenty days after his arrival within the same, he shall enter into a bond with two freeholders as sureties."[3] This would effectively prevent the immigration of blacks unless they were in the employ of someone who required their labor. Other provisions specified that no person of color could become an artisan, mechanic, or shopkeeper unless the person obtained a license from a judge of a district court. Licenses could cost $100 or more at a time when the average annual wage of a male cotton mill worker was $285. It was clear that the provision was designed to eliminate all economic opportunity for African Americans aside from agricultural work.

Black residents of the state who were unemployed or without a permanent address were considered vagrants, as was anyone who could not produce $10 when required to by officials—of course, only those of color were required to meet this provision. Vagrants were liable to fine or imprisonment. If the fine could not be paid the person was bound to a term of labor in lieu of the fine. This usually took the form of required work on a local plantation, a state only superficially different from that of a plantation slave. The new constitution made free use of the terms "master" and "servant," requiring that "servants shall not be absent from the premises without the permission of the master" and the servants must assist their master "in the defense of his own person, family, premises, or property."[4] The purpose, of course, was to create a restrictive system as close as possible to that of slavery.

Further attempts to limit effects of Thirteenth Amendment and the participation of Africans in the social and economic life of the South came in the form of "Black Codes." Much like the South Carolina constitution, their purpose was to eliminate potential black political power and severely curtail economic opportunity. One of these appeared in Opelousas, Louisiana, specifying that "no negro or freedmen shall be allowed to come within the limits of the town of Opelousas without special permission from his employers.... Whoever shall violate this provision shall suffer imprisonment and two days work on the public streets, or pay a fine of five dollars." Further, any person of color found on the streets of the town after 10:00 p.m. was subject to the same penalties. But that was not all. The ordinance continued:

> No negro or freedman shall be permitted to rent or keep a house within the limits of the town under any circumstances.... No negro or freedman shall reside within the limits of the town ... who is not in the regular service of some white person or former owner.... No public meetings or congregations of negroes or freedmen shall be allowed within the limits of the town.... No negro or freedman shall be permitted to preach, exhort, or otherwise declaim to congregations of colored people without a special permission from the mayor or president of the board of police.... No freedman ... shall be allowed to carry firearms, or any kind of weapons.... No freedman shall sell, barter, or exchange any article of merchandise within the limits of Opelousas without permission in writing from his employer.... Every negro [is] to be in the service of some white person, or former owner.[5]

Bolstered by the Black Codes, backed by state and local governments largely in the hands of ex–Confederates, owners of large land holdings began to reassert themselves as they moved to recreate a new form of plantation. Owners divided their land into small parcels of twenty to fifty acres that were large enough to support a single family. In most cases, ex-slaves who had worked on the plantation were assigned one of these plots of land, along with seed and other supplies, in return for payment of one-half of their crop to the land owner. This was referred to as "sharecropping." The landowner essentially rented the land in return for a share of the crop. The sharecroppers could also purchase supplies on credit from the landowner, but at very high interest rates which sometimes reached as much as 70 percent per year. The result was a system of perpetual debt that reduced the sharecroppers to a state as close to slavery that was then legally possible.

At the same time that Southern legislatures moved to place severe limits on residents of African descent, some whites began to organize secret local organizations to oppose federal reconstruction through intimidation of both blacks and any whites who supported them. Styling themselves by a number of intriguing names such as Men of Justice, the Pale Faces, the Constitutional Union Guards, the White Brotherhood, and the Order of the White Rose, these groups were comprised mostly of ex–Confederates who sought to keep resistance alive. Of these the Ku Klux Klan became the most widely known, gradually absorbing nearly all of the smaller local factions. Organized in Tennessee in May 1866, it described itself as "an institution of Chivalry, Humanity, Mercy, and Patriotism."[6] It was none of these. The Klan used terror, whippings, lynchings and other forms of intimidation against blacks. Whites who supported the Republican Reconstruction policies were economically and socially ostracized, denied jobs, and often intimidated. The most important goal was to keep black men from voting so that ex–Confederates could maintain political control. In April 1867 a general meeting of local organizations held in Nashville, Tennessee, elected former Confederate cavalry general Nathan Bedford Forrest as its "Grand Wizard of the Empire."

This depiction of members of the Ku Klux Klan was published in *Harper's Weekly* on February 19, 1868 (*Harper's Weekly*).

The purpose of the Black Codes, the Klan, and other similar Southern strategies was to severely limit the freedom of movement and the rights of freedmen, deny them equality before the law, and eliminate any real economic options so that they could be forced back to the plantations where their lives would be little better than they had been before emancipation.

Congressional Moderates in Control

In December 1865, Johnson announced that all of the Southern states had met the conditions he established for resuming their status as states and the Union was restored, despite the fact that several had refused to renounce Confederate debts (a matter that would be resolved by the Supreme Court decision, *Texas v. White*, 1869) or otherwise not fully accepted Johnson's conditions, including Mississippi which refused to ratify the Thirteenth Amendment. Every government Johnson approved was all-white and each restricted the civil and political rights of black residents. This provoked further heated debate and animosity between the all-white Democratic governments in the Southern states, and their Democratic allies in Congress, against the Republicans who favored free labor and the extension of civil and political rights to ex-slaves. A joint Congressional committee comprised of six members from the Senate and nine from the House of Representatives announced that Congress would not recognize the state governments approved by the president and that only Congress had the authority to admit states to the Union.

When Congress reconvened on December 4, 1865, representatives from the presidentially-approved Southern states arrived to take their places in the House and Senate. When Congress adjourned the previous spring a bloody civil war was raging, the North had over a million men under arms, and there was a Northern, Republican, anti-slavery president in the White House. When they arrived in December the conditions were quite different. The war was over, the armed forces were being quickly discharged with little over 100,000 left in service, and the executive branch was now under the control of a Southern, Democrat who, before the Thirteenth Amendment, had been a slave owner. To make matters even less palatable to the Republicans, the Southern politicians waiting to take their seats included 58 former Confederate Congressmen, six cabinet members, five colonels, eight generals, and Confederate Vice President Alexander Stephens. As if to rub salt in the wound, some of the former rebel officers even arrived wearing their old uniforms. Republicans, and some Northern Democrats, were furious. Since Article I, Section 5 of the Constitution conveys to the houses of Congress the right to determine their own membership,[7] when the roll was called to begin the sessions the names of all of the would-be representatives from the states Johnson had certified were omitted, affectively denying them seats.

With the return of Congress clashes between the lawmakers and the president were only a matter of time. Despite the efforts of Northern Republicans, the all-white Southern state governments approved by Johnson acted swiftly to deny civil and political rights to blacks and to restrict them to occupations as agricultural laborers. One of the steps Republicans took in an attempt to thwart the Black Codes was to introduce a bill providing an indefinite extension of authorization for the Freedman's Bureau. Designed to provide ex-slaves with education, medical care, legal assistance, and other services, the reauthorization provided for trial by a military commission of anyone accused of violating the civil rights of freedmen. Republicans argued that this was necessary because it was otherwise impossible for freedmen to obtain a fair trial in the South. Adopted by both the House and Senate, Johnson vetoed the proposed legislation arguing that trial by military commissions violated the Fifth Amendment when civil courts were functioning or in peacetime and, in any case, Congress had no valid power to legislate without the participation of the eleven Southern states the president had approved. Congress overrode the veto.

In July of 1866, Republicans in Congress adopted the Southern Homestead Act in an attempt to address land issues. Led by Thaddeus Stevens in the House of Representatives, they argued that land ownership would give ex-slaves a positive step toward economic independence and equality. The legislation opened over 46 million acres of public land in Alabama, Arkansas, Florida, Louisiana, and Mississippi for sale to blacks or to whites who had been loyal to the Union during the war at the low price of $1.25 per acre. Originally offered in 80-acre lots, in 1868 the size of the parcel increased to 160 acres. As with the original Homestead Act, settlers were required to live on the land and improve it for five years to secure final ownership.

In a more direct assault on the proliferation of Black Codes, Congress also adopted the Civil Rights Act of 1866 that sought to extend federal protection to civil rights cases. First, the act clarified that

This Alfred R. Waud drawing appeared in *Harper's Weekly* under the title "The Freedman's Bureau." It shows a United States army officer, representing the Freedman's Bureau, holding back a mob from attacking ex-slaves (Library of Congress).

all persons born in the United States and not subject to any foreign power, excluding Indians not taxed, are hereby declared to be citizens of the United States; and such citizens, of every race and color, without regard to any previous condition of slavery or involuntary servitude, except as a punishment for crime whereof the party shall have been duly convicted, shall have the same right, in every State and Territory in the United States, to make and enforce contracts, to sue, be parties, and give evidence, to inherit, purchase, lease, sell, hold, and convey real and personal property, and to full and equal benefit of all laws and proceedings for the security of person and property, as is enjoyed by white citizens.[8]

Thaddeus Stevens, a Republican representative from Pennsylvania, was a Congressional leader in the fight for the elimination of slavery and the granting of civil and political rights to people of African descent (Library of Congress).

This provision provided a legal basis for black citizenship and equal enjoyment of the enumerated rights with white citizens. It went on to include provisions designed to enforce equal protection, provide penalties for those who violated its provisions, and specify that the United States Supreme Court was the final arbiter in cases arising from the act. This, its supporters hoped, would serve as an effective antidote to the growing racial discrimination in the South. Johnson vetoed the bill in the belief that it exceeded constitutional limits and was an unwarranted intrusion on the rights of the states. Congress passed the bill over Johnson's veto.

Although Republicans were pleased with the legislative victory, many of them were apprehensive that a legal challenge might invalidate key provisions of the law. The Thirteenth Amendment had clearly eliminated slavery from the national landscape by writing it into the Constitution. But early American immigration and naturalization law provided that only white people could become citizens and the Dred Scott decision had reinforced this notion by clearly stating that people of African ancestry were *not* citizens. In 1866 of the nine justices who returned that decision, three were still on the court and all three had concurred with the decision. Republicans feared the result if a legal action regarding the new law came before the Court. In short, the Supreme Court could overturn the intentions of Congress and the North in passing the Thirteenth Amendment. The solution appeared to be a new Constitutional amendment that would specifically address the citizenship question.

As Congress debated its options, during the summer of 1866 serious racial riots occurred in Memphis, New Orleans, and elsewhere in the South, convincing many Northerners that stricter measures would be required to protect the freedmen. One of the proposals was a Fourteenth Amendment to define citizenship and support Federal enforcement of civil rights, essentially the purposes of the Civil Rights Act of the same year but codified as part of the Constitution itself. Republicans submitted the new proposal to Congress in June 1866. Since Republicans feared that many Northerners were skeptical of black social and political equality, the authors had to craft something that would appeal to enough people to be approved. Although they attempted to make approval of the Fourteenth Amendment a condition for individual Southern states to rejoin the Union, Johnson rightly argued that this was unconstitutional since they were requiring what they claimed were conquered territories to vote for a Constitutional amendment despite the fact that the same Constitution plainly stated that only *states* can vote on amendments. It was an excellent point and one that Republicans were concerned that the Supreme Court might sustain if a case regarding the issue was brought before it. With this in mind, moderates attempted to fashion what they considered to be a compromise measure that would gain Southern support.

Section 1 of the amendment addressed the citizenship issue by stating that "all persons born or naturalized in the United States and subject to the jurisdiction thereof, are citizens of the United States and of the State wherein they reside." It further provided that "no State shall make or enforce any law which shall abridge the privileges or immunities of citizens of the United States; nor shall any State deprive any person of life, liberty, or property, without due process of law; nor deny to any person within its jurisdiction the equal protection of the laws."[9] This section established that people of African ancestry, if born in the United States, were in fact citizens and that all citizens enjoyed equal protection of the same rights. This was meant to bring civil rights enforcement under the purview of the federal government and in fact it has functioned as the cor-

This drawing from *Frank Leslie's Illustrated Newspaper* depicts women's suffragette leaders meeting with the House of Representatives Judiciary Committee in an attempt to have women granted the right to vote in the new amendment. Women were not accorded the right to vote until the Nineteenth Amendment in 1919 (Library of Congress).

nerstone for all modern civil rights legislation and federal enforcement. In short, the Fourteenth Amendment transformed citizenship from state to national determination and brought the rights of the Constitution and the Bill of Rights under national citizenship.

Section 2 is what the measure's authors viewed as a compromise. "Representatives shall be apportioned among the several States according to their respective numbers, counting the whole number of persons in each State, excluding Indians not taxed." This provision eliminated any vestige of the Three-Fifths Compromise, but in doing so it added a potential twenty new Southern seats in Congress, an ironic "bonus" for losing the war. However, then the section went on to say something quite interesting.

> But when the right to vote at any election for the choice of electors for President and Vice President of the United States, Representatives in Congress, the Executive and Judicial officers of a State, or the members of the Legislature thereof, is denied to any of the male inhabitants of such State, being twenty-one years of age, and citizens of the United States, or in any way abridged, except for participation in rebellion, or other crime, the basis of representation therein shall be reduced in the proportion which the number of such male citizens shall bear to the whole number of male citizens twenty-one years of age in such State.[10]

This is very interesting because it does *not* prevent states from denying the right to vote; rather, it appears to assume that they might do exactly that. And therein is the compromise. If the Southern states were to disenfranchise people, the only penalty they would suffer was loss of representation in the House.

Everyone knew the group likely to be disenfranchised. But there was one group that stood to win regardless of what any Southern state chose to do. If one was of African descent and a state decided to allow blacks to vote it was presumably good for those of African ancestry. If the state decided against allowing blacks to vote then it was not good for those of African ancestry. But looking at the matter from the perspective of Republicans, if the state allowed blacks to vote these would undoubtedly be almost exclusively Republican votes because no African American would vote for Democrats who had supported slavery during this period. On the other hand, if blacks were disenfranchised it would mean that although more Democrats would be elected the state would lose representation in the House, thereby leaving fewer Democrats to contend against Republican representatives in Congress. Either way, Republicans would win. It was a compromise they could well afford to make.

The remaining sections of the amendment disqualified from office ex–Confederates (who could apply to Congress for reinstatement) and repudiated the Confederate debt. In the end, some 627,000 whites and 703,000 blacks were registered to vote throughout the South in the wake of the amendment, with those of African ancestry forming majorities in Alabama, Georgia, Louisiana, Mississippi, and South Carolina.

Tennessee ratified the Fourteenth Amendment on July 19, 1866, and was readmitted to the Union by Congress, but Johnson continued to argue that the South had already been "restored" by presidential action and any action by Congress without Southern representatives participating was illegal. Congress responded that the president had acted unconstitutionally in usurping the function of the "reconstruction" from Congress. Johnson, holding fast to his position that Congress was acting illegally, advised the other Southern states to reject compromise and the Fourteenth Amendment and await the results of the fall 1866 election. The president was convinced that Northerners were tired

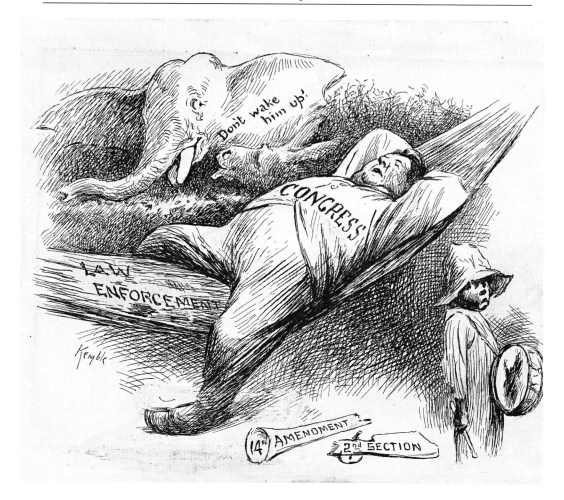

This Edward W. Kemble drawing portrays a Republican elephant cautioning against awakening a slumbering Congress. Beneath the hammock lies a broken weapon labeled "14th Amendment, 2nd Section." The cartoon criticizes the lack of enforcement of black voting rights (Library of Congress).

of the continuing controversy over the Reconstruction and would vote against the radicals in Congress. Following the election, he assured Southerners, moderates would be in control of Congress and a better "deal" could be arranged. With this, although 1866 was not a presidential election year, the campaign became largely a referendum on Johnson's leadership.

Johnson seriously misjudged Northern feelings. Moderate Republicans were furious that their efforts to find some compromise had been rejected. "The last of the sinful ten," remarked Representative James A. Garfield of Ohio, referring to the remaining ten ex–Confederate states, "has, with contempt and scorn, flung back into our teeth the magnanimous offer of a generous nation. It is now our turn to act."[11] Then it became worse. Johnson incited ire among both Republicans and the general Northern population when a letter he wrote to the Provisional Governor of Mississippi, William L. Sharkey, was stolen and published. In it the president said: "If you could extend the elective franchise to all persons of color who can read the Constitution of the United States in English and

Appearing in *Harper's Weekly* on May 26, 1866, this Alfred R. Waud drawing was labeled "Scenes in Memphis, Tennessee, During the Riot—Burning a Freedmen's School-House" (Library of Congress).

write their names, and to all persons of color who own real estate values at not less than $250 and pay taxes thereon, you would completely disarm the adversary."[12] While one would think Republicans would be happy with Johnson's call for black enfranchisement, they found the appeal weak, merely asking in an almost pleading manner, and more importantly, they focused on the last phrase—"you would completely disarm the adversary." Adversary? Who was the adversary? Clearly, Johnson meant the Republicans. Throughout the North this was taken as confirmation of Johnson's pro–South intentions.

Residents of the Northeast also favored Republican policies on industrial development, while those in the Northwest backed Republican support for internal improvements and homestead legislation. Looking at Johnson's actions toward the South, many throughout the North believed the accusations that Johnson was a rebel at heart, especially in the wake of a series of serious race riots in New Orleans, Memphis, and other Southern locations during the summer. When the votes were tallied, 42 Republicans and only eleven Democrats were returned to the Senate, 143 Republicans and 49 Democrats to the House. The Republicans won a sweeping victory, returning a veto-proof two-thirds majority in both houses of Congress. When the new Congress convened in December it established the Joint Committee on Reconstruction of the South. The radicals would now be in a controlling position, there would be no further negotiation, the only discussion would be among Republicans on what terms to impose on the South as conditions for the return to the Union and to Congress of the former Confederate states.

11

Radical Reconstruction

Following the election of 1866, on January 22, 1867, Congress adopted a law providing for a special session of the newly elected Congress to convene in March after every election. This allowed the new Republican dominated legislature to meet nine months earlier than previously. Republicans immediately used their control of both houses to impose their own Reconstruction plan on the South. What would be known as the First Reconstruction Act began:

> *Whereas*, no legal State governments or adequate protection for life or property now exists in the rebel States of Virginia, North Carolina, South Carolina, Georgia, Mississippi, Alabama, Louisiana, Texas, and Arkansas; and whereas, it is necessary that peace and good order should be enforced in said States until loyal and republican State governments can be legally established; Therefore—
>
>   *Be it enacted by the Senate and House of Representatives of the United States of America in Congress assembled*, That said rebel States shall be divided into military districts and made subject to the military authority of the United States as hereinafter prescribed; and for that purpose Virginia shall constitute the first district; North Carolina and South Carolina the second district; Georgia, Alabama, and Florida the third district; Mississippi and Arkansas the fourth district; and Louisiana and Texas the fifth district.[1]

The legislation eliminated civil government in these respective military districts and gave the military governors responsibility for state voter registration, with Africans eligible to register and vote. Whites who had held public office before 1861 and supported the Confederacy were disqualified from voting or holding elective office. The military governors were also empowered to hold elections and oversee development of new state constitutions that would be required to include black suffrage. These new state constitutions would also be required to ratify the Fourteenth Amendment as a condition for re-admittance to the Union. Based on the new state constitutions, new legislatures needed to be formed that extended the franchise to Africans according to the criteria for national voter rights under the Fourteenth Amendment. When these requirements had been fulfilled, the former Confederate states could apply for readmission to the Union.

Johnson once again raised the issue of legality by his vetoing the bill, explaining that Congress was requiring political units that it claimed were not states to act as if they were states for the purpose of ratifying an amendment when legitimately only a legally constituted state within the Union could exercise this authority. He had a good point. Nevertheless, Congress overrode the veto on March 2, 1867.

Although the new law promised to place the Reconstruction under Congressional control, Congress feared that the president, by virtue of his role as commander-in-chief of the armed forces, might circumvent the statute by issuing orders directly to the new military governors. This would allow Johnson to order the military governors to ignore any Congressional directives. To address this, Congress adopted the Command of the Army Act requiring the president to issue all military orders through the General of the Armies, a position then occupied by U.S. Grant, and not directly to military governors or other military personnel. When President Johnson attempted to replace Secretary of War Edwin Stanton, a leader of the radical Republicans who Johnson thought was undermining his policies, with one of his own supporters, Congress responded with the Tenure of Office Act in 1867. After overcoming yet another presidential veto, the legislation required that "every person holding any civil office to which he has been appointed by and with the advice and consent of the Senate, and every person who shall hereafter be appointed to any such office, and shall become duly qualified to act therein, is, and shall be entitled to hold such office until a successor shall have been in like manner appointed and duly qualified."[2] In other words, any person appointed to office by the president with the consent of the Senate was entitled to remain in that office until the Senate approved a new appointee. This was designed to prevent Johnson from replacing Secretary of War Edwin Stanton, or any other cabinet appointee, without the approval of the Republican-controlled Senate.

In August 1867 Johnson again attempted to remove Stanton from office but Congress refused to approve the move. By this time it was obvious that the president was a "lame duck" in the worst sense, powerless to effect his own policies or to prevent the Radical Republicans from pursuing their own agenda. Johnson began to characterize the Radicals as "factious, domineering and tyrannical." They responded by labeling Johnson a "drunken imbecile" and a "ludicrous boor."[3] Relations between the two branches of government continued thereafter to be either uncivil or none at all.

In February 1868, Johnson made a second attempt to remove Stanton. From the White House to wrote to the Secretary of War on February 21: "By virtue of the power and authority vested in me as President by the Constitution and laws of the United States, you are hereby removed from office as Secretary for the Department of War, and your functions as such will terminate upon receipt of this communication. You will transfer to Brevet Major General Lorenzo Thomas, Adjutant General of the army, who has this day been authorized and empowered to act as Secretary of War *ad interim*, all records, books, papers, and other public property now in your custody and charge."[4] This was a clear violation of the Tenure of Office Act. The president followed his missive to Stanton with an order to all military governors instructing them to report directly to the president, a violation of the Command of the Army Act.

Stanton barricaded himself in his office and refused to leave. The House of Representatives responded quickly, if perhaps less dramatically, on February 24 by voting 126 to 47 to impeach the president for "high crimes and misdemeanors." Although the impeachment proceedings mostly addressed the issue of the Tenure of Office Act, there were a host of other presidential actions to which Northern Republicans objected. Johnson had vetoed some twenty bills approved by Congress. He continually had attempted to subvert Congressional authority for the reconstruction. He had recommended to state political leaders in the South that they refuse to approve the Fourteenth Amendment. He had failed to enforce federal laws in the South that would offer protections to ex-slaves. He had ordered the eviction of ex-slaves from land upon which they had been settled through federal authority. Clearly, there were many reasons for Northern Republicans to be unhappy with Johnson.

Impeachment is the first of two stages in a process by which a legislative body may remove a government official from office. For the executive branch, only those who have allegedly committed "treason, bribery, or other high crimes and misdemeanors" may be impeached. Although treason and bribery are obvious, the Constitution is silent on what constitutes "high crimes and misdemeanors."[5] Several scholars of the Constitution have suggested that Congress alone may decide for itself what constitutes an impeachable offense under these terms.

In the first step, the House of Representatives passes "articles of impeachment" by a majority vote. The articles constitute the formal allegations. Upon their passage, the defendant has been "impeached." This process is similar to a grand jury where evidence is presented to see if there is sufficient reason to conduct a trial. If there is, the person is "indicted" on specific charges and a trial is held to determine guilt or innocence. In the case of impeachment, the Senate conducts the trial of the accused. With a president, the Chief Justice of the United States presides over the proceedings with conviction requiring a two-thirds majority vote.

The House adopted eleven articles of impeachment. Articles I charged,

> That said Andrew Johnson, President of the United States, on … [February 21, 1868]…, at Washington, in the District of Columbia, unmindful of the high duties of his office, of his oath of office, and of the requirement of the Constitution that he should take care that the laws be faithfully executed, did unlawfully, and in violation of the Constitution and laws of the United States, issue an order in writing for the removal of Edwin M. Stanton from the office of Secretary for the Department of War, said Edwin M. Stanton having been theretofore duly appointed and commissioned, by and with the advice and consent of the Senate of the United States, as such Secretary.[6]

Articles II through VIII generally supported the same charge, illegally removing Stanton from office.

Article IX accused Johnson of violating the Command of the Army Act by issuing orders directly to Brevet Maj. Gen. William H. Emory, commanding the Department of Washington to "unlawfully prevent Edwin M. Stanton, then being Secretary for the Department of War, from holding said office and discharging the duties thereof."[7]

Articles X–XI charged the president with libeling Congress through "intemperate, inflammatory and scandalous harangues." Article X asserted that the president, "unmindful of the high duties of his office and the dignity and proprieties thereof, and of the harmony and courtesies which ought to exist and be maintained between the executive and legislative branches of the government of the United States, designing and intending to set aside the rightful authority and powers of Congress, did attempt to bring into disgrace, ridicule, hatred, contempt, and reproach the Congress of the United States … and to excite the odium and resentment of all the good people of the United States against Congress." Article XI specified that on August 18, 1866, the president in a public speech declared that "the thirty-ninth Congress of the United States was not a Congress of the United States authorized by the Constitution" since it did not include all of the states and consequently he was not obliged to adhere to its legislation "except in so far as he saw fit to approve the same."[8]

The Senate gave Johnson only ten days to prepare his defense. On May 16, the Senate voted 35–19 in favor of conviction, one short of the two-thirds vote required to convict. Seven Republicans joined all of the Democrats in voting "no." Of the seven, none who chose to run for re-election when their terms expired was returned to office. For the balance of President Johnson's term in office, he was irrelevant to the political process. Con-

A ticket to the impeachment proceedings of President Andrew Johnson (Library of Congress).

gress largely ignored him or any proposals he made, and continued to pass whatever legislation it cared to over his veto.

Election of 1868

Given the widely-held perception of Andrew Johnson as pro–South, coupled with the public humiliation of the impeachment trial, there was no possibility that the Democrats would nominate him for another term in office. Yet the party remained conservative at heart, seeking a candidate who would carry on its opposition to Republican Reconstruction and the growing federal influence in the economy. They chose Horatio Seymour, governor of New York, who had supported the Crittenden Compromise in 1861 and then, although supporting the Union, became a leading critic of the Lincoln administration. Following the war, he had supported Johnson's opposition to Republican attempts to support the civil and political rights for people of African ancestry. As a running mate the Democrats selected Frank P. Blair of Missouri, a former Republican who left the party in opposition to its Reconstruction policy.

The Democratic platform stressed a swift reintegration of the South into the national political fabric and repayment of the United States war debt in greenbacks, the latter designed to appeal to debtors, farmers, and the working class. They hoped that by raising economic issues Northerners who were becoming more interested in domestic issues would identify with their proposals rather than with the continuance of the Radical Republican Reconstruction agenda.

Meanwhile, Republicans continued to ride the horse of Southern treachery and culpability for starting the war and for the assassination of Lincoln. What better standard bearer for this platform than the commanding general who led the United States armies to victory, Ulysses S. Grant? As a running mate for the Illinoisan they chose Schuyler Colfax from neighboring Indiana, an odd choice only in that they did not attempt to balance the ticket sectionally by tapping someone from the northeast. Colfax, thoroughly anti-slavery in sentiment, was a founder of the Republican Party and served in the House of Representatives during the war, becoming Speaker in 1863. Although they condemned Democratic financial proposals as "inflationary," the Republicans spent most of their energy "waving the bloody shirt." The phrase referred to a major campaign focus on blaming the Democrats for the Civil War, praising the party of Lincoln for saving the Union and ending slavery, and arguing that continuation of the radical plan for reconstruction was necessary to be sure that the South did not overturn the verdict of the Civil War through political intrigue.

Seymour broke tradition by personally campaigning vigorously rather than relying on his supporters to do so as had been the previous tradition. The Democrats portrayed Grant as an unqualified drunkard, a butcher, a speculator, and attacked him in explicitly racist terms as a "Negro-lover" and worse. His running mate was assailed as anti–Catholic because of his earlier brief affiliation with the Know-Nothing movement. Although Grant did no active campaigning, his theme of "let us have peace" conflicted with the general Republican approach of accusing Seymour and the Democrats of disloyalty during the war, spreading the rumor that insanity ran in Seymour's family, and charging Blair with Southern sympathies even though he had fought to keep Missouri in the Union and served as a federal general during the war. In addition, Republicans successfully disenfranchised many white Southerners in the states controlled by the Reconstruction governments, while registering blacks to vote. In short, there was enough mud-slinging and corruption to go around.

Harper's Weekly **celebrates the election of U.S. Grant as president (Library of Congress).**

When the results were in, Grant received 3,012,833 popular votes and 214 electoral votes to Seymour's 2,703,249 popular and 80 electoral votes. Although the electoral vote margin was substantial, the popular vote was closer than might have been imagined considering the circumstances of the election. Republicans looking forward to the midyear election in 1870 and the next presidential canvass two years later could not help but be concerned. In 1868 the party lost two governorships and their majority in Congress decreased. Worse, Grant had carried the popular vote by a margin of only 309,584, a mere 5.4 percent of the 5,716,082 ballots cast. Since there were some 703,000 blacks registered to vote in the Southern states—forming majorities in Alabama, Florida, Louisiana, Mississippi, and South Carolina—it was apparent that black votes had pushed him over the top. Given the link between Republicans and emancipation, as well as the efforts of Republicans on behalf of ex-slaves, nearly all of these votes would have gone to Grant. It is reasonable to conclude, as some historians have, that without the black votes Grant would not have won. It was obvious to Republicans that their continued political ascendancy might depend very much on their continued control of the Southern states, and that could only happen with the assurance of African votes, and with maintenance of the federal occupation and military governorships of the remaining "unreconstructed" states.

The Grant Administration

Ulysses S. Grant took the oath of office as the eighteenth president of the United States on March 4, 1869. In his inaugural address he observed that "the country having just emerged from a great rebellion, many questions will come before it for settlement in the next four years which preceding Administrations have never had to deal with. In meeting these it is desirable that they should be approached calmly, without prejudice, hate, or sectional pride, remembering that the greatest good to the greatest number is the object to be attained." The national debt incurred in preserving the Union must be paid in full, something which ought to be a point of "honor" and "national pride." After pledging to respect all foreign nations, he further promised to pursue "proper treatment of the original occupants of this land" including a pathway to "ultimate citizenship." He closed with comments on one of the more emotional issues of the day:

> The question of suffrage is one which is likely to agitate the public so long as a portion of the citizens of the nation are excluded from its privileges in any State. It seems to me very desirable that this question should be settled now, and I entertain the hope and express the desire that it may be by the ratification of the fifteenth article of amendment to the Constitution. In conclusion I ask patient forbearance one toward another throughout the land, and a determined effort on the part of every citizen to do his share toward cementing a happy union; and I ask the prayers of the nation to Almighty God in behalf of this consummation.[9]

Following the inauguration and the seating of the new Congress, Republicans turned their attention back to the Reconstruction as Grant had asked. It had become obvious that those Southern states that had already resumed their normal status within the Union were rapidly creating legal means of disenfranchising those of African ancestry despite the fact that the states doing so would, under the Fourteenth Amendment, lose representation in the House in proportion to the people disqualified. Republicans, who wanted to champion black voting rights, proposed a new amendment, the third resulting from the Civil War and its aftermath. But there were some serious political problems that promised to make the new effort difficult.

Adoption of a Constitutional amendment required a three-forth majority vote of the states with each state having one vote, or 28 of the existing 37 states. There were nine Northern states that allowed blacks to vote and the Republicans controlled ten Southern states through federal occupation. The latter could be forced to vote in favor of an amendment, but that would total only nineteen votes, nine short of the required majority. One problem was that some Northern states did *not* allow blacks to vote and the Republicans were reluctant to bring the issue before voters in those states for fear of provoking angry disputes and public referendums. By bringing the matter before Congress they hoped to avoid open clashes that might break out if they left the matter to individual states. In Congress they could fight one battle with a better chance of success, but there was a problem. It was a lame duck Congress in which Republican power was about to be diluted. If no measure could be adopted soon, the chance to do so at all might be lost.

Radical Republicans generally favored a "universal" approach, a positive statement that guaranteed the right to vote to all adult male citizens. But this would be much more difficult to push through given the need to attract nine more votes. Because of this, and the problems noted above, it was agreed that the best chance of adopting anything rested with an "impartial" approach, a negative statement that guaranteed no discrimination based on certain conditions. The new Fifteenth Amendment gained passage in February 1869 and was declared ratified in March 1870. It read:

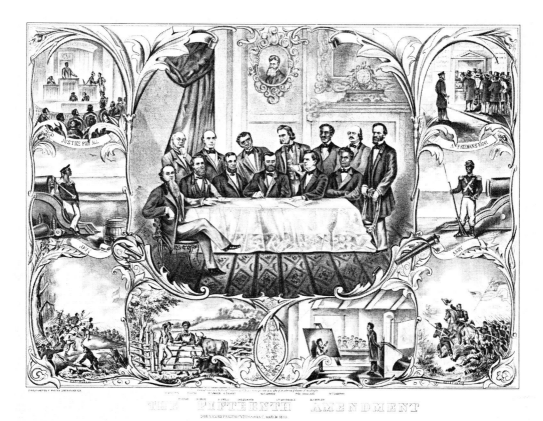

Republicans were hopeful that the Fourteenth and Fifteenth Amendments would lead to new opportunities for people of African ancestry (Library of Congress).

Section 1—The right of citizens of the United States to vote shall not be denied or abridged by the United States or by any state on account of race, color, or previous condition of servitude.
Section 2—The Congress shall have power to enforce this article by appropriate legislation.

The problem with this approach was that it really did not guarantee that any people of African heritage would be able to vote. A state could easily circumvent the spirit of the amendment by simply finding some way in which to disenfranchise people that did not *appear* to discriminate based on the prohibited categories. Some states adopted poll taxes knowing that most black residents were poor and could not pay the fee. The law applied to everyone in theory but in practice disproportionally affected potential black voters. A favorite tactic used throughout the South was the literacy test. Arguing that people ought to be able to pass a literacy test to vote to insure that they could understand the pertinent issues, framers of these laws reasoned that since they applied to everyone they did not specifically target any group because of "race, color, or previous condition of servitude."

One problem its proponents faced with the literacy test was that there were some 500,000 whites in the South who were illiterate and stood to be disenfranchised under the new laws. The solution was to create exceptions, the most widespread of which was the "grandfather clause." Under this provision, anyone who could prove that their grandfather voted would be exempt from the literacy test requirement. Again, the argument was that this applied to everyone so it did not violate the new amendment. In theory, "yes," but in practice, "no." Since it was illegal for black residents to vote in the Southern states prior to the end of the Civil War it was impossible for those people to provide the required proof because none of their grandfathers could have voted. This once again created a situation where the reality was that those of African ancestry could be disenfranchised with no real legal recourse.

In 1870, 1871, and again later in 1875 Republicans pushed through Congress amendments to the original Civil Rights Act of 1866 in attempts to secure basic rights for freed African Americans. The first two attempted to enforce voting rights including implementing federal supervision of voter registration and elections. The Enforcement Act of 1870 made interference with constitutionally guaranteed civil rights a felony, provided fines and imprisonment for people obstructing qualified voters, and gave Federal courts jurisdiction over these matters. A year later the Second Enforcement Act allowed Federal courts to supervise elections and made interference a Federal offense.

The Ku Klux Klan Act of 1871 strengthened the Enforcement Acts by defining unlawful combinations against the government and allowing the president to suspend *habeas corpus* and permitting use of military force in areas where unlawful disenfranchisement existed. President Grant used this to declare martial law in nine counties in South Carolina where federal troops arrested suspected violators. The 1875 statute, proposed by Charles Sumner, addressed other rights, specifying the right of all people to access to public accommodations, transportation, service on juries, and the right to file suit for damages should these be denied. In 1883 five civil rights cases were combined into a Supreme Court decision which held that the Fourteenth Amendment applied only to states, not to private individuals and thus the 1875 statute was unconstitutional. It would be the last civil rights legislation adopted by Congress until 1957.

Republicans had been successful in adopting the three Constitutional amendments, enacting civil rights legislation, and providing assistance to ex-slaves through the Freedman's

Bureau and other federal programs, but by the 1870s many Northern voters wanted reconciliation with the South, especially merchants. Although Grant was in office, he was not a hard-liner. He too favored reconciliation as reflected in his campaign slogan "Let us have peace." With the adoption of the Fifteenth Amendment, Reconstruction was no longer a unifying priority for Northern Republicans. Economic issues had come to the fore: the extension of the nation's railroad network, government support for manufacturing, "hard" versus "soft" money, the Homestead Act, and other public land issues.

The one lingering issue from the war also had an economic basis, the "Alabama Claims," the U.S. government's financial claims against Great Britain for the aid that it had given to the Confederacy. During the war, Confederate commerce raiders built or refitted in British ports caused serious damage to the U.S. merchant fleet. As a result, many shippers resorted to registering their ships in foreign countries to avoid capture or sinking by the rebels. In doing this, they found their ships could often be registered much less expensively abroad than at home and the Northern shipping industry never fully recovered as many owners continued to register their vessels abroad in the postwar years. Blockade runners, similarly constructed or assisted by Britain and its empire, continued to smuggle badly needed military and medical supplies into the Confederacy until its very last days, no doubt prolonging the war.

The most successful of the raiders was the CSS *Alabama*. Launched at a British shipyard in July 1862, in 23 months of service it captured 58 Northern merchant ships before being sunk by the USS *Kearsarge* off Cherbourg, France, in June 1864. In total, eighteen

THE APPLE OF DISCORD AT THE GENEVA TRIBUNAL.

Thomas Nast's caustic cartoon on the Geneva Tribunal that met to negotiate a settlement of the "Alabama Claims" appeared in *Harper's Weekly* (Library of Congress).

commerce raiders, also constructed in British shipyards, accounted for 257 Northern vessels sunk of captured. The value of the ships was estimated at $6,500,000, with lost cargo adding another $19,000,000 in losses.

Following the war, the U.S. government demanded restitution from Britain for these losses. Senator Charles Sumner went so far as to claim that British aid had prolonged the war for two full years and the British ought to be liable for payment of all costs associated with half of the war. Graciously, he suggested that rather than pay the impossibly enormous sum of $2,125,000,000, the U.S. would accept Canada in payment of the debt. It took seven years following the conclusion of the war to settle the differences between the two nations. Under the Treaty of Washington in 1871, Britain expressed "regret" (it did not "apologize" as the U.S. wished) and both sides agreed to establish a commission to arbitrate their differences, including boundary and fishing disputes. As a result, Britain eventually paid the U.S. $15.5 million and gave up claims to the San Juan Islands between British Columbia and the state of Washington. Other boundary issues were also settled, as were fishing rights off the New England and Canadian coasts with fishermen from each country having access to each other's waters for ten years. With this, the last of the international complications arising from the war were put to rest.

Contrasting Views of the Reconstruction

The Republican Reconstruction governments relied for support on people of African descent, white Northerners who moved South after the war, and white Southerners who had either always been pro–Union or were postwar converts. To Northerners, those who went South in the wake of the war were usually portrayed as men of principle whose motivations were to assist the ex-slaves in successfully adapting to their new status as free people and in the process aid in the economic, social, and political renewal of the South.

Most Southerners had an entirely different view. "Yankees" who came south were labeled "carpetbaggers" from the suitcases they carried and were portrayed as corrupt adventurers out for political and economic exploitation. Southerners who cooperated with the Reconstruction governments were "scalawags" who betrayed their race, their state, and their section for the sake of personal gain. The most famous of the latter was former Confederate general James Longstreet who became a Republican and supporter of President Grant. No doubt it was for this, rather than his actual battlefield performance, that Southern promoters of the "Lost Cause" chose to place most of the blame for the loss at Gettysburg on his shoulders. The description offered by James Bryce provides a good example of the Southern view: "Such a Saturnalia of robbery and jobbery has seldom been seen in any civilized country, and certainly never before under the forms of free self-government. The coloured voters could hardly be blamed for blindly following the guides who represented to them the party to which they owed their liberty…. But nine-tenths of the illicit gains went to the whites. Many of them were persons of infamous character who ultimately saved themselves from justice by flight."[10]

In truth, while some Northerners no doubt came South looking for profit of one form or another, members of the clergy, teachers, and others did indeed seek to assist former slaves. Business people arrived who were interested in establishing cotton textile factories or other manufacturing concerns beneficial not only to them but to the unem-

RECONSTRUCTION OF THE SOUTH.

ployed where the enterprises were located and to the diversification of the Southern economy. Among the latter were Union Army veterans attracted by the opportunity for economic investment or the more moderate climate of some of the South. Likewise, scalawags were often pragmatists interested in doing what they could to help rebuild the South.

Some carpetbaggers and scalawags were unscrupulous schemers, but they enjoyed no monopoly on those traits. The South Carolina legislature under Federal control voted $1,000 to cover the gambling losses of the Speaker while graft and waste were commonplace in many of the Reconstruction governments. On the other hand, the governor of Mississippi appointed by President Johnson embezzled $62,000 and that state's "Redeemer" treasurer set a record for that era by pilfering $316,000. Political corruption could be found in both major parties.

Election of 1872

Although Grant remained popular as the presidential canvass approached in 1872, the liberal wing of the Republican Party was unhappy over the lack of progress on civil service reform or moderating the high tariff. In protest they nominated Horace Greeley, editor of *New York Tribune*, to oppose Grant on a theme of "a more honest government." Oddly, the Democrats also nominated Greeley despite the fact that he had excoriated Southern Democrats in his newspaper and did not support the Democrats tariff policy. The hope was that by siphoning off enough Republican votes they might be successful in replacing Grant who supported the Republican Reconstruction policies. The Democrats also chose to run a number of "regional" candidates for vice president rather than a single nominee hoping that popular local candidates would attract regional votes to the ticket. Eliminating some minor candidates, the final tally for the two main opponents appeared to be a runaway Grant victory.

Candidate	Popular Vote	Electoral Vote
U. S. Grant (R)	3,597,132	286
Horace Greeley (D)	2,834,079	3

A closer look at the results show the Republican margin of victory was only 763,053, or 11.9 percent. Given the larger population in the Northern states and the Republican control of some of the Southern states where black residents were enfranchised and many whites disenfranchised, this is a surprisingly slight majority.

Recurring Scandals Damage the Administration's Credibility

Although Grant himself was personally honest, he proved a much weaker political leader than he was when directing the Union armies to victory on the battlefield. His first administration was relatively calm, but after his re-election in 1872 an economic

Opposite, top: **Northerners pictured the Reconstruction as a period of providing new opportunities, especially for former slaves.** *Opposite, bottom:* **In this Southern view of Reconstruction, the "carpetbagger" governor of Louisiana, assisted by African Americans, is seen murdering the state while Pres. Grant does nothing (both illustrations, Library of Congress).**

"This is a white man's government," read the caption on this Thomas Nast political cartoon in *Harper's Weekly*. Quoting the Democratic Party Platform he continued: "We regard the Reconstruction Acts (so called) of Congress as usurpations, and unconstitutional, revolutionary, and void" (Library of Congress).

downturn beginning with the Panic of 1873, caused by over speculation in railroads and over expansion of industry and agriculture, naturally led people to blame his administration. Some 5,000 businesses failed by the end of the year with attending unemployment fueling labor unrest and popular discontent. Farmers, miners, and debtors blamed the economic recession on the Coinage Act of 1873 that ended the coinage of silver, a move they believed resulted from government pandering to financial interests.

Worse, a series of scandals rocked the government beginning with the so-called "Salary Grab Act" in which Congress attempted to double the president's salary to $50,000 and increase the salaries of some government officials, including Congress, by between $5,000 to $7,500. A public furor resulted in repeal of the raises in January 1874 except for the president and Supreme Court justices. An exposé by the *New York Sun* made public the Crédit Mobilier scandal. The Crédit Mobilier was a dummy corporation set

"You took it" read the caption on this cartoon from *Frank Leslie's Illustrated Newspaper* as the politicians all point to each other in "That Salary Grab" (Library of Congress).

up by promoters of the Union Pacific Railroad to divert profits to owners and their allies in Congress who were in a position to vote to approve grants to railroads. Among those censured by the House of Representatives for their part in the affair were Reps. Oakes Ames of Massachusetts and James Brooks of New York. Vice President Schuyler Colfax, the new vice presidential nominee Henry Wilson, and Rep. James A. Garfield (who would later become president) were all accused of wrongdoing but escaped censure. As a result, the public began to question government credibility and support for big business.

In May 1875, the *St. Louis Democrat* exposed conspiracy to defraud the government of distillery tax revenue. Known as the "Whiskey Ring," the scheme involved revenue agents taking bribes to cut or to forego collection of the excise tax on distilled alcohol. Some 238 people were indicted, with 110 convicted. Among those indicted was Orville Babcock, President Grant's private secretary, who was saved from possible conviction through the president's intervention. Over $3 million in tax revenue was eventually recovered. Although no evidence surfaced to suggest any involvement in the scheme by the president, his stature was certainly injured by the far-reaching scandal.

Nor was this the end. In 1876 Secretary of War William W. Belknap was impeached by the House for corruption in managing the Indian trading posts, but the Senate refused to convict after Belknap resigned. In the same year, Representative James G. Blaine was investigated for accepting favors from the Union Pacific Railroad while he was Speaker of the House. Other financial scandals also fed into an atmosphere of distrust and a general feeling of political corruption. The recurring scandals resulted in declining support for the Republican Party, and a serious split within its own ranks that led to formation of a liberal reform wing.

The Elections of 1874 and 1876

With the economic recession and some of the scandals beginning to come to light, Republicans lost 85 seats in House of Representatives in the 1874 Congressional elections and with them their majority. Overall, Republicans lost 96 seats in Congress with Democrats picking up 94 of those and independents the other two.

Party	Total Seats	Change	%
Democratic	182	+94	62.1
Independent	8	+3	2.7
Republican	103	−96	35.1
Totals	293	+1	100.0

As the next presidential election neared, Republicans found themselves much less confident of victory. Democrats appeared for the first time since before the Civil War to have a real opportunity to reclaim the presidency.

To carry their banner, the Republicans went seven ballots at their convention before nominating another former Union army general, Rutherford B. Hayes of Ohio, who was known as a moderate. The vice presidential nomination went to William A. Wheeler, a New York district attorney known for this anti-corruption activities and member of the U.S. House of Representatives. The Republican platform once again "waved the bloody shirt," calling for continued control of the South, but also proposed civil service reform in an attempt to address criticism over the recent scandals, and supported an investigation into the affects of Asian immigration, an issue important in the Pacific coast states.

The Democrats nominated New York governor Samuel J. Tilden, a conservative, with Thomas A. Hendricks, an Indiana attorney, as his running mate. Their platform called for an end to the occupation and Reconstruction in the South, an end to land grants for railroads, and a restriction of Asian immigration. During the campaign the Democrats accused Hayes and the Republicans of corruption, while the Republicans countered with the familiar charges that the Democrats were the party of treason.

By the 1876 election, the Civil War had been over for eleven and a half years and many Northerners were wearying of the Reconstruction. More important to the manufacturing areas were the economy, internal improvements, and other issues not related to the war and the military occupation. When the votes were counted, Tilden led in both the popular and electoral vote, but there were also twenty disputed electoral votes.

Rutherford B. Hayes of Ohio, a former Union Civil War general, carried the banner for the Republicans in 1876 (Library of Congress).

	Popular Vote	*Electoral Vote*
Tilden	4,284,020	185
Hayes	4,036,572	166
Disputed		19

One vote from Oregon was contested because the Republican Elector John W. Watts was a postmaster and thus, as a federal official, ineligible to serve. Since the governor of the state was a Democrat, he took advantage of the disqualification to appoint a fellow Democrat to fill the vacancy changing Oregon's electoral vote from 3–0 for Hayes to two for Hayes and one for Tilden. Since Tilden needed only one of the disputed electoral votes to become president, this change would place the Democrat in the White House. Naturally, Republicans challenged the obvious political move.

The other nineteen disputed votes came from Florida, Louisiana, and South Carolina where two separate sets of electors

The Democrats chose Samuel J. Tilden, the governor of New York and a wartime critic of the Lincoln administration, as their standard bearer (Library of Congress).

were filed, one by the Reconstruction government and one by opponents of the military government. Corruption abounded on both sides. Republicans claimed their results were the legitimate voting tallies, while Democrats claimed theirs reflected the actual will of the people because a large number of Democratic voters had been disenfranchised. The Democratically-controlled House of Representatives sent voting inspectors to the South, but Republican governors controlled the three states in question and refused to cooperate. Republicans in Congress demanded that the votes be counted in accordance with Article II, Section 1, of the Constitution which stipulates that "the President of the Senate shall, in the presence of the Senate and House of Representatives, open all the certificates, and the votes shall then be counted." This would place determination of *which* votes to count in the hands of the Republican vice president and thus give Hayes the election. Democrats responded by demanding that the election go to the House since Article II, Section 1, of the Constitution states: "if no person have a majority, then from the five highest on the list the said House shall in like manner choose the President." This would give Tilden the edge since his party controlled the House.

To address the growing crisis, Congress adopted the Electoral Commission Act in January 1877 by a vote of 47–17 in the Senate and 191–86 in the House. The legislation established a special Electoral Commission comprised of five members of the House, five from the Senate, and five Supreme Court justices. The mixture would include seven Republicans, seven Democrats, and Justice David Davis who was an independent. Assuming a party-line vote, this would effectively place election of the next president in Davis's hands. Unwilling to trust to the judgment of a single independent, before the Commission could meet the Republican-controlled Illinois legislature elected Davis to a vacant Senate seat. He accepted, requiring him to give up his position on the Court and with it his seat on the Commission. Since all of the other Supreme Court justices were Republicans, the final composition of the Electoral Commission was eight Republicans and seven Democrats. Not surprisingly, when the Commission voted on which of the disputed ballots to accept the tally was eight to seven in every case with all twenty votes going to the Republican Hayes giving him a majority of one, 186–185.

The Compromise of 1877

Democrats were outraged by what they considered a corrupt process that stole the election from the candidate who received the majority of the popular vote. Some threatened a new civil war, while others threatened legal actions that might tie up the government indefinitely or even postpone the inauguration of the new president. Amid these threats, leaders of the Southern Democrats approached both candidates about their views for the future. They asked the Democrat Tilden if he would end the military Reconstruction, appoint a Southerner to the Cabinet, and provide federal money for internal improvements in the South. Although the South had traditionally opposed the use of federal funds for internal improvements, the destruction of the Civil War left the South in a state of economic despair. Harbors were blocked with sunken ships, railroads destroyed, and public buildings burned. It was important to them to obtain financial assistance if their economy was to recover. Tilden agreed to end the Reconstruction and appoint Southerners to the Cabinet, but he was reluctant to promise federal funds for internal improvements since the Democratic Party had traditionally opposed the idea.

In this *Harper's Weekly* cartoon, Thomas Nast provides the caption "A truce—not a compromise, but a chance for high-toned gentlemen to retire gracefully from their very civil declarations of war" (Library of Congress).

When the Southerners approached Hayes, he agreed to end the military occupation and Reconstruction of the South, to appoint a Southerner to the Cabinet, and to appoint Democrats to patronage positions in the South. In agreeing to withdraw troops from the South, it was understood that Africans would not be disenfranchised in the Southern states where they were actually voting and participating in government. This understanding lasted until the 1890s when a new generation attained political power in the South and undermined the civil rights of African Americans through enactment of Jim Crow laws, reflective of the Black Codes of an earlier generation. Since the Republicans had always supported the use of federal funds for internal improvements, Hayes also had no problem agreeing to that request. In return, Southern Democrats withdrew their objections, selling out their own candidate, and agreed to acquiesce in Hayes taking office as the next president. In this way the two groups *least* likely to cooperate, Southern Democrats and Northern Radical Republicans, combined their support of Hayes to continue Republican control of the presidency leaving Northern Democrats powerless to stop the deal. All they could do was derisively refer to the new chief executive as "Rutherfraud," "His Fradulency," and "His Accidency."

With the compromise, known as "the act of settlement," the crisis passed. Hayes took the oath of office on March 3, 1877, and the following month he issued orders removing troops from the South. The Reconstruction was officially over.

12

The Legacy of Sectionalism, Civil War and Reconstruction

Human history is a progression of cause-and-effect relationships. The eventual outcomes of the process that unfolded during the period of Sectionalism, Civil War and Reconstruction changed the fundamental social, economic and political foundations of the United States, with effects often felt even today.

Military and Naval Developments

Some writers have called the Civil War the first modern war. More properly it can be said that it reflects a transition period between the old Napoleonic form of combat and the new modern modes of warfare. Throughout most of the conflict professionally-trained officers used the same linear battlefield tactics employed earlier in the century, despite the obvious increased killing power of the rifled muskets and artillery that predominated in the major engagements. By the end of the war the enormous casualty rates forced some adaptations, most notable the use of field fortifications. By the summer of 1864 it was said that if the Army of Northern Virginia were given two hours it could throw up formidable field works in any location it occupied. This, as well as the more permanent fortifications of cities like Richmond and Petersburg, certainly presaged the trench warfare that emerged in World War I. The repeating rifles and Gatling gun first employed in the war was a first stage in the development of the automatic weapons and machine guns that proved so devastating on European battlefields fifty years later. Although stationary balloons had been used for military observation earlier in Paris, France, they were used in the field for the first time by the Union Balloon Corps during the Civil War, foreshadowing the reconnaissance role of aircraft in the First World War. Interestingly, a German observer with the Union army at the time, Count Ferdinand von Zeppelin, later brought the idea to Europe where he founded the Zeppelin airship company.

Similarly, there had been an attempt to use a submarine in the American Revolution, but the first submarine to sink an enemy warship was the CSS *Hunley*, which also held the dubious distinction of being the first submarine lost in combat. The submarine would evolve into its World War I iteration so devastatingly lethal to Allied shipping. The Korean Admiral Yi Sun-Shin had used an armored ship in combat in the late sixteenth century, but the first engagement between ironclad warships took place in 1862 in Hampton Roads, Virginia, when the USS *Monitor* and CSS *Virginia* fought to a draw. The navies of the Great War would fight for control of the oceans with later versions of these first rudimentary vessels. Likewise, later generations of the naval mines (called "torpedoes" in the Civil War) that sank an estimated forty Union ships would develop into not only mines, but modern submarine torpedoes, and various land versions of the stationary mine.

The telegraph was for the first time used in the field for rapid military communication, with one estimate that 15,000 miles of telegraph lines were employed during the war for military purposes. The railroad was not only used extensively for the movement of troops, equipment, and supplies, but entire railroad lines were constructed exclusively for specific military purposes. New York Gen. Daniel Butterfield authored "Taps," which is still very much in use today, and also designed the first system of corps and division badges to distinguish the various commands. A Pennsylvania-born surgeon, Dr. Jonathan Letterman, is often known as the "Father of Battlefield Medicine" for his innovative organization of medical procedures while serving as Medical Director of the Army of the Potomac. His improvements in the processes of removing wounded from the battlefield, providing rapid triage close behind the lines, and then evacuating them to field hospitals was far in advance of anything previously employed. And the use of photography brought the war's destruction home to civilian audiences in more graphic images than ever before.

Dr. Jonathan Letterman developed many innovations in battlefield medical procedures (U.S. Army Medical Museum).

Political and Legal Consequences

Politically, the war led to a nearly complete change in political power and direction within the nation. In the Executive Branch this can be seen quite unmistakably. In the 32 years between 1828 and 1860, three Whigs and five Democrats held the presidency, but two of the Whigs—William Henry Harrison and Zachary Taylor—died in office after serving only a total of fifteen months leaving a Whig presidency for only slightly over five years during this period. In comparison, in the 72 years from the election of Lincoln in 1860 to that of Franklin Roosevelt in 1932, only three Democrats (including Andrew Johnson who actually ran on the National Union ticket) held the office as opposed to twelve Republicans. Of the 72 years, Republicans held roughly a 61 to 13 edge. The same change in control can be seen in the Congress. In the former era Democrats controlled the Senate and the House each by a 27 to five margin. In the latter this was reversed with the Republicans controlling the Senate by a 60–11 margin (with one tie) and the House by 48–24. The consequence of this was that national control passed in large part from

Southern, Democratic, pro-agriculturalists to Northern, Republican, pro-industrialists. As a result, the government turned dramatically in favor of federal assistance to business and commercial interests.

The Northern victory led to passage of what have been called the "Civil War Amendments"—the Thirteenth, Fourteenth, and Fifteenth Amendments to the Constitution. Together, these abolished slavery, defined citizenship, provided for equal protection, and eliminated discrimination in voting rights based on race, color, and "previous condition of servitude." The Fourteenth Amendment is the basis for all of the civil rights legislation enacted since that time and forms the foundation for laws barring discrimination and promoting equal opportunity today.

Because of the war the critical issue of "implied powers" versus "States' Rights" was settled in favor of the former. Consequently, the power and reach of the federal government grew exponentially in the wake of the war, eventually affecting almost every facet of a citizen's life. Having in effect seceded from secession, West Virginia joined the Union as the 35th state in June 1863, followed by Nevada the next year. The Federal government created the "absentee ballot" to enable those in the armed forces to vote, while the Northern victory reasserted the supremacy of the federal government over the states contained in Article VI of the Constitution.

Legally, there were also landmark decisions that would have a bearing on future interpretations of the Constitution. At the beginning of the war President Lincoln ordered the arrest and imprisonment of Southern sympathizers in Maryland without charges being preferred and without trial, arguing that he had the right to do this as commander-in-chief during a national emergency. In its *Ex Parte Merryman* ruling the U.S. Supreme Court declared Lincoln's suspension of the writ of *habeas corpus* to be unconstitutional, upholding Constitutional guarantees of the writ and prohibitions against unlawful restraint while asserting that only Congress could suspend these, not the president, and only in time of national emergency.[1]

Later in the war, General Ambrose P. Burnside ordered the arrest of anyone making disloyal statements or aiding the enemy. When Clement L. Vallandigham, a leading anti-war activist, urged people to ignore what he believed was an illegal order Burnside ordered his arrest and trial before a military court. Following his conviction, Vallandigham appealed to the Supreme Court only to have it decline to hear the case in *Ex Parte Vallandigham* since military court proceedings were not reviewable. In a similar case a Federal military commander declared martial law in southern Ohio and Indiana, arrested Southern sympathizers, and conducted trials in military courts. In *Ex Parte Milligan* the Supreme Court found unconstitutional the use of military courts when civilian courts were open and operating and there was no imminent threat of invasion.[2]

Finally, a fundamental legal issue of the Civil War was whether a state could legally leave the Union once it had joined. During the conflict the Confederate government of Texas sold a number of United States bonds that the state possessed. Following the war various claimants attempted to secure payment for the bonds, but Texas filed suit for the recovery of the bonds arguing that they had been illegally possessed and sold. In *Texas v. White* the Supreme Court found in that the debts were not valid because the government controlling the state during the war had no legal authority binding on the legitimate federal and state authorities. In the majority opinion, Chief Justice Salmon P. Chase found that the Union of the States never was a purely artificial and arbitrary relation. It began among the Colonies, and grew out of common origin, mutual sympathies, kindred principles, similar interests, and geographical relations. It was confirmed and strengthened by the necessities of war, and received definite form and character and sanction from the Articles of Confederation. By these, the Union was solemnly declared to "be perpetual." And when these Articles were found to be inadequate to the exigencies of the country, the Constitution was ordained "to form a more perfect Union." It is difficult to convey the idea of indissoluble unity more clearly than by these words. What can be indissoluble if a perpetual Union, made more perfect, is not?[3]

Secession, the Court ruled, is illegal. Therefore, the rebel government of Texas had no legal authority to legislate and any acts of that government were not binding on the legally constituted post-war state government.

Social and Economic Consequences

With Southern representatives absent from Congress during the war, the North was able to enact legislation providing for internal improvements. The Morrill Land Grant Act provided federal aid to establish land grant colleges in each state. Originally agricultural and mechanical colleges, these are today some of the most prestigious public universities in the country. The Republican Congress created the Department of Agriculture, authorized the construction of the transcontinental railroad, established the United States National Banking System, set aside land for the first national park at Yosemite, launched the Freedman's Bureau to assist ex-slaves, adopted the homestead legislation opening 270 million acres spurring a westward movement that eventually provided free land to 1.6 million homesteaders.

With so many men away in the armed forces, women began to move into jobs they never held before. When farmers went off to war their wives took over full management of their land with all the additional mental and physical work that implied. In urban areas women had for decades been a mainstay in the textile mills, but now their employment extended into manufacturing and sales positions few had previously occupied. One of the most critical new roles taken on by women was that of nursing in hospitals serving the wounded and the ill. Female nurses working with male patients was rare in antebellum America, but that changed forever because of the wartime need for trained medical personnel. This included the first female physician ever employed by the U.S. Army.

Despite the political disputes, the Republican Reconstruction governments instituted

Justin S. Morrill of Vermont was the father of the Morrill Land Grant Act that established the system of Land Grant state universities (Library of Congress).

the first system of public education in the South, built roads and railroads, introduced social services to support the poor, wrote state constitutions that were more democratic, and expanded women's opportunities. The most significant "ethnic" consequence of the Civil War era was its impact on African Americans. As a direct result of the Union victory, some four million people were freed from bondage. Citizenship was redefined specifically to include those of African heritage and Congress attempted to protect the rights of African Americans, although the period of "Jim Crow" legislation provided the South with means to circumvent most of these attempted protections. Colleges were founded and supported by Northern philanthropists to provide opportunities for higher education for African Americans including Atlanta University (Georgia, 1865; today Clark Atlanta University), Talladega College (Alabama, 1865), Fisk University (Nashville, 1866), Howard University (Washington, D.C., 1867), Hampton Institute (Virginia, 1868), and Tougaloo College (Mississippi, 1869). The war also spurred the first movement of Africans from the South to cities in the North, and to a lesser extent to the West in search of new opportunities. In Chicago, for example, the population of African ancestry rose from some 4,000 in 1870 to 7,400 in 1880, and 14,800 in 1890.

Financially, the war brought a dramatic increase in government spending. Economic researchers Claudia Goldin and Frank Lewis estimated that the combined cost of the war for both North and South was some $6.652 billion including $3.3 billion in direct costs, $1.8 billion in economic losses, and $1.5 billion in destruction. To this they add $3.709 billion in indirect costs, including the lost value of emancipated slaves, for a total cost of $10.361 billion. Roger Ransom estimated that the per capita cost for the North was approximately $150, about one year of income for the average worker, while per capita Southern expenses were a crushing $376. Looking at the United States government debt alone, it rose from only $65 million in 1860 to a massive $2.7 billion in 1865. On top of this, estimates by Goldin and Lewis suggest that the direct cost to the South was $3.285 billion.[4] By 1866 the war and its immediate aftermath cost the North some $6.19 billion, a figure that rose to $11.5 billion by 1910 when interest on loans, veterans benefits, and other post-war expenses were included. The cost continued to escalate after 1910 because of these same factors. The enormous debt led to the printing of paper money, a dramatic rise in tax rates, and the imposition of new taxes.

Although historians disagree on the issue, the war and the Northern victory spurred a dramatic growth in industry that led to the United States becoming the leading industrial nation in the world. Some 22,000 miles of rails were laid during the war. The expansion of railroads and standardization of gauges promoted postwar industry and the westward movement. During the war stock in the Erie Railroad ballooned from $17 to $126, while the Michigan Central increased from $40 to $150. Some railroads paid dividends during the war that totaled more than their entire capital investment at the outbreak of hostilities. Soft coal production increased 36 percent, hard coal 10 percent, and pig iron 23 percent. After the First Battle of Bull Run the federal government pumped $3.2 billion into industry including more than $1 billion in contacts. The fortunes made by industrial leaders during the war—for example, John D. Rockefeller, Andrew Carnegie, Philip Armour, J. P. Morgan, Cornelius Vanberbilt, and Cyrus McCormack—provided them with the capital to grow their businesses following the conflict and to contribute to what has been identified as an "industrial revolution." Technological developments such as the Bessemer process for making steel (1864) transformed that industry. Although the war decimated the Southern economy, the aftermath brought federal and Northern investment, a restructuring of the Southern railway system, and the beginning of gradual economic diversification which would eventually lead to a stronger, more resilient economy firmly tied to the rest of the nation.

Yet, for all of its decisive changes, a major disappointment of the era was the ultimate failure to solve the nation's racial problems. Thus, the Reconstruction ended through political compromise, not because it had succeeded in achieving its original goals. With the creation of the Freedman's Bureau, passage of the Thirteenth, Fourteenth, and Fifteenth Amendments and the Civil Rights Act of 1866, and other actions taken on behalf of the nation's population of African descent, most Northerners believed they had provided well for the ex-slaves. Faced with losing votes because the people of the North had become more interested in economic and other issues, and were no longer responding to their "bloody shirt" rhetoric, Republicans abandoned their attempts to guarantee civil rights for Africans. No further serious moves would be made to restore and protect African American civil rights until the 1950s. In the meantime, so-called "Redeemer" governments gradually reinstituted white supremacist rule in the South, ultimately disenfranchising Africans wholesale. So tightly did the Democrats continue to control the South that the majority of Southern states voted Democratic in every presidential election until 1964, resulting in the term "Solid South" to refer to its political allegiance. In the process, race relations continued to be a serious national divide that would not begin to be addressed until the advent of the modern Civil Rights Movement after World War II.

State	Date of Readmission	Date of Democratic "Redeemer" Control
Tennessee	1866	1869
North Carolina	1868	1870
Alabama	1868	1874
Arkansas	1868	1874
South Carolina	1868	1877
Florida	1868	1877
Louisiana	1868	1877
Virginia	1870	1869
Georgia	1870	1871
Texas	1870	1873
Mississippi	1870	1876

Americans Interpret Their National Trauma

The French sociologist Maurice Halbwach posited that "individual memory can only be recalled in the social framework within which it is constructed." In his essay "Historical Memory and Collective Memory" he distinguished between two differing types of memory: collective memory and historical memory. Collective memory exists within a specific group at a specific time and place and is maintained only so long as there are people living who have direct knowledge of events that they share in common. Historical memory exists when all of the witnesses are deceased. It is the manifestation of a lost past, a past that no longer exists as a collective memory. It is the difference between a lived memory and a constructed memory.[5]

With Halbwach's distinction in mind, how did those who lived through the events interpret them? What caused the traumatic events that shaped their lives? The answer depended largely on the section of the country to which on owed allegiance. To Confederate President Jefferson Davis it was Northern aggression against the property rights of slave

owners, combined with lack of respect for States' Rights, which sparked the national conflagration. His vice president, Alexander Stephens, likewise defined the root cause of the
war in political terms with the North being the aggressor through its promotion of the cen-
tralization of power despite the clear support for States' Rights implicit in the Tenth Amendment. Confederate Secretary of State Robert Toombs likewise believed the North the
antagonist, but focused more on economic inequity arguing that Federal economic policies
favored the North at the expense of the South. Rebel Postmaster General John H. Reagan
also focused on economics, arguing that the South was paying "tribute" to the North through
Federal policies promoting internal improvements, the revenue and navigation laws, and
Northern monopolies on manufacturing and shipping. All of these, he asserted, drained the
legitimate income of the South to support the North. Whether political or economic in
nature, Southern leaders were united in viewing this as "the War of Northern Aggression."

The perspective of these leaders was that while the South had supported in a mul-
tiplicity of ways the Constitution of 1787 as it had been approved, the North had aggressively altered the Constitution in numerous ways and imposed those changes on the
nation. This was the terrible aggression that they believed the North had illegally and
unconstitutionally imposed on the South, that directly interfered with Southern domestic
institutions, that made it impossible for the South to live together in peace with the
North, and that resulted in the South seeking its own destiny outside of the United States.

To a certain extent, President James Buchanan agreed that the North was to blame
for the conflict, arguing that it was a needless war kindled by the continual agitation of
Republicans and anti-slavery "fanatics" for causing the emotional pot to boil over. Not
surprisingly, most Northerners disagreed with both the Southern interpretations and the
conclusions of the former president. United States Secretary of State William H. Seward
identified the cause as an "irrepressible conflict" between a free labor system established
by divine law and a slave labor system resting on unnatural degradation. It was the Southern system that was promoting something immoral and aberrant, not the North. Similarly,
Massachusetts Senator Henry Wilson, later to become vice president in the Grant administration, contended in his *History of the Rise and Fall of the Slave Power in America*[6] that
the war was caused by an evil conspiracy of slave owners to subvert American ideals,
using repression and violence to stifle any dissent. Both of these arguments rested on the
anti-slavery viewpoint articulated during the war by Frederick Douglass that the conflict
"has its root and its sap, its trunk and its branches, and the bloody fruit it bears only
from the one source of all abounding abomination, and that is slavery."[7] Although there
were other causes identified and arguments made, the majority reflected the prewar sectional divide. Southern participants focused mainly on issues of politics, constitutionality
and economics, while supporters of the North viewed it as a moral disagreement over
slavery, the preservation of which was so important to the South that it was willing to
begin a devastating fratricidal war to destroy the nation.

In large part, these arguments were echoed by participants in their writing following
the war. In the immediate aftermath of the war, Northern historians, led by George Ban-
croft and John Draper, placed the blame squarely on slavery and the personal interests
of Southern leaders. The North was blameless, having fought for freedom and the rule
of law against the evils of the rebellious South. However, another narrative also emerged
from postwar Southern writers who had lived through the four-year struggle. This began
with Edward A. Pollard, a Virginia journalist, who authored two books picturing the
South as a romanticized "Lost Cause." Pollard defended his section as a genteel, non-

competitive, agrarian society, a "distinctive civilization" with "higher sentimentalism, and its superior refinements of scholarship and manners" in which "capital ... protected labour." The South was "a peculiar and noble type of civilization" based on "notions of chivalry" characterized by "polished manners" and "many noble and generous virtues." By contrast, the North was coarse and materialistic, bent only on profit.[8] This was the *Birth of a Nation-Gone with the Wind* image of the Old South, a genteel society of large plantations, cultured living, and profitable agriculture supported by happy laborers content with their lot in life. It was, at least in part, a portrait engineered to justify the Southern viewpoint that all was well in the South until Northern agitation and aggression provoked the war. The "Lost Cause" literary movement begun by Pollard proved amazingly resilient, forming the basis for a mythology that depicted the South as a heroic, outnumbered people forced to fight for their rights against Northern aggression.

Reflections of the "Lost Cause" interpretation repeatedly emerged in innumerable portrayals of the Old South in literature and later in movies and on television. Another significant element in promoting this view, especially in the 1880s and 1890s, was the United Daughters of the Confederacy (UDC) that was, according to the Southern Poverty Law Center, responsible for the erection of some 718 memorial monuments to honor those who fought in behalf of the Confederacy. Through these and other means the UDC and similar groups have contributed significantly to keeping alive the Confederate perspective of Northern aggression as well as Southern hostility to African Americans.[9]

In 1872 Currier & Ives published this lithograph titled "The Last Cause." A ghostly image of a Confederate battle flag hovers above a man mourning the dead with a rundown farm house and fence to the left background (Library of Congress).

The second element of Halbwach's dichotomy was the constructed memory of later generations who lack the perspective of participant observation. In contrast to "Collective Memory," this "Historical Memory" was created by people with no direct connection to the events they are writing about. Americans have interpreted the Civil War in various ways, many of them dependent on the background of the researcher or the time in which the interpretation originated. In general, these have been divided into three general categories: those who support a Northern view of the causes, those that support a Southern view, and those who are more-or-less neutral by describing it as a needless conflict.

Aside from the partisan interpretations, the latter years of the nineteenth century also launched the beginning of a new genre of historical memory oriented more toward reconciliation. During the later nineteenth century, an increasing number of veterans reunions, especially those at Gettysburg which began to take on the form of national commemorations, brought together in peace the aged warriors in blue and gray to promote healing and understanding.[10] Mirroring this move toward downplaying sectional divisions, historians began to take a more "neutral" view of the antebellum era rather than point fingers of responsibility. Those who pursued this line generally spoke of the war as an "irrepressible conflict" resulting from differing political-economic structures, or occasionally from inept politicians who failed to find an acceptable compromise to avert the tragedy. The classic example of the latter was James G. Randall's *The Civil War and Reconstruction*[11] that viewed the war as a needless conflict caused by blundering politicians caught up in the rhetoric of abolitionism and States' Rights.

The last reunion of the blue and gray occurred in Gettysburg in 1938, the 75th anniversary of the battle that helped decide the conflict. Some 1,870 veterans attended, including 25 who had been in the battle (Library of Congress).

Domestic economics dominated the two decades between 1920 and 1940; the former the economic prosperity of the "Roaring Twenties" and the latter the despair of the Depression. During these years people's minds focused on economics and historical interpretations of the Civil War were no different. The most influential of these was *The Rise of American Civilization* in which Charles and Mary Beard argued that the war resulted from Northern dominance of the economy through manufacturing, commerce and finance. Slavery, they asserted, was merely one symptom of that fundamental economic cause. "The Second American Revolution," they wrote, "while destroying the economic foundations of the slaveowning aristocracy, assures the triumph of business enterprise."[12] Another example of this was Frank L. Owsley's "The Irrepressible Conflict."[13] A product of the Southern agrarian anti-capitalism of the 1930s, Owsley, not surprisingly, viewed the South as a victim of Northern economic and cultural aggression through insistence on high tariffs, restriction of slavery from much of the western lands, and opposition to the rights of the states.

With the rise of the modern Civil Rights Movement after World War II, the issue of slavery again came to the fore as the nation focused on issues of civil and political rights. This was reflected in the preeminent historical interpretations of that era. Allan Nevins's massive six-volume study *Ordeal of the Union*[14] recognizes the failures of leadership, but refocuses attention on the rising emotional divide over slavery, naming it as the underlying cause of the discord. Similarly, Avery O. Craven emphasized irrationalism—Southern nationalism and Northern abolitionism—as a causal factor, but also identified slavery as the primary issue of disagreement. Eugene Genovese's *The Political Economy of Slavery* argued that the slave economy produced "a class of slaveholders with a special ideology and psychology, and the economic power to impose their values on society as a whole."[15] This led to increasing Southern political aggressiveness and ultimately to war. This is a somewhat different twist on slavery causation, but in its general conclusion privileges slavery once again as the most important cause of the conflict. And finally, Eric Foner examined the ideology of "free labor" and its essential conflict with the slave labor system in his *Free Soil, Free Labor, Free Men: The Ideology of the Republican Party Before the Civil War*.[16] All of these works, as well as derivatives of each, once again brought slavery to the forefront in an era when race relations dominated the national news.

Today, the era of Sectionalism, Civil War and Reconstruction remains one of the most heatedly debated periods in American history, although its transformational influence on postwar America cannot be doubted.

Chapter Notes

Chapter 1

1. For John Rolfe, see Murray N. Rothbard, *Conceived in Liberty* (Auburn, AL: Ludwig von Mises Institute, 2011), 52.

2. For literacy rates, see Kenneth A. Lockridge, *Literacy in Colonial New England: An Enquiry into the Social Context of Literacy in the Early Modern West* (New York: W.W. Norton, 1974).

3. E. H. Scott, ed., *Journal of the Constitutional Convention, Kept by James Madison* (Chicago: Scott, Foresman and Company, 1893), 74.

4. Article I, Section 2, of the United States Constitution.

5. Reproduced in the Avalon Project at http://avalon.law.yale.edu/18th_century/debates_710.asp (accessed July 9, 2015).

6. Quoted from Max Farrand, ed., *The Records of the Federal Convention of 1787* (New Haven: Yale University Press, 1911), II, 364.

7. Sedition Act, July 14, 1798, reproduced in the Avalon Project at http://avalon.law.yale.edu/18th_century/sedact.asp (accessed July 17, 2015).

8. Francis W. Halsey, ed., *Great Epochs in American History: Described by Famous Writers from Columbus to Roosevelt* (New York: Funk & Wagnalls Company, 1912), V, 147.

9. Gary John Kornblith, *Slavery and Sectional Strife in the Early American Republic, 1776–1821* (New York: Rowman & Littlefield, 2010), 155.

10. Junius P. Rodriguez, ed., *Slavery in the United States: A Social, Political, and Historical Encyclopedia* (Santa Barbara, CA: ABC-CLIO, Inc., 2007), I, 333.

11. "South Carolina Ordinance of Nullification," in Melvin Yazawa, ed., *Documents for America's History* (Boston: Bedford/St. Martin's, 2011), I, 257–58.

12. *Ibid.*, 58.

13. Fred L. Israel and Jim F. Watts, eds., *Presidential Documents: The Speeches, Proclamations, and Policies that Have Shaped the Nation from Washington to Clinton* (New York: Routledge, 2000), 71–76.

14. *Ibid.*, 76.

Chapter 2

1. For the growth of the cotton industry in the U.S., see "The Growth of the Cotton Industry in America," https://www.sailsinc.org/durfee/earl2.pdf.

2. For the Irish arrival and early years in America see Oscar Handlin, *Boston's Immigrants, 1790–1865; a Study in Acculturation* (Cambridge: Harvard University Press, 1941).

3. Carl Wittke, *Refugees of Revolution: The German Forty-Eighters in America* (Philadelphia: University of Pennsylvania Press, 1952).

4. For the Second Great Awakening, see Timothy L. Smith, *Revivalism and Social Reform: American Protestantism on the Eve of the Civil War* (Baltimore: Johns Hopkins University Press, 1980); Whitney R. Cross, *The Burned-over District: The Social and Intellectual History of Enthusiastic Religion in Western New York, 1800–1850* (Ithaca, NY: Cornell University Press, 1982); Charles Hambrick-Stowe, *Charles G. Finney and the Spirit of American Evangelicalism* (Grand Rapids, MI: Eerdmans, 1996); Nathan O. Hatch, *The Democratization of American Christianity* (New Haven: Yale University Press, 1989).

5. Gerald Sorin, *Abolitionism: A New Perspective* (New York: Praeger Publishers, 1972), 45.

6. Richard L. Manzelmann, "Revivalism and Reform," in *The History of Oneida County* (Utica: Oneida County, 1977), 54.

7. Keith J. Hardman, *Charles Grandison Finney, 1792–1875, Revivalist and Reformer* (Syracuse: Syracuse University Press, 1987), 273.

8. Manzelmann, "Revivalism and Reform," 53.

9. Charles Grandison Finney, "The Pernicious Attitude of the Church on the Reforms of the Age," *The Oberlin Evangelist*, January 21, 1846.

10. Bernard A. Weisberger, *They Gathered at the River: The Story of the Great Revivalists and Their Impact Upon Religion in America* (Boston: Little, Brown, 1958).

11. C. S. Griffin, *The Ferment of Reform, 1830–1860* (New York: Thomas Y. Crowell Company, 1967).

12. Timothy L. Smith, *Revivalism and Social Reform: American Protestantism on the Eve of the Civil War* (New York: Harper & Row, 1965).

13. T. Bailey, D. Kennedy, and L. Cohen, *The American Pageant* (Boston: Houghton Mifflin Company, 1998). Other studies differ, but the percentage of slaves in the United States was by all accounts small compared to the rest of the hemisphere. Stephen Behrendt estimates it at 6.45 percent in his article "Transatlantic Slave Trade," *Africana: The Encyclopedia of the African and African American Experience* (New York: Basic Civitas Books, 1991).

14. Theodore Weld, *American Slavery as It Is: Testimony of a Thousand Witnesses* (New York: American Anti-Slavery Society, 1839), 43.

15. *Ibid.*, 40.

16. *Ibid.*, 49.

17. *Ibid.*, 28.

18. *Ibid.*, 29.

19. *Ibid.*, 33.

20. For a good source on urban slavery see Richard C. Wade, *Slavery in the Cities: The South 1820–1860* (Oxford: Oxford University Press, 1969).

21. For the distribution of slaves in 1860 see the U.S. census at https://www.census.gov/history/www/reference/maps/distribution_of_slaves_in_1860.html.

22. For information on exports from the U.S. Treasury Department, see "Foreign Commerce of the United States as Affected by Civil War," *New York Times*, February 28, 1862.

23. *The Liberator*, No. 1, January 1, 1831.

24. *The Pro-Slavery Argument: As Maintained by the most Distinguished Writers of the Southern States, Containing the Several Essays, on the Subject, of Chancellor Harper, Governor Hammond, Dr. Simms, and Professor Dew* (Charleston: Walker, Richards, 1852), 451–62.

25. E. N. Elliott, *Cotton is King, and Pro-slavery Arguments; Comprising the Writings of Hammond, Harper, Christy, Stringfellow, Hodge, Bledsoe, and Cartwright, on this Important Subject* (Augusta, GA: Abbot & Loomis, 1860), 898.

26. For Angelina Grimké, *Letters to Catharine E. Beecher in reply to an Essay on Slavery and Abolitionism addressed to A. E. Grimké by the Author* (Boston: Isaac Knapp, 1838).

27. William Wilson, "The Great American Question" (1848), accessed February 28, 2015, at http://memory.loc.gov/cgi-bin/query/r?ammem/rbaapc:@field(DOCID+@lit(rbaapc34000div0)).

28. Elliott, *Cotton is King*.

29. Milton C. Sernett, *Abolition's Axe: Beriah Green, Oneida Institute, and the Black Freedom Struggle* (Syracuse: Syracuse University Press, 1986), 112; Charles A. Hammond, *Gerrit Smith: The Story of a Noble Life* (Geneva, NY: Press of W. F. Humphrey, 1908), 36; Eric Foner, *Free Soil, Free Labor, Free Men: The Ideology of the Republican Party Before the Civil War* (New York: Oxford University Press, 1978), 302; *National Party Conventions 1831-1972* (Washington, D.C.: Congressional Quarterly, 1976), 25.

30. Sernett, *Abolition's Axe*, 114.

31. Foner, *Free Soil, Free Labor, Free Men*, 81; Sernett, *Abolition's Axe*, 109, 117; Stewart Mitchell, *Horatio Seymour of New York* (Cambridge: Harvard University Press, 1938), 68; letter, Smith to Salmon P. Chase, May 31, 1842, Gerrit Smith Papers, Syracuse University.

32. Gerald Sorin, *The New York Abolitionists: A Case Study of Political Radicalism* (Westport, CT: Greenwood Publishing Corporation, 1971), 113; Sernett, *Abolition's Axe*, 55.

33. *National Party Conventions*, 25; Sernett, *Abolition's Axe*, 117; Milton C. Sernett, *North Star Country: Upstate New York and the Crusade for African American Freedom* (Syracuse: Syracuse University Press, 2002), 118.

34. Joshua R. Giddings, *Speeches on Congress by Joshua R. Giddings* (Boston: John P. Jewett and Company), 1853), 151–52, 275.

35. John C. Calhoun, "The Clay Compromise Measures," speech in the U.S. Senate, March 4, 1850, from http://www.nationalcenter.org/CalhounClayCompromise.htmll.

36. Richard Harrison Shryock, "Georgia and the Union in 1850" (Philadelphia: University of Pennsylvania, 1926, PhD dissertation), 344.

Chapter 3

1. For the Fugitive Slave Act see Project Avalon at Yale Law School, http://avalon.law.yale.edu/19th_century/fugitive.asp.

2. Gerrit Smith's speech at an anti–Fugitive Slave Law meeting in Syracuse, New York, January 9, 1851, can be found at the Gilda Lehrman Institute of American History, https://www.gilderlehrman.org/collections/240b686d-6023-4c3d-b54e-725128101991.

3. Thomas R. Dew, *Review of the Debate in the Virginia Legislature of 1831 and 1832* (Richmond: T. W. White, 1832), 106–07; see also *From The Pro-Slavery Argument: As Maintained by the most Distinguished Writers of the Southern States, Containing the Several Essays, on the Subject, of Chancellor Harper, Governor Hammond, Dr. Simms, and Professor Dew* (Charleston: Walker, Richards, 1852), 451–62.

4. King James version of the Bible, 1 Peter 2:18–20.

5. Dew, *Review of the Debate*, 106–07; *The Pro-Slavery Argument*, 451–62.

6. James A. Colaiaco, *Frederick Douglass and the Fourth of July* (New York: Palgrave Macmillan, 2006), 52.

7. For the Kansas-Nebraska Act see John R. Wunder and Joann M. Ross, eds., *The Nebraska-Kansas Act of 1854* (Lincoln: University of Nebraska Press, 2008).

8. Salmon P. Chase, "Appeal of the Independent Democrats in Congress to the People of the United States," Towers' Printers, January 19, 1854.

9. *Congressional Globe*, May 22, 1854, 1254, 1321.

10. Peter Jarvis, "Abolitionism in Oneida County," unpublished ms., Oneida County Historical Society, Utica, NY, 1968, 5.

11. *Utica Morning Herald*, June 15, 1854.

12. *Utica Morning Herald*, June 16, 1854.

13. Charles Sumner, "Crime Against Kansas," *The Works of Charles Sumner* (Boston: Lee and Shepard, 1870–1873), IV, 125–249.

14. *Ibid.*

15. Charles Sumner, *The Crime Against Kansas: The Apologies for the Crime. The True Remedy* (Boston: John P. Jewett & Company, 1856).

16. James Daley, ed., *Landmark Decisions of the U.S. Supreme Court* (Mineola, NY: Dover Publications, 2006), 75.

17. *Southern Enterprise* (Greenville, South Carolina), March 26, 1857.

18. Quoted in Stanley I. Kutler, *The Dred Scott Decision: Law or Politics?* (Boston: Houghton Mifflin Company, 1967), 111.

19. Alfred R. Conkling, *The Life and Letters of Roscoe Conkling, Orator, Statesman, Advocate* (New York: Charles L. Webster & Company, 1889), 30.

20. *Utica Herald*, editorial March 10, 1857, 2.

21. Mitchell Snay, *Horace Greeley and the Politics of Reform in Nineteenth-Century America* (New York: Rowman & Littlefield, 2011), 125.

22. Quoted in Kutler, *Dred Scott Decision*, 70.

23. See http://www.bartleby.com/268/9/16.html.

24. See http://www.digitalhistory.uh.edu/disp_textbook.cfm?smtID=2&psid=3283.

25. Quote from Chester G. Hearn, *Companions in Conspiracy: John Brown & Gerrit Smith* (Gettysburg, PA: Thomas Publications, 1996), 53.

26. Hearn, *Companions in Conspiracy*, 54.

27. *Political Debates Between Hon. Abraham Lincoln and Hon. Stephen A. Douglas in the Celebrated Campaign of 1858 in Illinois* (Columbus: Follett, Foster and Company, 1860), 26.

28. *Letters and Addresses of Abraham Lincoln* (New York: Howard Wilford Bell, 1903), 105.

29. *Political Debates Between Abraham Lincoln and Stephen A. Douglas in the in the Celebrated Campaign of 1858 in Illinois* (Cleveland: The Burrows Brothers Company, 1894), 116.

30. Hearn, *Companions in Conspiracy*, 55.

31. Hearn, *Companions in Conspiracy*, 41, 49; Lawrence J. Friedman, "The Gerrit Smith Circle: Abolitionism in the Burned-Over District," *Civil War History*, Vol. 26, No. 1 (March 1980), 36.

32. Louis DeCaro, Jr., *John Brown Speaks: Letters and Statements from Charlestown* (Lanham, MD: Rowman & Littlefield, 2015), 19.

33. John Morley, ed., *The Fortnightly Review*, Vol. XXI (new series; January 1–June 1, 1882; London: Chapman and & Hall, Ltd., 1882), 259.

34. James Redpath, ed., *Echoes of Harper's Ferry* (Boston: Thayer & Eldridge, 1860), 98.

35. Harold Bloom, ed., *Henry David Thoreau* (New York: Infobase Publishing, 2007), 16.

36. Jonathan Daniels, *They Will Be Heard: America's Crusading Newspaper Editors* (New York: McGraw-Hill, 1965), 150.

37. Quoted in Stephen B. Oates, *To Purge this Land with Blood: A Biography of John Brown* (Amherst: University of Massachusetts Press, 1984), 320.

38. E. N. Elliott, *Cotton Is King*.

39. *Congressional Globe*, 36th Congress, 1st Session, 658–59.

40. *Congressional Globe*, 36th Congress, 1st Session, 658–59.

41. *The Charleston Mercury*, June 9, 1860.

42. Quoted in Paul F. Boller, Jr., *Presidential Campaigns: From George Washington to George W. Bush* (Oxford: Oxford University Press, 2004), 110.

Chapter 4

1. "Ordinance of Secession" (1860), South Carolina Department of Archives and History, Columbia, SC.

2. "Amendments Proposed in Congress by Senator John J. Crittenden: December 18, 1860," The Avalon Project, Yale Law School, http://avalon.law.yale.edu/19th_century/critten.asp.

3. *New York Tribune*, March 27, 1861.

4. James Buchanan, *The Works of James Buchanan: Comprising His Speeches, State Papers, and Private Correspondence* (Philadelphia: J. B. Lippincott Co., 1908–1911; John Bassett Moore, ed.), 178.

5. Lynda Lasswell Crist and Mary Seaton Dix, eds., *The Papers of Jefferson Davis* (Baton Rouge: Louisiana State University Press, 1992), Vol. 7, 45–51.

6. *Ibid.*

7. *New York Tribune*, March 27, 1861.

8. "First Inaugural Address of Abraham Lincoln," The Avalon Project, Yale Law School, http://avalon.law.yale.edu/19th_century/lincoln1.asp.

9. *Ibid.*

10. *Ibid.*

11. *Ibid.*

12. Anderson's father had served at Ft. Moultrie in Charleston during the American Revolution.

13. A native of Louisiana, Beauregard had finished second in the 45-man West Point class of 1838. A twice wounded veteran of the Mexican War, he earned two brevets for gallantry in action.

14. Lincoln's call for 75,000 volunteers to put down the rebellion can be found at History Central, http://www.historycentral.com/documents/Callvol.html.

15. *The War of the Rebellion: A Compilation of the Official Records of the Union and Confederate Armies* (Washington: U.S. Government Printing Office, 1902), Series III, Vol. I, 72.

16. "Kentucky Refuses Troops," *New York Times*, April 16, 1861.

17. *Harper's New Monthly Magazine*, Volume 23, 120.

18. Letter, Lincoln to Orville H. Browning, September 22, 1861, in Roy P. Basler, ed., *Collected Works of Abraham Lincoln* (New Brunswick, NJ: Rutgers University Press, 1953), Vol. 4, 532.

Chapter 5

1. Herman Hattaway and Archer Jones, *How the North Won: a Military History of the Civil War* (Urbana: University of Illinois Press, 1991).

2. See David Donald, ed., *Why the North won the Civil War* (Baton Rouge: Louisiana State University Press, 1973).

3. See Frank Owsley and Harriet Chapell Owsley, *King Cotton Diplomacy: Foreign Relations of the Confederate States of America* (Tuscaloosa: University of Alabama Press, 2008).

4. For an analysis of Civil War costs see Claudia D. Goldin and Frank D. Lewis, "The Economic Cost of the American Civil War: Estimates and Implications," *Journal of Economic History*, Vol. 35, no. 2 (Jun., 1975), 299–326.

5. *Ibid.*

6. See Douglas B. Ball, *Financial Failure and Confederate Defeat* (Urbana: University of Illinois Press, 1991); Richard C. K. Burdekin and Farrokh Langdana, "War Finance in the Southern Confederacy, 1861–1865," *Explorations in Economic History*, Vol. 30, no. 3 (July 1993), 352–76.

7. See Ella Lonn, *Foreigners in the Union Army and Navy* (New York: Greenwood Press, 1969); Ella Lonn, *Foreigners in the Confederacy* (Chapel Hill: University of North Carolina Press, 2002).

8. Wilhelm Kaufmann, *Die Deutschen im amerikanischen Bürgerkriege Sezessionskrieg 1861–1865* (München: Oldenbourg, 1911).

9. Despite the name, only a handful of the men were of Polish origin, most were of Irish and German origin or ancestry from the New Orleans area.

10. See Patricia L Faust, ed., *Historical Times illustrated Encyclopedia of the Civil War* (New York: Harper-Perennial, 1991); "Civil War Army Organization," The Civil War Trust, https://www.civilwar.org/learn/articles/civil-war-army-organization.

11. Quoted in E. B. Quiner, *The Military History of Wisconsin: A Record of the Civil and Military Patriotism of the State in the War for the Union* (Chicago: Clarke & Co., 1866), 210.

12. Quoted in Joseph K. Barnes, *The Medical and Surgical History of the War of the Rebellion (1861–65)* (Washington: U.S. Government Printing Office, 1870), I, Appendix, 45.

13. *Ibid.*

14. Mark H. Dunkelman, *Brothers One and All: Esprit de Corps in a Civil War Regiment* (Baton Rouge: Louisiana State University Press, 2004), 235. The soldier was Dwight More in the 154th New York.

15. Barnes, *Medical and Surgical History*.

16. See George Worthington Adams, *Doctors in Blue: the Medical History of the Union Army in the Civil War* (Baton Rouge: Louisiana State University Press, 1996); Joseph K. Barnes. ed., *The Medical and Surgical History of the War of the Rebellion, 1861–65* (Washington, D.C.: U.S. Government Printing Office, 1875–1883).

17. William Keen, "Military Surgery in 1861 and in 1918," *Annals of the American Academy of Political and Social Science*, Vol. 80, *Rehabilitation of the Wounded* (Nov. 1918), 11–22.

18. Carl Schurz, *The Reminiscences of Carl Schurz* (London: John Murray, 1909), III, 39.

19. See Adams, *Doctors in Blue*; Barnes, *Medical and Surgical History*.

20. "Important from Missouri: Proclamation of Gen. Fremont," *The New York Times*, September 1, 1861.

21. Born in Troy, New York, Hunter was a Military Academy graduate who confided his anti-slavery views in correspondence with Lincoln in 1860. The two became close enough that the president elect invited Hunter to accompany him on the train to Washington following Lincoln's election. Although promoted to colonel of the 6th U.S. Cavalry, Hunter served only three days in that position before being elevated by the president to the rank of brigadier general. Wounded at First Bull Run, he was promoted to major general and assigned to division command under Frémont.

22. Born a Kentuckian, Johnston graduated from West Point, served with distinction in the Texas war for independence, and fought in the Mexican War under Gen. Zachary Taylor.

23. Grant had served as a quartermaster in the Mexican War with a relatively undistinguished career thereafter, mostly spent manning outposts in the west. Failing at several business ventures and depressed over being separated from his family back east, Grant took to drink and eventually resigned under pressure in 1854. Civilian life was not kind to him and he finally eked out a subsistence-level living at various jobs until he took a position as a clerk in a leather store his father owned. Unsuccessful in gaining reinstatement in the army when the war broke out, he voluntarily began recruiting soldiers in his home state of Illinois until Governor Richard Yates appointed him to recruit and train the state's volunteers. With the support of Illinois Congressman Elihu B. Washburne, Grant eventually gained appointment as colonel of the 21st Illinois and promotion to brigadier general to date from May 17, 1861. Frémont assigned him to organize Federal troops at Cairo.

24. An Ohioan, Buell graduated from West Point in 1841. He served in the Mexican War where he was wounded at Churubusco and earned three brevet promotions. Following the war he served in the army Adjutant General's Office and then in California. At the beginning of the war he was involved in organizing what would become the Army of the Potomac before being assigned to command the Department of the Ohio and

the army named after the same river. His promoted to brigadier general ranked from the same date as that of U.S. Grant.

25. A graduate of the U.S. Military Academy, McDowell had served as an aide-de-camp in the Mexican War after which he taught tactics at West Point. In 23 years of military service, he had never led so much as a squad in actual combat.

26. Beauregard had also graduated from West Point and served in the Mexican War, but his service was leading combat troops where he suffered two wounds and earned two brevets for gallantry in action. In January 1861 he was serving as superintendent at West Point, but his orders were revoked when Louisiana seceded. Beauregard protested then left for home while billing the U.S. government for his train fare. Appointed the first brigadier general in the Provisional Army of the Confederate States, after his service in South Carolina he was sent to northern Virginia to command troops in the defense of the border with the North.

27. A veteran of service in Florida and the Mexican War where he was wounded five times and earned three brevets for gallantry, Johnston resigned his commission as a brigadier general and Quartermaster General of the U.S. Army when his native Virginia left the Union, the highest ranking army officer to "go south."

28. R. A. Brock, ed., "The Signal Corps in the Southern States Army," *Southern Historical Society Papers*, Vol. XVI (Richmond: Southern Historical Society, 1888), 94.

29. There are many renditions of what Bee said and meant. This one was the version given by Gen. Pierre G. T. Beauregard. Derek Smith, *The Gallant Dead: Union and Confederate Generals Killed in the Civil War* (Mechanicsburg, PA: Stackpole Books, 2005), 7.

30. For the Revenue Act of 1861 see The Gilder Lehrman Institute of American History, https://www.gilderlehrman.org/history-by-era/american-civil-war/timeline-terms/revenue-act-1861.

31. *Congressional Globe*, July 24, 1861, 247.

32. For the First Confiscation Act see The Gilder Lehrman Institute of American History, https://www.gilderlehrman.org/history-by-era/african-americans-and-emancipation/timeline-terms/first-confiscation-act.

33. A Pennsylvanian and Military Academy graduate, McClellan earned two brevets in the Mexican War after which he was dispatched as a U.S. observer to the Crimean War. While there he took note of the special saddle used by Hungarian Hussars. Bringing this information back with him he developed the "McClellan Saddle" for use by the American army. Returning to civilian life in 1857, he used the engineering skills he learned in the army to gain a position as chief engineer and vice president of the Illinois Central Railroad and in 1860 accepted a position as president of the Ohio and Mississippi Railroad.

34. Edward McPherson, *The Political History of the United States of America During the Great Rebellion: From November 6, 1860, to July 4, 1864; Including a Classified Summary of the Legislation of the Second Session of the Thirty-sixth Congress, the Three Sessions of the Thirty-seventh Congress, the First Session of the Thirty-eighth Congress, with the Votes Thereon, and the Important Executive, Judicial, and Politico-military Facts of that Eventful Period; Together with the Organization, Legislation, and General Proceedings of the Rebel Administration* (Washington, D.C.: Philip & Solomons, 1864), 349.

Chapter 6

1. A native of Kentucky who finished eighth of 41 graduates in his West Point class of 1826, Johnston had considerable military experience. He fought in the Black Hawk War, the Texas War of Independence, the Mexican War, and the Mormon Rebellion in Utah, while also serving two years as Secretary of War for the Republic of Texas. The outbreak of the Civil War found him in California commanding the Department of the Pacific, but he soon resigned his position to accept an appointment as the second-ranking general officer in the Confederacy.

2. Born in Westernville, New York, Halleck graduated from the Military Academy third in his class in 1839 acquiring along the way the nickname "Old Brains." After earning a brevet for his services in California and Mexico during the Mexican War, he resigned his commission in 1854 and settled in California where he became wealthy through his law practice and land speculation. When the war erupted General-in-Chief Winfield Scott appointed him a major general in the regular army, which made him the fourth highest ranking officer, and assigned him to command the important Department of the Missouri.

3. An Ohioan, Grant graduated from West Point in 1843 and earned a brevet for bravery in the Mexican War where he served with distinction in the attack on Mexico City. Following the war his star declined. He married, but his assignments required him to move frequently, separating the couple for long periods of time. In 1854 he resigned under a cloud when suspected of imbibing too freely in intoxicating liquors. After failing in several occupations including farming, he finally took a clerkship in his father's leather shop in Galena, Illinois. When the war began he unsuccessfully sought appointment to the U.S. army, including being snubbed by Gen. George B. McClellan, finally accepting an appointment to recruit and train Illinois volunteers offered by the state's governor. Through the intervention of the influential Congressman Elihu B. Washburne, he finally received an appointment as colonel of the 21st Illinois Volunteer Infantry. When he proved successful, Washburne again interceded, convincing President Lincoln to appoint him brigadier general to date from May 17, 1861. Assigned to the command of Cairo, Illinois, he captured Paducah, Kentucky, through fast marching, bringing himself to the attention of his superiors.

4. Floyd was a Virginian who graduated from South Carolina College. He served in the Virginia legislature, was elected to a term as governor, and in 1857 was appointed Secretary of War by President James Buchanan. In that position he was implicated in a financial scandal and later accused of purposely repositioning military supplies and equipment into southern arsenals in anticipation of the beginning of the war.

5. A slaveholding Tennessean who was a noted attorney and political leader, Pillow had served as a major general in the Mexican War and received the gratitude of the Confederate Congress for his conduct at the Battle of Belmont in Missouri in 1861.

6. *The War of the Rebellion: A Compilation of the Official Records of the Union and Confederate Armies* (Washington, D.C.: U.S. Government Printing Office, 1882), Series I, Vol. VII, 161 [hereafter *OR* for Official Records].

7. Brooks D. Simpson, *Ulysses S. Grant: Triumph Over Adversity, 1822–1865* (Minneapolis, MN: Zenith Press, 2014), 134.

8. Lewis Wallace was born in Indiana, grew up to be a journalist and attorney, then fought in the Mexican War. He led the 11th Indiana as its colonel at Romney and Harpers Ferry before being promoted to brigadier general in September 1861 and major general in March 1862. Following the war the authored the immensely popular novel *Ben Hur.*

9. Thomas L. Livermore, *Numbers and Losses in the Civil War in America 1861–65* (New York: Kraus Reprint Co., 1969).

10. A Tennessean married to a Virginian, appointed a midshipman when he was only nine years old, Farragut served in the War of 1812, being wounded and captured while serving aboard the USS *Essex* off Valparaiso, Chile. After serving in the West Indies, during the Mexican War he commanded the sloop USS *Saratoga* on blockade duty off the Mexican gulf coast. Following the war he was placed in command of the construction of what would become the Mare Island Navy Yard near San Francisco. The emotional atmosphere of the 1860 election found him assigned to the naval base at Norfolk, Virginia. Despite his Southern birth, and that of his wife, he moved his family north after announcing his allegiance to the United States.

11. A brigadier general in the Massachusetts militia at the outbreak of the war, a position he attained largely through his considerable political connections, Butler was an influential prewar politician who raised a force that quickly occupied Annapolis and Baltimore at the beginning of the war. This coup did much to open the way for reinforcements to move into the nation's capital, as well as to save Maryland for the Union. Following that he led a force that successfully captured two forts along the North Carolina coast before returning to Massachusetts to raise additional forces. Designated to lead the military portion of the New Orleans expedition because of his earlier successes, he was ironically a prewar Democrat who favored accommodation with the South, had nominated Jefferson Davis for the presidency, and later backed John C. Breckinridge.

12. A native of the District of Columbia, Lovell came from a long line of military men dating back to the Revolution. He graduated from the Military Academy in 1842 and was wounded twice in the Mexican War where he earned a brevet. After resigning in 1849 he became the deputy street commission in New York City where he was also active in the local militia before resigning to head south in September 1861.

13. *OR*, Series I, Vol. X, Part II, 531.

14. Born in Scotland, Pinkerton was a former Chicago detective and the co-founder of a detective agency. In the latter capacity he investigated a series of train robberies which brought him into contact with the vice president and chief engineer of the Illinois Central Railroad, one George B. McClellan, and the company's attorney, Abraham Lincoln. Following the 1860 election, Pinkerton accompanied the president-elect to Washington in charge of his security.

15. John C. Waugh, *Lincoln and McClellan: The Troubled Partnership Between a President and His General* (New York: Palgrave Macmillan, 2010).

16. A prominent Massachusetts politician who had served as an anti-slavery representative in Congress and Republican governor of his state, Banks was a political appointee with no real prior military experience.

17. Thomas was a Virginian who, as a child, had been forced to flee his home and hide in the woods with his mother and sisters during the Nat Turner uprising. He

graduated from West Point in 1840, served in the Seminole War and the frontier wars where he was wounded, and earned two brevets in the Mexican War. When he refused to "go South" after Virginia's secession, his family tuned his picture to the wall and never spoke to him again. After the war his sisters declined to attend his funeral telling those who inquired that their brother had died in 1861.

18. Pope had been appointed to the Military Academy from Illinois, graduating in 1842 and spending considerable time on surveying projects in the west. Earning one brevet in the Mexican War, he was jumped from captain to brigadier general on May 17, 1861, when the war required a rapid expansion of the army. He was related by marriage to the family of Mary Todd Lincoln.

19. A Virginian who graduated from the Military Academy in 1830, Magruder served in the Seminole War, earned two brevets in the Mexican War, but resigned his commission as a captain to accept appointment as a colonel in the Confederacy in May 1861. After gaining plaudits for the Battle of Big Bethel on June 10, he was promoted to brigadier general and four months later to major general.

20. A Virginian, Johnston graduated from West Point in 1829 after which he gained considerable combat experience in the Black Hawk War and the Seminole War where he served as aide-de-camp to General Winfield Scott, was wounded twice and received a brevet promotion to captain. Wounded five times in the Mexican War, he earned three more brevets and led the final assault on Chapultepec at Mexico City. Following the war he held several positions including army Inspector General. When he went south in April 1861 he was appointed brigadier general in the Confederate army and major general of Virginia forces commanding the combined army that won the First Battle of Bull Run in July of that year.

21. Born in South Carolina, Longstreet was raised in Alabama from where he was appointed to the Military Academy. Graduating in 1842, he served in the Mexican War where he was wounded and earned two brevets. Having lead a brigade at First Bull Run he was, like so many others, rapidly promoted to command much larger units including this multi-division assault on the Federal position south of the Chickahominy.

22. Lee came from distinguished Virginia ancestry descended from a prominent early colonist named Richard Lee who arrived in 1639 and quickly became a prosperous planter who served in the colony's House of Burgesses. Lee's father, Maj. Gen. Henry Lee, popularly known as "Light Horse Harry," had become a hero leading cavalry troops in the American Revolution, moving on after the war to serve as governor of Virginia and then as a member of its delegation to Congress. Yet, despite the illustrious pedigree, poor investments and financial mismanagement eventually landed Henry in debtor's prison. Robert Edward was born in 1807, two years before his father was incarcerated, so he began life with few of the advantages one might associate with the prominence of his family. His early years were spent in a house in Alexandria, Virginia, his father passing away when he was only eleven years old. Lee's mother received support from a relative named William Henry Fitzhugh who later arranged an appointment for the youth to West Point. Lee graduated in 1829 second in his class. He spent much of his early military career on various engineering projects but distinguished himself as a member of Gen. Winfield Scott's staff during the

campaign against Mexico City earning a brevet promotion to major for his actions at the Battle of Cerro Gordo and being wounded in the storming of Chapultepec at the Mexican capital. He finished the war with additional brevet promotions to lieutenant colonel and colonel. In 1852 he was appointed superintendent of the Military Academy and three years later assigned as second in command of the 2nd Cavalry operating in Texas. He was at home in Arlington, Virginia, when the radical abolitionist John Brown attacked the United States arsenal at Harpers Ferry in October 1859. President James Buchanan assigned Lee to command the force of Marines sent to capture him, with then-Lt. James Ewell Brown ("Jeb") Stuart as his assistant. Back in Texas when the war began, he returned to Virginia where he accepted promotion to the rank of colonel at the end of March 1861, but a month later offered his services to his state. Sent to western Virginia, he was defeated at the Battle of Cheat Mountain before being appointed military advisor to President Davis.

23. An 1854 graduate of the Military Academy from Virginia, Stuart served on the frontier where he was seriously wounded and in Kansas during the unrest following the Kansas-Nebraska Act. After leading the assault at Harpers Ferry that captured John Brown, he resigned in May 1861 to accept a commission in the Virginia troops, being promoted to brigadier in September 1861.

24. A Floridian who graduated from West Point in 1845, before the war Smith earned two brevets in the Mexican War, taught mathematics at West Point, and served on the frontier where he was wounded.

25. William S. Rosecrans was born in Ohio. He graduate from West Point in 1842 after which he undertook various engineering assignments and served on the faculty at the academy until his resignation in 1854 to engaged in civilian engineering and the coal and oil business. When the war began he served on McClellan's staff before being named colonel of an Ohio regiment which he led in the fighting at Rich Mountain in western Virginia. Appointed brigadier general, he was promoted to major general in March 1862

26. John Codman Ropes, *The Army Under Pope* (New York: Charles Scribner's Sons, 1885), 160.

27. See http://www.arlingtoncemetery.net/ssturgis.htm.

28. Born in Indiana, Burnside was an 1847 graduate of the Military Academy who served in the Mexican and Indian Wars but resigned his commission in 1853 to go into private business manufacturing breech-loading rifles in Rhode Island. When this failed he accepted a position as treasurer of the Illinois Central Railroad where he came in contact with George McClellan. With the outbreak of war he accepted appointment as colonel of the 1st Rhode Island Volunteer Infantry. Promoted to brigadier general, he successfully led an invasion of the North Carolina coast earning promotion to major general.

29. For the Emancipation Proclamation, see The Avalon Project, Yale Law School, http://avalon.law.yale.edu/19th_century/emancipa.asp.

30. Duncan Andrew Campbell, *English Public Opinion and the American Civil War* (Suffolk, United Kingdom: Royal Historical Society, the Boydell Press, 2003), 132.

31. Some argued that since some Northern commanders were freeing slaves in those areas conquered by the North, Lincoln was concerned that his authority

to act would be co-opted by some of his generals and, hence, needed to act or he would be viewed as ignoring the issue of slavery.

32. Susan-Mary Grant, *The War for a Nation: The American Civil War* (London: Routledge, 2006), 169.

Chapter 7

1. A native of Pennsylvania, Pemberton was one of the few northern-born federal officers who chose to cast their lot with the South, no doubt due to his wife being from Virginia. A Military Academy graduate in 1837, he fought in the Seminole War and earned two brevets in the Mexican War where he served as aide-de-camp to Gen. William J. Wirth. After operating on the frontier, he resigned in April 1861 and received rapid promotion in the Confederate forces.

2. Born in Hadley, Massachusetts, Hooker graduated from West Point in 1837 and served as a staff officer in the Mexican War where he earned brevets from first lieutenant all the way to lieutenant colonel, a record unmatched by any other officer in the service. He resigned in 1853 to take up farming in California but obtained a commission as brigadier general on May 17, 1861. Although he amassed a creditable record during McClellan's campaign on the peninsula, his public persona was greatly aided by a press report that appeared in the newspapers under the heading "Fighting—Joe Hooker." Although it simply meant to identify that fighting had taken place involving Hooker's troops, forever after the general would be known as "Fighting Joe Hooker."

3. Walter H. Hebert, *Fighting Joe Hooker* (Indianapolis: Bobbs-Merrill Company, 1944), ii–iii.

4. Oliver Otis Howard, *Autobiography of Oliver Otis Howard, Major-General, United States Army* (New York: Baker & Taylor Company, 1907), Part 2, 348.

5. Stephen W. Sears, *Chancellorsville* (Boston: Houghton Mifflin Company, 1996), 120.

6. *OR*, Series I, Vol. XXV, Part 1, 39.

7. *OR*, Series I, Vol. XXV, Part 2, 328.

8. A native of Leeds, Maine, Howard graduated from the Military Academy in 1854 and then served as an assistant professor of mathematics there. As a colonel commanding a brigade at First Bull Run his troops were routed but he emerged with a promotion to brigadier general. Personally courageous, he lost an arm at Fair Oaks during the Peninsula Campaign. He rose to division command at Antietam and in the reshuffling when Hooker took over the army he was raised, by virtue of seniority, to command the Eleventh Corps.

9. Devens was a Harvard graduate and political appointee to general who was twice wounded earlier in the war. Von Steinwehr graduated from the Brunswick Military Academy and had served in the Prussian army. Schurz, a German revolutionary and a popular German-American leader who campaigned vigorously for Lincoln in 1860, was rewarded with appointment as U.S. Minister to Spain and later a brigadiership as one of the "political" generals.

10. Abner Doubleday, *Chancellorsville and Gettysburg* (New York: Charles Scribner's Sons, 1885), 22.

11. A New York politician, Sickles was a Tammany Hall Democrat who gained a great deal of prewar notoriety by murdering his wife's lover who happened to be the son of Francis Scott Key, author of "The Star Spangled Banner." His attorney, Edwin M. Stanton, none other than the Secretary of War in the Lincoln administration, was able to successfully argue "temporary insanity," saving his client from any punishment other than social banishment. As a "War Democrat," he supported the administration's effort to vanquish the rebellion, raising the "Excelsior Brigade" from his native state, rising through the Peninsula Campaign and Antietam to command a division at Fredericksburg and then the Third Corps by virtue of his seniority.

12. Noah Brooks, *Washington in Lincoln's Time* (New York: Rinehart, 1958), 57.

13. *Final Report Made to the Secretary of War, by the Provost Marshal General, of the Operations of the Bureau of the Provost Marshal General of the U.S., from the Commencement of the Business of the Bureau, March 17, 1863, to March 17, 1866; the Bureau Terminating by Law August 28, 1866* (Washington: 1866), 165–212.

14. Donald P. Kommers, John E. Finn, Gary J. Jacobsohn, *American Constitutional Law: Essays, Cases, and Comparative Notes* (Lanham, MD: Rowman & Littlefield, 2004), 182.

15. Frank Moore, ed., *The Rebellion Record: A Diary of American Events* (New York: G. P. Putnam, 1863), Vol. 5, 579.

16. William Farina, *Ulysses S. Grant, 1861–1864: His Rise from Obscurity to Military Greatness* (Jefferson, NC: McFarland, 2007), 146–47.

17. John Y. Simon, ed., *The Papers of Ulysses S. Grant* (Carbondale: Southern Illinois University Press, 1982), 197.

18. Ewell was born in Georgetown in the District of Columbia, was appointed to West Point from Virginia, graduating in 1840, and earned a brevet promotion during the Mexican War. After resigning his commission in May of 1861 he served in most of the major engagements in the Virginia area including First Bull Run, the Valley Campaign under Jackson, the Peninsula Campaign, and Groveton where he was seriously wounded, losing a leg.

19. Hill, a native Virginian, graduated from the Military Academy in 1847. He served in the Seminole War and Mexican War but resigned in April 1861. He was promoted to major general after performing well at Williamsburg and continued to exhibit solid leadership abilities during the rest of the Peninsula Campaign. Under Jackson in the Valley Campaign he earned a reputation for fast movement, his command being referred to as the "Light Division" because of its speedy marching. It was exactly this quality which allowed Hill to come up just in time to roll back Burnside's assault at Antietam that initially appeared to be delivering a fatal blow to Lee's defense.

20. Edward G. Longacre, *The Cavalry at Gettysburg: A Tactical Study of Mounted Operations* (Lincoln: University of Nebraska Press, 1993), 149.

21. *OR*, Series I, Vol. XXVII, Part 2, 692.

22. *OR*, Series I, Vol. XXVII, Part 1, 44.

23. Samuel Livingston French, *The Army of the Potomac from 1861 to 1863* (New York: Publishing Society of New York, 1906), 371.

24. *OR*, Series I, Vol. XXVII, Part 1.

25. *OR*, Series I, Vol. XXVII, Part 1.

26. Born the son of an American merchant in Cadiz, Spain, Meade graduated from West Point in 1835 and served in the Mexican War where he was awarded a brevet. With the outbreak of the Civil War he commanded a brigade on the Peninsula where he was seriously wounded and at Second Bull Run. He led a division at Antietam and Fredericksburg, being promoted

to command the Fifth Corps at Chancellorsville. Somewhat critical of Hooker, when the messenger arrived to apprise him of his appointment to command the army facing Lee he first thought the purpose of the late-night communication was to place him under arrest.

27. Born in Kentucky but appointed to the Military Academy from Illinois, he graduated in 1848 too late to participate in the Mexican War. He was assigned to duty on the frontier and in the Utah Expedition of 1857–58 before being promoted to major and assigned to the Inspector general's office in Washington. When Maj. Gen. John Pope came east he obtained a commission as brigadier general for Buford and assigned him to command the reserve cavalry brigade in his Army of Virginia. Severely wounded at Second Bull Run, he was promoted to McClellan's chief of cavalry and served in that capacity under Burnside at Fredericksburg.

28. Duane Schultz, *The Most Glorious Fourth: Vicksburg and Gettysburg, July 4, 1863* (New York: W. W. Norton, 2002), 208.

29. Born in New York, Doubleday graduated from the Military Academy in 1842, and served in the Seminole and Mexican War. The spring of 1861 found him a member of the garrison of Fort Sumter in Charleston harbor when the Confederates opened fire, inaugurating the Civil War. Tradition says that he aimed the first gun that responded to the bombardment. In any event, he gained considerable fame, was promoted to brigadier general, and served at Second Bull Run, Antietam, Fredericksburg, and Chancellorsville.

30. *OR*, Series I, Vol. XXVII, Part 3, 463.

31. Charles H. Howard, Letters, William E. Brooks Collection, Library of Congress.

32. A Pennsylvanian who graduated from West Point in 1840, he had lengthy experience on the frontier, during the Seminole War, in the Mexican War where he earned a brevet, and in Kansas during the civil war that broke out there over the Kansas-Nebraska question. Having served with the Army of the Potomac since its inception, he fought on the Peninsula, and at Antietam, Fredericksburg, and Chancellorsville.

33. *OR*, Series I, Vol. XXVII, Part 2, 44.

34. A native of New York, Warren graduated from West Point in 1850. He participated in the army's actions on the Peninsula, Second Bull Run, Antietam, and Fredericksburg.

35. Greene was an 1823 graduate of the Military Academy and taught mathematics and engineering at West Point before resigning to work on the engineering and construction of railroads.

36. Julia Lorrilard Safford Butterfield, *A Biographical Memorial of General Daniel Butterfield* (New York: The Grafton Press, 1904), 260.

37. A native of Georgia, Hardee graduated from the Military Academy in 1838 and saw service in the Seminole War, on the frontier, and in the Mexican War where he was captured and earned two brevets. Hardee spent two years studying at the French cavalry school in Saumur, served as commandant of cadets at West Point where he taught tactics, and authored the respected *Rifle and Light Infantry Tactics.*

38. Polk, a relative of President James K. Polk and a bishop in the Episcopal Church, was a North Carolinian who graduated from the Military Academy in 1827. One of the founders of the University of the South, he was a West Point classmate of Jefferson Davis who offered him a commission as major general in the opening weeks of the war. During the early months he had the distinction

of defeating Grant at Belmont, Missouri, then personally led four charges while commanding the Confederate right at Shiloh under his Military Academy roommate, Albert Sidney Johnston. Second in command at Perryville, he also fought at Stones River.

39. Sherman was a native of Ohio who graduated from the Military Academy in 1840 and served in California during the Mexican War. He resigned in 1853 to go into private life, 1860 finding him the superintendent of a military academy in Louisiana that later became Louisiana State University. Sherman enjoyed excellent political connections. His brother John was a long-serving and influential United States Senator while Sherman himself married the daughter of Senator Thomas Ewing who initially secured for him his appointment to West Point. After leading a brigade at First Bull Run he gained promotion to brigadier general and was sent to the western theater of operations. Often critical of administration policy, he also incurred the wrath of the press that turned upon him with particular venom spreading the rumor that he was insane and nearly ruining his military career. Due in large part to his political connections, and his excellent conduct at Shiloh under the eye of Grant, Sherman survived and was promoted to major general in May 1862. He and Grant became close friends as well as sharing a mutual respect for each other's abilities, leading Grant to trust him with independent commands during the Vicksburg campaigns.

40. John William Jones, ed., *Life and Letters of Robert Edward Lee: Soldier and Man* (New York: The Neale Publishing Company, 1906), 280.

41. For the Gettysburg Address see The Avalon Project, Yale Law School, http://avalon.law.yale.edu/19th_century/gettyb.asp.

42. Roy P. Basler, ed., *The Collected Works of Abraham Lincoln* (New Brunswick: Rutgers University Press, 1953), Vol. 7, 55.

43. *Ibid.,* 54.

Chapter 8

1. Abraham Lincoln, State of the Union Address, December 8, 1863, http://www.presidency.ucsb.edu/ws/index.php?pid=29504.

2. Banks had been a politician before the war, serving in Congress from 1853 to 1857 and then as governor of Massachusetts. His political connections brought him appointment as a brigadier general of volunteers in May 1861, after which he served in the Shenandoah Valley against Stonewall Jackson, whom he defeated at the Battle of Kernstown. Jackson returned the favor by defeating Banks at Cedar Mountain during the Second Bull Run Campaign. Banks replaced Maj. Gen. Benjamin Butler as head of the Department of the Gulf.

3. The owner of a large Louisiana sugar plantation, he was especially well educated for the time having studied in Europe and at both Harvard and Yale, graduating from the latter in 1845. He served in the Louisiana state senate from 1856 to 1861 and voted in favor of leaving the Union during the state secession convention.

4. A Tennessee native, Forrest was born into poverty but managed against all odds to become wealthy by dealing in cotton, livestock, and slaves. After raising a cavalry force at his own expense, he was seriously wounded covering the retreat from Shiloh. When he clashed with Bragg he was reassigned, but was nevertheless promoted to major general in December 1863.

5. John Allan Wyeth, *Life of Lieutenant-General Nathan Bedford Forrest* (New York: Harper & Brothers, 1908), 344.

6. *OR*, Series 1, Vol. 38, Part 1, 115–17.

7. *OR*, Series 1, Vol. 38, Part 3, 675–83.

8. C. Vann Woodward, ed., *Mary Chestnut's Civil War* (New Haven: Yale University Press, 1981), 482–83.

9. A native of Kentucky, Hood graduated from the Military Academy in 1853. Ironically, his classmates included James B. McPherson and John M. Schofield, while the artillery instructor at West Point while he was there was George H. Thomas. All three of these led armies under Sherman. McPherson commanded the Army of the Tennessee, Schofield led the Army of the Ohio, and Thomas headed the Army of the Cumberland. Hood earned a reputation for aggressiveness leading a force on the Peninsula that would become famous as "Hood's Texas Brigade" and soon advanced to division command under Longstreet. Often considered the "shock troops" of the corps, Hood gained further fame for arriving from Harpers Ferry in the nick of time to save Lee's army at Antietam. Hood was severely wounded by an artillery shell at Gettysburg, losing the use of his left arm. At Chickamauga he again was in the thick of the attack but suffered another debilitating wound necessitating the amputation of his right leg only a few inches below the hip. Longstreet recommended his promotion to lieutenant general because of his conspicuous bravery, which the Confederate Congress approved. Davis appointed him to command a corps under Johnston despite the physical infirmities.

10. Quoted in Russell Frank Weigley, *The American Way of War: A History of United States Military Strategy and Policy* (Bloomington: Indiana University Press, 1973), 143.

11. Vincent J. Esposito, ed., *The West Point Atlas of American Wars: Volume 1 1689–1900* (New York: Frederick A. Praeger, 1960), 122.

12. Quotes from Gordon C. Rhea, *The Battle of the Wilderness May 5–6, 1864* (Baton Rouge: Louisiana State University Press, 1994), 421–22.

13. Esposito, *West Point Atlas*, 125.

14. See Gordon C. Rhea, *The Battles for Spotsylvania Court House and the Road to Yellow Tavern, May 7–12, 1864* (Baton Rouge: Louisiana State University Press, 1997), 93–95.

15. Wright was a native of Connecticut who graduated second in his West Point class of 1841. After teaching French and engineering at the Military Academy, he supervised various harbor and coastal defense construction projects. Serving as the chief engineer under McDowell at First Bull Run, he gained promotion to brigadier in September 1861 and major general in July 1862, serving at Gettysburg and in the Mine Run Campaign.

16. Quoted in *New York Tribune*, May 13, 1864; Charles Carleton Coffin, *Redeeming the Republic: The Third Period of the War of the Rebellion, in the Year 1864* (New York: Harper & Brothers, 1889), 112.

17. Horace Porter, *Campaigning with Grant* (New York: Century Company, 1897), 111.

18. Quoted in Noah Andre Trudeau, *Southern Storm: Sherman's March to the Sea* (New York: HarperCollins, 2008), 508.

19. *OR*, I, XLIII, I, 37.

20. For Ex Parte Milligan, see Robert Bruce Murray, *Legal Cases of the Civil War* (Mechanicsburg: Stackpole Books, 2003), 76–84.

21. E. B. Long and Barbara Long, *The Civil War Day By Day: An Almanac, 1861–1865* (Garden City, NY: Doubleday, 1971).

Chapter 9

1. For the Thirteenth Amendment, see The Avalon Project, Yale Law School, http://avalon.law.yale.edu/18th_century/amend1.asp#13.

2. Hampton was a wealthy South Carolina planter who had outfitted the Hampton Legion at his own expense early in the war, served as a prominent cavalry commander in the Army of Northern Virginia, and replaced Jeb Stuart when he was killed at Yellow Tavern in May 1864.

3. For Lincoln's Second Inaugural Address, see The Avalon Project, Yale Law School, http://avalon.law.yale.edu/19th_century/lincoln2.asp.

4. Douglas Southall Freeman, *R. E. Lee: A Biography* (New York: Charles Scribner's Sons, 1934), Vol. IV, 36.

5. John R. Maass, *The Petersburg and Appomattox Campaigns, 1864–1865* (Washington, D.C.: Center of Military History, 2015), 53.

6. Michael E. Haskew, *Appomattox: The Last Days of Robert E. Lee's Army of Northern Virginia* (Minneapolis, MN: Zenith Press, 2015), 7.

7. Ulysses S. Grant, *Personal Memoirs of U.S. Grant* (New York: Charles L. Webster & Company, 1886), Vol. 2, 627.

8. *Ibid.*

9. *Ibid.*

10. *Ibid.*

11. *Ibid.*

12. *Ibid.*

13. *Ibid.*, 628.

14. *Ibid.*

15. Jones, *Life and Letters*, 376.

16. John R. Peacock III, "Keeping the Faith: Douglas Southall Freeman, 1886–1953" (PhD dissertation, Louisiana State University, 1990), I, 14.

17. J. David Hacker, "A Census-Based Count of the Civil War Dead," *Civil War History*, Vol. 57, no. 4 (December 2011), 306–47. The administrator of the 1870 census estimated that as many as 850,000 had died, but that figure was rarely cited. Most historians believe the earlier 620,000 figure is undoubtedly too low.

18. Quoted in Daniel Nasaw, "Who, What, Why: How many soldiers died in the U.S. Civil War?" *BBC Magazine*, April 4, 2012, http://www.bbc.com/news/magazine-17604991.

Chapter 10

1. Roy P. Basler, et al., eds., *Collected Works of Abraham Lincoln* at http://www.abrahamlincolnonline.org/lincoln/speeches/last.htm.

2. Kenneth M. Stampp, *The Era of Reconstruction, 1865 to 1877* (New York: Alfred A. Knopf, 1965).

3. The 1865 South Carolina constitution may be found at http://www.carolana.com/SC/Documents/South_Carolina_Constitution_1865.pdf.

4. *Ibid.*

5. The St. Landry's Parish Black Code of 1865 can be found in U.S. Congress, Senate Executive Document No. 2 (Washington, D.C.: Government Printing Office, 1865), 93–94.

6. Walter L. Fleming, *Documentary History of Reconstruction: Political, Military, Social, Religious, Educational & Industrial 1865 to the Present Time* (Cleveland: Arthur H. Clark Company, 1907), II, 347.

7. The section reads: "Each House shall be the Judge of the Elections, Returns and Qualifications of its own Members...."

8. For the Civil Rights Act of 1866, see *U.S. Statutes at Large*, Vol. 14:27.

9. For the Fourteenth Amendment, see The Avalon Project, Yale Law School, http://avalon.law.yale.edu/18th_century/amend1.asp#14.

10. *Ibid.*

11. *Congressional Globe*, 39th Congress (January 1867), 1104.

12. *Harper's New Monthly Magazine* (New York: Harper & Brothers, 1897), Vol. XCIV, 213.

Chapter 11

1. For the First Reconstruction Act see History Central at http://www.historycentral.com/documents/FirstReconstructionAct.html.

2. Richard Zuczek, ed., *Encyclopedia of the Reconstruction Era* (Westport, CT: Greenwood Press, 2006), Vol. 1, 795.

3. James Edward Pollard, *The Presidents and the Press* (New York: Macmillan, 1947), 406; George Brown Tindall, *America: A Narrative History* (New York: W.W. Norton, 1984), 684.

4. Paul H. Bergeron, ed., *The Papers of Andrew Johnson: September 1867-March 1868* (Knoxville: University of Tennessee Press, 1996), 620.

5. United States Constitution, Article II, Section 4.

6. *Proceedings in The Trial of Andrew Johnson, President of the United States, Before the United States Senate* (Washington, D.C.: F. & J. Rives and Geo. A. Bailey, 1868), 3.

7. *Ibid.*, 4–5.

8. *Ibid.*, 7.

9. Ulysses S. Grant: "Inaugural Address," March 4, 1869. Gerhard Peters and John T. Woolley, The American Presidency Project, http://www.presidency.ucsb.edu/ws/?pid=25820.

10. James Bryce, *The American Commonwealth* (New York: Macmillan, 1910), II, 498–99.

Chapter 12

1. For the Merryman case see Paul C. Bartholomew, *Summaries of Leading Cases on the Constitution* (Totowa, NJ: Littlefield, Adams & Co., 1973).

2. For the Vallandigham case see Murray, *Legal Cases*, 62–74. For the Milligan case see Murray, *Legal Cases*, 76–84.

3. Texas *v.* White, 74 U.S. 700 (1868), Cornell University Law School, Supreme Court Collection, https://www.law.cornell.edu/supremecourt/text/74/700. The majority vote of the Court was 5–3. For additional information see Murray, *Legal Issues*, 149–59.

4. Claudia D. Goldin and Frank D. Lewis, "The Economic Cost of the American Civil War: Estimates and Implications," *The Journal of Economic History*, Vol. 35, No. 2 (June 1975), 299–326; Roger L. Ransom, "The Economics of the Civil War," http://web.mnstate.edu/stutes/Econ411/Readings/civil.htm.

5. See Maurice Halbwach, "Historical Memory and Collective Memory," in Maurice Halbwach, *The Collective Memory* (New York: Harper and Row, 1980 [transl. by F. J. Ditter, Jr. & V. Y. Ditter from 1950 French edition]).

6. Henry Wilson, *History of the Rise and Fall of the Slave Power in America* (Boston: James R. Osgood and Co., 1872).

7. Quoted in Philip S. Foner, *The Life and Writings of Frederick Douglass* (New York: International Publishers, 1975), Vol. 3, 244–46.

8. Edward A. Pollard, *The Lost Cause: A New Southern History of the War of the Confederates* (New York: E. B. Treat & Co., 1866), 46–52.

9. From the Southern Poverty Law Center at https://www.splcenter.org/20160421/whose-heritage-public-symbols-confederacy. The site also lists 109 public schools named for Robert E. Lee, Jefferson Davis or other Confederate leaders; 80 counties and cities named for Confederates; 9 official Confederate holidays in six states; and 10 U.S. military bases named for Confederates.

10. Unfortunately, understanding only went so far. In nearly all cases African American veterans were not invited so as not to offend Southern sensitivities.

11. Randall, James G., *The Civil War and Reconstruction* (Boston: D. C. Heath and Company, 1937).

12. For the Beards' analysis, see Charles and Mary Beard, *The Rise of American Civilization* (New York: Macmillan, 1927), II, 166–92.

13. Frank L. Owsley, "The Irrepressible Conflict," in Twelve Southerners, *I'll Take My Stand: The South and the Agrarian Tradition* (New York: Harper, 1930).

14. Allan Nevins, *Ordeal of the Union* (New York: Charles Scribner's Sons, 1947–1971).

15. Eugene D. Genovese, *The Political Economy of Slavery: Studies in the Economy and Society of the Slave South* (Middletown, CT: Wesleyan University Press, 1989), 8.

16. Eric Foner, *Free Soil, Free Labor, Free Men: The Ideology of the Republican Party Before the Civil War* (New York: Oxford University Press, 1970).

Bibliography

Adams, George Worthington, *Doctors in Blue: The Medical History of the Union Army in the Civil War* (Baton Rouge: Louisiana State University Press, 1996).

Bailey, T., D. Kennedy, and L. Cohen, *The American Pageant* (Boston: Houghton Mifflin Company, 1998).

Ball, Douglas B., *Financial Failure and Confederate Defeat* (Urbana: University of Illinois Press, 1991).

Barnes, Joseph K., *The Medical and Surgical History of the War of the Rebellion (1861–65)* (Washington: U.S. Government Printing Office, 1870).

Bartholomew, Paul C., *Summaries of Leading Cases on the Constitution* (Totowa, NJ: Littlefield, Adams & Co., 1973).

Basler, Roy P., ed., *The Collected Works of Abraham Lincoln* (New Brunswick: Rutgers University Press, 1953).

Beard, Charles, and Mary, *The Rise of American Civilization* (New York: Macmillan, 1927).

Behrendt, Stephen, "Transatlantic Slave Trade," *Africana: The Encyclopedia of the African and African American Experience* (New York: Basic Civitas Books, 1991).

Bergeron, Paul H., ed., *The Papers of Andrew Johnson: September 1867–March 1868* (Knoxville: University of Tennessee Press, 1996).

Bloom, Harold, ed., *Henry David Thoreau* (New York: Infobase Publishing, 2007).

Boller, Jr., Paul F., *Presidential Campaigns: From George Washington to George W. Bush* (Oxford: Oxford University Press, 2004).

Brock, R. A., ed., "The Signal Corps in the Southern States Army," *Southern Historical Society Papers,* Vol. XVI (Richmond: Southern Historical Society, 1888).

Brooks, Noah, *Washington in Lincoln's Time* (New York: Rinehart, 1958).

Bryce, James, *The American Commonwealth* (New York: Macmillan, 1910).

Burdekin, Richard K. C., and Farrokh Langdana, "War Finance in the Southern Confederacy, 1861–1865," *Explorations in Economic History,* Vol. 30, no. 3 (July 1993), 352–76.

Butterfield, Julia Lorrilard Safford, *A Biographical Memorial of General Daniel Butterfield* (New York: The Grafton Press, 1904).

Calhoun, John C., "The Clay Compromise Measures," speech in the U.S. Senate, March 4, 1850, from http://www.nationalcenter.org/CalhounClayCompromise.htmll.

Campbell, Duncan Andrew, *English Public Opinion and the American Civil War* (Suffolk, United Kingdom: Royal Historical Society, the Boydell Press, 2003).

Chase, Salmon P., "Appeal of the Independent Democrats in Congress to the People of the United States," Towers' Printers, January 19, 1854.

"Civil War Army Organization," The Civil War Trust, https://www.civilwar.org/learn/articles/civil-war-army-organization.

Coffin, Charles Carleton, *Redeeming the Republic: The Third Period of the War of the Rebellion, in the Year 1864* (New York: Harper & Brothers, 1889).

Colaiaco, James A., *Frederick Douglass and the Fourth of July* (New York: Palgrave Macmillan, 2006).

Conkling, Alfred R., *The Life and Letters of Roscoe Conkling, Orator, Statesman, Advocate* (New York: Charles L. Webster & Company, 1889).

Crist, Lynda Lasswell, and Mary Seaton Dix, eds., *The Papers of Jefferson Davis* (Baton Rouge: Louisiana State University Press, 1992).

Crittenden Amendments, December 18, 1860, The Avalon Project, Yale Law School, http://avalon.law.yale.edu/19th_century/critten.asp.

Cross, Whitney R., *The Burned-over District: The Social and Intellectual History of Enthusiastic Religion in Western New York, 1800–1850* (Ithaca, NY: Cornell University Press, 1982).

Daley, James, ed., *Landmark Decisions of the U.S. Supreme Court* (Mineola, NY: Dover Publications, 2006).

Daniels, Jonathan, *They Will Be Heard: America's Crusading Newspaper Editors* (New York: McGraw-Hill, 1965).

DeCaro, Jr., Louis, *John Brown Speaks: Letters and Statements from Charlestown* (Lanham, MD: Rowman & Littlefield, 2015).

Dew, Thomas R., *Review of the Debate in the Virginia Legislature of 1831 and 1832* (Richmond: T. W. White, 1832).

Donald, David, ed., *Why the North Won the Civil War* (Baton Rouge: Louisiana State University Press, 1973).

Doubleday, Abner, *Chancellorsville and Gettysburg* (New York: Charles Scribner's Sons, 1885).

Dunkelman, Mark H., *Brothers One and All: Esprit de Corps in a Civil War Regiment* (Baton Rouge: Louisiana State University Press, 2004).

Elliott, E. N., *Cotton is King, and Pro-slavery Arguments; Comprising the Writings of Hammond, Harper, Christy, Stringfellow, Hodge, Bledsoe, and Cartwright, on this Important Subject* (Augusta, GA: Abbot & Loomis, 1860).

Emancipation Proclamation, The Avalon Project, Yale Law School, http://avalon.law.yale.edu/19th_century/emancipa.asp.

Esposito, Vincent J., ed., *The West Point Atlas of American Wars: Volume 1 1689–1900* (New York: Frederick A. Praeger, 1960).

Farina, William, *Ulysses S. Grant, 1861–1864: His Rise from Obscurity to Military Greatness* (Jefferson, NC: McFarland, 2007).

Farrand, Max, ed., *The Records of the Federal Convention of 1787* (New Haven: Yale University Press, 1911).

Faust, Patricia L., ed., *Historical Times Illustrated Encyclopedia of the Civil War* (New York: HarperPerennial, 1991).

Final Report Made to the Secretary of War, by the Provost Marshal General, of the Operations of the Bureau of the Provost Marshal General of the U.S., from the Commencement of the Business of the Bureau, March 17, 1863, to March 17, 1866; the Bureau Terminating by Law August 28, 1866 (Washington: The Office, 1866).

Finney, Charles Grandison, "The Pernicious Attitude of the Church on the Reforms of the Age," *The Oberlin Evangelist*, January 21, 1846.

First Confiscation Act, The Gilder Lehrman Institute of American History, https://www.gilderlehrman.org/history-by-era/african-americans-and-emancipation/timeline-terms/first-confiscation-act.

First Reconstruction Act, History Central, http://www.historycentral.com/documents/FirstReconstructionAct.html.

Fleming, Walter L., *Documentary History of Reconstruction: Political, Military, Social, Religious, Educational & Industrial 1865 to the Present Time* (Cleveland: Arthur H. Clark Company, 1907).

Foner, Eric, *Free Soil, Free Labor, Free Men: The Ideology of the Republican Party Before the Civil War* (New York: Oxford University Press, 1978).

Foner, Philip S., *The Life and Writings of Frederick Douglass* (New York: International Publishers, 1975).

Fourteenth Amendment, The Avalon Project, Yale Law School, http://avalon.law.yale.edu/18th_century/amend1.asp#14.

Freeman, Douglas Southall, *R. E. Lee: A Biography* (New York: Charles Scribner's Sons, 1934).

French, Samuel Livingston, *The Army of the Potomac from 1861 to 1863* (New York: Publishing Society of New York, 1906).

Friedman, Lawrence J., "The Gerrit Smith Circle: Abolitionism in the Burned-Over District," *Civil War History*, Vol. 26, No. 1 (March 1980), 18–38.

From The Pro-Slavery Argument: As Maintained by the most Distinguished Writers of the Southern States, Containing the Several Essays, on the Subject, of Chancellor Harper, Governor Hammond, Dr. Simms, and Professor Dew (Charleston: Walker, Richards, 1852).

Fugitive Slave Act, The Avalon Project, Yale Law School, http://avalon.law.yale.edu/19th_century/fugitive.asp.

Genovese, Eugene D., *The Political Economy of Slavery: Studies in the Economy and Society of the Slave South* (Middletown, CT: Wesleyan University Press, 1989).

Gettysburg Address The Avalon Project, Yale Law School, http://avalon.law.yale.edu/19th_century/gettyb.asp.

Giddings, Joshua R., *Speeches on Congress by Joshua R. Giddings* (Boston: John P. Jewett and Company, 1853).

Goldin, Claudia D., and Frank D. Lewis, "The Economic Cost of the American Civil War: Estimates and Implications," *The Journal of Economic History*, Vol. 35, No. 2 (June 1975), 299–326.

Grant, Susan-Mary, *The War for a Nation: The American Civil War* (London: Routledge, 2006).

Grant, Ulysses S., "Inaugural Address," March 4, 1869, in Gerhard Peters and John T. Woolley, The American Presidency Project, http://www.presidency.ucsb.edu/ws/?pid=25820.

_____, *Personal Memoirs of U. S. Grant* (New York: Charles L. Webster & Company, 1886).

Griffin, C. S., *The Ferment of Reform, 1830–1860* (New York: Thomas Y. Crowell Company, 1967).

Grimké, Angelina, *Letters to Catharine E. Beecher in reply to an Essay on Slavery and Abolitionism addressed to A. E. Grimké by the Author* (Boston: Isaac Knapp, 1838).

Hacker, J. David, "A Census-Based Count of the Civil War Dead," *Civil War History*, Vol. 57, no. 4 (December 2011), 306–47.

Halbwach, Maurice, "Historical Memory and Collective Memory," in Maurice Halbwach, *The Collective Memory* (New York: Harper and Row, 1980 [transl. by F. J. Ditter, Jr., & V. Y. Ditter from 1950 French edition]).

Halsey, Francis W., ed., *Great Epochs in American History: Described by Famous Writers from Columbus to Roosevelt* (New York: Funk & Wagnalls Company, 1912).

Hambrick-Stowe, Charles, *Charles G. Finney and the Spirit of American Evangelicalism* (Grand Rapids, MI: Eerdmans, 1996).

Hammond, Charles A., *Gerrit Smith: The Story of a Noble Life* (Geneva, NY: Press of W. F. Humphrey, 1908).

Handlin, Oscar, *Boston's Immigrants, 1790–1865; a Study in Acculturation* (Cambridge: Harvard University Press, 1941).

Hardman, Keith J. *Charles Grandison Finney, 1792–1875, Revivalist and Reformer* (Syracuse: Syracuse University Press, 1987).

Haskew, Michael E., *Appomattox: The Last Days of Robert E. Lee's Army of Northern Virginia* (Minneapolis, MN: Zenith Press, 2015).

Hatch, Nathan O., *The Democratization of American Christianity* (New Haven: Yale University Press, 1989).

Hattaway, Herman, and Archer Jones, *How the North Won: A Military History of the Civil War* (Urbana: University of Illinois Press, 1991).

Hearn, Chester G., *Companions in Conspiracy: John Brown & Gerrit Smith* (Gettysburg, PA: Thomas Publications, 1996).

Hebert, Walter H., *Fighting Joe Hooker* (Indianapolis: Bobbs-Merrill Company, 1944).

Howard, Oliver Otis, *Autobiography of Oliver Otis Howard, Major-General, United States Army* (New York: Baker & Taylor Company, 1907).

Israel, Fred L., and Jim F. Watts, eds., *Presidential Documents: The Speeches, Proclamations, and Policies that Have Shaped the Nation from Washington to Clinton* (New York: Routledge, 2000).

Jarvis, Peter, "Abolitionism in Oneida County," unpublished manuscript, Oneida County Historical Society, Utica, NY.

Jones, John William, ed., *Life and Letters of Robert Edward Lee: Soldier and Man* (New York: The Neale Publishing Company, 1906).

Kaufmann, Wilhelm, *Die Deutschen im amerikanischen Bürgerkriege Sezessionskrieg 1861–1865* (München: Oldenbourg, 1911).

Keen, William, "Military Surgery in 1861 and in 1918," *Annals of the American Academy of Political and Social Science*, Vol. 80, Rehabilitation of the Wounded (Nov. 1918), 11–22.

Kommers, Donald P., John E. Finn, Gary J. Jacobsohn,

American Constitutional Law: Essays, Cases, and Comparative Notes (Lanham, MD: Rowman & Littlefield, 2004).

Kornblith, Gary John, *Slavery and Sectional Strife in the Early American Republic, 1776–1821* (New York: Rowman & Littlefield, 2010).

Kutler, Stanley I., *The Dred Scott Decision: Law or Politics?* (Boston: Houghton Mifflin Company, 1967).

Letters and Addresses of Abraham Lincoln (New York: Howard Wilford Bell, 1903).

Lincoln, Abraham, First Inaugural Address, The Avalon Project, Yale Law School, http://avalon.law.yale.edu/19th_century/lincoln1.asp.

_____, Second Inaugural Address, The Avalon Project, Yale Law School, http://avalon.law.yale.edu/19th_century/lincoln2.asp.

Livermore, Thomas L., *Numbers and Losses in the Civil War in America 1861–65* (New York: Kraus Reprint Co., 1969).

Lockridge, Kenneth A., *Literacy in Colonial New England: An Enquiry into the Social Context of Literacy in the Early Modern West* (New York: W.W. Norton, 1974).

Long, E. B., and Barbara Long, *The Civil War Day By Day: An Almanac, 1861–1865* (Garden City, NY: Doubleday, 1971).

Lonn, Ella, *Foreigners in the Confederacy* (Chapel Hill: University of North Carolina Press, 2002).

_____, *Foreigners in the Union Army and Navy* (New York: Greenwood Press, 1969).

Maass, John R., *The Petersburg and Appomattox Campaigns, 1864–1865* (Washington, D.C.: Center of Military History, 2015).

Manzelmann, Robert L., "Revivalism and Reform," in *The History of Oneida County* (Utica: Oneida County, 1977).

McPherson, Edward, *The Political History of the United States of America During the Great Rebellion: From November 6, 1860, to July 4, 1864; Including a Classified Summary of the Legislation of the Second Session of the Thirty-sixth Congress, the Three Sessions of the Thirty-seventh Congress, the First Session of the Thirty-eighth Congress, with the Votes Thereon, and the Important Executive, Judicial, and Politico-military Facts of that Eventful Period; Together with the Organization, Legislation, and General Proceedings of the Rebel Administration* (Washington, D.C.: Philip & Solomons, 1864).

Mitchell, Stewart, *Horatio Seymour of New York* (Cambridge: Harvard University Press, 1938).

Moore, Frank, ed., *The Rebellion Record: A Diary of American Events* (New York: G. P. Putnam, 1863).

Moore, John Bassett, ed., *The Works of James Buchanan: Comprising His Speeches, State Papers, and Private Correspondence* (Philadelphia: J. B. Lippincott Co., 1908–1911).

Morley, John, ed., *The Fortnightly Review,* Vol. XXI (London: Chapman and & Hall, Ltd., new series, January 1–June 1, 1882).

Murray, Robert Bruce, *Legal Cases of the Civil War* (Mechanicsburg: Stackpole Books, 2003).

Nasaw, Daniel, "Who, What, Why: How many soldiers died in the US Civil War?" *BBC Magazine,* April 4, 2012, http://www.bbc.com/news/magazine-17604991.

National Party Conventions 1831–1972 (Washington, D.C.: Congressional Quarterly, 1976).

Nevins, Allan, *Ordeal of the Union* (New York: Charles Scribner's Sons, 1947–1971).

Oates, Stephen B., *To Purge this Land with Blood: A Biography of John Brown* (Amherst: University of Massachusetts Press, 1984).

"Ordinance of Secession" (1860), South Carolina Department of Archives and History, Columbia, SC.

Owsley, Frank L., "The Irrepressible Conflict," in Twelve Southerners, *I'll Take My Stand: The South and the Agrarian Tradition* (New York: Harper, 1930).

_____, and Harriet Chapell Owsley, *King Cotton Diplomacy: Foreign Relations of the Confederate States of America* (Tuscaloosa: University of Alabama Press, 2008).

Peacock, John R., III, "Keeping the Faith: Douglas Southall Freeman, 1886–1953" (PhD dissertation, Louisiana State University, 1990).

Political Debates Between Hon. Abraham Lincoln AND Hon. Stephen A. Douglas in the Celebrated Campaign of 1858 in Illinois (Columbus: Follett, Foster and Company, 1860).

Pollard, Edward A., *The Lost Cause: A New Southern History of the War of the Confederates* (New York: E. B. Treat & Co., 1866).

Pollard, James Edward, *The Presidents and the Press* (New York: Macmillan, 1947).

Porter, Horace, *Campaigning with Grant* (New York: Century Company, 1897).

The Pro-Slavery Argument: As Maintained by the most Distinguished Writers of the Southern States, Containing the Several Essays, on the Subject, of Chancellor Harper, Governor Hammond, Dr. Simms, and Professor Dew (Charleston: Walker, Richards, 1852).

Proceedings in The Trial of Andrew Johnson, President of the United States, Before the United States Senate (Washington, D.C.: F. & J. Rives and Geo. A. Bailey, 1868).

Quiner, E. B., *The Military History of Wisconsin: A Record of the Civil and Military Patriotism of the State in the War for the Union* (Chicago: Clarke & Co., 1866).

Randall, James G., *The Civil War and Reconstruction* (Boston: D. C. Heath and Company, 1937).

Ransom, Roger L., "The Economics of the Civil War," http://web.mnstate.edu/stutes/Econ411/Readings/civil.htm.

Redpath, James, ed., *Echoes of Harper's Ferry* (Boston: Thayer & Eldridge, 1860).

Revenue Act of 1861, The Gilder Lehrman Institute of American History, https://www.gilderlehrman.org/history-by-era/american-civil-war/timeline-terms/revenue-act-1861.

Rhea, Gordon C., *The Battle of the Wilderness May 5–6, 1864* (Baton Rouge: Louisiana State University Press, 1994).

_____, *The Battles for Spotsylvania Court House and the Road to Yellow Tavern, May 7–12, 1864* (Baton Rouge: Louisiana State University Press, 1997).

Rodriguez, Junius P., ed., *Slavery in the United States: A Social, Political, and Historical Encyclopedi*a (Santa Barbara, CA: ABC-CLIO, Inc., 2007).

Ropes, John Codman, *The Army Under Pope* (New York: Charles Scribner's Sons, 1885).

Rothbard, Murray N., *Conceived in Liberty* (Auburn, AL: Ludwig von Mises Institute, 2011).

Schultz, Duane, *The Most Glorious Fourth: Vicksburg and Gettysburg, July 4, 1863* (New York: W. W. Norton, 2002).

Schurz, Carl, *The Reminiscences of Carl Schurz* (London: John Murray, 1909).

Scott, E. H., ed., *Journal of the Constitutional Convention, Kept by James Madison* (Chicago: Scott, Foresman and Company, 1893).

Sears, Stephen W., *Chancellorsville* (Boston: Houghton Mifflin Company, 1996).

Sernett, Milton C., *Abolition's Axe: Beriah Green, Oneida Institute, and the Black Freedom Struggle* (Syracuse: Syracuse University Press, 1986).

_____, *North Star Country: Upstate New York and the Crusade for African American Freedom* (Syracuse: Syracuse University Press, 2002), 118.

Shryock, Richard Harrison, "Georgia and the Union in 1850" (Philadelphia: University of Pennsylvania, 1926, PhD dissertation).

Simon, John Y., ed., *The Papers of Ulysses S. Grant* (Carbondale: Southern Illinois University Press, 1982).

Simpson, Brooks D., *Ulysses S. Grant: Triumph Over Adversity, 1822–1865* (Minneapolis, MN: Zenith Press, 2014).

Smith, Derek, *The Gallant Dead: Union and Confederate Generals Killed in the Civil War* (Mechanicsburg, PA: Stackpole Books, 2005).

Smith, Timothy L., *Revivalism and Social Reform: American Protestantism on the Eve of the Civil War* (New York: Harper & Row, 1965).

Snay, Mitchell, *Horace Greeley and the Politics of Reform in Nineteenth-Century America* (New York: Rowman & Littlefield, 2011).

Sorin, Gerald, *Abolitionism: A New Perspective* (New York: Praeger Publishers, 1972).

_____, *The New York Abolitionists: A Case Study of Political Radicalism* (Westport, CT: Greenwood Publishing Corporation, 1971).

South Carolina Constitution of 1865, http://www.carolana.com/SC/Documents/South_Carolina_Constitution_1865.pdf.

Stampp, Kenneth M., *The Era of Reconstruction, 1865 to 1877* (New York: Alfred A. Knopf, 1965).

Sumner, Charles, "Crime Against Kansas," *The Works of Charles Sumner* (Boston: Lee and Shepard, 1870–1873).

_____, *The Crime Against Kansas: The Apologies for the Crime. The True Remedy* (Boston: John P. Jewett & Company, 1856).

Texas v. White, 74 U.S. 700 (1868), Cornell University Law School, Supreme Court Collection, https://www.law.cornell.edu/supremecourt/text/74/700.

Thirteenth Amendment, The Avalon Project, Yale Law School, http://avalon.law.yale.edu/18th_century/amend1.asp#13.

Tindall, George Brown, *America: A Narrative History* (New York: Norton, 1984).

Trudeau, Noah Andre, *Southern Storm: Sherman's March to the Sea* (New York: HarperCollins, 2008).

Wade, Richard C., *Slavery in the Cities: The South 1820–1860* (Oxford: Oxford University Press, 1969).

Waugh, John C., *Lincoln and McClellan: The Troubled Partnership Between a President and His General* (New York: Palgrave Macmillan, 2010).

Weigley, Russell Frank, *The American Way of War: A History of United States Military Strategy and Policy* (Bloomington: Indiana University Press, 1973).

Weisberger, Bernard A., *They Gathered at the River: The Story of the Great Revivalists and Their Impact Upon Religion in America* (Boston: Little, Brown, 1958).

Weld, Theodore, *American Slavery as It Is: Testimony of a Thousand Witnesses* (New York: American Anti-Slavery Society, 1839).

Wilson, Henry, *History of the Rise and Fall of the Slave Power in America* (Boston: James R. Osgood and Co., 1872).

Wilson, William, "The Great American Question" (1848), at http://memory.loc.gov/cgi-bin/query/r?ammem/rbaapc:@field(DOCID+@lit(rbaapc34000div0)).

Wittke, Carl, *Refugees of Revolution: The German Forty-Eighters in America* (Philadelphia: University of Pennsylvania Press, 1952).

Woodward, C. Vann, ed., *Mary Chestnut's Civil War* (New Haven: Yale University Press, 1981).

Wunder, John R., and Joann M. Ross, eds., *The Nebraska-Kansas Act of 1854* (Lincoln: University of Nebraska Press, 2008).

Wyeth, John Allan, *Life of Lieutenant-General Nathan Bedford Forrest* (New York: Harper & Brothers, 1908).

Yazawa, Melvin, ed., *Documents for America's History* (Boston: Bedford/St. Martin's, 2011).

Zuczek, Richard, ed., *Encyclopedia of the Reconstruction Era* (Westport, CT: Greenwood Press, 2006).

Index